A Dictionary of the

Internet

DARREL INCE

OXFORD
UNIVERSITY PRESS

OXFORD
UNIVERSITY PRESS

Great Clarendon Street, Oxford OX2 6DP

Oxford University Press is a department of the University of Oxford. It furthers the
University's objective of excellence in research, scholarship, and education by
publishing worldwide in

Oxford New York

Auckland Bangkok Buenos Aires Cape Town Chennai
Dar es Salaam Delhi Hong Kong Istanbul Karachi Kolkata
Kuala Lumpur Madrid Melbourne Mexico City Mumbai Nairobi
São Paulo Shanghai Singapore Taipei Tokyo Toronto

Oxford is a registered trade mark of Oxford University Press in the UK and in certain
other countries

Published in the United States by Oxford University Press Inc., New York

British Library Cataloguing in Publication Data

Data available

Library of Congress Cataloging in Publication Data

Data available

ISBN 0-19-280460-X

10 9 8 7 6 5 4 3 2 1

Typeset in 7.5/8.5pt OUPSwiftLight by
Kolam Information Services Pvt. Ltd, Pondicherry, India

Printed in Great Britain by
Clays Ltd
Bungay, Suffolk

OXFORD PAPERBACK REFERENCE

A Dictionary of the

Internet

Darrel Ince is currently Professor of Computing at the Open University. He is the author of 28 books, which include *Programming the Internet with Java*, student textbooks, research monographs, and an edition of the computing papers of Alan Turing.

Oxford Paperback Reference

The most authoritative and up-to-date reference books for both students and the general reader.

Contents

Preface

This dictionary has its roots in a question I was once asked during a consultation visit to an oil company. A senior member of the technical staff asked me what Dynamic HTML[1] was. In trying to find out the answer I discovered that, while there were a number of good computing dictionaries, there were only a few dictionaries that were solely devoted to Internet technology; those that I consulted contained around a few hundred Internet terms with quite a lot of padding provided by general computing terms. This is my attempt to remedy the situation.

In the dictionary I have included terms which fall into the following broad categories:

- Terms associated with Web technology, for example *Web server*, *Web page*, and *deep link*.

- Terms associated with ecommerce. This is a fledgling area in terms of terminology, but a rapidly increasing one. I have taken the term *ecommerce* to broadly mean the use of Internet technology for business purposes. This not only encompasses what most readers might perceive of ecommerce: retail Web sites, but also includes applications such as those associated with supply chain management and virtual private networks.

- Terms associated with Internet infrastructure, such as those associated with the TCP/IP suite of protocols that implement the basic transmission mechanisms that drive the Internet.

- Terms associated with distributed processing and distributed systems. A distributed system is a collection of computers linked by a disparate collection of transmission media; the World Wide Web is probably the simplest yet largest example of such a system. Distributed systems are huge: for example the Web-based system for the Sydney Olympic Games consisted of over 600 servers, 800 network switches, 13 million lines of code and, at its peak, received 1.2 million page hits on its Web servers. The last four years has seen a huge increase in the use of Internet technology in distributed system development and it would be a major omission not to include terms from this area.

- Terms associated with Internet security. The Internet is an open system and hence is more prone to attack. I have included terms associated with the majority of attacks and technologies used to guard against intrusion.

- Jargon which is employed by the users of chat rooms, newsgroups, and senders of emails. A dictionary which claimed to cover the Internet would be incomplete without a coverage of the more popular items of jargon which have emerged over the last decade, words and phrases such as *demoware*, *Zen mail*, *denizen*, and *shovelware*.

- Abbreviations. The Internet is awash with abbreviations—there's even a self referential abbreviation TLA[2]. The reason for the large number of abbreviations is that the Internet is a textual medium where its users communicate by pressing keys on a

---

[1] It is a term used to describe the augmentation of the markup language HTML with facilities which allow dynamic processing such as that associated with animations. There is an entry within the dictionary for this term.
[2] It stands for Three Letter Acronym.

keyboard and clicking a mouse; the former activity is a lot more efficient when abbreviations are used, even though it can lead to some degree of obfuscation.[3]

It is also worth detailing what I have *not* included. First, with a few exceptions, I have steered away from commercial products. Many products last for a short time and a printed dictionary would not be able to keep pace with this. I have, however, included references to products such as Internet Explorer which will be with us for some time— at least until the next edition of the dictionary.

I have also steered clear of general computing terms. The only exceptions are when a term is extensively used within the dictionary, such as *byte*, and where a term is worth highlighting because of its connection with the Internet; for example there is a short entry on the computer operating system UNIX because it was the first operating system to contain Internet programming facilities.

Finally, I would like to thank Gordon Davis, Kim Fowler, Blaine Price, and Mike Richards, four colleagues who provided entries for the dictionary and Prof. David Barron for painstakingly reading the dictionary and providing many suggestions. I would also like to thank all the members of newsgroups and chat room participants who tolerated my near silent presence[4] and my occasional questions about a particular piece of jargon.

I hope you enjoy using this book—I certainly enjoyed researching and writing it.

DARREL INCE
MILTON KEYNES 2000

---

[3] It has led to a form of written communication known as Weblish, for which there is an entry in the dictionary.
[4] A process known as lurking.

AAA server A server which provides AUTHENTICATION, AUTHORIZATION, and accounting services for financial transactions. Such servers are normally used within ECOMMERCE applications. For example, they are used to check that a particular user has been authorized to make a particular transaction, such as a debit transaction in a credit card payment system.

abbreviation The Web and the Internet float on a flood of abbreviations. They are often used to save time when posting to a NEWSGROUP or writing an EMAIL. This dictionary contains most of the common abbreviations used in such forums: *see*, for example, AFAIK and BBL.

ABI *See* APPLICATION BINARY INTERFACE.

above the fold When a WEB PAGE is displayed in a BROWSER the area of the page that is displayed is referred to as being above the fold. The contents that lie below are known as BELOW THE FOLD. The term is derived from the newspaper industry where the fold refers to the paper fold in broadsheet paper.

absolute link A HYPERLINK in a WEB PAGE which specifies the full path to the Web page being linked rather than a RELATIVE LINK; that is, each folder needed to traverse to the page is specified. So if a Web page is found in folder A within folder B which is in folder C, then the path to the page is C/B/A. Absolute links are problematic when the directories in which the pages are contained are moved or renamed, as it leads to BROWSERS being unable to find these pages. Because of this, most professional WEB SITES use RELATIVE LINKS.

absolute path A list of directories and a file that specifies the path to a WEB PAGE from a particular FOLDER. So, for example, if a Web page is contained in folder C which is stored in folder B which, in turn, is stored in folder A, then the path

to the page is A/B/C. When a user clicks on a HYPERLINK or specifies a path which is an absolute path, the page specified by this path is displayed on a BROWSER. Absolute paths are usually frowned on by professional WEB DESIGNERS since, if it is necessary to move pages which are specified in this way, the Web pages in which they are referenced need to be modified. Because of this, most professional Web pages contain RELATIVE LINKS.

acceptable use policy A synonym for AUTHORIZED USE POLICY.

access To access a network such as the Internet means to gain access to the facilities of the network, such as WEB SERVERS and FILE SERVERS. The process is achieved via a LOG-IN. Users who can access a network are usually given ACCESS RIGHTS which determine the range of resources they can access and what they can do with them. For example, they might only be allowed to read and write to certain FILES.

access control The process of ensuring that only authorized users are allowed access to a computer network. There are a number of techniques which are employed for this including PASSWORDS and DIGITAL SIGNATURES. For example, passwords are used to limit access to a system to those users who have been given ACCOUNTS.

access control list Data containing information about the services and resources in a DISTRIBUTED SYSTEM that users are allowed to access. For example, such a list would contain the names of users or USER GROUPS who would be allowed to read or write to certain files in the system. This is one of the devices used to control access to a distributed system.

access number The telephone number that is used when the user of a network employs DIAL-UP ACCESS to access the facilities of that network.

access profile A collection of data about the user of an ECOMMERCE application which is used by an AAA SERVER in order to identify the data and authorize any financial transactions that are initiated by it. This data normally includes the user's name, PIN, and PASSWORD.

access provider Another, less frequently used, name for an INTERNET SERVICE PROVIDER or ISP. The term is sometimes used to describe companies that provide Internet service providers with wholesale access to the Internet.

access right The collection of rights that the user of a DISTRIBUTED SYSTEM has for accessing the system. For example, a user may have access rights to read and write files in certain directories in a subset of the computers that make up the system. A NETWORK OPERATING SYSTEM ensures that any attempt to access resources outside those specified in the access rights of a user are prevented.

access token A security device which is usually attached to the COM port of a computer and which allows access to the system to which the computer is connected. It is often used in connection with SMART CARDS. *See also* DONGLE.

accessware A generic term used to describe the software that regulates ACCESS to a network to authorized users. It includes components of a software system that check PASSWORDS and mediate access to resources such as SERVERS and FILES. Such software resides in a NETWORK OPERATING SYSTEM.

account When a user is allowed access to a networked computer system they are associated with a collection of data known as an account. An important item of data associated with an account is the PASSWORD of the user. Accounts have a number of functions, one of which is to keep track of the use made of the resources in a system—in this case data—such as when a user carries out a LOG-IN or a LOG-OFF associated with the account. Accounts are also used for billing in commercial environments.

account management A sub-discipline of NETWORK MANAGEMENT. It consists of monitoring the resource usage (files, processor time, access time) of a network, ascribing the usage to users or groups of users and, in a commercial environment, billing these users for the resources they have employed. The level of sophistication of account management depends on the organization that is managing the network. A large commercial organization with many divisions and departments which have separate budgets requires a large amount of account management, while an INTERNET SERVICE PROVIDER that charges a flat rate for access has a low level of account management.

account name A series of letters and digits which uniquely identifies an ACCOUNT on a computer or on a network.

ACH *See* AUTOMATED CLEARING HOUSE.

ACID *See* ATOMICITY CONSISTENCY ISOLATION DURABILITY.

ACK *See* ACKNOWLEDGEMENT.

acknowledged datagram service A DATAGRAM SERVICE where the successful receipt of the data associated with the service is acknowledged and some form of acknowledgement data passed to the computer that sent the original data. This ensures that the computer that sent the data does not have to resend it.

acknowledgement A term, almost invariably known as ACK, which is used to describe the acknowledgement that a computer or hardware device on a network sends back to another computer when it receives a packet of data. The receipt of this acknowledgement is a signal that the data does not have to be sent again.

ACL *See* ACCESS CONTROL LIST.

ACM *See* ASSOCIATION FOR COMPUTING MACHINERY.

acoustic coupler A technology that was used to convert electrical signals from a computer signal to sound which was then transferred across a telephone line. This sound was then reconverted into the original signal at the other end of the line. Acoustic couplers were one of the first technologies used to connect computers to a network. They are now very rarely used and have been superseded by electronic MODEMS.

active attack An intrusion into a computer network which attempts to delete or modify the data stored on the computers which form part of the network. This is one of the most serious forms of attack since many companies' operations critically depend on data. *See also* PASSIVE ATTACK.

Active Channel® The most popular implementation of the CHANNEL DEFINITION FORMAT, a standard which enables a broadcaster to generate content in real time to a BROWSER. Active Channel technology was developed by the Microsoft Corporation. The user of this technology is able to receive Web content in real time as it is broadcast. It is an example of PUSH TECHNOLOGY where a SERVER broadcasts information to a CLIENT rather than the client asking for the information.

active code or **active content** Synonyms for EXECUTABLE CONTENT or ACTIVE CONTENT.

Active Database Object® A technology developed by the Microsoft Corporation which allows ACTIVE SERVER PAGES to access databases. It allows the users of a BROWSER to interact with large databases: for example, the user of a retail ECOMMERCE application would be able to browse a database of products looking for potential purchases using this technology. It is often abbreviated to ADO.

Active Desktop® A term coined by the Microsoft Corporation to describe the integration of the desktop with the Internet. When INTERNET EXPLORER 4 was developed, Microsoft made the decision to make the desktop the primary means of organizing Internet-related information. For example, it enabled the user to place shortcuts to favourite WEB SITES on the desktop rather than as BOOKMARKS in a BROWSER.

active repeater 1. A hardware device that amplifies light signals which travel down a fibre optic communication line. The active repeater receives a light signal and converts it into an electrical signal which is then amplified to full strength and retransmitted as a light signal. This prevents the light signals from becoming weaker and weaker. *See also* OPTICAL REPEATER.
2. Occasionally used for an amplification device attached to other communications media.

Active Server Pages® A technology pioneered by the Microsoft Corporation which triggers processing at a WEB SERVER when a WEB PAGE is requested by a BROWSER. Normally when a browser requests a page from a WEB SERVER it is sent directly back to the browser. Active Server Page technology triggers some processing, such as inserting topical data, when a Web page which has the FILE EXTENSION ASP is requested. The server examines the file, identifies any SCRIPTS that need to be executed, executes them and inserts the results into the Web page. A typical example of an application that might use ASP technology is network monitoring, where pages which have dynamic information embedded in them that describes the current state of a network can be sent back to a SYSTEM ADMINISTRATOR. This technology is similar in intent to that of SERVER SIDE INCLUDES. It is usually referred to as ASP.

Active X® An important technology which is mainly used for the embedding of EXECUTABLE CONTENT within a WEB PAGE. The technology was developed by Microsoft, primarily for its own INTERNET EXPLORER browser. The intent is the same as that of APPLETS: executing program code within a Web page. The executable code is known as an ACTIVE X CONTROL. A typical use for Active X is for embedding a simple spreadsheet within a Web page which can then be used by the user of a browser. One of the problems with Active X software is that it can potentially modify files on a computer and hence is a ready-made host for VIRUSES. In order to prevent this, Active X controls are packaged with a DIGITAL CERTIFICATE which provides confidence that a reputable software developer has produced the control. The Active X approach to security is in contrast to that used by JAVA for APPLETS where a SANDBOX is used.

Active X Control The name given to the program code which is normally embedded in a WEB PAGE using ACTIVE X technology. *See* EXECUTABLE CONTENT.

activity monitor A form of VIRUS DETECTION SOFTWARE which monitors the running of a computer and reports any suspicious activities, such as an attempt to alter basic OPERATING SYSTEM information like a PASSWORD FILE. The term is sometimes used to describe software which is used to monitor any unusual activity on a computer system that could indicate a possible intrusion: for example, a day user attempting to LOG-IN after midnight.

actor singer waiter Webmaster The Internet version of the actor/singer/waiter who is filling in on table-waiting jobs until he or she can get a break in films: in effect someone who is occupying a menial job in the expectation of gaining a lucrative Internet-based position such as a WEBMASTER.

adaptive digital pulse code modulation A COMPRESSION technique in which the difference between electronic signals is stored rather than a compressed version of the actual values of the signals. If a signal does not vary much, this is a highly effective way of compressing a signal.

adaptive Huffman coding A dynamic variant of HUFFMAN CODING for data COMPRESSION that can adjust the representation of characters depending on local properties of the text that is being processed. For example a file might contain natural language text and computer programs. An adaptive Huffman compression scheme would use one transformation for the natural language and another for the programs. The technique is also known as the FGK ALGORITHM.

adaptive Lempel Ziv Welsh coding A variant of the LEMPEL ZIV WELSH CODING method for data COMPRESSION which uses a dictionary with variable length entries.

adaptive routing algorithm When a ROUTER uses an adaptive routing algorithm to decide the next computer to which to transfer a PACKET of data, it examines the traffic conditions in order to determine a route which is as near optimal as possible. For example, it tries to pick a route which involves communication lines which have light traffic. This strategy is in contrast to a NON-ADAPTIVE ROUTING ALGORITHM.

ADC *See* ANALOGUE TO DIGITAL CONVERSION, ANALOGUE TO DIGITAL CONVERTER, or AUTOMATIC DATA CAPTURE.

additional server A NAME SERVER used for the INTERNET DOMAIN NAME SERVICE which would be used if a PRIMARY SERVER and a SECONDARY SERVER are unable to carry out their functions.

add-on virus The most common form of VIRUS. It functions by adding program code to the code of the computer which has been infected. It usually alters the START-UP FILE of the infected computer so that the virus code is executed first before the normal code which starts up the computer. Such a virus is activated when the computer is first booted up after infection; the virus code then carries out some potentially destructive act such as deleting important files.

address book A collection of EMAIL user addresses stored in a simple database associated with an email program. An address book allows the user of the program to find EMAIL ADDRESSes and transfer them quickly to an email. Entries in an address book could be those of individual users or groups of users.

address harvester A program used by SPAMMERs in order to find and store EMAIL addresses which can then be used to send spam mail. These harvesters are BOTS which wander over WEB SITES, NEWSGROUPS, BULLETIN BOARDS, PROFILES, CHAT ROOMS, and MEMBER DIRECTORY areas that are used by INTERNET SERVICE PROVIDERS. They function in a simple way, in that they read text and look for strings which match the format of an email address. A common way to defeat such software programs is somehow to disguise an email address, at the same time making it obvious to the reader that it is an address, for example by inserting the word 'dot' for full stops in the domain and separating the name of the recipient from the address of the DOMAIN NAME by some intervening text. This technique is known as a SPAMBLOCK.

address resolution Each computer in a network has a physical address. Address resolution is the term used to refer to the process of looking up that address given a computer's INTERNET PROTOCOL ADDRESS (IP address). So, for example, if some data is to be sent to a computer which specifies its IP address, then this address needs to be converted into the computer's real address for the computer to receive it correctly. In order to do this the ADDRESS RESOLUTION PROTOCOL is used.

Address Resolution Protocol A PRO-TOCOL used to convert an INTERNET PROTOCOL ADDRESS (IP address) to the physical address of a device on a network. The correspondence between the IP address and the physical device is stored in a table known as an ARP CACHE.

adhocracy A term used to describe companies that do not rely on job descriptions, hierarchy, standards, and procedures; rather, workers in the company carry out tasks because they need to be done. Adhocracies have, in the past, mainly been found in creative industries such as advertising. However, they have started to appear in companies which are associated with the Internet. Computer networks encourage this form of working since information can be easily shared between staff, thus obviating the need for formal meetings.

adjacency search A search using a SEARCH ENGINE which looks for documents containing words that are located physically close to each other; for example, a search for a document which has the words 'judo' and Japan' close to each other in a WEB PAGE.

administrative address To subscribe to a MAILING LIST or request information from the list, this is the EMAIL ADDRESS to which to send messages. For example, a common way of subscribing to a mailing list is to send an email to an administrative address with the message 'Subscribe'. This would then ensure that the sender was registered with the list.

administrative log-in The process whereby the SYSTEM ADMINISTRATOR of a networked system carries out a LOG-IN. Often, this form of log-in is carried out by the system administrator providing a well-known account name such as SYSADMIN and a password such as SYS. This form of log-in is often used by intruders to gain access to a system because they can often guess the administrator's account name and password and assume his or her privileges. A wise system administrator disables administrative log-ins and logs in as a normal user but with greatly enhanced PERMISSIONS and ACCESS RIGHTS.

administrivia Small tasks associated with some Internet activity, such as maintaining a MAILING LIST.

ADN Abbreviation used for Any Day Now in CHAT ROOMS, EMAILS, and NEWSGROUPS. It is usually used as a cynical reaction to the propensity of software companies to announce a software product which they claim is only a few weeks from being released when, in reality, it usually emerges in a year or so.

ADO® *See* ACTIVE DATABASE OBJECT.

ADPCM *See* ADAPTIVE DIGITAL PULSE CODE MODULATION.

ad server A server that maintains BANNER ADVERTS for a collection of WEB SERVERS. It has a number of functions: it loads the adverts into selected WEB PAGES, ensures that a wide variety of adverts are presented, and keeps statistics on the effectiveness of the adverts in terms of the number of CLICKS that are made on them by the users of browsers.

ADSL *See* ASYMMETRICAL DIGITAL SUBSCRIBER LINES.

ad space Space on a WEB PAGE which is reserved for advertising, normally BANNER ADVERTS.

Advanced Encryption Standard The replacement for the DATA ENCRYPTION STANDARD.

Advanced Network and Services A consortium formed by publishers, universities, and INTERNET SERVICE PROVIDERS set up to promote the use of technologies such as the WORLD WIDE WEB in education, for example by promoting EBOOKS and TELEPRESENCE systems in education.

Advanced Networked Systems Architecture A research group, often known as ANSA, which was established in Cambridge, England in 1984. They have had a major effect on the specification and design of distributed systems. Their ANSA Reference Manual is an excellent source book for those involved in both the hardware and software aspects of DISTRIBUTED SYSTEMS.

Advanced Research Projects Agency An agency of the US Department of Defense which sponsored much of the early research which eventually came to fruition as technologies used on the Internet. The research was motivated by the US government's need for computer communications which could survive high levels of conventional or nuclear attack.

Advanced Research Projects Agency Network A network, more commonly known as ARPANET, which was the forerunner of the Internet. In the 1970s it was the proving ground for many of the technologies that are currently used on the Internet. The network was funded by the ADVANCED RESEARCH PROJECTS AGENCY.

Advanced Streaming Format® A Microsoft technology used for media storage.

advert auction An ONLINE AUCTION where WEB SITES submit space on their WEB PAGES which are available for adverts—usually BANNER ADVERTS—and advertisers bid for these spaces.

advertisement filter A program which removes BANNER ADVERTS from WEB PAGES. Such adverts are often a visual intrusion and this type of software is used to clean up Web pages. Often such software is not totally reliable; usually it removes most adverts, but not all of them.

advertorial Advertising found on the WORLD WIDE WEB which is designed to fit in with the editorial content and style of a WEB PAGE. This is a technique which is often used in conventional publishing

but has also spread rapidly to Web publishing.

advert server A SERVER which stores a large number of BANNER ADVERTS in files. These adverts are requested by code inserted into a WEB PAGE. Such servers can be relatively simple, sending adverts to a page on a periodic basis, or sophisticated, sending adverts of a certain category and for differing lengths of time. Effectively an advert server acts as a special-purpose FILE SERVER which uses PUSH TECHNOLOGY.

ad view A single advert which appears without scrolling on a WEB PAGE. It is sometimes known as an IMPRESSION.

aero In 2000 seven new DOMAIN NAMES were created. aero was one of these. It is intended for use within the aero industry.

AES *See* ADVANCED ENCRYPTION STANDARD.

AFAICT Abbreviation for As Far As I Can Tell used in CHAT ROOMS, EMAILS, and NEWSGROUPS. It is used to indicate a small degree of doubt about the statement which it precedes.

AFAIK Abbreviation for As Far As I Know used in CHAT ROOMS, EMAILS, and NEWSGROUPS. Like AFAICT it is used to indicate some degree of doubt about the statement which it precedes.

affiliate program An alternative term for ASSOCIATE PROGRAM.

AFK Abbreviation for Away From Keyboard used in CHAT ROOMS, EMAILS, and NEWSGROUPS. It is used to indicate that the person who has written it has temporarily left the computer. It is usually used in chat rooms when, for example, a comfort break is taken. It is occasionally used in other forums to inform other users that a long break is to be taken, for example to go on holiday.

agent A program which helps a user carry out some computer-related task. For example, an agent might be used to remind the user of a network that he or she should be sending a message to another user by a certain time. There are a number of categories of agents.

REACTIVE AGENTS just respond to stimuli. A simple example of this type of agent is one that initiates a sound such as a beep when an email arrives. A DELIBERATIVE AGENT is one that uses some knowledge of an application area such as airline ticket booking to aid the user in carrying out a task such as booking an airline ticket or scheduling a meeting. This type of agent usually employs artificial intelligence technology. COLLABORATIVE AGENTS are collections of agents which work together. For example, an agent which carries out the process of planning the diary of a user may collaborate with an agent used for booking airline tickets in order to achieve an optimal spread of a user's time for a journey. A MOBILE AGENT is a program which moves from one computer to another carrying out some task for a user. For example, such an agent, used by a computer manufacturer, might visit the sites of components suppliers, find out how many components are in stock, and then return to its home computer and order an optimal mix of components to minimize some function of delivery time and price. Agents are very similar in concept to BOTS; indeed the two communities overlap considerably, and there is no consistent definition of what is a bot and what is an agent.

agent name delivery The process of developing a WEB SITE in such a way that SEARCH ENGINES are not sent to the HOME PAGE seen by normal visitors, but to a page containing SPAMDEXING material. The page is optimized in such a way that the site features prominently in a search using a search engine. Usually technologies such as SERVER SIDE INCLUDES are used for this. It is also known as BAIT AND SWITCH. The page that provides the search engine with data is called a GATEWAY PAGE.

aggregate buying site A shopping WEB SITE which puts a number of people together, all of whom want to buy the same item, for example a refrigerator. The site keeps details of how many people want to buy a certain item and then use this information to drive the price down with the company selling the product. The more people want to buy the item the further the price is driven down.

aggregated loan scam A common scam found on the Internet where participants are told of a scheme which aggregates all their debts into one loan at an advantageous interest rate. When the participants sign up for the loan they discover that the small print on an obscure WEB PAGE commits them to a large number of hidden charges which make the total cost of the loan larger than any of the loans and debts they are currently committed to. Often such scams are notified to users via SPAM.

aiff A FILE EXTENSION for the aiff sound format found on the Internet. It is used to indicate that a particular FILE contains sounds which are to be played using the audio generation facilities on a computer.

AIM *See* ASSOCIATION FOR INTERACTIVE MEDIA.

AIUI Abbreviation for As I Understand It used in CHAT ROOMS, EMAILS, and NEWS-GROUPS. Like AFAICT it indicates some degree of hesitancy about the statement that it normally precedes.

AKA Abbreviation for Also Known As used in CHAT ROOMS, EMAILS, and NEWS-GROUPS. Conventionally it is used to indicate an alternative name for a product; less conventionally it is used pejoratively, as in 'Operating system X AKA Crapware'. Sometimes it is placed in a SIG FILE to indicate a nickname: for example, 'Darren Tompkinson AKA The Vicious Reaper'.

alerting service A service which a user can subscribe to which delivers electronic news on a regular basis, or whenever an event of interest to the user occurs. For example, there are a number of WEB SITES associated with newspapers that provide emails which notify a subscriber of news to match their interests. Another example of an alerting service is one which emails a WEBMASTER when a Web site cannot be connected to a BROWSER, usually because of some hardware or software failure.

alert protocol A PROTOCOL used by the SECURE SOCKETS LAYER (SSL); it is used to transmit basic messages between the BROWSER and SERVER that are communicating using SSL. For example, it enables

algorithm 8

one of the participants to signal to the other that no more information is going to be sent.

algorithm A documented series of steps which leads to the transformation of some data. For example, in order to calculate the sum of a series of numbers a possible algorithm would involve repeatedly adding the numbers to be summed to a running total. Computer programs are a manifestation of algorithms which allow them to be executed very quickly.

alias A sequence of characters in a UNIFORM RESOURCE LOCATOR that stands for a much longer sequence of characters. For example the URL http://www.open. ac.uk/~studentdetails contains the alias ~studentdetails which could stand for the sequence of characters mainfiles/secondyear/computing/projects/coursem99 that designates the file containing the HYPERTEXT MARKUP LANGUAGE text for a WEB PAGE. When a WEB SERVER encounters a URL which has an alias in it, it substitutes the sequence of characters for the alias. Aliases are used in order to reduce the amount of typing that users of a BROWSER have to carry out when initially they want to access a Web page.

alignment A term used to describe the way that text is positioned on a WEB PAGE or on a conventional, paper-based page; there are a number of alignment options including left, centred, and right.

ALIWEB A search engine which is distinguished from its contemporaries such as ALTA VISTA by the fact that it does not automatically index sites. If a WEBMASTER wants a site to be indexed by ALIWEB then he or she must write a special file. Because of the difficulty of doing this, ALIWEB has a much smaller database than search engines such as LYCOS and has suffered in popularity.

all in one search engine A term used to describe a METASEARCH ENGINE.

almost face-to-face computer-mediated conferencing A form of computer conferencing which approaches the quality of face-to-face conferencing. A good example of this type of conferencing is CU SEEME. See SYNCHRONOUS COMPUTER-MEDIATED CONFERENCING and ASYNCHRONOUS COMPUTER-MEDIATED CONFERENCING.

alpha geek The most knowledgeable or proficient GEEK in a company. Usually they have a huge depth of knowledge about one particular technology, for example JAVA or ACTIVE X.

alpha software Software that is not thoroughly tested by the developer before it is released to customers; see also BETA SOFTWARE. Alpha software usually contains serious errors, while beta software contains annoying but relatively minor errors.

alt This designates those NEWSGROUPS which discuss alternative topics; these topics are often adult in nature, are of a bizarre nature, or promote alternative lifestyles.

alta visitor A visitor to a WEB SITE who has entered the site via a SEARCH ENGINE rather than by other means, such as via a GURU SITE. The term is a play on the words ALTA VISTA, one of the most popular SEARCH ENGINES.

Alta Vista One of the most powerful SEARCH ENGINES at present. It was originally developed by the now defunct Digital Equipment Corporation (DEC). The engine emerged from a project which originated in one of the DEC research labs that had developed very powerful software for keeping track of EMAILS. Reputedly the name came from the fact that, when the project was discussed, the whiteboard that was used contained the unerased second word of Palo Alto which was then modified and concatenated with Vista.

alt text The text associated with a graphic image contained in a WEB PAGE. This text is seen when the image is being loaded and has not yet appeared. It is often seen when a mouse is passed over the image.

Amaya The experimental Web BROWSER used by the WORLD WIDE WEB CONSORTIUM to explore future extensions to both SERVER technology and to MARKUP LANGUAGES such as HTML and XML. For example, it has been used to test out the PNG graphics format. It represents the browser equivalent of the WORLD WIDE WEB CONSORTIUM experimental WEB SERVER known as JIGSAW. One of its features not found on other browsers is that it can show what a page looks like on another mainstream browser.

Amazon effect A term sometimes used to describe an ECOMMERCE company which attracts large amounts of investment funding even though its profits are small or non-existent. The term is derived from one of the most prominent examples of this effect, the online bookstore Amazon.

AMBW Abbreviation for All My Best Wishes used in CHAT ROOMS, EMAILS, and NEWSGROUPS. Normally used to sign off an email or a session in a chat room.

American National Standards Institute The US organization which is responsible for setting standards. It consists of private, governmental and non-governmental organizations such as research labs. Standards produced by the American National Standards Institute, usually abbreviated to ANSI, are often adopted by the INTERNATIONAL STANDARDS ORGANIZATION. Curiously it has not been involved in a major way in the setting of Internet and World Wide Web standards.

American Registry for Internet Numbers An American organization, often abbreviated to ARIN, which manages the dispensing of INTERNET PROTOCOL ADDRESSes to North America, South America, the Caribbean, and sub-Saharan Africa. It is one of three organizations around the world which does this, the others being the RÉSEAUX IP EUROPÉENNE NETWORK COORDINATION CENTRE and the ASIA PACIFIC NETWORK INFORMATION CENTRE.

American Standard Code for Information Interchange A standard which defines an alphanumeric set of characters storable within 7 bits. This standard virtually dominates the computer industry. It is usually abbreviated to ASCII. Its main competitor is UNICODE.

America Online hell A collection of computer programs which was used by CRACKERS to carry out unauthorized

ACCESS to the system run by the INTERNET SERVICE PROVIDER America Online (AOL). Also known as AOHell.

amplifier An electronic circuit which is used to increase the strength of an ANALOGUE SIGNAL; without such a device the signal would eventually become so weak that it could not be detected. Amplifier technology is a very mature engineering technology.

amplitude modulation The process whereby a DIGITAL SIGNAL is sent over a TRANSMISSION LINE by changing the amplitude of a sine wave known as a CARRIER.

analogue signal A signal which consists of a continuously varying voltage. For example, the signals which are generated by sources of sound are analogue signals. Before being processed by a computer such signals have to undergo ANALOGUE TO DIGITAL CONVERSION. Analogue signals are in contrast to DIGITAL SIGNALS which consist of discrete values of zeroes and ones.

analogue to digital conversion The process whereby an ANALOGUE SIGNAL such as a voice recording consisting of continuously varying waves is converted into a binary DIGITAL SIGNAL. This is carried out by splitting the signal into a series of exact values represented by a binary number, a process called QUANTIZATION.

analogue to digital converter A hardware device or a program running on a computer which takes continuously varying ANALOGUE SIGNALS such as voice data and converts them into a discrete DIGITAL SIGNAL.

analytical buyer A term used in connection with ECOMMERCE. It describes an online buyer who is experienced in searching the Internet for information such as the prices of products and services. Analytical buyers are proficient in technologies such as SEARCH ENGINES and SEARCH BOTS and are knowledgeable about GURU SITES relevant to their search.

anchor An area on a WEB PAGE which, when clicked by the user of a BROWSER, displays the WEB PAGE which is referred to by the URL associated with the anchor. An anchor can be a TEXT ANCHOR or a GRAPHIC ANCHOR. *See also* ANCHOR IMAGE.

anchor image A graphic embedded in an HTML PAGE underneath which is embedded a HYPERLINK. Clicking on the image results in the page referenced in the link being displayed on a BROWSER. A typical image might be that of a BUTTON.

angel A term prevalent in SILICON VALLEY to describe investors in Internet start-up companies. It was originally used to describe the backers of theatrical productions.

angry fruit salad A description given to a WEB PAGE or WEB SITE which contains a large amount of visually distracting media such as ANIMATIONS and VIDEO CLIPS. As Web technology has developed this problem has become more prevalent. Initially, in the early days of the World Wide Web, it was applied to Web pages which contained BLINKING TEXT but now encompasses pages containing large amounts of animation, rapidly changing BANNER ADVERTS, and SOUND CLIPS. *See also* BLENDO PAGE and WORST OF THE WEB.

ANI *See* AUTOMATIC NUMBER IDENTIFICATION.

animated GIF A primitive technology used to provide ANIMATIONS, particularly on WEB SITES. It consists of sequentially displaying a series of GIF graphics which differ only slightly from each other to give the impression of movement. The technology is essentially an electronic version of the flick books which children use to produce simple animations, where each page of the book contains a slightly different image. *See also* GIF ANIMATION TOOL.

animation The process of providing some form of moving video. There are a number of technologies that are used for animation, ranging from simple ones such as GIF ANIMATION to much more complex multimedia packages which provide a whole gamut of facilities including sound and video.

anime A form of Japanese GRAPHIC IMAGE which is particularly suited to publication on the WORLD WIDE WEB.

Annie A WEB PAGE that has not been changed for a considerable time. The term is derived from the comic book character Annie who was a poor forgotten orphan. Such a page is also known as an ORPHAN ANNIE. The term has also been applied to an INVISIBLE PAGE which is not linked to any other Web pages. *See also* COBWEB SITE.

annotation Notes that a user can add to a WEB PAGE. The notes are stored locally on a CLIENT and can be accessed when a user reads the page with a BROWSER.

announcement newsgroup Specialized NEWSGROUPS which are devoted to announcing commercial products, commercial services, and new WEB SITES. These provide a much more acceptable way of advertising a product than activities such as SPAMMING.

annoyance bot A BOT which intrudes into a CHAT ROOM and carries out some annoying act such as sending obscene messages to participants.

anonymizer site A WEB SITE which allows you to use the facilities of the Web without disclosing your identity. Such sites are employed by users who do not wish to leave information about their identity on the Internet. This prevents SPAMmers sending unsolicited EMAIL to you or CYBERSTALKERS contacting you. Such a site is an example of the use of a PROXY SERVER.

anonymous FTP The name given to the process whereby a user is able to copy a file from a FILE SERVER using the FILE TRANSFER PROTOCOL without having to pass through the normal ACCESS CONTROLS of the server. Usually this is achieved by the use of a special account name and an arbitrary PASSWORD or no password at all. FTPing a file is expedited by means of placing software or data that can be downloaded into an area of the file store of a SERVER known as a PUBLIC DIRECTORY.

Anonymous Internet Mercantile Protocol There are a large number of PROTOCOLS which have been developed to handle secure interaction between a buyer and a seller on the Internet. This is one of the best known. It was developed by the US company AT and T.

anonymous posting A POSTING made to a NEWSGROUP where the poster does not divulge his or her identity. This is usually carried out via an ANONYMOUS REMAILER SERVICE. There are usually two reasons for anonymous postings: the first is that the poster does not want to attract SPAM, and the second is that the poster does not directly want to be associated with the opinions expressed in the posting. For example, the posting may be a critical comment on the company that he or she works for.

anonymous remailer service A service which acts as a mail intermediary. It allows users to send mail to a destination anonymously so that SPAMMers cannot discover an EMAIL ADDRESS and send unwanted EMAIL. Such a service is normally used for sending POSTINGS to NEWSGROUPS. Some INTERNET SERVICE PROVIDERS offer anonymous email services, as does DEJA-NEWS. There are also a number of WEB SITES which offer the service free.

anorak A term used as an alternative to NERD in the United Kingdom.

ANSA *See* ADVANCED NETWORKED SYSTEMS ARCHITECTURE.

ANSI *See* AMERICAN NATIONAL STANDARDS INSTITUTE.

answer mode The state of a MODEM when it receives signals from a computer system.

anti-aliasing The process of adding extra colours or shading to an image in order to minimize the jagged images found in digital graphics. Most graphic packages contain facilities which enable the user to carry out anti-aliasing. Although it is mainly used for colour images it can also be used for black and white images.

anti-spam software Software which prevents the receipt of unsolicited EMAIL. There are two categories of anti-spam software. The first category prevents SPAM emails from being read by the user of an EMAIL READER. This type of software examines the header of an email; the part of the email that lists the sender; and the text of the message. It then rejects any emails which the user has notified as potential spam by comparing the contents of the email with a list of keywords, phrases, and known spammers' addresses. These are set up by the user prior to using the software. This type of software can operate either by scanning a MAIL SERVER prior to emails being downloaded to the reader or by scanning mail which has been received by the reader. When spam is identified by a tool at the reader the tool places it in a special folder which can be perused by the user or just ignored and periodically deleted. Anti-spam software which examines mail in a mail server should be used with care since such software has been known to delete mail which is genuine. Programs in the second category of anti-spam software are used to process a spam email in order to determine where it has been sent from so that the recipient can mail a protest to the sender or the INTERNET SERVICE PROVIDER that hosts the user. There are a few anti-spam software programs on the market which combine both the functions of filtering email and determining the address of the sender.

anti-virus software Software which monitors a computer and its files in order to detect any VIRUS intrusions that have occurred. Such software, for example, examines system files to see if they have been modified.

anycast address An IP ADDRESS which is used in the IPV6 replacement for TCP-IP. It identifies a number of interfaces on a single computer connected to the Internet.

AOHell An abbreviation for AMERICA ONLINE HELL.

Apache One of the most popular WEB SERVERS. It is distributed as FREEWARE. It was originally based on a server developed by the NATIONAL CENTER FOR SUPERCOMPUTING APPLICATIONS. It is almost certainly the most popular Web server currently in use. Its name is derived from the fact that the first few versions had a large number of PATCHES applied to them.

API *See* APPLICATION PROGRAMMING INTERFACE.

APNIC *See* ASIA PACIFIC NETWORK INFORMATION CENTRE.

applet A program, written in JAVA, that can be embedded in a WEB PAGE using special TAGS. When a BROWSER links to that page, the page, along with the applet, is transferred to the computer on which the browser resides. The applet starts executing when the area in which it resides on the page comes within the browser window. Applets can carry out a diverse number of functions. For example, they are used for ANIMATIONS, for FORMS processing, and for access to remote databases. One of the potential problems with applets is that they are programs transferred to a computer from the SERVER containing the Web page in which they are embedded. This means that applets could, theoretically, provide a means whereby VIRUSES could be spread from one computer to another. In order to prevent this, the original designers of the applet mechanism have severely limited the actions which an applet can carry out; for example, they are not allowed to read from or write to a file, in effect using a SANDBOX. In later versions of the language DIGITAL SIGNATURES are used as a mechanism for preventing destructive access to a computer. When applets first appeared they revolutionized the development of WEB PAGES: until then such pages had consisted of text, some very primitive animations, and some forms processing which was carried out by the server on which a Web page resided, rather than the client. Since applets have appeared, a large number of other technologies have emerged which achieve much of what was intended by applets, for example ACTIVE X and SCRIPTING LANGUAGES. *See also* JAVA APPLET RATING SERVICE.

appletviewer A program which executes an APPLET. It processes an HTML file containing the applet, removes the HTML statements and then carries out the execution. It is a much more efficient way of debugging applets than using a conventional browser, which has a high overhead associated with it. The appletviewer is part of the standard distribution kit for JAVA, produced by Sunsoft.

application binary interface A software interface that allows programs such as CLIENTS and SERVERS to gain access to the facilities of the operating system in which they are executed.

applicationcentric EDI The augmentation of conventional EDI technology with security technology such as CRYPTOGRAPHY in order to enable the transfer of confidential data across the Internet. The use of the Internet as a medium for ELECTRONIC DATA INTERCHANGE brings many performance gains; however, there are potential security problems with sending data over an open network, Applicationcentric EDI is an attempt to nullify these disadvantages.

Application Channel A conduit through which updated versions of a software product can be loaded into a computer using PUSH TECHNOLOGY. It is associated with the OPEN SOFTWARE DESCRIPTION language originally developed by the Microsoft Corporation.

application gateway An application gateway connects two applications via the APPLICATION LAYER in the TCP-IP architecture. An example of such a gateway is one which forwards EMAIL written using one format to a mail box which requires another format.

application interface A set of modules which can be called by a programmer in order to exercise the FUNCTIONS of the system in which the modules are embedded. For example, an EMAIL package would have an application interface which would allow programmers to write programs to send and receive email. *See also* APPLICATION PROGRAMMING INTERFACE.

application layer A layer in the OSI REFERENCE MODEL. It is the layer in which applications such as SERVERS and NEWSREADERS reside. These applications produce and consume data which is sent to and received from lower layers. In CLIENT SERVER COMPUTING systems this is the layer where a client resides. There is also a layer known as the application layer in the TCP-IP architecture; this combines the functions of the APPLICATION LAYER, the

PRESENTATION LAYER, and the SESSION LAYER in the OSI model.

application monitor A form of VIRUS DETECTION SOFTWARE which monitors the execution of programs to see whether they are exhibiting behaviour which is similar to that of VIRUSes: for example, carrying out the deletion of important files.

application programming interface A set of software facilities that enable programmers to develop programs which interact with the software that provides the interface. For example, a word processor might have an application programming interface that allows a programmer to enhance and customize it.

application server A computer and a collection of software which communicates with a WEB SERVER and which provides those services associated with application programs such as accessing databases or files or carrying out complex calculations.

application service provider A company which not only offers the facilities of an INTERNET SERVICE PROVIDER, but also services such as WEB DESIGN, WEB SITE PROMOTION, and accounting. Such a company is usually the first stop for a conventional company that wishes to enter the field of ECOMMERCE.

Archie This can be regarded as the parent of all SEARCH ENGINES. It was developed in 1990 for UNIX systems and enabled users to locate and retrieve files from FTP SERVERS around the embryonic Internet. It is now of historical interest.

ArchitextSpider The SPIDER associated with the Excite SEARCH ENGINE.

archive A collection of files which are often compressed and which are usually available through the use of ANONYMOUS FTP. Such files are found in FTP SERVERS or FILE SERVERS. A typical archive might contain SHAREWARE software.

archive site A SERVER which stores files that are generally available to the users of technologies such as ANONYMOUS FTP. Increasingly WEB SITES are being used for archival purposes.

ARIN *See* AMERICAN REGISTRY FOR INTERNET NUMBERS.

armoured virus A VIRUS which attempts to subvert any attempts by VIRUS DETECTION SOFTWARE to discover them. The main way they do this is by adding confusing and complex code to the infected computer along with the real virus code.

ARP *See* ADDRESS RESOLUTION PROTOCOL.

ARPA *See* ADVANCED RESEARCH PROJECTS AGENCY.

ARPANET *See* ADVANCED RESEARCH PROJECTS AGENCY NETWORK.

ARP cache A table which stores the mapping from INTERNET PROTOCOL ADDRESSES to real computer addresses within part of a TCP-IP network. It is used by the ADDRESS RESOLUTION PROTOCOL before data is sent to a receiving computer.

ARP spoofing A form of SPOOFING whereby the ARP CACHE is overwritten by an intruder in order to fool a computer into thinking that a remote computer is trusted by a network. The ARP cache contains the hardware address and name of computers on a network. ARP spoofing involves overwriting the physical address of a specified trusted computer with that of an intruding computer.

ARR *See* AUTOMATIC REPEAT REQUEST.

article Another name for a POSTING.

arts In 1997 the Internet Ad Hoc committee proposed a number of new names for DOMAINS. Arts is one of these; it represents art and cultural entities.

ASAP Abbreviation for As Soon As Possible used in CHAT ROOMS, EMAILS, and NEWSGROUP.

asbestos Employed by NEWSGROUP users to indicate that they are expecting a FLAME: for example, 'I know that I should wear asbestos knickers when I say this.'

ascender Used in typography for the part of a lower case letter that is higher than the letter x. It is used in connection with the letters b, d, f, h, k, l, and t.

ASCII *See* AMERICAN STANDARD CODE FOR INFORMATION INTERCHANGE.

ASCII armoured The ability of the PRETTY GOOD PRIVACY system to send ASCII text which has been encrypted using EMAIL.

ASCII art A collective term used to describe pictures, sometimes pornographic, which have been produced by just using the ASCII character set. They are often found within SIGNATURE FILES.

ASCIIbetical order An ordering of data based on the ASCII codes of the data rather than on alphabetical ordering.

Asia Pacific Network Information Centre The organization which dispenses INTERNET PROTOCOL ADDRESSES to users in Asia and the Pacific area. The other organizations that do this are RÉSEAUX EUROPÉENNE NETWORK COORDINATION CENTRE and AMERICAN REGISTRY FOR INTERNET NUMBERS. It is often abbreviated to APNIC.

ask Synonymous with 'question' when used as a noun. For example 'What's the ask?' means 'What's the question?'.

Ask Jeeves One of the most popular SEARCH ENGINES that uses free format text to frame a query. It provides an interesting facility, in that questions being posed to Jeeves by other users are displayed on its HOME PAGE. There is also a junior version of this search engine.

ASL Abbreviation for Age Sex Location used in CHAT ROOMS, EMAILS, and NEWSGROUPS. It is normally used in CHAT applications to ask a participant for some of their personal details.

ASN See AUTONOMOUS SYSTEM NUMBER.

ASP See ACTIVE SERVER PAGES®.

assicon A ribald version of EMOTICONS involving the depiction of the backside using keyboard characters. For example (!) stands for a tight ass, while (_x_) stands for kiss my ass.

assigned number A number assigned to a specific port on a computer by the INTERNET ASSIGNED NUMBER AUTHORITY. For example, the DEDICATED PORT 25 is associated with the SIMPLE MAIL TRANSFER PROTOCOL. This means that any computer connected to the Internet can expect email traffic associated with the simple mail transfer protocol to be delivered through this port.

associate program An agreement between one Web-based company and another, whereby one company pays the other for every visitor to its site who has come from the other company's site. For example, the first company may sell CDs and the other may run a GURU SITE for some category of music. Associate programs enable targeted sets of Web users to flow into a commercial WEB SITE which directly addresses its interests. The pioneers of associate programs have been bookshops such as Amazon and CD shops such as CD Paradise. The payment to a Web site which has delivered customers can be based on a PAY-BY-CLICK MODEL or a PAY-BY-PURCHASE MODEL. The former is based on paying a small amount, usually a few cents or pence, when a visitor visits a Web site; the latter is based on an actual sale made. Being an associate usually entails placing HYPERLINKS prominently on WEB PAGES or adding a customized interface supplied by the associated Web trader. A company which has a large number of associates can be overwhelmed with the process of tracking clicks. This has led to a new type of company, the CLICK INTERMEDIARY, which manages the accounting process. Much higher amounts can be earned by using a pay-by-purchase model. Here, revenue is based on a percentage of the purchase made by a customer directed by one Web site to another. Typically a commission would be around 5 to 10 per cent of the purchase price. As with pay-by-click, the organization of pay-by-commission may require a large amount of investment of time, and so specialized PURCHASE INTERMEDIARY companies have sprung up to administer such schemes.

Association for Computing Machinery The premier US professional society for computer scientists. It has over 80,000 members in both industry and academia. It is usually abbreviated to ACM.

Association for Interactive Media A large US trade organization which promotes the use of the Internet for business.

Their Web site issues free newsletters about Internet business. It is often abbreviated to AIM.

Association of Shareware Professionals A professional association of SHAREWARE developers which has, as its main aim, the promotion of shareware as an alternative to commercially bought software.

asymmetric cryptography A collection of cryptographic methods which rely on more than one KEY. Almost certainly the best known of these is PUBLIC KEY ENCRYPTION. This requires the use of two keys: a PUBLIC KEY and a PRIVATE KEY.

Asymmetrical Digital Subscriber Lines One of the fastest technologies for connecting to the Internet. It offers speeds in excess of 1.5 Mbs as compared with other fast technologies such as ISDN which has speeds of around 128 Kbps. Currently this form of technology is being offered to business customers or via wholesale agreements to INTERNET SERVICE PROVIDERS. The technology holds out great promise, but is being implemented very slowly both in the USA and the UK; for example, in the United Kingdom time on ADSL networks is only initially being sold to INTERNET SERVICE PROVIDERS. It is, however, expected that the technology will eventually percolate down to a mass market. The technology is regarded as asymmetric in that the speeds for UPLOADING are slower than those for DOWNLOADING. It is often abbreviated to ADSL.

asynchronous communication The transmission of data over a communication medium where the time at which a character of the data is sent is not determined by the timing of the sending or receiving of a previous character. This is in contrast to SYNCHRONOUS COMMUNICATION.

asynchronous computer-mediated conferencing A form of COMPUTER-MEDIATED CONFERENCING where participation in a conference does not require the participants to come together at the same time. Typical examples of this include EMAIL and NEWSGROUPS.

With this form of conferencing messages can be sent at any time and read at any time: they do not need to be interlaced or replied to immediately as with SYNCHRONOUS COMPUTER-MEDIATED CONFERENCING.

asynchronous learning The use of media in DISTANCE LEARNING which does not impose a REAL TIME interaction between the student and the teacher. Examples of such media include EMAIL, CONFERENCING SOFTWARE, and NEWSGROUPS.

Asynchronous Transfer Mode A high-performance network technology which, as its name suggests, relies on ASYNCHRONOUS COMMUNICATION. This technology uses fixed size packets known as CELLS. When data is sent using this method a connection is first established and all the cells that make up the data follow the same path through the network. The delivery of these cells is not guaranteed; however, the order in which they are sent is: a cell which is delivered is always received by the recipient computer after a received cell which was dispatched before it. Networks based on Asynchronous Transfer Mode, often known as ATM, are organized in the same way that WIDE AREA NETWORKS are organized: with transmission lines and ROUTERS. The technology is flexible and fast: flexible because it can handle data which is sent at a constant rate, such as audio data, as well as data sent at a variable rate; and fast because it is capable of speeds in the gigabits range. Although ATM is usually discussed in the context of wide area networks, it is also capable of being used as a base technology for local area networks which are increasingly finding their bandwidth being used up by more and more complex applications.

asynchronous transmission The transmission of data which does not require coordination between the receiver computer and the sending computer.

ATB Abbreviation for All The Best used in CHAT ROOMS, EMAILS, and NEWSGROUPS. It is usually used to terminate an email or a session in a chat room.

At Home A broadband network which was designed for fast data access over cable television transmission lines. Often known as @Home.

ATM *See* ASYNCHRONOUS TRANSFER MODE.

atomic commit protocol Complex TRANSACTIONS often consist of a number of individual operations which, for example, update and query a number of distributed databases. It is important either that all these operations succeed or, if there is a problem with one or more of them, that they all fail and do not leave the distributed system in an incorrect state. An atomic commit protocol ensures that this happens. It involves querying the state of each of the servers involved in a distributed transaction.

atomicity This term describes the fact that a DISTRIBUTED TRANSACTION either completes, or fails and has no effect at all. So, for example, if a transaction involves the updating of a number of distributed databases then either all the databases are updated or, for example, if a failure occurs on one of the computers involved in the transaction, none of the databases are updated. Atomicity is an important property of a distributed transaction along with CONSISTENCY, ISOLATION, and DURABILITY.

atomicity consistency isolation durability These are properties that a DISTRIBUTED TRANSACTION should have. *See* ATOMICITY, CONSISTENCY, ISOLATION, and DURABILITY. The term is usually abbreviated to ACID. Without having these properties a transaction usually leaves a distributed system in an inconsistent state: for example, in a banking system it might leave one of the accounts incorrectly updated.

atomic multicast A form of MULTICASTING in which a message sent by a source computer is either received by all its recipients or none at all. Such a form of multicasting is often used in fault-tolerant systems which use DATA REPLICATION.

at party A party with restricted attendance: usually HACKERS who have some form of network address. In the past such parties were restricted to serious hackers

and were very popular; however they have now declined drastically since many more users have network addresses. The term is based on the @ sign in an EMAIL ADDRESS.

at sign The @ symbol. It is normally used to separate a user name and a DOMAIN within an EMAIL ADDRESS: for example D.C.Ince@freeserve.co.uk. However, it is also increasingly being used within names of ECOMMERCE companies.

attachment A file which is sent as part of an EMAIL message. Such files have been frequently used to infect computers with VIRUSES.

attachment encoding The coding method used to transform a BINARY FILE to a form in which it can be placed as an ATTACHMENT in an EMAIL. UUENCODE is an example of an attachment encoding.

attack An attempt to overcome the security provisions of the network of a computer network. Attacks can be ACTIVE ATTACKS which alter the data stored on the network, for example deleting a critical FILE, or PASSIVE ATTACKS which just read sensitive data passing through TRANSMISSION LINES.

attenuation The loss of energy as a signal travels down a TRANSMISSION LINE. As a signal becomes more and more attenuated it becomes more and more difficult to read and process. The solution to attenuation problems is the use of AMPLIFIERS or REPEATERS.

attribute Used in the HYPERTEXT MARKUP LANGUAGE to modify the effect of a TAG. For example, the FONT tag can be modified by a SIZE attribute which changes the default size of text expressed in that font. The tag <FONT SIZE = +1> increases the size of the font used to display text by one measure.

au A FILE EXTENSION for the au sound format found on the Internet.

audio clip A collection of sounds which can be integrated into a WEB PAGE. Normally, the user of a BROWSER who wishes to hear the sounds has to employ a PLUG-IN which integrates with the technology used to encode the sounds. Such clips are infrequently used as they can massively increase the DOWNLOAD time of a Web page. STREAMING TECHNOLOGY which plays sounds as they are loaded aims to minimize this problem. Currently there are a number of proprietary technologies that can be used for sound.

audiographic teleconferencing A form of TELECONFERENCE which involves both the establishment of an audio link and a visual link via a shared WHITE BOARD.

audio plug-in A PLUG-IN which enables the user of a BROWSER to listen to sound stored in a file which conforms to one of the well-known sound standards such as MIDI. The best known of these plug-ins is LIVEAUDIO, although there are many commercial and SHAREWARE audio plug-ins available.

audio streaming The process of playing an AUDIO CLIP as it is being sent to a BROWSER in REAL TIME. This improves the LOAD TIME of the WEB PAGE compared with older audio technologies where the whole of the audio clip had to be transferred to the browser before it could be played.

audit file A FILE which contains data about events which have occurred in a system. For example the file may contain details of all the attempted LOG-INS made to the system: the name of the person making the log-in, the CLIENT which he or she used, the time when it occurred, and the password employed. Such files are often used for security purposes: for example, the file described above would be used to check for any unauthorized logins. Audit files can also be associated with applications. For example, a banking system has an audit file which contains data about the various transactions that have occurred with user accounts.

audit log file An alternative term for an AUDIT FILE.

audit trail The data which can be extracted from a SYSTEM LOG or an AUDIT FILE and which can provide information about potential security violations. Most NETWORK OPERATING SYSTEMS enable the contents of an audit trail to be varied dynamically: one day it may be configured to contain data about attempted log-ins on the system, while on other days it may

contain the locations of CLIENTS which call on the service provided by a SERVER.

AUI connector A 15-pin connector which can be found on ETHERNET cards and which is used for attaching a variety of cables to such a local area network including COAXIAL CABLE and FIBRE OPTIC CABLE.

AUP *See* AUTHORIZED USE POLICY.

authentication The process of convincing a network that a person is who he or she claims to be. This follows the process of IDENTIFICATION. Devices that are used for authentication include PASSWORDS, PERSONAL IDENTIFICATION NUMBERS, smart cards, and BIOMETRIC IDENTIFICATION SYSTEMS.

authentication server A SERVER which dispenses KEYS used for the sending of secure messages over a network. Such a server would use some highly secure technology such as PUBLIC KEY ENCRYPTION. Authentication server is also a term used to describe a server which mediates user access to a network.

authorization The process of ensuring that the user of a network has received permission to use the facilities of the network that are in his or her ACCESS PROFILE. Authorization follows the processes of IDENTIFICATION and AUTHENTICATION.

authorized use policy The conditions which an INTERNET SERVICE PROVIDER specifies for any user who wishes to make use of its facilities. They usually include the prohibition of: sending libellous material, making an unauthorized attempt to infiltrate another computer system or another user's area on the service provider's system, distributing pornography, distributing copyrighted material, harassing other computer users, sending SPAM mail, taking part in a PONZI SCHEME or a CHAIN LETTER SCAM, publishing private information such as credit card numbers, using unauthorized or illegal copies of software, and selling illegal commodities such as banned drugs. Such an agreement also includes standard clauses such as those that specify conditions regarding payment or non-payment of fees to the provider. Often abbreviated to AUP.

authorizing certificate A DIGITAL CERTIFICATE which provides some information about the properties of a person. For example, a WEB SITE which sells adult material might require an authorizing certificate from their customers to demonstrate that they are over eighteen.

automated clearing house A means whereby businesses can issue invoices to each other and pay for goods and services which have been supplied. Transfers of invoices and financial payments are usually carried out using VALUE-ADDED PRIVATE NETWORKS. Automated clearing house payments are usually high volume and low value compared with those processed by the clearing houses used by major banks.

automatic data capture The ability to capture data or information without manual intervention. There are a host of technologies which can be used for this, ranging from venerable ones such as barcodes to technically sophisticated technologies such as VOICE RECOGNITION and the use of BIOMETRIC IDENTIFICATION SYSTEMS.

automatic lockout Some OPERATING SYSTEMS allow the SYSTEM ADMINISTRATOR to specify the number of incorrect LOG-INS that are allowed to an ACCOUNT before the operating system prevents any more attempts to log-in, even by a valid user of the account. The process of preventing access is known as automatic lockout. It is a primitive security measure which acts as a first line of defence in a networked system.

automatic number identification Digital telephone systems are now able to detect the number of a telephone which is initiating a call. This is known as automatic number identification; it is increasingly being used to ensure that only telephones whose number matches a list of authorized phones are allowed to carry out DIAL-UP ACCESS to a network. It is also known as CALLING LINE IDENTIFICATION.

automatic repeat request This is a primitive form of error correction that is used in MODEMS.

autonomous system A collection of computers which are operated by a single organization and which communicate using an INTERIOR GATEWAY PROTOCOL. In such a system a NETWORK ADMINISTRATOR can define DOMAINS and allocate individual INTERNET PROTOCOL ADDRESSES to users.

autonomous system number In an AUTONOMOUS SYSTEM this is an INTERNET PROTOCOL ADDRESS that is assigned by the network to an individual computer in the network. It is sometimes abbreviated to ASN.

autoresponder A program which sends out prewritten EMAIL messages to any email address from which it receives email. A typical use for such a program is to inform the senders of email that the recipient has gone on holiday and will answer their emails sometime in the future.

avatar 1. The icon representing the user of a virtual reality system. It is normally displayed in the window of a user's computer.
2. The representation of a user of a MUD system.

AYSOS An insulting abbreviation for Are You Stupid Or Something used in CHAT ROOMS, EMAILS, and NEWSGROUPS.

B

B2B *See* BUSINESS TO BUSINESS.

B2B market This is a market run by computers and often mounted on a WEB SITE. It provides facilities for companies to buy products cheaply from other companies who act as suppliers. Suppliers who post their prices on such a site will have them displayed with those of other suppliers. B2B markets have been confined to small categories of commodities such as steel products associated with fabrication. B2B is an abbreviation for Business to Business.

B2C *See* BUSINESS TO CUSTOMER.

B4 A HAKSPEK abbreviation for Before used in CHAT ROOMS, EMAILS, and NEWSGROUP.

B4N A HAKSPEK abbreviation for Bye For Now used in CHAT ROOMS, EMAILS, and NEWSGROUP. Used to terminate an email, newsgroup POSTING, or a session in a chat room.

backbone A very high-speed transmission line in the Internet which other networks can connect to.

backbone cabal The group of systems administrators who, in 1987, removed much of the chaos of NEWSGROUPS by replacing the form of naming adopted until then by a hierarchic form of description. *See also* THE GREAT RENAMING.

back door Synonymous with TRAPDOOR: a device which allows the developer of an ENCRYPTION technology to easily decrypt messages sent using that technology.

back end database A DATABASE which is fronted by a WEB SERVER and can be accessed by BROWSERS that connect into the server. Such databases are usually employed in ECOMMERCE applications: for example, an online bookstore stores details of books on a back end database which can be browsed by users looking for a specific book. Increasingly mainstream database management systems provide facilities for databases to be easily connected to a Web server.

back end process A process which is carried out behind the facade of the Web interface presented to an ECOMMERCE user. These processes are usually carried out by conventional non-Internet technologies. For example, a typical back end process which is carried out behind a WEB SITE that sells some product is inventory maintenance, where sales are deducted from stock and new deliveries of products are added to stock. Such a process would be carried out using conventional database management software.

backing up The process of saving data on a computer or in a network by copying to some safe storage medium such as a CD. A number of backup programs and utilities exist, either as part of a computer's OPERATING SYSTEM or as stand-alone programs. There are also a number of BACKUP SITES on the World Wide Web which allow users to back up their files remotely.

backplane The circuit board on a computer to which other circuit boards can be connected.

backslash The character ' \ '. Also known as a REVERSE SLASH.

backup The transfer of FILES which are stored on a computer to some long-term archival medium such as a CD ROM. Backup is carried out in order to mitigate the effect of a disastrous event such as a hard disk becoming damaged.

backup site A WEB SITE which offers a backup service for your files which ensures that if a catastrophe hits your own computer and the files are destroyed you can recover them from the backup site. The site takes any of your files and stores them at some highly secure installation—sometimes at two or more installations. Users of this service usually employ the FILE TRANSFER PROTOCOL to send and recover files from a backup site. Users of a backup site pay a fee, usually monthly or annually.

bacteria Forms of VIRUS. Bacteria are programs which replicate themselves and then start executing: carrying out some processor- or memory-intensive task such as reading from a file. Each replicated virus then reproduces itself again. Eventually the number of these viruses reaches the point where the computer is unable to cope with their demands and CRASHES or exhibits extremely sluggish behaviour. They are also known as RABBITS.

bait and switch A synonym for AGENT NAME DELIVERY.

bamf A term associated with VIRTUAL REALITY systems or MUDS. In the former it refers to the sound made when a person teleports out of the vicinity of the hearer; in the latter it is used when a MUD user is redirected to another location.

bandwidth The range of frequencies which can be passed through a communication line with an acceptable ATTENUATION. It can also be used in EMAILS and POSTINGS to indicate that not enough resources are available for a task: for example, 'I have to report that the software will not contain this feature: we did not have enough bandwidth on the project to complete this.' The term has also passed into general usage to describe the quantity of data that can be sent down a transmission line: the bigger the bandwidth the faster the line.

Bandwidth Conservation Society A group which has been set up with the aim of showing how WEB PAGES can be developed with clean backgrounds that can be read by users with limited vision. Such pages also download a lot faster than those which make use of large, sophisticated graphics.

bandwidth junkie Someone who is obsessed with the speed of their Internet connections. It usually refers to the type of computer user who is the first to purchase or lease a fast, new transmission technology such as ISDN.

bandwidth theft A form of HYPERLINKing which goes beyond that normally found in the WORLD WIDE WEB. It occurs when the designer of a WEB SITE links to a GRAPHIC IMAGE, AUDIO CLIP, or VIDEO CLIP on your Web site in their Web site. In effect they are using your WEB SERVER as an extra storage medium for their WEB PAGES. *See also* SHALLOW LINK and DEEP LINK.

bang An exclamation mark used to express surprise in a POSTING.

banner A graphical element on a WEB PAGE which has a greater length than width. Often banners span the whole of a page. Banners normally have a HYPERLINK embedded in them. The main use of banners is in implementing BANNER ADVERTS where the embedded hyperlink is to the company WEB SITE which is referred to in the advert.

banner advert Adverts which have become prevalent on the WORLD WIDE WEB. The term 'banner' comes from the fact that they straddle a WEB PAGE. Such adverts almost invariably contain hot spots which, when clicked, take the user to the site whose services or products are being advertised. Banner adverts are placed on a WEB SITE for a number of reasons: the advertiser has paid the owner of the site; the owner and the advertiser have come to an agreement about payment every time the advert is clicked; or a product or service has been purchased; or because the site is hosted by an INTERNET SERVICE PROVIDER who is not charging the site owner and, in lieu of this, places adverts on the site.

banner advertising The process of displaying BANNER ADVERTS into a WEB SITE.

banner auction An ONLINE AUCTION in which BANNER ADVERTS are sold to WEB SITES that have space for them.

banner exchange The process whereby two or more WEB SITES exchange BANNER ADVERTS. This leads to a greater exposure for the adverts.

barf mail BOUNCE MESSAGES which have bounced a large number of times during their progress through a number of EMAIL systems. Such messages will often contain large amounts of incomprehensible routing information which details the paths that the message has taken through the Internet. Barf is American slang for the act of vomiting.

Barney page A WEB PAGE which has been developed quickly in order to take advantage of some fast-moving trend. It is named after the mechatronic doll Barney which, when it was released, quickly inspired a large number of commercial WEB SITES.

baseband A type of communication in which data transmission is carried out across a single channel. The best example of this type of communication occurs in ETHERNET networks.

baseband signalling A method of transmission where only one signal occurs on a communication medium at one time.

base font A FONT which is the default font for a document or WEB PAGE. Most software for producing documents and Web pages allows the user to specify what the base font is to be. Often it is Times New Roman.

baseline The line on which the letters of a text rest. Some letters, for example g, have portions known as DESCENDERS which fall below the baseline.

basic access A term used to describe the way that terminals and telephones are connected into a digital network.

basic rate interface This is by far and away the most popular version of the INTEGRATED SERVICES DIGITAL NETWORK technology. It uses the standard telephone jacks found in homes and businesses.

bastion *See* BASTION HOST.

bastion host A computer which stands between a secure network and the Internet. It protects the computers in the secure network from attack since an intruder has to circumnavigate the security controls on the bastion host before it can contact a computer residing on the secure network. A bastion host is often referred to simply as a bastion.

batch The collecting together of a series of files into a single group for transmission across a network. Usually the files have had some COMPRESSION method applied to them.

baud A measure of the number of times a signal on a transmission line changes state in one second. The higher the baud rate the faster signals are transmitted.

baud barf The random characters that are displayed on a monitor or VDU when some problem with transmission lines or transmission equipment occurs. Barf is American slang for the act of vomiting.

BBIAB Abbreviation for Be Back In A Bit used in CHAT ROOMS. It is used to indicate that the user has left his or her computer temporarily.

BBIAF Abbreviation for Be Back In A Few used in CHAT ROOMS. It is usually followed by a unit of time as in 'BBIAF minutes'. It is used to indicate that the user has left his or her computer temporarily.

BBL Abbreviation for Be Back Late used in CHAT ROOMS. It is used to indicate that the user has left his or her computer temporarily.

BBN Abbreviation for Bye Bye for Now used in CHAT ROOMS. Used to terminate a session in the chat room.

BBS Abbreviation for BULLETIN BOARD Site.

BCC Abbreviation for BLIND CARBON COPY.

B channel One of the wires in an INTEGRATED SERVICES DIGITAL NETWORK service. The service usually offered to home users and small businesses has two wires.

BCNU A HAKSPEK abbreviation for Be Seeing You used in CHAT ROOMS, EMAILS, and NEWSGROUP. Prevalent in chat rooms, but also used a little in email messages.

beam Derived from the *Star Trek* film series. It is used as a verb to describe the electronic transfer of a file between computers as in 'The software company beamed me a PATCH to the PLUG-IN when we discovered the security problem with it.'

Because Its Time Network This was a network which carried email and which connected over 200 US universities. It was eventually merged with the COMPUTER SCIENCE NET to become the CORPORATION FOR RESEARCH AND EDUCATIONAL NETWORKING. It was normally abbreviated to BITNET. It is now defunct.

beggarware A term sometimes used to refer to SHAREWARE.

bells and whistles The advanced features of a program or system. The provision of facilities to produce charts in a spreadsheet program is an example of the provision of bells and whistles. A comparative term: one person's bells and whistles may be another person's essential features.

below the fold When a WEB PAGE is initially displayed in a BROWSER the area of the page that is not displayed is referred to as below the fold. The term comes from the newspaper industry and originally referred to the paper which lay below the fold in a broadsheet.

BEO *See* BETTER ETHICS ONLINE.

Beowulf cluster A number of middle range personal computers connected together by network technology and which have been configured to be as powerful as a supercomputer. The term was invented by the American computer scientist Thomas Sterling.

BER *See* BIT ERROR RATE.

Berkeley Internet Name Domain An early DOMAIN NAME SERVER which was developed at the University of California at Berkeley. Such servers keep data on domain names and physical addresses of computers on the Internet. Many computers on the Internet still run versions of this server. It is usually abbreviated to BIND.

Berkeley Software Distribution A version of the UNIX operating system that was the first to contain TCP-IP facilities. It was developed at the University of California at Berkeley. It is often referred to as BSD.

best of the Web A generic description of those WEB SITES which are devoted to showing other Web sites that demonstrate exemplary design and good content.

They are listed under various names including What's Cool, Top Sites, What's Hot, Hot Picks, and so on.

beta software Software which is released to a number of customers before it is offered for sale. It is tested by these customers in realistic conditions. *See also* ALPHA SOFTWARE. Usually beta software contains many more errors than the finally released software; however, these errors are not serious.

Better Ethics Online A non-profit-making organisation which has been set up to promote the responsible use of the Internet and which provides advice and guidance on issues such as SPAMMING and SOFTWARE COPYRIGHT. Often abbreviated to BEO.

bevel A technique which is used to give the impression that a GRAPHIC IMAGE is raised. It is achieved by applying highlighting colours and a shadow.

beyond the banner Used by advertising companies to describe other media that can be used for advertising apart from BANNER ADVERTS, such as the use of advertising in EMAIL newsletters.

BFN Abbreviation for Bye For Now used in CHAT ROOMS. Usually employed to sign off a chat room session.

BFT *See* BINARY FILE TRANSFER.

BHOF Abbreviation for Bald Headed Old Fart used in CHAT ROOMS, EMAILS, and NEWSGROUPS. Usually used to describe someone who professes a belief or hazards an opinion derived from earlier times: for example, someone who states that MAINFRAME COMPUTERS still have a role to play in computing.

BIF Abbreviation for Basic In Fact used in CHAT ROOMS, EMAILS, and NEWSGROUPS. It is used to indicate some proposition for which there is overwhelming evidence.

biff To notify someone that EMAIL has arrived. It originated from the name of a BSD UNIX operating system utility.

big book The US equivalent of the UK telephone yellow pages. It is used to look up details of US companies.

big endian Someone who supports the placing of the largest byte first in a numeric encoding scheme. This is in contrast to a LITTLE ENDIAN. The Internet has seen a number of heated discussions between both groups: an example of a HOLY WAR.

Bigfoot A SEARCH ENGINE that can be used for finding people on the Web.

bill presentment A business term. It is used to describe the process of sending and processing a bill or invoice to a customer. Increasingly the Internet is being used for this type of business, usually via third-party companies. Such companies normally present the bills of large companies that have big customer bases such as electricity supply companies.

bin A FILE EXTENSION for the executable programs.

binary A problem for which there are only two solutions.

binary file A file which contains only binary digits. The commonest type of binary file contains an executable program.

binary file transfer The process of transferring a BINARY FILE from one computer to another.

binary large object An entity which is large in terms of memory size. A typical binary large object would be a VIDEO CLIP. They are often referred to as BLOBs.

BIND *See* BERKELEY INTERNET NAME DOMAIN.

binding 1. The association of a name with a resource on a network. For example, associating IP ADDRESSES with a DOMAIN NAME is an example of binding. **2**. The process whereby a CLIENT is associated with a SERVER: for example, a client used for handling transactions for a travel company might be permanently bound to a dedicated server which carries out the processing of transactions.

binding data Binding is the process of associating a SERVER with a particular CLIENT that can access it. The data that describes which servers a client can be bound to and under what conditions is known as binding data. This data is normally stored in a FILE.

binhex A technique used to convert non-ASCII files into ASCII for transmission over a network.

biometric identification system A system which uses some physical human characteristic to determine the identity of the user of a computer system. Typical characteristics that have been used include: typing characteristics such as the speed of typing or the number of errors made; the image of a face; fingerprints; hand shape; handwriting characteristics; voice properties; DNA patterns; and eye characteristics such as the pattern of blood vessels in the retina. Often this technique is used with some other form of identification such as a PASSWORD.

biosensor An electronic device attached to the user of a VIRTUAL REALITY system. Such devices provide feedback to the system about the state of the user's body: for example, whether he or she has moved their head.

biot An AGENT which can travel over a NETWORK looking for simulated environments which it can interact with; for example, by reproducing itself or feeding. Biot technology is in its early stages, but it may form the basis of computer games in the future.

BIOYIOP Abbreviation for Blow It Out of Your IO Port used in CHAT ROOMS, EMAILS, and NEWSGROUPS. A term of abuse which pejoratively describes a remark by another user; it is the electronic version of blow it out of your ass.

birthday attack An attack on a CRYPTOGRAPHY system. It is based on the mathematics behind the fact that you would need 183 people in a single room for there to be a better than even chance of one of them having the same birthday as yourself; but only require 23 people for there to be more than an even chance that two have the same birthday.

BIS *See* BIOMETRIC IDENTIFICATION SYSTEM.

B-ISDN *See* BROADBAND INTEGRATED SERVICES DIGITAL NETWORK.

bit Abbreviation for BInary digiT: either a one or a zero.

bit bucket The mythical place where lost EMAIL messages end up. It is sometimes used in connection with any loss of media during transmission.

bitcaster A radio station that broadcasts live and in real time on the WORLD WIDE WEB.

BITD Abbreviation for Back In The Day used in CHAT ROOMS, EMAILS, and NEWSGROUPS. Used to express nostalgia for a lost age: for example, 'BITD when we used mainframes and there were no NEWSGROUPS whose members insulted each other.'

bit error rate The figure which describes the number of errors expected or measured in a transmission across a network. It is usually expressed as a per-second figure.

bit hose A slang term used to describe cabling employed in a computer network.

bitloss A jargon term used to describe the loss of data during network transmission or the loss of data within the memory of a computer. *See also* BIT BUCKET.

bitmap A graphic which is made up of a number of PIXELS. An example of a bitmap format is the GRAPHICS INTERCHANGE FORMAT. *See* BITMAPPED GRAPHIC.

bitmapped font A FONT whose characters are stored as a series of dots rather than as a set of instructions to draw the character. A problem that such fonts suffer from is the inability to make them larger or smaller.

bitmapped graphic A way of defining graphic images by storing information about each PIXEL in a series of bits. For example, each pixel may have information stored about its colour, saturation level, and brightness. Bitmapped graphics are stored in the same way that a computer displays the image: as a block of pixels. This means that the display of bitmapped graphics is computationally very easy. It is one of the major graphics formats used on the Internet: GIF is a bitmapped graphic format.

BITNET A network which was based on the VNET network that was used to link IBM centres throughout the world. It was developed in the early 1980s and is now virtually defunct. Its full name was BECAUSE ITS TIME NETWORK. The BITNET network was managed by the CORPORATION FOR RESEARCH AND EDUCATIONAL NETWORKING and did not use TCP-IP as its PROTOCOL. The network still lives on in the BITNET II network which uses TCP-IP to connect computers together.

bitnik An Internet user who uses a public computer terminal such as those found in a CYBERCAFÉ.

bitoon A mythical place where data lost in transmission ends up. It has also been used as a personal term of abuse in NEWSGROUPS. *See also* BIT BUCKET.

bitraking Used to describe the process of carrying out investigative journalism using the facilities of the Internet. The term has also been used to describe investigative journalism about issues connected with the Internet. It is the electronic version of muckraking.

bitslag As the Internet has increased in size the amount of information in it has increased hugely. This means that, for example, the user of a SEARCH ENGINE recovers a large amount of useless information in response to a SEARCH QUERY. This useless information is known as bitslag.

bits per second A measure of the speed of a communications medium. Usually abbreviated to bps.

bitstorm A high level of traffic—usually encountered over a short period—which is sufficient to slow down the service offered by SERVERS. *See also* FLASH CROWD.

biz In 2000 seven new DOMAIN NAMES were created. biz was one of these. It is intended for use within the show business industry.

BL An abbreviation for Belly Laugh used in CHAT ROOMS, EMAILS, and NEWSGROUPS. Normally it is used as an adornment to a pejorative sentence about a user, some software technology, or a particular issue.

black hat A HACKER who carries out criminal acts such as entering a forbidden network. *See also* WHITE HAT.

black hole A mythical location in a network where lost data or EMAILS end up. *See also* BIT BUCKET and BITOON.

Black Thursday The day that the COMMUNICATIONS DECENCY ACT was passed. This US Act attempted to limit the freedoms that Internet users had before the Act was passed.

black widow A JAVA APPLET which carries out some malicious act on your computer: for example, carrying out a DENIAL OF SERVICE ATTACK by running in a loop for a long time and tying up valuable computer resources. Such programs are introduced into a system via the WEB PAGE on which they reside. A black widow is also known as a MALICIOUS APPLET. *See also* CRAPPLET. It is also the name of a METASEARCH ENGINE.

blatherer An EMAIL user or a participant in a CHAT ROOM or NEWSGROUP who sends long emails or sends long POSTINGS.

bleam To send data over a network. *See also* BEAM.

bleeding edge A term used for a project which is at the leading edge of technology but which can make the company developing the product vulnerable. Sometimes used by an individual when he or she is using recently released technology: for example, a beta release of an OPERATING SYSTEM. A play on the term 'leading edge'.

blendo page A WEB PAGE which contains a diverse amount of different media including, for example, scanned images, sound bites, and video. It is normally used to describe poorly designed pages which have had little thought put into them about reconciling the different media; consequently, the use of the term should be assumed to be derogatory. *See also* ANGRY FRUIT SALAD, EYE TRASH, and WORST OF THE WEB.

blind carbon copy A copy of an EMAIL message which is sent to a number of recipients. It is similar to a CARBON COPY; however, it differs in that the recipients

of the email are unaware of the identities of any of the other recipients. Usually abbreviated to BCC.

blind signature An ECOMMERCE scheme which uses electronic TOKENS that do not have the identity of their holder associated with the token. This is the equivalent of the use of paper money and coin in conventional merchandising.

blinking text Text in a WEB PAGE which is displayed, then disappears for a short time, and then reappears, or which regularly changes its colour. It is regarded by the vast majority of WEB DESIGNERS and users as hugely distracting. In the early days of the WORLD WIDE WEB it was the only form of animation available to designers. *See also* ANGRY FRUIT SALAD, EYE TRASH, and WORST OF THE WEB.

B list An abbreviation for BOZO LIST. A list of EMAIL senders that you wish your email program to ignore. Such a list is held in a FILE that is consulted by an email program. When an email program encounters an email from the member of a B list it is either deleted or placed in a special FOLDER. It is also known as a KILL LIST.

blivet A DENIAL OF SERVICE ATTACK which uses an area of a NETWORK which has no access controls: for example, shared file space or a PUBLIC DIRECTORY.

bloatware A term used for software which has too many functions and which is so large that it occupies too much space on a computer or has an inordinately long response time.

BLOB *See* BINARY LARGE OBJECT.

block A collection of data that is transmitted through a network as a single unit.

block cipher An ALGORITHM used in symmetric key encryption which transforms a block of data each time the algorithm is applied. One of the most best-known block cipher algorithms is the DATA ENCRYPTION STANDARD developed by the US government.

blocking software Software which is used to block access to WEB SITES which are considered inappropriate for the user of a BROWSER to access. The criteria used by blocking programs are quite diverse including: a list of banned Web sites, those sites which contain certain words such as 'sex' or sites that are identified by a CONTENT RATING SYSTEM such as the PLATFORM FOR INTERNET CONTENT SELECTION. Such systems provide a series of KEYWORDS which the blocking software recognizes thus preventing access to Web pages.

blog 1. Jargon term for a WEB LOG FILE: a FILE used to monitor the usage of WEB SITES which are stored on a WEB SERVER.
2. An intransitive verb to describe the process of creating a Web log or part of a Web log.

blowing your buffer To lose a train of thought or a thread in a conversation. A buffer is an area of computer memory to which data is sent to make it ready for processing by some device such as a monitor. In technical terms to blow a buffer means that the data stored there is lost or corrupted.

blue badge Used to describe a permanent Microsoft employee. It is derived from the blue identification badge worn. *See also* TURNING BLUE and ORANGE BADGE.

Bluetooth A technology which enables home devices such as burglar alarms, cookers, and mobile phones to be connected together. The technology was developed by two scientists employed by the Ericsson company in Sweden. It works by connecting devices together via radio waves.

BNC connector A connector used to connect together devices using 10Base2 CO-AXIAL CABLE.

BOAT Abbreviation for Bit Of A Twat used in CHAT ROOMS, EMAILS, and NEWSGROUPS. Usually found in alt newsgroups.

Bobo the Webmonkey Used to describe any incompetent WEB DESIGNER. Someone who, for example, develops pages containing ANGRY FRUIT SALAD.

body 1. The part of an EMAIL which contains the message; it excludes parts such as the HEADER.
2. The part of a WEB PAGE that is displayed in a BROWSER.

body type The FONT that is used for displaying the main text of a document or a WEB PAGE. This is often the Times New Roman font.

BOFH Abbreviation for Bastard Operator From Hell. Often used to describe a SYSTEM ADMINISTRATOR who has little tolerance for inexperienced users and is occasionally used to describe heavy-handed MODERATORS of NEWSGROUPS. The term originated in the days when MAINFRAME COMPUTERS were prevalent and when the users of such computers were very reliant on the operators to run their programs. Many operators, tired by irregular shift patterns, would take their unhappiness out on the users and came to be known as bastard operators from hell.

bogon A badly formed packet which is sent though a NETWORK, often causing havoc. These packets are often caused by a malfunctioning piece of hardware such as a ROUTER. The term is derived from the book *The Hitch-hiker's Guide to the Galaxy*.

bogon filter A piece of hardware or software which eliminates or minimizes the flow of BOGONS in a NETWORK, a bogon being a badly formed, corrupted packet of data.

bogus marketing scheme The huge expansion of the Internet has meant that a large number of illegal schemes have been instigated by criminals. Bogus marketing schemes involve a user of the Internet helping to market some product which, its inventor claims, will make large amounts of money. In order to participate in such a scheme the user has to pay a fee to establish themselves as a distributor or a local agent. Once the money has been paid the criminal disappears or provides samples of the product which fall very far short of the claims made.

BOHICA Abbreviation for Bend Over Here It Comes Again used in NEWSGROUPS. The term has been used in a number of contexts, probably the most common one being to warn someone who has made a POSTING that a FOLLOW-UP which repeats another follow-up critical of the poster is to follow.

boilerplate Another name for a STYLE SHEET or TEMPLATE. It is a term used widely outside the Internet, for example in printing and document processing.

boil the ocean A phrase used in NEWSGROUPS to describe an impossible task: for example, 'Perhaps your scheme to connect all the computers together in the Internet in order to communicate with alien intelligence is a bit ambitious. Try something less difficult like boiling the ocean.'

bookmark 1. A marker used in a BROWSER to point at a WEB SITE which enables the user of the browser quickly to return to that site without typing in its UNIFORM RESOURCE LOCATOR. It functions just like a conventional bookmark.
2. Used in speech to make a note of a person, place, or idea: for example, 'I found John very interesting and bookmarked him' or 'Great idea I'll bookmark it.'

bookmark portal This is a PORTAL which allows users to store BOOKMARKS that can be accessed from any Internet device. It allows, for example, users to access bookmarks from any part of the world and does not require a browser on which the bookmarks are stored.

book ramping Some online booksellers allow visitors to their site to write reviews of the books that they sell. Book ramping is when a favourable review is written by the author or by a member of the publisher's staff; usually the reviewer hides behind an EMAIL ADDRESS which does not betray their identity. An activity similar to the much more serious one of SHARE RAMPING.

book site This is a WEB SITE that sells EBOOKS. At present there are only a few of these sites. Industry observers predict book sites as a major growth area as soon as technologies for implementing viable ebook readers are devised.

Boolean connective A symbol or word used to construct a complex SEARCH QUERY for a SEARCH ENGINE. Typical connectives include NOT, AND, and OR. For example, the query 'Java AND Privacy OR Security' searches for any documents which contain the words 'JAVA' and 'Privacy' or the word 'Security'. Boolean connectives are also used within programming languages to determine whether a section of code in a program is to be executed.

BOOP An abbreviation describing the top echelon of Microsoft. It stands for Bill and the Office Of the President, Bill being Bill Gates the chair of the company.

boot The process of starting up a computer's OPERATING SYSTEM. This normally occurs when a computer is switched on and is carried out by a small program, usually referred to as the boot program. It can also be initiated by pressing the reset button on a computer. Very occasionally the word is used in a non-technical way as in 'I was out late last night and it took me a long time to boot up this morning.'

boot off Used to describe the interruption of a connection to a network, for example where the amount of NOISE on the TRANSMISSION LINE is so large that a connection cannot be maintained, as in 'The line noise was so high that the server booted me off.' It is sometimes used to describe the suspension of a user by an INTERNET SERVICE PROVIDER. *See also* UNDER MOUSE ARREST.

boot sector The area of a PC disk which contains information about the formatting of the disk and a small program known as the boot program which starts up the computer when it is switched on. The boot sector is one of the targets of BOOT VIRUSES.

boot virus A VIRUS which stores itself on the BOOT SECTOR of a disk and contains a program which is executed when the computer containing the disk is started up. This program carries out some malicious act such as deleting important FILES.

Border Gateway Protocol A PROTOCOL that is used for the ROUTING between a SUBNET and the Internet. It has superseded the EXTERIOR GATEWAY PROTOCOL.

bot A program that carries out some repetitive or periodic task for a user. Typical tasks include finding email addresses for SPAMMING programs, gathering WEB PAGE statistics, providing updates for a user when stock prices change, EMAIL FILTERing, and maliciously sending a POSTING to any NEWSGROUP that it encounters. *See also* CANCELBOT, CHATTERBOT, NEWS BOT, and GOVERNMENT BOT. Bots are similar to AGENTS; indeed there is no hard and fast rule for determining whether a program is a bot or an agent. The derivation of the word is unclear. Two derivations place it as a shortened form of the word 'robot' and as an abbreviation for 'Box o' Tricks'.

bot moderation Being a MODERATOR for a MODERATED NEWSGROUP can be a very time-consuming task. In order to help with this task BOTS have been developed which filter out irrelevant POSTINGS to newsgroups. The process of using such devices is known as bot moderation.

botrunner Someone who employs a BOT on the Internet: for example, a financial analyst who uses a bot to gather up-to-date news on certain stocks or shares.

bot war What happens when CHAT BOTS invade a CHAT ROOM and start trying to establish some dominance; usually this results in the normal users of the room deserting.

bounce When an EMAIL cannot be delivered an error message is sent to the sender which usually includes some or all of the message; the email is then said to have bounced. There are a number of reasons for bounces occurring, including hardware faults and the recipient's email account having been deleted.

bounce message The message that is transmitted to the sender of an EMAIL when it cannot be delivered to its recipient: for example, when the recipient's email address has been deleted. The message contains some indication of why delivery did not occur and data on the route that the message took. *See also* BOUNCE and ROUTER DROPPINGS.

bowl A typographical term used to describe the curved line that encloses or partially encloses a space in letter. The letter 'a', for example, contains a bowl.

bozo filter A FILTER used in connection with an EMAIL PROGRAM or a NEWSREADER which filters mail or POSTINGS from users whose contributions or mailings you would prefer not to read. Such a filter either deletes the emails or places then in a special FOLDER. Such a collection of users is known as a BOZO LIST or B LIST.

bozo list A list of users whose contributions to a NEWSGROUP or whose EMAILS you do not want to read. A FILTER uses such a list to delete postings and emails or places them in a special directory.

bozotic Adjective used to describe stupid or ludicrous behaviour such as CROSSPOSTING to a large number of NEWSGROUPS. It is derived from Bozo the clown, a famous circus performer. *See also* BOZO FILTER and BOZO LIST.

bps Abbreviation for BITS PER SECOND.

BRB Abbreviation for Be Right Back used in CHAT ROOMS. Used when a participant wishes to take a short break.

breath of life packet A PACKET which is sent to any of the computers in an ETHERNET which have CRASHed. The purpose of the packet is to resuscitate and restart the malfunctioning computers.

BRI *See* BASIC RATE INTERFACE.

brick and mortar company A term used in ECOMMERCE documents to describe a conventional company which does not use network technology for dealing with customers, preferring to meet them face to face in a shop or in an office. *See also* CLICKS AND MORTAR.

bridge A hardware device which allows data to flow between two networks, usually LOCAL AREA NETWORKS. It examines the destination address of data that flows through it and forwards it to the network that it bridges if the address matches. If it does not, then the data is sent to other networks which contain bridges so that they can check whether the data is intended for them.

bridge page Another name for a GATEWAY PAGE.

British Computer Society The premier British professional organization for computing personnel.

broadband A term derived from the telephone world where it refers to any signal higher than 4 kHz. However, in the computing world the term is usually used to describe any cable network which employs analogue transmission.

Broadband Integrated Services Digital Network A technology for WIDE AREA NETWORKS which provide a sufficient bandwidth for those applications which have, in the past, swamped conventional networks: applications such as VIDEO ON DEMAND. B-ISDN, as it is often known, uses facilities provided by another technology known as ASYNCHRONOUS TRANSFER MODE.

Broadband ISDN *See* BROADBAND INTEGRATED SERVICES DIGITAL NETWORK.

broadband Web A future vision of the WORLD WIDE WEB where all connections, including those to the home, are via very high-speed communication lines. There are still major barriers to instant service from a WEB SITE, ranging from problems with WEB SERVER technology to the slow speed of the cables used to connect a telephone into the local exchange. The broadband Web is what will occur when all these problems have been solved. *See also* LAST MILE PROBLEM.

broadcasting The sending of data or messages from one computer to all the computers in a network. MULTICASTING which involves the sending of data and messages to a subset of computers is a variant of this.

broadcast network A computer network which has a single communication channel. A PACKET sent by one computer is received by all the other computers on the network. The packets that are sent contain the address of the receiving computer; each computer checks this field to see if it matches its own address. If it does not then it is usually ignored; if it does then it is read. Broadcast networks are usually small, localized networks known as LOCAL AREA NETWORKS.

broadcast quality video Video signals which are transmitted at a speed in excess of 30 frames per second at a resolution of 800 by 640 PIXELS.

broadcast storm It is possible to create a special message which, when received by a network, results in all the computers in the network replying to it or retransmitting it. The result of this is that the network becomes unusable. This is known as a broadcast storm; it often occurs when an item of software or hardware malfunctions.

broken graphic A clickable graphic in a WEB PAGE which contains a BROKEN LINK. When the user clicks on such a graphic an error message is returned.

broken link A HYPERLINK in a WEB PAGE to another page which no longer exists; when clicked by the user of a browser such a link generates an error message. There are a number of reasons for broken links. Two common ones are that the file referenced in the link no longer exists or that the SERVER hosting the file is out of action. *See also* BROKEN GRAPHIC.

broken pipe What happens when the DOWNLOADing of some data is fatally interrupted. There are a number of reasons for this including heavy network traffic or a hardware failure. The term was originally used in connection with failures which occurred during the use of the Netscape Navigator BROWSER; however, it is gradually being used in connection with failures associated with any type of software which transfers data.

broket Jargon used to describe angle brackets made from the characters < and >. Such characters are used as brackets for TAGS in the HYPERTEXT MARKUP LANGUAGE. Derived from 'broken bracket'.

brouter A network device that can function both as a ROUTER sending data to a destination network and a BRIDGE connecting two networks.

browse To view a number of WEB PAGES using a BROWSER. *See also* SURFING.

browser A computer program which requests files from a WEB SERVER. The files are marked up using the HYPERTEXT

MARKUP LANGUAGE and are formatted by the browser. HYPERLINKS in the text of the file, when clicked, will enable the user of the browser to display the file that the link refers to. There are a large number of browsers in existence, although the vast majority of users employ either INTERNET EXPLORER or NETSCAPE NAVIGATOR. As well as displaying text, a browser also displays graphics, although this can take some time to download since graphics occupy a large amount of memory; to counteract this browsers can be configured not to display graphics. There are also some browsers which are not designed for the processing of graphics which are very fast, the best known being LYNX. In the early days of the WORLD WIDE WEB, browsers such as MOSAIC just displayed text; however, there are now a large number of PLUG-INS which enable a browser to process a wide variety of media including VIDEO CLIPS, AUDIO CLIPS, and ELECTRONIC PAPER formats. Programs known as EXECUTABLE CONTENT can now be embedded in WEB PAGES using technologies such as JAVA and ACTIVE X. These programs interact with the browser to produce effects such as animations, provide forms, or interact with BACK END PROCESSES such as database updating.

browser cache An area of memory where WEB PAGES which have been recently accessed are stored. Caches are used to increase the efficiency of a browser in that they allow the user to revisit recently browsed pages without their being transferred over slow Internet connections.

browser caching The process whereby WEB PAGES which have been viewed are stored on some local storage medium such as a hard disk. Often users of a BROWSER return to these pages after visiting other pages. By storing them in an area on the computer running the browser they are retrieved much more quickly than if they were transferred anew over the Internet. Browsers normally allow the user to configure the amount of storage used for visited pages. The local storage used to contain the pages is known as the CACHE.

browser war A term used to describe the marketing war between the Microsoft Corporation and the Netscape Corporation over their respective browsers INTERNET EXPLORER and NETSCAPE NAVIGATOR which took place in the mid 1990s. Many ordinary users of browsers were drawn into this war, mainly in newsgroups where the discussion of the relative merits of the browsers often spilled into discussion about the ethics of the companies involved, a prime example of a RELIGIOUS WAR.

brute force attack Any criminal attempt to access a computer system by the repeated execution of some action. An example of this is an attempt to decipher a message which has undergone ENCRYPTION by repeatedly trying a large number of keys for DECRYPTION. If the encryption method is secure a successful attack using brute force would have to employ a prohibitively large amount of computer power. Brute force attacks on schemes such as the DATA ENCRYPTION STANDARD and the SECURE SOCKETS LAYER have been successful. They have often been carried out with the active support of the developers of the schemes; however, the resources required and the time taken for the attack have been so prohibitively high that the systems are regarded as secure. The term can also be used to describe attacks on a computer network which are based on SCANNING ATTACKS.

BSA *See* BUSINESS SOFTWARE ALLIANCE.

BSD *See* BERKELEY SOFTWARE DISTRIBUTION.

BSD UNIX A variant of the OPERATING SYSTEM known as UNIX. It was developed by staff of the Computer Science Research Group at the University of California, Berkeley. It has become one of the most popular platforms for Internet development.

BSF Abbreviation for But Seriously Folks used in CHAT ROOMS, EMAILS, and NEWSGROUPS. Used to indicate that the preceding text should be regarded as irony or humour.

BSOD Abbreviation for Blue Screen Of Death used in CHAT ROOMS, EMAILS, and

NEWSGROUPS. This is the display which is shown on a monitor when a Windows operating systems experiences a fatal error.

BTA Abbreviation for But Then Again used in CHAT ROOMS, EMAILS, and NEWSGROUPS. Normally used in liberal debate where the writer wishes to give the impression of fairness.

BTDT Abbreviation for Been There Done That used in EMAILS and NEWSGROUPS. Normally used to warn someone that a particular action will not result in its intended effect.

BTW Abbreviation for By The Way used in CHAT ROOMS, EMAILS, and NEWSGROUPS.

BUAA Abbreviation for Big Ugly ASCII Art. This refers to the use of ASCII characters in drawing very large letters, for example making the letter H from a large number of small ASCII H characters. This practice used to be prevalent in the days when the results of computer programs were delivered as printouts, but has markedly declined. Sometimes it is seen in SIG FILES.

buddy list A service which informs you when a friend or relative has logged on to the Internet. Once you have been notified of this you can engage in ONLINE CHAT with them. It is associated with INSTANT MESSAGING and requires a special program to create the list.

buffer An area of memory where data is stored, either before it is sent into a network to some device such as printer, or before being read by a computer as part of the processing of the data.

buffer page A WEB PAGE used for marketing. It is the page that is displayed when a user clicks on a BANNER ADVERT. Such pages are normally stored on the WEB SERVER which contains the banner advert and usually contain material pertinent to the banner advert such as a special marketing offer for a product or service.

bullet A large dot used in WEB PAGES and other documents to indicate one of the items in a list of textual objects.

bullet clicker A derogatory term used to describe the novice user of a browser who

clicks the BULLET points in a WEB PAGE under the mistaken impression that they are links to other pages.

bulletin board A bulletin board functions very much like a NEWSGROUP with the users of the board sending messages to it; these are then displayed to all those who access the bulletin board. It is a low-tech solution to providing a forum for users whose numbers are too small or whose focus of interest is too arcane to be supported by a NEWSGROUP. Often bulletin boards are used by companies who employ them to support their products or services.

bump To remind someone about something they meant to do: for example, 'You need to bump John about updating his Web site.'

burglar alarm Software that issues a warning when an intruder enters a computer system, such as by sending an EMAIL to the SYSTEM ADMINISTRATOR. Often used in conjunction with a HONEY POT.

burst page Synonym for BANNER ADVERT.

bus network A simple way to organize the hardware in a network. It consists of a single transmission pathway, with each device in the network attached to the pathway by a connector. Each device on the network has a unique address; if the software controlling the connector senses a packet of data it checks the address in that packet. If the address is the same as the address of its device it is passed to that device; if it is not then it is passed further along the bus for other devices to examine.

Business Software Alliance A consortium of software publishers and developers which aims to eliminate SOFTWARE PIRACY. The name is occasionally abbreviated to BSA.

business to business Used in connection with ECOMMERCE. It describes commercial transactions that are carried out between two businesses such as those associated with FINANCIAL EDI: for example, the purchase of components from a supplier by a car manufacturer. This is one of the most profitable areas of the Internet, which enables companies to make large efficiency gains in their SUPPLY CHAINS. Often abbreviated to B2B.

business to customer Used in ECOMMERCE to describe financial transactions which occur between individual customers and a business which uses the Internet for trade, for example the buying of a book from an online bookseller. *See also* BUSINESS TO BUSINESS. It is often abbreviated to B2C.

button A rectangular or rounded WIDGET which, when clicked by a mouse, initiates some action. For example, a button is often used on a WEB PAGE to send FORM data to a SERVER for processing.

buzzword bingo A version of the popular bingo game which takes place in meetings organized in large high-tech companies. Here, each member of the audience is secretly given a computer-generated card of ABBREVIATIONS and buzzwords; every time that one of these is mentioned it is deleted from a card. The winner is the person who deletes the full card or who has the most deletions. There are a number of apocryphal stories of participants standing up and shouting 'bingo' in the middle of a meeting when they have won. The term occasionally surfaces in EMAILS; for example, someone might claim to be the buzzword bingo winner after a particular email or POSTING full of abbreviations has appeared. There is a variant of buzzword bingo where everyone in a meeting is assigned a word and the person whose word is uttered most often gains a prize.

BWL Abbreviation for Bursting With Laughter used in CHAT ROOMS, EMAILS, and NEWSGROUPS. A response to a statement which is perceived to be completely wrong.

BWQ Abbreviation for Buzz Word Quotient used in CHAT ROOMS, EMAILS, and NEWSGROUPS. Usually used to pour scorn on a posting or email which contains a large number of ABBREVIATIONS. *See also* BUZZWORD BINGO.

BWTHDIK Abbreviation for But What The Heck Do I Know used in CHAT ROOMS, EMAILS, and NEWSGROUPS.

BWYM Abbreviation for Be With You Momentarily used in CHAT ROOMS. It usually indicates that the user has interrupted their participation by carrying out some other task such as adjusting screen resolution or setting the options on a piece of software.

byte A unit of storage equivalent to 8 BITS.

bzzt wrong A term taken from popular TV or radio quiz programmes to indicate the response of the quizmaster when a contestant provides a wrong answer. Usually the bzzt is the sound some buzzers make while the word 'wrong' is spoken by the quizmaster. It is often used in NEWSGROUPS by a participant to indicate that another participant has made an incorrect statement: for example, 'bzzt wrong, the browser was released in 1996 not in 1994 as you claim.'

C

C++ An OBJECT-ORIENTED PROGRAMMING LANGUAGE used for system programming and scientific programming. It is being increasingly used to develop Internet applications, primarily via ACTIVE X technology although its use lags well behind JAVA. The language is a superset of the programming language C. An example of a RELIGIOUS WAR is that carried out by proponents of C++ and those of the programming language Java.

C2 audit The process of writing system activity to a LOG FILE in a format demanded by the C2-LEVEL SECURITY standard. It involves logging activities such as opening a file, closing a file, and changing a DIRECTORY. Such an audit can consume huge amounts of file space and requires special-purpose tools to interpret the information written to the log file.

C2-level security A US government standard which is applicable to OPERATING SYSTEMS. Its base requirement is that users and applications need to be authenticated before they are allowed to use a resource administered by the operating system, for example a database. Operating systems which can demonstrate this are awarded a C2 certificate.

CA *See* CERTIFICATE AUTHORITY.

cable modem A MODEM which is able to connect from the home to the cable provided by cable TV companies. It currently allows downloads from the Internet at speeds approaching 10 Mbits/s.

cablese A form of abbreviated text used by journalists when they had to send articles and messages to their newspaper from another country. Cablese arose because telegraph messages were charged on a per-word basis. Occasionally cablese turns up in EMAIL as a way of reducing the time taken to type a message.

cable system operator A company which operates a CABLE TELEVISION service.

cable television The technology of delivering television-quality pictures to the home using BROADBAND technology. Such technology is becoming prevalent in areas with dense populations and is seen as one way to deliver fast Internet access to homes. Previously the technology used for delivering television was uni-directional—the pictures were just sent to the television set, with nothing being sent the other way—and so was unsuitable for the bi-directional signals that, for example, are required for Web access. Consequently one of the major efforts that cable television operators have made, and are making, has been to replace old cabling with bi-directional cabling which is suitable for Internet access.

cache An area of memory or a FILE in a computer which is used for storing data, text, graphics, or programs that are frequently accessed by users. By using a cache, efficiency is improved since it minimizes the number of slow connections that might be required to retrieve the data from its source—often the Internet. *See* SITE CACHING, BROWSER CACHING, and CACHING.

cache hit What occurs when the data required by a software process can be found in a CACHE and does not require retrieval from a slow storage medium. A request for a WEB PAGE which is currently held in a BROWSER CACHE would be an example of such a hit.

cache miss What occurs when the data required by some software process cannot be found in a CACHE and requires retrieval from some slow storage medium. For example a request for a WEB PAGE which is not currently held in BROWSER CACHE and which requires it to be transferred from the Internet using a slow connection is an example of a cache miss.

caching The process of storing frequently used data, programs, or text which is normally stored in a medium to which access is slow, in a medium to which access is faster. For example, storing a frequently accessed FILE in an area of computer memory is an example of caching. *See also* SITE CACHING, BROWSER CACHING, and CACHE.

caching policy The rules which are used to determine what items are to be stored in a CACHE and how long they are to remain. For example, a WEBMASTER has to make a number of decisions about the cache which holds WEB PAGES in a CACHING WEB SERVER. A typical decision is how long to keep pages in a cache before refreshing them by recopying them from their remote WEB SERVER. Another decision concerns which pages to cache: typically the Webmaster would ensure that any pages with a UNIFORM RESOURCE LOCATOR which indicates that their server is close to the caching server would not be cached; he or she would also decide that very frequently accessed pages would be cached. All these decisions and many others form part of a caching policy.

caching proxy server A SERVER which acts as an intermediary between a set of browsers and the Web. When a WEB PAGE is requested by a BROWSER it is first stored in the caching proxy server and then sent on to the browser that requested it. The server always ensures that popular pages requested by the browsers are stored locally in its file store. This means that access to these pages is very fast since there is no need for the pages to be brought across slow external communication lines. *See also* CACHING, PROXY, and SITE CACHING. Caching proxy servers are also used for implementing FIREWALLS.

caching Web server An alternative term for a CACHING PROXY SERVER.

calendar server A SERVER which usually forms part of a GROUPWARE package; it holds the diaries of a number of people centrally in such a form that, for example, meetings can be easily arranged when every person's diary for a particular day is free.

call back A technique which is used to establish that a user of a computer network is using a valid phone number and

is not MASQUERADING. After the user has dialled the computer which allows access to the network it disconnects the user and then redials what should be a valid telephone number.

call detail reporting 1. The reporting and storage of data about connections made by the users of a LOCAL AREA NETWORK.
2. The reporting and storage of data concerning the connections made by phone users of a telephone network.

call for votes A voting procedure used to determine whether a new Usenet NEWSGROUP should be created. During the voting period any participant in a Usenet newsgroup is allowed to vote for or against. If, at the end of the voting period, a potential newsgroup has 100 more votes for than against and has gained at least two thirds of the votes then it is created. Sometimes the term is abbreviated to CFV.

calling line identification The ability of a computer to detect the number of a phone making a call. Usually abbreviated to CLI; it is also known as AUTOMATIC NUMBER IDENTIFICATION.

CAN or Campus Area Network A collection of Local Area Networks within a localized environment such as a university.

can To abort a program running on a NETWORK, for example a program which attempts a DENIAL OF SERVICE ATTACK or a program which has been written so badly that it starts using too many network resources.

cancelbot A BOT that periodically examines postings to NEWSGROUPS cancelling those which look like SPAM. Also known as a ROBOCANCELLER.

cancelbunny A name given to semi-mythic users who delete postings to newsgroups. They do this for a variety of reasons ranging from the material's potential copyright infringement to its pornographic content. Cancelbunnies are also known as CANCELPOODLES or CANCELMOOSES.

cancelmoose A mythical Internet user who wages war against SPAM in NEWSGROUPS. To do this the cancelmoose uses a CANCELBOT to delete any POSTINGS to a newsgroup that he or she regards as spam.

cancelpoodle Another name for a CANCELMOOSE.

CAP *See* COMPETITIVE ACCESS PROVIDER.

Captain Crunch A famous CRACKER who used a free whistle given away with the American Captain Crunch breakfast cereal to imitate pay phone tones in order to make illegal phone calls.

carbon copy A copy of an EMAIL sent to recipients other than the main recipient of the email. Usually abbreviated to CC.

careware SHAREWARE for which the author usually suggests that payment should be made to some charitable institution.

carrier 1. Another name for a phone connection to a network.
2. A signal that can be used to carry another signal over a transmission line. For example, in analogue systems a sine wave signal is used to carry data which may be the subject of AMPLITUDE MODULATION or FREQUENCY MODULATION.
3. A phone company.

carrier sense multiple access collision avoidance One of the ways devices on a network access the network in order to transmit data, for example when sending a message to a SERVER or sending a reply to a CLIENT. Using this technique each device signals to the other devices on the network its intention to transmit before it carries out the procedure. This enables other devices which might be about to send data to hold back so that data packets do not cause a collision when two of them are simultaneously released into the network. *See also* CARRIER SENSE MULTIPLE ACCESS COLLISION DETECTION.

carrier sense multiple access collision detection A technique whereby computers on a network transmit data into the network over a transmission line. A computer using this technique first checks that the transmission line is not carrying data; if it is not then the transmitted data is released into the network. If another computer issues data at the same time and a collision occurs, then each computer rolls back, waits for a random time period, and attempts to retransmit. *See also* CARRIER SENSE MULTIPLE ACCESS COLLISION AVOIDANCE.

Cartesian coordinate system A way of locating objects in either two- or three-dimensional space by specifying their X (horizontal) position, Y (vertical) position and Z (through) position. It is used in graphics and in positioning text on documents. *See, for example*, Z ORDER.

cascade A series of messages which reply to a message which has been sent to a BULLETIN BOARD system.

cascading style sheets Cascading style sheets, more commonly known as CSS, are used as a STYLE SHEET facility in HTML. They can also be used in conjunction with SCRIPTING LANGUAGES such as JAVASCRIPT to change the format of an HTML document as a user interacts with the document. They form part of version 4 of HTML and enable the Web designer to define a standard visual identity for pages which have a similar function. For example, a style sheet could be used to define an entry in an ONLINE CATALOGUE and then be applied to individual Web pages containing sales information so that they look the same. Style sheets can be defined in a separate file or can be included in an HTML file that is to be browsed. They can be constructed by hand, but this is a tedious and error-prone process. Fortunately, there are a number of special-purpose software tools available for the definition of CSS style sheets and many WYSIWYG EDITORS provide facilities for their semi-automatic construction.

cascading style sheets level 1 A subset of the CASCADING STYLE SHEETS standard which is supported by the major BROWSERS.

cast shadow This is similar to a DROP SHADOW. However, the graphic artist uses techniques which enhance the perspective of the GRAPHIC IMAGE associated with the shadow.

cat 5 Cabling that can be used for a variety of transmission technologies including ASYNCHRONOUS TRANSFER MODE and TOKEN RING technology.

catatonic A word used to describe a computer or network that does not respond to user actions such as clicking a mouse or pressing the return key. A catatonic computer or catatonic network is usually suffering from a major hardware or software problem.

catenet An obsolete term that was used to describe a WIDE AREA NETWORK consisting of a number of SUBNETS. The term is derived from a contraction of the term 'concatenated network'. Sometimes it is written as catnet.

CC A common abbreviation for CARBON COPY or COURTESY COPY.

CCIRN See COORDINATING COMMITTEE FOR INTERCONTINENTAL RESEARCH NETWORKS.

CCITT See CONSULTATIVE COMMITTEE FOR INTERNATIONAL TELEPHONE AND TELEGRAPH.

CDA See COMMUNICATIONS DECENCY ACT.

CDF See CHANNEL DEFINITION FORMAT.

CDF file A FILE which contains information about a channel defined by the CHANNEL DEFINITION FORMAT®. It defines the properties of a channel that is to broadcast to a BROWSER and also includes information such as the update schedule of the channel.

CDMA See CODE DIVISION MULTIPLE ACCESS.

CDPD See CELLULAR DIGITAL PACKET DATA.

CDR See CALL DETAIL REPORTING.

CDSA See COMMON DATA SECURITY ARCHITECTURE.

cell The basic unit of data sent in an ASYNCHRONOUS TRANSFER MODE network. A cell is 53 bytes long of which 5 bytes are used for header information. The term is also generally used to describe PACKETS which are small.

cell padding The control of white space around a TABLE in a WEB PAGE. Cell padding has been extensively used by Web designers to format text and graphics on a Web page where the text and graphics

are embedded in tables. However, its use is declining with the increasing availability of WYSIWYG AUTHORS. This is an example of a SHIM. See also PIXEL SHIM.

Cellular Digital Packet Data A wireless technology that allows the transmission of data over unused parts of the telephone network. In order to do this a special-purpose modem is needed. Users of this service are normally charged on a per packet basis. This technology is frequently referred to as CDPD.

censorware A term, almost always used pejoratively, for BLOCKING SOFTWARE.

central office A location where a telephone company terminates telephone lines and establishes switching equipment so that they can be connected to other networks. An American term.

Centre for Democracy and Technology A non-profit-making organization which concerns itself with privacy and individual rights and liberty on the Internet.

CERN See CONSEIL EUROPÉEN POUR LA RECHERCHE NUCLÉAIRE.

CERN image map format One of the two IMAGE MAP formats that are used for SERVER SIDE IMAGE MAPS. Such a format describes the data that should be contained in the WEB SERVER file that is consulted when an image map is clicked in a BROWSER. The other format is the NCSA IMAGE MAP FORMAT.

CERT See COMPUTER EMERGENCY RESPONSE TEAM.

CERT advisory A bulletin produced by the COMPUTER EMERGENCY RESPONSE TEAM which details a security incident such as a virus being spread through a network, and provides information such as: a description of the problem, information that helps a computer site determine whether the incident is affecting it, and any modifications that are required to overcome problems created by the incident.

certificate authority A reputable organization such as the US Postal Service which issues DIGITAL CERTIFICATES that authenticate a user's identity or some data associated with a user such as their address.

certificate revocation list A CERTIFICATE AUTHORITY has to keep a list of all those DIGITAL CERTIFICATES that it has issued but are not valid. Such a list is known as a certificate revocation list. It is often referred to as a CRL.

certified delivery server A SERVER which provides a NON-REPUDIATION service for EMAIL: it provides information on whether a particular email was received and whether a genuine attempt to deliver it was made.

CFML *See* COLD FUSION MARKUP LANGUAGE.

CFN Abbreviation for Chow (Ciao) For Now used in CHAT ROOMS. Used to indicate that the originator is terminating their interaction with the room.

CFV *See* CALL FOR VOTES.

CGI *See* COMMON GATEWAY INTERFACE.

CGI bin A DIRECTORY on a UNIX-based WEB SERVER which stores the CGI SCRIPTS which are executed when an access is made to the server. Such scripts carry out processing associated with the WEB PAGE that is currently being processed: for example, reading data submitted in a form and depositing it in a database.

CGI programming The process of programming a WEB SERVER so that it can interact with other applications such as DATABASE MANAGEMENT SYSTEMS. *See also* CGI SCRIPT and CGI BIN. In the past the chosen language for this type of programming was PERL. However, most servers now support Java SERVLETS and because of this there has been a very small decline in the use of Perl. The term is an abbreviation of COMMON GATEWAY INTERFACE, part of a Web server that needs to be accessed in order to carry out any non-trivial processing such as reading a FORM.

CGI script A program that is executed when a WEB SERVER wants to carry out some processing that requires an interface to an application such as a database management system. For example, when the user fills in details in an HTML FORM and sends that form to the server a CGI script is the program that normally carries out the processing associated with the form. CGI scripts can now be written in a variety of languages although the most popular language used has been PERL.

CGM *See* COMPUTER GRAPHICS METAFILE.

CGUI *See* CUSTOMIZABLE GRAPHICAL USER INTERFACE.

chained transaction A TRANSACTION which consists of a series of further transactions that are executed sequentially. For example, a chained transaction might consists of a transaction to look up data in a database, a second transaction to look up some further data in another database, and a final transaction which updates a third database based on the results of the first and second transactions. Such transactions are easier to program than those which consist of a number of parallel transactions.

chain letter scam A semi-criminal activity in which a user of the Internet receives an EMAIL which contains the name and addresses of a number of other users. The letter asks for a sum of money to be sent to the first name on the list and asks the recipient to remove this name and add their own at the bottom of the list. Finally the recipient is asked to send the letter to a number of friends. Theoretically the recipient can make a large amount of money just by sending a small amount of money and reposting. This never happens: most recipients do not bother with chain letters, do not send money, and may even replace the name at the top of the email with their own. Such scams are as old as the postal service, but they have been given a new fillip by the mass use of email.

Challenge Handshake Authentication Protocol An AUTHENTICATION protocol that is used when connecting to an INTERNET SERVICE PROVIDER. It provides a high degree of security against unauthorized intrusion. It is much more secure than its predecessor the PASSWORD AUTHENTICATION PROTOCOL. It is often abbreviated to CHAP.

challenge response A security technique by which the user of a network is asked a question to which the computer knows the answer, such as the maiden name of the user's mother. If the user gives the wrong response then he or she is regarded as an intruder. The questions and corresponding responses are stored when the user first registers with the network.

Change Cipher Spec Protocol A PROTOCOL which is used in the SECURE SOCKETS LAYER. This technology uses cryptographic methods to send data between a CLIENT and a SERVER. The protocol is used to inform the participants that the previous ENCRYPTION ALGORITHM used for communication between the BROWSER and the SERVER is to be replaced by a new one.

change detection The process of auditing a computer system to check whether sensitive files have been changed by an intruder. One of the first things that an intruder does after a successful entry to a networked system is to change files in the system so that the next time that he or she enters the system it will be easier. For example, intruders might change a user file which gives them enhanced privileges or change a PASSWORD FILE so that they can enter the system masquerading as a regular user. There are a number of commercially available CHANGE DETECTION TOOLS that are available. Change detection is also known as EDIT DETECTION.

change detection tool A software tool used by SYSTEM ADMINISTRATORS to check whether any sensitive files held in a networked system have been subject to unauthorized change. They are periodically used to check sensitive files such as START-UP FILES.

channel An alternative name for a TRANSMISSION LINE.

Channel Definition File® A FILE which contains details about how much content is to be downloaded and how frequently it is to be broadcast for WEBCASTING. The format of these files is defined by a WORLD WIDE WEB CONSORTIUM standard.

Channel Definition Format Channel Definition Format, often known as CDF, is a technology specified by the WORLD WIDE WEB CONSORTIUM which enables CONTENT PROVIDERS, such as news channels like CNN, to continually download content to the desktop of a computer. The subscriber to one of these channels receives content which changes as new events are reported by the content provider. This technology was one of the first large-scale applications of the EXTENSIBLE MARKUP LANGUAGE.

channel hopping The process of moving from one INTERNET RELAY CHAT channel to another very quickly. Often carried out by participants looking for sexual contacts.

channel op A very common term used for a CHANNEL OPERATOR: the person who manages a CHAT ROOM or a series of chat rooms.

channel operator Someone who has special privileges associated with one or more INTERNET RELAY CHAT channels. For example, they may be allowed to suspend users for inappropriate behaviour. They are usually referred to as CHANNEL OPS.

CHAP *See* CHALLENGE HANDSHAKE AUTHENTICATION PROTOCOL.

charge back A financial transaction associated with credit card processing. It involves a customer's credit card account being credited rather than debited. Normally this happens when a problem with a particular physical transaction occurs, such as when a product that has been purchased by credit card is returned to the vendor because it is defective. Charge back transactions have been one of the main targets of intruders into ecommerce systems; a typical crime would involve a perpetrator issuing a number of illegal charge backs to his or her credit card and then using the funds built up to purchase goods.

charityware SHAREWARE for which the author suggests payment is made to a charity.

chat The process of communicating with other users of the Internet in REAL

TIME. The most common way of doing this is via CHAT ROOMS or MULTI USER DUNGEONS. There are a variety of reasons for using a chat room, ranging from companionship to sexual contact. A number of companies have implemented chat rooms on their WEB PAGES so that their customers can engage in online dialogue about the products or services sold by the company.

chat bot Malicious BOTS which intrude into CHAT ROOMS and carry out acts such as sending large amounts of text to the screens of the chat room participants. When a number of these bots intrude into a chat room and interact with each other a BOT WAR occurs; when this happens the human participants usually leave. *See also* ANNOYANCE BOT, FLOOD BOT, CLONE BOT, and INVITATION BOT.

chat channel The medium used to carry out a conversation which is taking place in an ONLINE CHAT environment.

chat client Software which the user of a CHAT ROOM needs to participate in the REAL TIME conversations that occur in a chat room. A chat client processes lines of text typed in by a chat room participant and sends them to a CHAT SERVER which then displays the text to the other participants and often displays the current state of the chat room, such as the identity of the participants who are currently in the room.

chat room The visual interface which displays the messages and responses of participants who are using ONLINE CHAT. Often chat rooms are implemented via WEB PAGES. Chat rooms are usually devoted to special topics such as US politics; however, there are a number of general chat rooms which are devoted to any issue the participants wish to bring up. Some chat rooms are sophisticated three-dimensional areas where participants can choose an icon known as an AVATAR to represent their presence in the chat room. Chatting normally occurs on a CHANNEL, and participants must join a channel before they can start talking to other users. Participants usually communicate by typing their contributions into a simple text box line by line.

chat server A SERVER which monitors the users of a CHAT ROOM. When one of the users sends a message to all the participants the server broadcasts the message to all the users. The main function of this type of server is thus reading and broadcasting the messages and responses in a chat room.

chat site A WEB SITE which hosts ONLINE CHAT. A big advantage of such a site is that all that is needed to use such a facility is a BROWSER. The disadvantage is that the subject of the online chat is often dictated by the owner of the site.

chatterbot A BOT which is a computer program that is capable of communicating with humans. The development of such bots is really an academic exercise in artificial intelligence. The aim of the developers of chatterbots is to construct a program which can pass the Turing test: that it cannot be distinguished from a human. Occasionally chatterbots are launched into CHAT ROOMS. They are normally detected very quickly.

cheapernet A slang term for TBASE2 wiring: thin ETHERNET cabling which employs coaxial technology.

checkout page A WEB PAGE that is used in an ECOMMERCE site that provides information about the items bought at the site. It also provides information about postage rates and special facilities such as gift wrapping. Normally such a page is associated with a SHOPPING CART where the checkout page processes the contents of the cart.

checkpointing The process of writing recovery data to some long-term storage medium. The data can be used to recover a DATABASE when it becomes corrupt or inconsistent due to hardware or software failure.

checksum A numeric quantity that is calculated from data that is sent over a network. For example, a very simple checksum might be the sum of the internal character codes which make up a message that is transmitted from one computer to another. Checksums are used to check that there has been no modification of data sent through a network due to factors such as hardware errors. The mechanism for checking this is to calculate the checksum of some data to be sent, send the data, and then send the checksum. The receiving computer then takes the data that was sent, recalculates the checksum, and compares it with the checksum that was sent. If they match, then there is a high probability that no change in the data has occurred, if they do not match the data has been corrupted during its journey from one computer to another. The choice of checksum method is critical: some methods like the one above, are too simple and occasionally fail to detect errors. CRYPTO-GRAPHIC CHECKSUMS are used to ensure that no illegal modification of data has occurred. Checksums are very similar in concept to MESSAGE DIGESTS and tend to be used in non-Internet circles.

Chernobyl packet A badly formed PACKET of data which causes a network to malfunction badly. Usually such packets are caused by a hardware error. *See also* BROADCAST STORM and NETWORK MELT-DOWN. The term is derived from the Russian nuclear accident at Chernobyl.

choke A device that restricts the free flow of data between networks. It is often implemented using a ROUTER. The main use of a choke is to prevent unauthorized intrusion into a network.

choke point A point in a computer network through which all or most of the traffic in the network flows. Such points are vulnerable to both CRACKERS and hardware failure. One of the main strategies of network designers is to minimize or eliminate the number of choke points.

chosen plaintext attack An attack on a network in which the intruder attempts to discover the KEY used for ENCRYPTION. This attack involves the intruder sending known messages to the computer which carries out the encryption and then intercepting the text that is created by the encryption process.

Christmas tree packet A packet of data for which every option is set in the PROTOCOL which is being used to send the data.

churn Jargon term often used in ECOM-MERCE to describe customer disloyalty: the ease with which the Internet enables a customer to move from one ecommerce retailer to another makes churn a major factor in the WEB DESIGN process.

CIAC *See* COMPUTER INCIDENT ADVISORY CAPABILITY.

CID Abbreviation for Consider It Done used in CHAT ROOMS, EMAILS, and NEWS-GROUPS. It also stands for Crying In Disgrace, used when someone admits to a wrong action or statement.

CIDR *See* CLASSLESS INTER DOMAIN ROUTING.

CIO Abbreviation for Check It Out used in CHAT ROOMS, EMAILS, and NEWS-GROUPS.

cipher The set of rules which is used to change a text—the PLAIN TEXT—into a form which cannot be read by an unauthorized person. For example, a very simple and easily breakable rule might be to replace one character by another in the text. The process of applying the rules is known as ENCRYPTION. The text that is created by encryption is usually known as the CIPHER TEXT.

cipher text The text which has been created when a message known as the PLAIN TEXT has undergone the process of ENCRYPTION. Once in this form it cannot be read by anyone who does not have the KEY for the encryption process used.

circuit Synonym for a TRANSMISSION LINE.

Circuit Switched Cellular A simple but expensive wireless technology that allows the user of a cellular phone to connect to a network; all that is required is a cellular modem which connects the portable phone to a computer.

circuit switched network A network where a single physical connection is established from a source which sends data to a receiver. This connection is established via some switching mechanism. The best example of such a network is the telephone system.

CIX *See* COMMERCIAL INTERNET EXCHANGE.

class A address An INTERNET PROTOCOL ADDRESS which is used to identify computers on a large SUBNETWORK. The network part of the address is stored as 7 BITS and the local address of the computer on the network is stored as 24 bits.

class B address An INTERNET PROTOCOL ADDRESS which is used to identify computers on a medium-sized SUBNETWORK. The network part of the address is stored as 14 BITS and the local address of the computer on the network is stored as 16 bits.

class C address An INTERNET PROTOCOL ADDRESS which is used to identify computers on a small SUBNETWORK. The network part of the address is stored as 21 BITS and the local address of the computer on the network is stored as 8 bits.

class D address An INTERNET PROTOCOL ADDRESS which is used to carry out MULTICASTING. The multicasting address is stored in 28 BITS.

classless interdomain routing One of the solutions being adopted to address the problem of the Internet running out of addresses in which smaller chunks of space are allocated to organizations that require an address. For example, if a site requires a CLASS B ADDRESS then it is given a block of CLASS C ADDRESSes instead. This solution is really only a temporary one compared with solutions such as IPv6.

clear text A synonym for PLAIN TEXT.

CLEC *See* COMPETITIVE LOCAL EXCHANGE CARRIER.

CLF *See* COMMON LOGFILE FORMAT.

CLI *See* CALLING LINE IDENTIFICATION.

click The process of placing a mouse cursor over some text or a graphic and pressing one of the mechanical switches which are found at the top of the mouse. Some action usually follows the process of clicking, for example the display of a WEB PAGE or the highlighting of text.

clickable region That part of an IMAGE MAP which is associated with a HYPERLINK. When this region is clicked, control is passed to the WEB PAGE referenced by the hyperlink.

click here The text that is often found in a WEB PAGE to indicate that some HYPERMEDIA link is embedded at that point. When the text is clicked a new WEB PAGE is often displayed.

click intermediary A third-party company that administers an ASSOCIATE PROGRAM which is based on a PAY-BY-CLICK MODEL. Typically this company provides links or custom interfaces to the affiliates of the program and carries out the accounting process involved in tracking and paying affiliates. *See also* PURCHASE INTERMEDIARY.

clickly A term sometimes found in EMAIL messages and POSTINGS to NEWSGROUPS. It means clicking quickly.

clicks and mortar The combination of conventional commerce and ECOMMERCE. For example, a number of industrial commentators have predicted that supermarkets will eventually rely on both ecommerce sales and conventional sales, with the ecommerce sales being of bulk commodity items such as tissues, breakfast cereal, and jam, and the conventional sales being of fresh products such as fruit, vegetables, fish, and meat.

clickstream The path the user of a BROWSER takes when navigating the WORLD WIDE WEB. A clickstream consists of individual visits to each WEB PAGE known as HITS. Clickstreams provide very valuable information for marketers about the tastes and habits of Internet users, for example the fact that many users visit one WEB SITE immediately after visiting another site.

click through The number of mouse clicks which a BANNER ADVERT has received. It is also known as a PAGE INFORMATION REQUEST.

click through rate A figure used to quantify how often a user visits a commercial WEB SITE from another site. For example, the term is often used to judge the effectiveness of BANNER ADVERTS. To judge this type of effectiveness a click through rate might be defined as the ratio of the number of times a user clicks a banner advert to visit the site associated with it to the number of times a visitor accesses the page containing the advert.

click wrap agreement A licensing agreement that is presented to the user of a WEB SITE which downloads software. The agreement is similar to those associated with conventional software products. Often the agreement requires some action from the user such as clicking a BUTTON.

client A program or computer that requests some service from a SERVER. For example, a BROWSER accessing WEB PAGES from a WEB SERVER acts as a client to that server and an FTP client asks for files to be downloaded from a FTP SERVER. *See* CLIENT SERVER COMPUTING.

client pull The process of transferring media in response to user actions, for example the DOWNLOADing of a WEB PAGE when a HYPERLINK in another page is clicked. This is in contrast to SERVER PUSH.

client server computing The combination of computers—often powerful computers—known as SERVERS which offer specialized services to a number of other computers known as CLIENTS. A typical service is a file service where a server provides files requested by clients. It is worth pointing out that the provision of services is usually a little more complicated: a server providing a service often calls on the facilities of another server. For example, a WEB SERVER hosting an ECOMMERCE application that entails selling a product usually calls on the services of a DATABASE SERVER which stores product information. A client server computing system has a number of characteristics. The first is that it should be capable of combining clients and servers running a variety of operating systems and hardware using standard PROTOCOLS. One of the reasons for the rise of TCP-IP, and its increased use in client server systems in the 1990s, has been its widespread availability on virtually every OPERATING SYSTEM. The second characteristic is that resources in such a system are shared: for example, a network operating as a client server system may contain a single database that is held on a database server accessed by clients, with the server

mediating and sharing the access to the data. The third characteristic is that servers are highly specialized in that they carry out one service; hence they can be optimized for that service alone. This leads to a near optimum performance that would not be achieved if a server were carrying out a large amount of general-purpose processing. The fourth characteristic is that scaling a client server system is relatively straightforward: more clients can be easily added to increase user access to a system and more powerful servers can be added to increase the power of the system. The fifth characteristic is that of TRANSPARENCY: that when a client asks for a service there is no need for the user of the client, or the programmer who developed the code that requests the service, to know the address of the server that provides the service. In order to implement this, client server systems usually contain a NAME SERVICE that maps symbolic names to the locations of resources. If a server address changes then all that needs to be done is to change the data stored by the server implementing the name service; no other program code needs to be changed. A sixth characteristic is that the relationship between a client and a server is asymmetric: clients issue requests for a service and servers wait for this request before responding. The final characteristic of a client server system is the fact that program code and data for services are maintained centrally at the server that provides the service; this means that there are no complications when such software needs to be updated. The client server model is increasingly becoming the de facto model for computer networks: for example, the WORLD WIDE WEB is a client server system, where the client is a computer that runs a browser and servers are WEB SERVERS that respond to requests from the clients for WEB PAGES. *See also* INTRANET and EXTRANET.

client side image map An implementation of an IMAGE MAP where the location of a link inside a graphic is stored and processed by a BROWSER running on a client computer. This is in contrast to a SERVER SIDE IMAGE MAP where the processing is carried out by the WEB SERVER.

Details of the image map are contained in the HTML file that is browsed; these details are similar in format to the IMAGE MAP DEFINITION FILES found on the WEB SERVERS which carry out the processing of server side image maps.

clip art Graphic images which can be cut or clipped from a library and placed in a document such as a WEB PAGE. There are a large number of clip art libraries in existence on the Internet; they are useful for users who have no formal design or art training. Many, however, represent the minimum in terms of style and timeliness.

clipper An abbreviation for CLIPPER CHIP.

Clipper chip A hardware device which encrypts and decrypts signals sent over a network. The chip was developed by the NATIONAL SECURITY AGENCY and has been the subject of much controversy, with civil liberties groups claiming it results in an invasion of privacy.

CLM Abbreviation for Career Limiting Move.

cloaking The process whereby the contents of one or more WEB PAGES are hidden from visitors to a WEB SITE in order to deter those visitors from copying or stealing the pages. Cloaking is usually carried out by not linking to these pages from publicly visible pages. If a user wishes to select a number of visitors to access cloaked pages then the visitors are supplied with the UNIFORM RESOURCE LOCATOR.

clock drift Computers usually contain crystal-based clocks. These clocks are often subject to clock drift, when their time becomes gradually more and more inaccurate. This provides problems for the designers of DISTRIBUTED SYSTEMS where TRANSACTIONS can be made up of individual accesses to SERVERS which have to occur in a certain temporal order. There are a number of solutions to this problem. They include ALGORITHMS which make allowances for known drift and PROTOCOLS for keeping clocks in step with each other. See, for example, the NETWORK TIME PROTOCOL.

clock synchronization The computers which make up a DISTRIBUTED SYSTEM contain clocks that are subject to time drift. One of the problems facing the developers of such systems is ensuring that TRANSACTIONS which consist of smaller transactions are carried out in a specified order. If some of the clocks in the computers that make up the system have drifted badly then there is a danger that the transactions will not be carried out in the right order and this will give rise to an inconsistent state. In order to overcome the problem a number of algorithms and PROTOCOLS have been developed to compensate for the drift in time. See, for example, the NETWORK TIME PROTOCOL.

clogging A type of DENIAL OF SERVICE ATTACK on a computer in a network. It involves the attacker establishing many thousands of connections to the attacked computer but not relinquishing them and hence not making them available to other users. This prevents legitimate users from making a connection. See, for example, SYN FLOODING.

clone bot A BOT which intrudes into a CHAT ROOM, carries out some malicious act such as issuing obscenities, and multiplies itself in order to make it difficult for the MODERATOR of the chat room to remove them.

closed network A network to which access is only allowed to users who have been authenticated. Typically this type of network uses technologies such as FIREWALLS, PROXY SERVERS, PASSWORDS, and FIREWALL ROUTERS to achieve this.

clothesline model A term used on connection with computer CONFERENCING and NEWSGROUPS. It describes a topic that is artificially introduced for discussion.

clustergeeking The activity of spending an inordinate time on a computer which is part of a cluster of computers: for example the computers found in a laboratory devoted to practical work in a university. Often used to describe the activities of users who engage in multiuser games.

clustering A technique used by some SEARCH ENGINES which ensures that each site has only one page reference stored in the INDEX. This means that there will not be multiple occurrences of the same site when the results of a SEARCH QUERY are displayed by the search engine.

CMC *See* COMPUTER-MEDIATED CONFERENCING.

CMIP *See* COMMON MANAGEMENT INFORMATION PROTOCOL.

CNET One of the largest content providers for the computer industry and for home computer users.

CNI *See* COALITION FOR NETWORKED INFORMATION.

CNP Abbreviation for Continued in my Next Post used in NEWSGROUPS.

Coalition For Networked Information A consortium of US governmental and educational bodies which was set up to promote the access and dissemination of information in networked environments.

coaster A term used to describe either a defective CD ROM or one, usually sent by an INTERNET SERVICE PROVIDER, which is not needed. The name derives from the fact that these CD ROMs are often used as mats for mugs of hot liquid.

coaxial cable Cable which consists of a single copper conductor at its centre enclosed by a braided metal shield and covered in a layer of plastic. The shield protects the main copper cable from electrical interference. Such cabling is difficult to install but is highly resistant to interference. The cable comes in two versions: thick coaxial cable and thin coaxial cable. The latter is often referred to as THINNET and the former as THICKNET. *See also* CHEAPERNET.

cobranding The appearance of two companies, usually via their respective logos, on a WEB SITE. There are a number of reasons why this might occur: for example, one company might have developed a major product, while the other might have developed some add-on for the product. Another reason is that one company might provide technical expertise and perhaps a customer base, while the other company might market a product to be sold to the customer base using its marketing expertise. *See also* COOPETITION.

cobweb site A WEB SITE which has not been updated for a long time. Sometimes it is referred to as a MORTUARY SITE.

COCA *See* COST OF CRACKING ADJUSTMENT.

code book The medium used to store a series of ONE TIME PASSWORDS. Typically a computer program generates a series of passwords which are used only once: after they have been used the computer system refuses to recognize them. The passwords, which are stored in the code book are given to a user in a number of forms ranging from a sheet of paper to a secure FILE which the user can access.

Code Division Multiple Access A technology used to implement cellular phone communication. Each conversation on such a system is split into a number of packets which are transmitted over the cellular system. It is also used for wireless Internet services.

Cof$ Abbreviation for Church of Scientology used in CHAT ROOMS, EMAILS, and NEWSGROUPS. This organization has a poor reputation among Internet users because of its propensity to sue the owners of sites who make scientology material readily available to users.

coffee cup holder A term of abuse used in connection with a very inexperienced user of the Internet. It is derived from a famous NEWSGROUP posting which complained about the size of the coffee cup holder on a computer (the poster was referring to the CD tray).

cold boot 1. To BOOT a computer by switching it on after it has been closed down for a period during which its circuits and devices have cooled down.
2. To boot a computer by switching on its power supply.

Cold Fusion Markup Language® An extension of the HYPERTEXT MARKUP LANGUAGE developed by the Allaire Corporation. It includes facilities for database access, programming logic and ERROR TRAPPING.

collaborative agent An AGENT which collaborates with other agents to carry out a task. These other agents can be simple REACTIVE AGENTS, other collaborative agents, or intelligent DELIBERATIVE AGENTS. Each has a degree of expertise about some area and calls upon the expertise of other agents in areas where it lacks knowledge. For example, an agent which carries out the process of periodically reorganizing a WEB SITE might collaborate with an agent which is able to carry out the physical partitioning of the files which make up the site and also with a simple REACTIVE AGENT which informs the WEBMASTER when the reorganization has been completed.

collaborative buying site A WEB SITE which co-ordinates the bulk buying of some commodity. The owner of the site usually puts up a particular product for sale and users then add their names to a list of potential buyers. As the list lengthens the cost to the buyers drops because the Web site owner has negotiated bulk deal discounts.

collision The event that occurs when two devices on a network send packets of data at the same time. The packets 'collide' in the transmission lines used in the network and the data needs to be resent. Different types of network have different ways of either avoiding this event or recovering from it.

collision detection The process whereby an ETHERNET discovers that two of the nodes on the network have sent a PACKET of data at the same time. When this happens the network takes some action to retransmit the data which could have collided. For example, the transmitters of the data may be delayed by a random time period before they retransmit.

colo An abbreviation for COLOCATION.

colocation The process of siting a server in some secure site rather than in an office. Colocation sites are highly secure, have major backup facilities and are heavily protected against natural disasters. The term is occasionally abbreviated to colo.

colour depth The number of colours that can be displayed in a PIXEL. The deeper the colour the larger the number of colours that can be used in a graphic but the slower it becomes to DOWNLOAD it to, say, a WEB PAGE.

COM® An abbreviation used to refer to the serial port of a personal computer. It is also a component technology developed by the Microsoft Corporation and a top-level DOMAIN NAME for companies.

Comdex The major show for commercial companies who sell hardware and software. Two conferences are held every year, usually in Atlanta and Las Vegas. *See also* CUMDEX.

comma delimited file A FILE in which the individual items in the file are separated by commas. *See also* TAB DELIMITED FILE. Many software packages such as spreadsheets can read and interpret data expressed in such a way.

command language A simple language which is conveyed to a program using simple text. The MSDOS command language is an example of such a technology, as is the UNIX command language. Users of such languages often pride themselves on their technical expertise in comparison with the users of technologies like graphical interfaces. Facility in a command language is a skill usually displayed by GEEKS.

comment Text in a program or WEB PAGE written in the HYPERTEXT MARKUP LANGUAGE which contains documentary information and is not processed by a compiler or BROWSER.

commerce bot A BOT which carries out some commercial activity such as tracking currency rates and signalling any unusual fluctuations or looking for the best price for a particular product.

CommerceNet A non-profit-making collection of organizations which acts as an industry body for ECOMMERCE companies. It carries out a number of functions including advocating the use of the Internet for commercial activities, coordinating the use of emerging technologies in ecommerce applications, and supporting pilot projects.

commerce server A SERVER which provides services needed by companies who wish to implement TRANSACTIONS that require a high level of security: for example, banks and companies that practise ETAILING. Such servers process credit cards and use security technology such as the SECURE SOCKETS LAYER.

commerce service provider A company which provides an individual or a business with all the facilities necessary to carry out ECOMMERCE. These include the provision of secure transaction facilities, the facilities provided by a COMMERCE SERVER, WEB SITE PROMOTION services, credit card handling facilities and WEB DESIGN expertise. Increasingly INTERNET SERVICE PROVIDERS, faced with major competition, are moving into this area.

Commercial Internet Exchange A large US trade organization for INTERNET SERVICE PROVIDERS and other companies that offer access to the Internet. Often abbreviated to CIX.

commit protocol Often a TRANSACTION in a distributed system involves the updating of a number of distributed databases. It is important that all these updates occur together correctly and that none fails to occur. If one does fail, then the whole of the transaction must fail and the databases affected by the transactions must be rolled back to their original state. A commit protocol enables this to happen.

committed A term used to describe a TRANSACTION which has resulted in the permanent storage of data associated with the transaction: in effect the transaction has been successfully completed with all its individual components having been successfully executed.

commoditization The transformation of a complex and difficult task to an easy one. For example, finding an insurance quote for a car used to be something a car owner entrusted to an expert insurance agent. Now there are many WEB SITES which bypass the broker and offer insurance quotes from a number of companies.

common carrier An American term used to describe a company that offers telecommunications services to the public.

Common Data Security Architecture An architecture for providing high security for transactions over the Internet. It makes extensive use of security certificates and portable digital tokens which store KEYS and carry out ENCRYPTION and DECRYPTION.

Common Gateway Interface A standard which defines the interface between a WEB SERVER and an application program such as a database program. It enables the server to interact with such a program during the process of sending and receiving WEB PAGES to and from a BROWSER. A typical CGI program would process a form, say a form associated with a GUEST BOOK that has been sent from a browser, check that the items typed in the form are correct and then update a database with the details held in the form. During the early history of Web servers CGI programming was the common means of carrying out processing that could not be accomplished by the browser. Usually this programming was carried out in the programming language PERL, although there are now a number of alternatives such as SERVLETS. *See also* SERVER API, NETSCAPE SERVER APPLICATION PROGRAMMING INTERFACE, INTERNET SERVER APPLICATION PROGRAMMING INTERFACE, FASTCGI, and APPLET.

Common Intermediate Format A standard for VIDEO CONFERENCING systems which supports data presented at a FRAME RATE of 30 FPS.

Common Logfile Format A format used to describe the contents of a WEB LOG FILE. It defines the individual items of data in the log file and the order in which they appear. It was defined by the NATIONAL CENTER FOR SUPERCOMPUTING APPLICATIONS and is the most popular log file format. *See also* EXTENDED LOGFILE FORMAT and IIS STANDARD LOG FILE FORMAT.

Common Management Information Protocol A standard which is aimed at providing the facilities that enable DISTRIBUTED SYSTEMS to be managed efficiently. Typical functions addressed by this standard include those associated with security, the management of individual computers, and the monitoring of performance.

Common Object Request Broker Architecture A DISTRIBUTED OBJECT technology which has been specified by a collection of companies and government organizations known as the OBJECT MANAGEMENT GROUP. CORBA, as it is more familiarly known, enables objects to be distributed within a network, with each object being capable of receiving messages from other objects. These objects are defined in a special-purpose language known as an INTERFACE DEFINITION LANGUAGE. There are a number of implementations of CORBA which allow distributed objects to be written in a variety of languages; this means that, for example, an object written using JAVA can communicate with an object written in C++. *See also* OBJECT REQUEST BROKER.

Communications Decency Act A controversial section of a US telecommunications reform bill which made illegal the transmission of lewd and obscene material. The broadness of the drafting of the legislation was such that it encompassed much more than pornography and led to major protests by users and communication companies. The Act was watered down by a US federal court. The day the Act was passed is known as BLACK THURSDAY.

communications port A connector usually found at the back of a personal computer which is used as a communications interface.

communications software The software that enables a computer to connect to a network and communicate with other computers on the network. It is a generic term which covers, for example, the software used to control a NETWORK INTERFACE CARD or a MODEM and software which provides an interface to the TCP-IP protocol.

communication subnet An alternative term for SUBNET.

comp An abbreviation which designates those NEWSGROUPS that discuss computing topics. They include some of the most active newsgroups on the Internet; however, the topics they discuss tend only to be understandable to professional users of computer technology.

companion virus A VIRUS which replaces a particular program in a computer and is executed when the user issues an instruction to execute the program. For example, it may replace a program which finds files and may result in the files that the user wishes to find being deleted.

comparison site A WEB SITE which, given a product request, returns with the cheapest price. Such sites operate in a number of ways: some send emails to the vendors who then have to respond by presenting the user with the cheapest price some time after a request has been made; some operate by scanning a stored DATABASE of product costs; and others operate by using a SHOPPING BOT.

competitive access provider A company which provides connections to a telephone network. Such companies compete with telephone companies. They are also known as COMPETITIVE LOCAL EXCHANGE CARRIERS.

competitive local exchange carrier A company which provides voice connections to conventional telephone networks. They compete with conventional phone companies. They are also called COMPETITIVE ACCESS PROVIDERS.

compiled programming language A programming language whose programs are converted into an executable form before being executed, in contrast to INTERPRETED PROGRAMMING LANGUAGES which are executed directly. Compiled programming languages are more efficient than their interpreted cousins. C is an example of a compiled programming language.

compiler A program which takes a program written in a source code such as JAVA and then converts it into machine code. This generated code is then executed by a computer. This is in contrast to INTERPRETERS which execute the program directly.

complete network A network in which every computer has a direct connection to every other computer. In this network a message sent from one computer to another does not have to travel via any intermediate computers.

Component Object Model® A component technology which has been developed by the Microsoft Corporation. It enables software developers to produce software components which can be reused time and time again. It gave rise to the DISTRIBUTED COMPONENT OBJECT MODEL. It is often abbreviated to COM.

compression The process of reducing the size of a file before sending it over a transmission line. Many transmission media on the Internet are still slow, and since compression algorithms are often efficient, large gains in transmission time can be achieved by a good compression program. When a file has been sent, a decompression program at its destination recovers the original file. Compression schemes are categorized into LOSSY COMPRESSION SCHEMES and LOSSLESS COMPRESSION SCHEMES. The former result in some of the information in a compressed file being lost; the latter results in no loss. Lossy compression schemes are used in applications where some small loss of data can be tolerated, for example when the file that is compressed contains graphical images which, when decompressed, are not discernibly different from the original, uncompressed image.

computationally secure A phrase used to describe a coding technique based on CRYPTOGRAPHY which cannot be broken using available technology in such a time that some gain, financial or otherwise, can be made.

computerate A combination of 'computer' and 'literate' used to describe someone who is familiar and practised with computer technology.

Computer Emergency Response Team More usually known as CERT. The CERT Coordination Center was set up by the Defense Applied Research Projects Agency at Carnegie Mellon University in 1988 after the INTERNET WORM seriously affected the Internet. It has the general brief to provide help and expertise when a major security incident affects the Internet. Originally the work of the team was confined to responding to security incidents. However, since then it has broadened and now includes: helping to start other incident response teams, the coordination of teams when a large-scale incident occurs, the provision of training, and the carrying out of research into computer security.

Computer Graphics Metafile A GRAPHIC FORMAT which defines a way of storing graphic images so that they can be displayed using a wide variety of output devices. Often abbreviated to CGM.

Computer Incident Advisory Capability An agency funded by the US government which provides computer security services to branches of the US government and contractors working on government projects.

computer-mediated communication Those technologies used for communication where the computer plays a major part. It includes NEWSGROUPS, CHAT ROOMS, EMAIL, and COMPUTER-MEDIATED CONFERENCING. Often abbreviated to CMC.

computer-mediated conferencing The use of a computer to carry out the basic functions associated with conferencing. These include receiving contributions for a conference, displaying them, and cataloguing contributions into topic areas.

Computer Professionals for Social Responsibility An organization of computing professionals, educators, and members of the public which is dedicated to the ethical use of computing. The organization is currently based in California.

Computer Science Net In the late 1970s the NATIONAL SCIENCE FOUNDATION saw that the ARPANET was having a major impact on computing and decided to set up a network known as the Computer Science Net for academics. This supported DIAL-UP ACCESS and had connections to the ARPANET. It was one of the precursors of the Internet and was finally merged with BITNET and administered by CREN. It is often abbreviated to CSNET.

computer sex The process of connecting two computers together using some physical connection medium such as a wire.

computer-supported cooperative work The use of Internet and DISTRIBUTED SYSTEM technology to support the work of a group of people who are often physically distanced from each other. The term encompasses everything from the simple use of MAILING LISTS to the use of sophisticated GROUPWARE. Two common uses of computer-supported cooperative work are VIRTUAL CORPORATIONS and TELEWORKING.

computer telephone integration The integration of computer technology and telephone technology, with the former controlling the latter. A good example of this is the call centre which uses a computer to take a customer through a series of steps until they reach the service they require. Another example of this technology is a UNIVERSAL MESSAGING SERVICE which enables a single telephone number to be used as a receiver of FAXes and phone calls and then forwards them to an EMAIL account. Computer telephone integration uses a number of technologies including speech recognition, speech synthesis, database, email, and FAX.

concentrator Computer hardware which acts as a connector for devices in a network. Most concentrators have the ability to amplify the electrical signals they receive as PACKETS pass through them.

concept search A search using a SEARCH ENGINE which looks for documents containing words that are conceptually related to a particular word rather than looking for documents containing the word itself.

concurrency control The actions that are taken in a DISTRIBUTED SYSTEM to ensure that the system is not left in an inconsistent state when TRANSACTIONS are carried out in parallel. For example, a transaction could be in the middle of carrying out some transformation on data when another parallel transaction uses this data before the first transaction has finished

with it. This can lead to the data being given an incorrect value. The aim of concurrency control is to ensure that the result of a series of transactions which are carried out in parallel is the same as if the transactions were carried out one after another. This is a property known as SERIAL EQUIVALENCE.

conferencing The process of asynchronous or synchronous discussion on a network. It can be used to describe the activities that are carried out in NEWSGROUPS or can be used to describe the use of CONFERENCING SOFTWARE which allows users to communicate with each other over a network in REAL TIME using technologies ranging from low-tech mechanisms such as keyboards to video cameras.

conferencing software A generic term used to describe any software which links a number of users together in a conference and which enables them to post submissions to a conference and read other users' contributions. The term is often used to include software which is used in connection with NEWSGROUPS.

confidential email system A generic term used to describe a system for sending and receiving EMAIL which uses CRYPTOGRAPHY to ensure that the mail is kept confidential. *See* PRETTY GOOD PRIVACY.

configuration management 1. A subdiscipline of NETWORK MANAGEMENT. It consists of identifying and tracking the various devices which make up a network such as ROUTERS, BRIDGES, and computers. **2**. A software engineering term that describes the management of versions of a software system.

confirmed service A service which is provided by a LAYER in a LAYERED ARCHITECTURE such as the INTERNET LAYERED ARCHITECTURE where some confirmatory response from an entity such as a computer is required. Connecting one entity to another across a network is an example of a confirmed service, since before data can flow between the two entities the second must have indicated that it agrees to be connected.

congestion control The processes that are used to reduce congestion in a network. This includes making decisions such as: deciding when to accept new TRAFFIC, when to delete packets and when to adjust the ROUTING policies used in a network.

connect The process of establishing contact with a network, usually the Internet, via an INTERNET SERVICE PROVIDER. After a user has been connected and authorized he or she can make full use of the facilities of the network.

connection hijacking The process whereby an intruder intercepts a connection between a user and a computer and takes over the role of one of the parties in the dialogue that takes place. For example, an intruder may mimic the user and carry out a number of financial transactions in the user's name which favours the intruder. Another example is where the intruder mimics the computer and gathers useful information such as the PASSWORD employed by the user.

connection laundering An attack on a computer by an intruder which uses another computer to achieve the intrusion. This is also known as NETWORK WEAVING.

connection-oriented service A service provided by a LAYER in a LAYERED ARCHITECTURE such as the INTERNET LAYERED ARCHITECTURE where, in order to provide the service, the layer has to connect to a receiver and send the data direct. This is in contrast to a CONNECTION-LESS SERVICE.

connectionless protocol A PROTOCOL which governs the sending of packets of messages into a network which are not sent via a connection, but transmitted into the network with their destination address. This is an efficient way of sending data; however, it is not reliable since if a packet is lost there is no way for the sender to determine this and resend the packet. The best-known connectionless protocol is the UNRELIABLE DATAGRAM PROTOCOL.

connectionless service A service provided by a LAYER in a LAYERED ARCHITEC-TURE such as the INTERNET LAYERED ARCHITECTURE where in order to provide

the service the layer sends chunks of data independent of other chunks of data sent. There is no guarantee that the individual items will arrive at their destination in the order in which they are sent.

connect time The amount of time that a user stays connected to a network, usually used to refer to a connection to the Internet.

Conseil européen pour la recherche nucléaire A European research centre for particle physics situated in Switzerland and France. It is the birthplace of the HYPERTEXT TRANSFER PROTOCOL, more commonly known as HTTP and the WORLD WIDE WEB. The centre had a massive demand for information from employees and HTTP was the result of a project to develop searching facilities for documentation over a network and to provide facilities for collaborative authoring. Usually abbreviated to CERN.

consistency Used to describe the property of a DISTRIBUTED TRANSACTION. It describes the fact that such a transaction must transform a DISTRIBUTED SYSTEM from one state to another consistent state. For example, in a banking system an account balance should be equal to the old balance of the account plus the sum of the credits minus the sum of the debits on the account. If this condition did not hold, for example because of a hardware error occurring when a transaction took place, then the bank database would not be consistent: it would show a number of credits, a number of debits and a new bank balance which would be inconsistent with respect to each other. This is an important property of a distributed system along with ATOMICITY, ISOLATION and DURABILITY. *See also* ACID.

Consultative Committee For International Telephone And Telegraph A world standards-making body which concerns itself with standards for telecommunications. In the 1990s it was renamed the INTERNATIONAL TELECOMMUNICATIONS UNION or ITU.

Consumer Fraud Alert Network An organization which alerts consumers to frauds, in particular those on the Internet.

contact card A card which is used for DIGITAL CASH.

container A TAG used in the HYPERTEXT MARKUP LANGUAGE which is delineated with an END TAG and which contains text. For example, the tag <H1> and its end tag </H1> delineate text that forms part of a major heading displayed in prominent letters when viewed by a BROWSER.

content The information found in a WEB SITE and the way in which it is structured. *See also* CONTENT PROVIDER.

content control The process of ensuring that certain types of CONTENT are not seen by certain groups of Internet users: for example, that sexual content is not viewed by children. To implement this requires some form of rating system, such as the PLATFORM FOR INTERNET CONTENT SELECTION, and BLOCKING SOFTWARE such as a specially configured BROWSER which recognizes the rating system.

contention The condition which sometimes occurs in some LOCAL AREA NETWORKS where two devices connected to a network are allowed to transmit data at the same time; when this condition holds there is a probability that a COLLISION will occur. There are a number of strategies that are used to avoid or recover from this condition. For example, each of the senders may be delayed for a different, random time period before resending.

content management system Software which enables a company to organize and maintain its Web site. For example such a system would enable the pages delivered to a user to be tailored to that particular user.

content network technology Any technology which attempts to make interaction with the Internet a more personal process. An example of this is the COOKIE which holds a personal profile of a user that might include their first name, credit card details, and INTERNET PROTOCOL ADDRESS. Another example is the PERSONALIZED NEWSPAPER which contains only details which are of interest to a specific Internet user.

content provider Either a WEB SITE or a company which owns a site that provides up-to-date information about a particular topic or set of topics. Content provider sites contain a wide range of information including, for example, job opportunities, holiday offers, news, games, guides to online ECOMMERCE sites, and specialized industry content such as that provided by a company such as CNET.

content rating The process of providing a description of the CONTENT of a WEB SITE. This is achieved by the use of a CONTENT RATING SYSTEM which provides a primitive language for describing the content and the level of a particular aspect of that content such as the degree of violence depicted.

content rating system A system used for rating and providing information about the contents of a WEB SITE. For example a content rating system provides information about the suitability of a Web site for children based on the level of sex, nudity, obscene language, and drug abuse. The most important standard for this is the PLATFORM FOR INTERNET CONTENT SELECTION. There are a number of specific schemes for content rating including NETSHEPPERD, RASCI, and SAFE FOR KIDS. Content rating systems are used by BLOCKING SOFTWARE to restrict or prevent the viewing of Web content. Such software consults some SCRIPT expressed in the language of the content rating system before making a decision about restriction.

context switch To change the subject.

contextual commerce The use of text masquerading as editorial content, usually in a WEBZINE, in order to sell a product on line. This is a common technique used in conventional publications such as magazines, but has started to appear in commercial WEB SITES.

convergence The coming together or integration of a number of technologies: for example, the convergence of the Internet and television to give rise to interactive television services, or the convergence of cellular telephone technology and the Internet to provide portable information services.

cookie A file that is stored on a client computer that is using a BROWSER. It is initially deposited there by a SERVER and is used to store information that might be required over one particular session or over a number of sessions with a browser. One use for cookies is to identify users and prepare customized Web pages for them. For example, a cookie might be used to store the identity of someone who has used an ECOMMERCE site that sells some commodity by taking credit card details and the name of the user. This cookie can then be read by a server next time the buyer uses the browser in order to personalize a greeting and to relieve them of the repetitive effort of providing credit card details. Another use for a cookie is in ETAILING sites where the cookie holds the contents of a SHOPPING CART. Cookies are used because HTTP is a stateless protocol: a message sent by a browser in HTTP has no knowledge of any previous message. The name 'cookie' derives from UNIX entities called magic cookies. These are pieces of data that are attached to a user or program and change depending on the actions taken by the user of the program. Sometimes cookies are referred to as PERSISTENT COOKIES because they stay in a computer for a long time rather than just one session. *See also* APPLET and SERVER API.

cookie file 1. A file containing a collection of FORTUNE COOKIES: pithy and wise sayings which greet a user when they LOG-IN to a system.
2. A term for the file used for COOKIE storage on a Web CLIENT.

cookie jar 1. The storage area where COOKIES are found: *see also* COOKIE FILE.
2. A term used by CRACKERS for a PASSWORD FILE.

cookie poisoning An attack on a computer system which involves the modification of a COOKIE, such as modifying the cookie so that it obtains credit card details.

cool An adjective which was extensively used in mainstream speech for a short period in the early 1960s. It fell into disuse until the 1990s when it was disinterred by Internet users to describe entities such as superior WEB SITES and software products.

It has now reemerged into mainstream use in a much bigger way than in the 1960s. *See* COOL SITE OF THE DAY.

Cool Site Of The Day A WEB SITE which regularly features other Web sites that are superior in terms of both content and design.

coop In 2000 seven new DOMAIN NAMES were created. coop was one of these. It is intended for use by cooperatives.

cooperative network A WIDE AREA NETWORK whose costs are borne by any organization that links into the network.

coopetition The formation of alliances —often temporary—by companies who are usually in competition with each other. A good example of this is the co-opetition of IBM, Sun, Apple, and Netscape for the promotion of the JAVA programming language. Sometimes it is called a cartel, particularly by those who oppose the companies who are carrying out the coopetition.

Coordinated Universal Time An international standard which defines the time throughout the world. Signals which send coordinated universal time values are broadcast regularly from land transmitters and satellites which can reach any part of the world. DISTRIBUTED SYSTEMS usually coordinate the clocks of their SERVERS and CLIENTS using this time standard. It is often found abbreviated as UTC (sic).

Coordinating Committee for Intercontinental Research Networks An organization that brings together North American and European research organizations who carry out research on networking technologies. Usually abbreviated to CCIRN.

copycat page A WEB PAGE that has been copied from a reputable site in order to attract gullible visitors who might then be the victims of some fraud. *See* COPYCAT SITE. The copycat page is often the HOME PAGE of a site and leads visitors into pages which have the same style but which have been developed for criminal intent.

copycat site A WEB SITE which has been designed to look like another site. Such sites are usually developed for criminal purposes: for example, they may mimic a reputable ECOMMERCE site and elicit credit card details from customers which are then used by the criminals responsible for the development of the site. More often than not the whole site is not replicated, just a few COPYCAT PAGES, with the remaining pages adopting the same style as the copycat pages.

copyleft A licensing system developed by Richard Stallman which allows users to modify the source code of a system provided they grant the same rights to those they pass the system on to. Copyleft is one of the basic tenets of the OPEN SOURCE MOVEMENT. It is derived from the word 'copyright', the use of 'left' differentiating it from that restrictive form of licensing.

CORBA *See* COMMON OBJECT REQUEST BROKER ARCHITECTURE.

core cancer The process that occurs when the memory of a computer (the core) is gradually corrupted by invalid data. It usually occurs because of badly written software. The term is derived from the term 'core memory', used in the early days of computing when memory was implemented as magnetic rings known as cores.

core page A page in a WEB SITE which summarizes some part of the site and provides links to other pages. For example a typical core page in an ECOMMERCE site might summarize products that are due to be released soon and contain links to these products. There is a school of WEB DESIGN which urges the use of a number of these core pages combined with ENTRY TUNNELS and EXIT TUNNELS in preference to the conventional design of a Web site using a HOME PAGE.

Corporation for Research and Educational Networking An organization that supports the use of computers and networking in education and research. It produces seminars and develops tools to enable educationalists and researchers to use the Internet effectively. It is often abbreviated to CREN.

cost of cracking adjustment As time proceeds computers become more power-

ful and the knowledge gained by CRACKERS increases. This means that the developers of security methods have to strengthen the technologies that are used to guard against intrusion. The cost of cracking adjustment is a term used to describe the number of BITS that need to be added to a key for an algorithm used in CRYPTOGRAPHY in order to keep it as secure as it was in the previous year of its existence. A general principle of cracking a KEY is that the larger the KEYSPACE the more difficult it is to crack the ENCRYPTION method based on it. Sometimes the term is abbreviated to COCA.

cost per thousand page views A standard measure used by the ECOMMERCE industry to measure banner advertising rates. It represents the amount of money an advertiser pays for every thousand times a page containing a BANNER ADVERT is viewed by the user of a BROWSER.

counter script A CGI SCRIPT which tracks the number of visitors to a WEB SITE and displays the current number on a WEB PAGE. Often these scripts produce graphics which intrude into the overall design of the page. They are usually frowned on by WEB DESIGNERS who, if their clients insist on their use, make them as small as possible. *See also* HIT SLUT.

country code A two-letter name used as a DOMAIN NAME. For example, UK is the country code for the United Kingdom. Originally country codes were intended for countries, but they can now be used for geographic entities such as Antarctica. This dictionary lists all the country codes in Appendix 1.

courtesy copy Another name for a CARBON COPY.

covert channel A means whereby someone who works inside an organization that uses a network can convey secret information to accomplices outside the organization. Including sensitive information using the letters within specific words of an innocent looking text file is an example of a covert channel.

CPE or Customer Premises Equipment Used by systems development companies to describe communications equipment which is found on a customer's premises.

CPS *See* ABBREVIATION FOR CHARACTERS PER SECOND.

CPU attack A form of DENIAL OF SERVICE ATTACK whereby a program is illegally sent into a network, replicates itself, and then hogs the processors of the computers on the network denying other programs a fair share of processor time. CPU stands for the central processing unit, the hardware device which carries out operations such as addition and the execution of programs.

cracker Someone who carries out unauthorized or criminal acts such as breaking into secure computer networks. The term was invented by HACKERS who found it distasteful to be associated with programmers who violated the security of a system.

cracking The unauthorized entry into a computer system, usually a networked system, in order to carry out some illegal act such as reading secure files or infecting the system with a VIRUS.

crack root The successful intrusion of a UNIX system where the intruder somehow gains SYSTEM ADMINISTRATOR privileges. The term 'root' is used to describe the highest level of privileges in UNIX.

crapplet A poorly written APPLET which is either full of errors, hogs the processor, or has little or no function. *See also* BLACK WIDOW.

crash When a computer crashes it becomes inoperable. The reason for it crashing could be a hardware or a software fault. The term is usually applied to a computer and sometimes applied to a network.

crawler Synonymous with SPIDER. A program which accesses the Internet, usually the WORLD WIDE WEB or NEWSGROUPS, gathering information for SEARCH ENGINES.

credit card scam An illegal scheme whereby a WEB SITE gains the credit card details of a user and where the developers of the site use these details to make illegal purchases. Often the site which captures the details is a COPYCAT SITE that mimics the site of a reputable company.

credit repair scam A common illegal activity found on the Internet. Users who have a poor credit record—for example, they may have defaulted on a credit card payment—are encouraged to pay for a service which it is claimed will restore their credit rating. Usually the perpetrators of this scam just pocket the money that is sent to them without doing anything. Often such schemes are notified to users via SPAM.

CREN *See* CORPORATION FOR RESEARCH AND EDUCATIONAL NETWORKING.

crippled version A version of a program which has had many of its FUNCTIONS disabled. Normally crippled versions are used for demonstration purposes. They are also distributed at no cost by software developers in the hope that the users of the software will buy the full version. *See also* CRIPPLEWARE.

crippleware Software that has had its main functions disabled or severely restricted. The term is usually used to describe free versions of software which provide basic functions and which are used to entice users to buy the fully functioning version.

CRL *See* CERTIFICATE REVOCATION LIST.

cross-post To post an article simultaneously to a number of NEWSGROUPS. Excessive cross-posting is regarded as a major sin by the users of newsgroups.

cross-roasting The process of POSTING an irrelevant entry in a NEWSGROUP which has already appeared in another newsgroup. The posting annoys the members of the newsgroup to the point where they FLAME the original poster. The term is derived from CROSS-POSTING: the legitimate use of posting to draw the attention of members of one newsgroup to a relevant posting in another newsgroup.

cross site scripting A general term used to describe attacks which rely on security subtleties that occur when a number of different computers running different operating systems also use a number of SCRIPTING LANGUAGES.

crosstalk An electromagnetic disturbance caused by a cable which affects any other cables which are close to it.

crunch To compress a FILE using some COMPRESSION algorithm. For example, 'I crunched the program before I sent it over the Net.'

cryptographic checksum A numeric quantity formed by applying an ALGORITHM to a message that is to be sent through a network. It is used to check that no modification of the message has taken place. The process for using a cryptographic checksum is as follows: the checksum is calculated from the message; the message is sent to some destination computer; the checksum is then encrypted and sent; the message and the checksum are both received at the destination computer; the checksum is decrypted; the destination computer recalculates the checksum using the received message and compares it with the decrypted value of the checksum that has been received; if the two checksums match, then there is a high probability that the message has not been tampered with; if they do not match, then tampering has occurred. *See also* CHECKSUM. A cryptographic checksum is also known as a MESSAGE DIGEST.

cryptography The study of secret codes. During the 1980s, as networks became larger and larger and were employed in more and more organizations, the application of cryptography became increasingly prevalent in computer communications. The advent of the Internet, an OPEN NETWORK, has meant that cryptography has become even more important and forms the security core of any application where sensitive data is to be transferred across an accessible network. A cryptographic method transforms a message containing sensitive data into one that cannot be read by someone who is not authorized to access it. To do this the text to be sent is transformed using a set of rules known as a CIPHER. The rules in the cipher can be varied according to a KEY which is provided by the sender of the text. The process of modifying text using a cipher is known as ENCRYPTION. Once a text has

been encrypted it is sent over a transmission line and decoded by its recipient who uses the key to transform the text back to its original form. This is a process known as DECRYPTION. The process described above, where the same key is used for decryption and encryption, is known as SYMMETRIC KEY ENCRYPTION. There is another form of encryption known as PUBLIC KEY ENCRYPTION where two keys, a PRIVATE KEY and a PUBLIC KEY, are used. Cryptography permeates the Internet. It is used in technologies which support ECOMMERCE; technologies such as the SECURE SOCKETS LAYER that provide for the safe bulk transport of data across the Internet; and it is used to provide authentication via DIGITAL SIGNATURES and in providing validation using DIGITAL CERTIFICATES.

cryptovirus A VIRUS that enters a computing system and carries out ENCRYPTION on the files in the system. The developer of the virus then usually contacts the organization whose computer has been infected demanding money for the password.

CSCW *See* COMPUTER-SUPPORTED COOPERATIVE WORK.

CSMACA or **CSMA-CA** *See* CARRIER SENSE MULTIPLE ACCESS COLLISION AVOIDANCE

CSMACD or **CSMA-CD** *See* CARRIER SENSE MULTIPLE ACCESS COLLISION DETECTION.

CSNET *See* COMPUTER SCIENCE NET.

CSP *See* COMMERCE SERVICE PROVIDER.

CSS *See* CASCADING STYLE SHEETS.

CSS1 *See* CASCADING STYLE SHEETS LEVEL 1.

CTI *See* COMPUTER TELEPHONE INTEGRATION.

CUL Abbreviation for See You Later used mainly in CHAT ROOMS.

CUL8ER A HAKSPEK abbreviation for 'see you later' used mainly in CHAT ROOMS. An alternative to CUL.

cul de site A WEB SITE which is a dead end in that it contains useless links or no links at all. A typical cul de site is one which has been developed by a student as an exercise.

Cumdex A trade exhibition organized by pornographic software vendors who were denied admission to COMDEX.

cup holder The tray of the CD drive of a computer; so-called because of the legend of the user who complained that the size was not quite right for his cup of coffee.

cursor dipped in x Used in an EMAIL to indicate a letter containing vitriolic content. For example 'he had his cursor dipped in bile'.

CU SeeME A free VIDEO CONFERENCING system which was developed by Cornell University in the United States (the CU in CU SeeME). It can be used in any network which supports Internet protocols and can be configured for a number of simultaneous users. It provides full video services, a CHAT facility, and WHITE BOARD communication. It is available for both Intel-based and Macintosh computers.

cusskiddie A derogative term used to describe an immature user who posts vulgar messages or profanities in a forum such as a NEWSGROUP.

customizable graphical user interface A program which aids the process of adding an extra layer to an existing program or system in order to make it look different to the user: for example adding a new interface to an existing OPERATING SYSTEM so that it looks like another operating system. Sometimes referred to as a SKIN and often abbreviated to CGUI.

cut and paste The process of removing some part of a document and placing it elsewhere, sometimes in a different position in the same document or in another document.

CYA Abbreviation for Cover Your Ass used in EMAILS and NEWSGROUPS. Usually employed as a warning to a user who has made a provocative statement.

CYAL8R A HAKSPEK abbreviation for 'see you later' used in EMAILS and NEWSGROUPS.

Cyberangels A group founded in 1995 by the International Alliance of Guardian Angels which provides advice to users of the Internet on security. Its remit includes education, crime prevention and Internet safety.

cyberbunny Someone who is very ignorant of computer technology but still takes it upon themselves to advise others, normally using technologies such as NEWSGROUPS and BULLETIN BOARD systems to do so.

cybercad The Internet version of a lounge lizard or gigolo.

cybercafé A cafe which, as well as providing food and drink, provides access to the Internet via PCs. Also known as an INTERNET CAFÉ.

cyberchondriac A user who is continually obsessed with the fact that his or her computer is malfunctioning. Normally such users commit mistakes through not reading software instructions or a manual; when their programs do not carry out an intended procedure they blame either the software or the hardware.

cybercide The killing of a character in an online game which is played over the Internet.

cybercrud **1**. Text overloaded with jargon and technical terms. **2**. Information found in an EMAIL message which should really be hidden from the reader: for example, text showing the route that the email message took before it arrived at the recipient's computer.

cyberia Used to describe an isolated existence where all you are aware of is the screen and keyboard of your computer. A state that is often achieved by programmers when developing or debugging software. *See also* CYBERSPACE.

cyberlaw The law as applied to the use of the Internet. It covers issues such as INTERNET COPYRIGHT, the use of DEEP LINKS and SHALLOW LINKS, and stalking on the Internet.

cyber luddite Internet users who are against the Internet and the WORLD WIDE WEB. They form a loose collection of academics, anarchists, and those opposed in principle to commercialism. They have little in common, with very few unifying characteristics, apart, perhaps, for a yearning for the early text-based days of the Internet when it was based on DIAL-UP LINES. Because of the nature of their views they are difficult to contact using electronic means such as EMAIL.

cybermediary An intermediate company which uses Internet technology to provide a service between a customer and one or more companies. A company offering competitive insurance over the WORLD WIDE WEB would be a good example of a cybermediary. Such a company would ask a customer for the details of the insurance required and then provide data about prices and policies from the insurance companies for which it acts.

cybermystic Someone who is concerned with the interface between Internet technology and mysticism: for example, someone who espouses views about the relationship between Eastern religion and the Internet.

cybernaut Someone who uses sensory devices to experience VIRTUAL REALITY worlds. It is more generally used to describe anyone who uses the Internet.

Cyber Patrol® This is commercial BLOCKING SOFTWARE used to restrict access to sites that have content which should be limited, for example sites with sexual content.

cyberphobia A fear of computers and the stress that this engenders. It normally arises from an inability to come to terms with the increasing use of the computer in the workplace.

cyberpork The funding given to large Internet systems developers by the US government.

cyberpunk A type of science fiction which is characterized by a dystopic vision of an oppressive society dominated by computer technology. Key to this vision is the existence in this society of a lawless sub culture owing much to the punk culture of the 1980s.

cyberrhea Excessive verbiage found in POSTINGS to NEWSGROUPS or in EMAILS.

cybersexism The intrusion of male-oriented culture and mores into the Internet, particularly prevalent on NEWSGROUPS.

cybersitter A term used to describe computer-literate students or schoolchildren who are used to teach the children of rich parents Internet skills.

cyberspace Originally devised by the author William Gibson. It describes the world of interlinked computers and the people who use them. *See also* CYBERIA.

cyberspeak Natural language augmented with technical terms such as APPLET, jargon such as DISK DANCER, and ABBREVIATIONS such as CUL. Employed by a hard core of Internet users. *See also* WEBLISH.

cyberstalker A user who pursues another user through the Internet, usually using EMAIL, making a nuisance of themselves.

cybersquatting The act of creating and buying a DOMAIN NAME which includes the name of a celebrity or a company within: for example, HarrisonFord.com. There are a number of motives for this. The buyer may, for example, want to embarrass the celebrity by posting inappropriate material on the site. There are also commercial reasons for buying a domain name: for example, a domain name which includes that of a start-up company that is predicted to be a success could be sold back to the company at a large profit. Another commercial reason is that sites with famous names attract visitors and can be adorned with advertising. The law which deals with trademarks is ambiguous about cybersquatting using celebrity names, although there have been a number of successful prosecutions against cybersquatters who have used company names.

cyberwoozle A term used by the security community to describe the act of monitoring and capturing data from a user's computer as they access the WORLD WIDE WEB. It is also known as INTERNET CHANNEL ENABLED THREAT.

cybrarian Someone who is skilled in searching the Internet for information and who sometimes earns a living from it.

cycle Used for time: for example, 'I could not find enough cycles today to finish my posting.' It is derived from the cycle that represents the heartbeat of computer.

cycle server A SERVER which is solely dedicated to running programs which consume a large amount of resources, for example file space or memory. Such servers are highly specialized and are usually optimized for the particular service they carry out.

cycle time The time it takes to bring a product to market. In the late 1990s the Internet injected much more efficiency into a number of economies by considerably reducing the cycle time of many products. *See also* INTERNET TIME and WEB YEAR.

CYO Abbreviation for see (C) You Online used in EMAILS and NEWSGROUPS. Normally used to indicate that the sender will meet the recipient in a CHAT ROOM or some other real-time forum.

cypherpunk Someone who believes that the ordinary citizen should be free to send messages which have been encrypted and that ENCRYPTION technology should be freely available.

D

DAC *See* DIGITAL TO ANALOGUE CONVERSION.

daemon A program that is executed on a computer but lies dormant until some condition occurs which it has been programmed to act upon. For example, the WEB SERVER daemon HTTPD lies dormant until a BROWSER communicates with the server asking for a WEB PAGE. When this communication occurs the daemon wakes up, finds the page requested by the browser, and sends it back to the CLIENT running the browser. *See also* HTTP DAEMON.

daisy chain Connecting a number of devices such as hard disk drives sequentially in a series, with the connection from one device leading to the next device on the daisy chain. Used both as a noun and a verb.

dancing baloney The use of some Web technology in order to cheer up an otherwise dull WEB SITE. Often this is used to impress a client or visitor to the site. An example of this is the use of ANIMATED GIF inserts or VIDEO CLIPS in a WEB PAGE.

DAP *See* DIRECTORY ACCESS PROTOCOL.

DAR *See* DYNAMIC ADAPTIVE ROUTING.

dark fibre Transmission lines, usually employing optical fibre technology, which have a very high BANDWIDTH and are only partially used or not currently used at all. Such transmission lines are laid down as an investment for the future.

dark side hacker A malicious HACKER, the implication here being that the hacker community is dedicated to the overall good of the Internet.

DARPA *See* DEFENSE ADVANCED RESEARCH PROJECTS AGENCY.

database A collection of data stored on some permanent medium which is structured in order to show the relationship between individual items within the database. For example, a banking database would contain data on accounts and customers, together with an indication of which accounts are associated with which customers. This is in contrast to a FILE which is just a loose collection of data on some permanent storage medium.

database management system A large collection of software which carries out the processes of storing, maintaining, granting access, archiving, and optimizing large collections of data stored in FILES. These files can be stored on the same computer or can be distributed across a number of computers; in the latter case the database management system is known as a distributed database management system. Database management systems have been in existence since the 1960s; the demands made upon them in distributed systems mean that they have become very sophisticated and complex pieces of software. The vast majority of database management systems now have interfaces to the WORLD WIDE WEB to enable BACK END PROCESSES to take place in ECOMMERCE systems.

database server A SERVER that responds to requests from CLIENTS which require data from the databases that it administers. Such servers have a number of functions. First, they interpret queries expressed in the STRUCTURED QUERY LANGUAGE programming language sent to it by a client, execute them, and send back the results. Second, they prevent the errors that occur when one user concurrently accesses data which is being accessed by another user. Third, they optimize queries. An SQL QUERY can be executed in a number of ways and the difference in response time can be very large. A good database server examines an SQL query and works out an execution plan which minimizes execution time. Fourth, they administer security. A good database server ensures that no user is allowed access to a database without authorization. Fifth, they administer backup and recovery procedures. A database server keeps a log of transactions, which is used to recover a database when some large problem occurs such as a gross system failure. This log keeps details of the transactions against databases and the parts of each database that were affected. When a problem occurs the recovery facility of the server finds a copy of the last saved database and then reapplies all the transactions held in the backup log.

data compression The process of reducing the size of a collection of data. There are three reasons for carrying out this activity: to save FILE space, to reduce the time taken for data to travel over a network connection, and to save space when backing up a file. There are a number of data compression algorithms in existence. They are categorized as either a LOSSY COMPRESSION SCHEME which results in some loss of the data or a LOSSLESS COMPRESSION SCHEME which results in no loss.

data diddling The unauthorized changing of data on a computer system: for example changing entries in an ACCESS CONTROL LIST. It is also known as TAMPERING.

Data Encryption Standard A US government standard for a BLOCK CIPHER which employs a 56-bit SECRET KEY. The algorithm used in this standard has been the subject of a large amount of controversy since there has been a suspicion that there is a TRAPDOOR in it that allows the US government to eavesdrop on parties using the technology. There is, as yet, no evidence for this, but the suspicion lingers on in the computing community. The algorithm has been broken by a BRUTE FORCE ATTACK; however the original designers of the algorithm always envisaged that this might happen and posited that the resources that would be required would be so large that it would be highly unlikely to happen in practice. This standard has now been replaced by the ADVANCED ENCRYPTION STANDARD.

data flow computer A large, very powerful computer that has a number of processors all physically wired together with a large amount of memory and backing storage. Such computers are highly parallel in that they can carry out a large number of tasks at the same time. They are in physical antithesis to CLIENT SERVER COMPUTING where processors are coupled via communication lines. Data flow computers are used to execute processor intensive applications such as those associated with areas like molecular biology and simulation.

dataglove An electronic device usually fitted to the users of a VIRTUAL REALITY system. It monitors the movement of the hand and the fingers of the user and enables the wearer to control some aspect of the system. For example, a dataglove might be used in a training application for handling radioactive materials.

datagram The basic unit of data that is sent out over a TCP-IP network.

datagram service This is a fast service which occasionally loses data, especially under high traffic conditions. The best example of such a service is that implemented by the USER DATAGRAM PROTOCOL and found on the Internet.

data integrity The accuracy and consistency of the data in a DISTRIBUTED SYSTEM. For example, in a banking system, the fact that the closing balance of all bank accounts is consistent with the opening balance and the sequence of debits and credits that have been applied to them is an example of data integrity.

Data Interchange Standards Association A body which organizes the work of the AMERICAN NATIONAL STANDARDS INSTITUTE on ELECTRONIC DATA INTERCHANGE.

data link layer A layer in the OSI REFERENCE MODEL which carries out the process of detecting errors that occur when data is transferred in a network; it also carries out the process of correcting transmission errors. The errors that it addresses are those that occur at the hardware level due, for example, to effects such as electrical and radio interference.

data management bot A BOT which carries out some form of processing on stored data. Typical examples are: a bot which finds the main keywords in a Web document or a bot which summarizes the important sentences in a Web document.

data mart A form of DATA WAREHOUSE which addresses one specific requirement of an enterprise; this is in contrast to a data warehouse which stores all the data pertinent to an enterprise's effective functioning. An example of a data mart might be a set of databases which store data only on past sales. Often data marts extract their data from an enterprise's data warehouse.

data mining The process of extracting useful information from a disparate collection of DATABASES, FILES, and other sources such as WEB PAGES. A typical data mining operation might be carried out by a bank to discover the financial profile of customers who opt for a particular type of credit card. Data mining software often uses some artificial intelligence technology and quite a lot of statistical theory.

data replication The duplication of data on a number of computers within a distributed system. There are a number of reasons for duplicating data. The first is that computers malfunction and go out of service; if only one computer held a single copy of an important set of data, then this would become immediately unavailable. Data replicated across a number of computers eliminates this problem. A second reason is to increase access time. Data can take a long time to travel over large computer networks, particularly WIDE AREA NETWORKS. In order to achieve fast response times such data is often replicated in computers that are close to those which access it: for example, the data might be contained on a computer which is connected via a LOCAL AREA NETWORK. Data replication is not free. One of the disadvantages of replicating data is that each of the files or databases containing the data must be kept up to date. This means that a network often has a large number of update messages flowing through it as users interact with the data, modifying and deleting records. Designing a distributed system containing replicated data so that it is reliable, achieves a good response time, and is not swamped by update traffic is still an art.

Data replication has achieved a major importance with the increasing use of network technology. There are now a large number of replication utilities which are either built into conventional database management systems or can be purchased as stand-alone programs. *See also* MIRROR SITE and MIRRORING TOOLS.

data replication manager A program which manages DATA REPLICATION in a DISTRIBUTED SYSTEM. This is software which keeps a number of databases containing replicated data in synchronization. Such software has two functions: first it ensures that when a database changes the change is broadcast to the other replicated databases in order to update them; second, it ensures that any query or update on a database waits until the database is in synchronization with the other replicated databases.

data shopper A type of AGENT which wanders over the Internet looking for useful data such as stock prices and financial reports.

data source object Software code, often abbreviated to DSO, that is embedded in an HTML PAGE which allows a user to have control over some data displayed on that page. For example, a DSO might allow a user to view a table in a different number of ways: by a sorted column, with specific rows omitted according to some criterion, or by some relationship between rows. Data source objects allow very much more control than is possible using pure HTML.

data switching exchange An alternative name for a ROUTER.

data vaulting The long-term storage of data which does not need to be accessed immediately.

data virus A virus which affects a file that contains data: for example, the START-UP FILES used by programs. The infection usually results in the program being disabled or its FUNCTIONality being compromised.

data warehouse A collection of data in a wide variety of formats including files expressed in HYPERTEXT MARKUP

LANGUAGE, SQL files, and text files. Data warehousing software enables users to recover files quickly and to make complex queries based on the contents of the files.

DAVIC *See* DIGITAL AUDIO VIDEO INTERACTIVE COUNCIL.

day trading The use of the Internet to buy and sell shares using online stockbrokers. The term is usually applied to the process of buying stocks and shares over a short period, sometimes less than a day. A number of ONLINE BROKERS provide facilities for day trading and there are a number of software packages that provide the day trader with enough information about share prices and movements to enable them to make informed decisions about buying or selling.

DBA Abbreviation for Doing Business As used in CHAT ROOMS, EMAILS, and NEWSGROUPS. Used to indicate a trade name or company name.

DCE *See* DISTRIBUTED COMPUTING ENVIRONMENT.

DCOM *See* DISTRIBUTED COMPONENT OBJECT MODEL®.

DDN *See* DEFENSE DATA NETWORK.

dead link A HYPERLINK in a WEB PAGE which no longer points to an existing page. Very few sites on the WORLD WIDE WEB employ LINK CHECKER software and so this is a common phenomenon, particularly in non-commercial sites. *See also* ORPHAN ANNIE and ORPHAN PAGE.

deadlock The process whereby two programs which are executing concurrently are both blocked waiting for each other to finish with a resource. For example one program may be holding a FILE and requires access to a file which the second program is holding, while the second program may be waiting for the file which is being held by the first program. Both programs are unable to proceed. When the programs are executing on separate computers this is known as DISTRIBUTED DEADLOCK. There are a number of ways of avoiding deadlock, but many of them are somewhat inefficient. Developing distributed systems which are both deadlock-free and efficient is an art.

dead tree A term of abuse which refers to the paper version of some online document. An example of its use is 'If you can't email the document as attachment then, if you have to, send it to me as a dead tree'. *See also* SNAIL MAIL and PMAIL.

deboursification The act of removing irrelevant or fake NEWSGROUPS from the header part of a POSTING.

debt collection scam A common Internet scheme which involves a user receiving an EMAIL threatening action over an unpaid debt. The email usually contains a telephone number which has to be called. When the recipient phones the number he or she is kept on hold for some time before the 'debt collector' admits a mistake. It is only when the recipient receives a phone bill does he or she realise that that they have been phoning a number on an ultra-high, premium payment telephone line, a proportion of which went to the debt collector.

decibel The logarithmic value of the ratio between two signals. It is often used as a measure of how free of interference a transmission line is. It is usually abbreviated to dB.

decision support system A system which is used to analyse historical data about a company's performance. Such a system produces reports on past performance and predictions of future performance. A typical question asked by such a system for a manufacturing company would be 'Which of our suppliers has been most reliable in delivering components?' Decision support systems are also used to analyse scenarios based on conditions which might hold in the future: for example, to provide data on the profitability of a bank based on a proposed increase in charges.

decryption The process of changing a text, the CIPHER TEXT, which has had ENCRYPTION applied to it so that it becomes unreadable, back to the original readable text: the PLAIN TEXT.

dedicated line A telecommunications line that is permanently connected to a network. This is in contrast to a DIAL-UP LINE which often functions as a conventional phone line as well as a connection to a network.

dedicated port A TCP-IP port that is associated with some dedicated function. Ports numbered below 255 are used as dedicated ports, for example port 110 is dedicated to processing applications which use the POP3 protocol for EMAIL and port 23 is reserved for TELNET. Dedicated ports are more commonly known as WELL-KNOWN PORTS.

deep link A HYPERLINK in a WEB SITE that is embedded a long distance from the site's HOME PAGE. For example, you may have to click on about ten or more links on higher-level pages to reach the link. One of the more controversial aspects of the issue of copyright on the Web is the degree to which it is legal for a company to develop WEB PAGES which contain such deep links: *see* INTERNET COPYRIGHT. A link which is close to the home page or is the UNIFORM RESOURCE LOCATOR of the home page is known as a SHALLOW LINK. *See also* BANDWIDTH THEFT.

deep space 1. If a program or computer does not respond to a user then it is said to have gone into deep space.
2. A term used in connection with someone who, for a number of reasons, does not reply to any form of verbal communication: For example, 'John was so distracted by the process of developing his WEB SITE that he was usually to be found in deep space.'

default browser The BROWSER which is used whenever a WEB PAGE is accessed, even though there may be a number of other browsers installed on the computer. It is relatively easy to adjust the operating system so that any browser becomes the default browser.

default home page This is the WEB PAGE that is displayed when a BROWSER is started up. Which page to display can be set by altering one of the browser options.

default mode Many software systems can be configured to behave in slightly different ways. For example, a BROWSER can be configured to reject any APPLETS which are contained in a WEB PAGE. The configuration of the software is adjusted by means of a number of settings which the user can easily access. When a program is in default mode its settings match those that were initialized when it left the software developer's premises. It is also used in a non-technical sense to describe someone who has not developed in his or her life: for example, 'John is a sad case. He is still in default mode.'

default password The PASSWORD that is delivered with a software product. Normally the password is easy to guess and hence is a target for CRACKERS.

Defense Advanced Research Projects Agency A military agency of the US government which funded the forerunner of the Internet in the 1970s. The network that it funded was the main focus of a research project to replace vulnerable telephone command and control centres with a computer network which had redundant data paths and could, consequently, not be destroyed by one of its nodes being attacked. The network was the subject of research and experimentation which led to the development of many of the technologies that are used today on the Internet such as the INTERNET PROTOCOL and the TRANSMISSION CONTROL PROTOCOL. The agency is usually referred to as DARPA.

Defense Data Network The part of the Internet that is connected to United States military bases, military agencies, and defence contractors. It is often abbreviated to DDN.

deflate A verb used to describe the process of compressing a file. *See also* INFLATE.

degradation of service attack An alternative name for a DENIAL OF SERVICE ATTACK.

DejaNews One of the best and oldest SEARCH ENGINES dedicated to accessing NEWSGROUPS. Not only does it provide reading facilities but also facilities for sending postings. One notable feature of DejaNews is the fact that postings can be anonymous in order to foil the ADDRESS HARVESTERS used by SPAM merchants. DejaNews is the old name of the engine. It is now called Deja.com.

delay distortion A term used to describe the fact that components of a signal may be delayed as they travel down a TRANSMISSION LINE.

delayed response media Internet media that require a long time delay in order to respond, rather than a real-time delay. NEWSGROUPS are an example of this.

deliberative agent An AGENT which has some knowledge of an application domain and is able to carry out a complicated task using this knowledge. For example, a manufacturing company which develops products from electronic components might use a deliberative agent that has knowledge about factors such as supplier reliability, supplier price, and supplier delivery times to decide on an optimal mix of orders for components so that the cost and time of production are minimized. Deliberative agents use an area of computer science known as artificial intelligence. This is the discipline which has, as its ultimate aim, the development of artefacts which exhibit some form of intelligent behaviour, albeit over a narrow application domain such as electronic component purchasing or air travel scheduling. The main technology used in intelligent agents is that associated with expert systems. These are intelligent programs which contain knowledge about a domain in a database known as rule base. This rule base contains statements such as 'If you order this component from supplier X then you will get a good price and reasonably good delivery time unless the component is of type Y, in which case the delivery time will be longer than three weeks.'

delisting The process of removing details of a WEB SITE from the INDEX used by a SEARCH ENGINE. There are a number of reasons for this, two of the most popular reasons being that the site could be unreliable or the owner of the site has attempted SPAMDEXing.

delivery failure What occurs when an EMAIL has not arrived at its intended destination. It has passed into ordinary use as a term to describe the fact that someone does not understand or ignores what you

are saying: for example, 'I told him not to use that browser, but unfortunately there was a delivery failure and he went ahead and did it.'

delta Used to indicate some period of time: for example, in 'I will post again. The delta will be about two days.' Derived from the mathematical use of the Greek delta symbol for a small quantity.

delurking The process of sending messages to a NEWSGROUP after LURKING.

demilitarized zone The area delineated by a FIREWALL which separates the outside world from valuable computer resources such as FILES or sensitive computers. The demilitarized zone acts as a barrier to those who want to make unauthorized intrusions into a network. It is constructed of a combination of hardware such as ROUTERS and software. Usually the term is used in connection with architectures which make use of a dual firewall where it describes the space between the two servers used.

demo account An ACCOUNT on a network which has been created for some demonstration purpose: for example, to show some software at a trade fair. Often these accounts have easy-to-remember PASSWORDS such as Demo or Sys and hence are easy to crack. Dormant demo accounts are often a target for intruders who then use them to gain access to the resources of a network.

demodulation The process of extracting the signal that has been added to a CARRIER by means of MODULATION.

demon Part of a program waits for an event to happen which it then responds to: for example, a section of JAVA code which waits for the end of a file transfer from a computer on a network. Similar to a DAEMON, the difference is that a daemon is a program and a demon is usually part of a program: for example a SUBROUTINE.

demo version A version of a program which can be used for a demonstration to an audience of potential buyers. Often demo versions are primitive versions of a real system and are usually error-ridden. The term is also used as a less pejorative

alternative to CRIPPLEWARE. *See also* DEMO-
WARE.

demoware A pejorative term used to describe barely functioning software. It is
derived from the fact that programs used
for demonstrations to a potential audience of buyers are often rudimentary and
only work if predefined functions of the
software are exercised in a particular
order. For example, 'I bought the news
reader that was recommended in the
newsgroup, but it was useless—worse
than demoware.'

denial of service attack An attack on
a computer system which results in the
service being offered to a user or a number
of users being severely degraded. Usually
this degradation is so serious that the
users are unable to interact effectively
with the computer that is the subject of
such an attack. An example of such an
attack is one where a VIRUS infects a computer and takes over the processor by executing a large number of high-priority
programs which carry out some slow process such as reading a FILE. This would
result in any user programs having their
access to the processor severely curtailed.
Another example is EMAIL FLOODING
where a large volume of EMAILS causes
major problems for an EMAIL SERVER.
Other examples include SYN FLOODING,
PING FLOODING, and BLACK WIDOW. It is
also known as a degradation of service
attack.

denizen A term of abuse sometimes applied to those regarded as being second-
class Internet users.

**Dense Wavelength Division Multi-
plexing** A technology which is used to
increase the BANDWIDTH over existing optical fibre transmission media. It works by
using MULTIPLEXING to transmit multiple
signals at different wavelengths.

depository directory A DIRECTORY
which is created by a SYSTEM ADMINISTRA-
TOR that can be used to store files created
by the users of FILE TRANSFER PROTOCOL
software. Such directories are now
frowned on by administrators since they
are often used to store illegal software,
pornographic images, and files of stolen

passwords that can be accessed by anyone
using the FTP facility. The collection of
illegal files in a depository directory is
often referred to as WAREZ.

deprecated tag A TAG in an earlier version of the HYPERTEXT MARKUP LANGUAGE
which has been replaced by another tag in
a later version. While the tag is not banned
there are usually strong recommendations that it should not be used. An
example of a deprecated tag is the
<CENTER> tag which is deprecated in
version 4 of the Hypertext Markup Language.

derf The process of gaining access to a
network by exploiting the fact that a user
has left his or her computer and not
logged off. The derfer uses the computer
to carry out acts such as reading private
files. The term is derived from reversing
the name of the original victim of this
crime.

DES *See* DATA ENCRYPTION STANDARD.

descender The part of a lower-case letter
that lies below the BASELINE. Only a few
letters have descenders: y and g are
examples.

desktop The area of the computer shown
by a Windows-based OPERATING SYSTEM.
Called the desktop because it attempts to
mimic the normal top of a desk holding
folders and documents.

DESX A modification to the DES SYMMET-
RIC KEY ENCRYPTION algorithm which considerably strengthens the algorithm.

device driver virus A VIRUS which in-
filtrates a computer via the device driver
software: the software used to control peripherals such as the keyboard. Happily
only early operating systems such as
MSDOS were susceptible to this type of
virus.

DHTML *See* DYNAMIC HYPERTEXT MARKUP
LANGUAGE.

dialler program A program which establishes DIAL-UP ACCESS to a network.
Usually such a program is associated with
a PROTOCOL such as the SERIAL LINE INTER-
NET PROTOCOL. Many dialler programs are
provided as part of an OPERATING SYSTEM.

dial-up access The use of a normal telephone line to gain access to a network, usually the Internet. The line is often also used for phone calls. See LAST MILE PROBLEM. This form of access is in contrast to using a DEDICATED LINE.

dial-up account The basic type of account provided by an INTERNET SERVICE PROVIDER. So called because access to the Internet is via a normal telephone line and a MODEM.

dial-up line A phone line which is not permanently connected to a network. This is in contrast to a DEDICATED LINE.

dial-up networking An early form of networking in which all connections were established by users dialling up a computer, or a computer dialling another computer using the conventional phone system. The Internet in the 1980s was an example of a network which was based on this form of networking.

diary site A WEB SITE which offers the diary facilities found in common diary applications: facilities such as entering appointments, deleting appointments, and finding blocks of time that are free. Such sites are popular with users who travel and who need to coordinate their diary with other users.

dick size war A slightly cruder name for a PENIS SIZE WAR: a series of EMAILS or POSTINGS which discuss some aspect of computer software or hardware which is connected to performance: for example, the speed of a browser. Most dick size wars tend to be irrelevant to the normal user of the Internet.

dictionary attack An attempt to enter a network illegally using a large number of PASSWORDS generated from a computerized dictionary. A CRACKER using this form of attack would repeatedly try to discover the passwords used in a system by repeatedly trying a series of passwords extracted from a dictionary and applying them to a PASSWORD FILE. This is a surprisingly successful way of entering a network illegally: studies carried out in the 1990s indicated that somewhere between 10 to 40 per cent of all passwords could be discovered using this form of attack.

dictionary flame The act of concentrating on the definition of terms rather than the content of an argument in a NEWSGROUP. Used by pedants, but also employed by newsgroup users who wish to subvert an argument.

differential cryptographic attack An attack on a computer system whereby the KEY used for the ENCRYPTION of messages is discovered by an intruder. The intruder sends a number of messages which differ only slightly, for example by transposing a small number of adjacent letters, and examining the encrypted text that has been produced by the computer system. Often this form of attack requires a number of sophisticated decoding programs.

differential encoding A SOURCE ENCODING technique used to achieve COMPRESSION of data. It is used when items of data vary only slightly. This means that adjacent items can be specified by data which describes their difference; this differential data is usually very much smaller than the data it describes.

differential fault analysis This is an attack on a computer system which carries out ENCRYPTION using some hardware device such as a CLIPPER CHIP. The attacker subjects the device to some environmental stress such as heat in order to make it malfunction and send erroneous messages. By monitoring these messages the intruder can discover information such as the KEY used or the ENCRYPTION ALGORITHM.

Diffie Hellman key agreement A PROTOCOL that allows two parties to exchange a KEY for SYMMETRIC KEY ENCRYPTION without the key value being directly transmitted. This technique applies a mathematical process to the key in order to disguise it. See also PUBLIC KEY ENCRYPTION.

digerati A collective term used to describe those who, through their entrepreneurial, journalistic, literary, or advocacy skills, have greatly contributed to the growth and awareness of the Internet. It includes people as diverse as Bill Gates of Microsoft and Kevin Kelly of WIRED magazine.

digest A collection of postings to a NEWS-GROUP or messages sent to a mailing list. Sometimes some editing takes place in that only those postings or messages of high interest are included. The digest is then either made available on a WEB PAGE or posted to another newsgroup. The preparation of a digest is usually carried out by a MODERATOR.

Digital Audio Video Interactive Council A European body which has been set up to administer and manage standards which govern the transmission of multimedia in Europe.

digital cash A generic term used to cover a number of technologies which have been proposed or developed to overcome the problem that occurs when small payments are made over the Internet, where the size of the payment is so small that it is economically infeasible to process the payment by conventional means. *See* MICROPAYMENT, MICROTRANSACTION, MICROMERCHANT, BLIND SIGNATURE, and ELECTRONIC TOKEN.

digital certificate A document with a DIGITAL SIGNATURE. Such a certificate is used to authenticate identity. Digital certificates are often signed by a trusted third party known as a CERTIFICATE AUTHORITY. Such a company provides a PRIVATE KEY and a PUBLIC KEY. The latter is used to carry out the DECRYPTION of the signature associated with the certificate; the former is used to carry out the ENCRYPTION. To enable digital certificates to be successful the certificate authority has to be of such a status that they can guarantee that the private keys that are used are securely stored. Virtually the only certificates in use on the Internet are those which conform to the x509 standard. Digital certificates can be categorized as IDENTIFYING CERTIFICATES, AUTHORIZING CERTIFICATES, TRANSACTIONAL CERTIFICATES, and TIME STAMPING CERTIFICATES.

digital coin An alternative term to DIGITAL CASH.

digital library An online repository of electronic texts. These texts may be highly specific, such as information sheets on hardware devices which are maintained on a WEB SITE or they may be similar to the texts held in a normal library. For example, there are a number of libraries which keep the texts of classic out-of-copyright books. *See* PROJECT GUTENBERG.

Digital Power Line Technology A technology jointly developed by Nortel and the British company Norweb which sends digital signals along a power line. The inventors of the technology have claimed speeds up to 1 Mbit/second. It effectively converts the power network into a massive LOCAL AREA NETWORK.

Digital Property Rights Language A language based on the EXTENSIBLE MARKUP LANGUAGE which supports commerce in digital works such as GRAPHIC IMAGES and EBOOKS, and supports access and user controls. It is often abbreviated to DPRL.

digital signal A signal which consists of discrete values sampled over a particular time frequency. So, for example, a digital signal may be made up of 32-bit values, each value representing the voltage of an ANALOGUE SIGNAL sampled every hundredth of a second.

digital signature A form of identification attached to a document which identifies the sender of the document. Digital signatures are normally associated with PUBLIC KEY ENCRYPTION and a mathematical function known as a MESSAGE DIGEST. The message digest is a process which is applied to the text that is to be signed and generates an integer value that has a very high probability of being unique. The sender of a signed document applies the message digest to a document and then uses a PRIVATE KEY to encrypt the value that is generated. Any recipient of the message would need to know the PUBLIC KEY associated with the private key and the method used for generating the message digest value. The recipient applies the public key to the integer value, calculates what this integer should be by applying the message digest algorithm to the text that has been sent, and then compares it with the decrypted value. If they match a correct signature has been received and the sender of the text has been identified; if they do not, then the signature has been forged. A number of message digest algorithms have been devised, including SECURE HASH ALGORITHM 1, MESSAGE DIGEST 2 and MESSAGE DIGEST 5.

Digital Signature Algorithm An algorithm which is used in the US government's DIGITAL SIGNATURE STANDARD. When applied to a message it generates two integers which need to be compared by the recipient of a message which has been signed using this technique. It is often referred to by its abbreviation: DSA. The algorithm can only be used for digital signatures, not for the transmission of data.

Digital Signature Standard A standard for DIGITAL SIGNATURES which has been developed by the US government, standardized as the DIGITAL SIGNATURE STANDARD and incorporated into a federal information processing standard. At its heart lies an algorithm known as the DIGITAL SIGNATURE ALGORITHM. The algorithm and standard are so closely bound up with each other that the terms 'digital signature algorithm' and 'digital signature' are used interchangeably.

digital store A term occasionally used to describe a WEB SITE which sells a product such as books or CDs.

Digital Subscriber Line A family of PROTOCOLS which were designed for the high-speed transmission of data over existing phone lines. The first practical implementation was that of INTEGRATED SERVICES DIGITAL NETWORK.

digital to analogue conversion The process of converting a digital signal consisting of a series of on–off states into a continuous value which can be processed by a device which normally uses this form of signal.

digital to analogue converter A hardware device or a program running on a computer which converts discrete DIGITAL SIGNALS to continuous ANALOGUE SIGNALS: for example, a device which converts from a digital representation of voice signals to an analogue version suitable for playing on loudspeakers.

digital wallet An alternative term for WALLET, a technology used within

browsers to provide facilities for financial transactions.

digital watermark Data that is embedded into media such as a graphic which is hidden from sight, but which can be recovered by executing a program that displays it. There are a number of uses for digital watermarking. The first is to show ownership. For example, the owner of a media object would place a watermark in that object using a PRIVATE KEY. If someone claimed ownership of the object the original owner could recover the watermark by DECRYPTION and prove ownership. The second use is to detect unauthorized duplication. The third use is to provide authentication and integrity verification in legal cases where the authenticity of a media object such as a photograph has to be demonstrated. The fourth use is to provide hidden content labelling: for example, a watermark could be used to provide subsidiary information about a photograph, such as who the subject was and when it was taken. The fifth use is in usage control where the watermark would be dynamic and would include a number which indicated how many copies should be taken of the media object. This figure would be decreased every time a copy was taken. Watermark technology is in its early days, but a number of products have been a released.

DIKU Abbreviation for Do I Know You? Used in EMAILS and NEWSGROUPS. It is often used when the sender of an email or a POSTING uses a PSEUDO.

direct connection A term synonymous with DEDICATED LINE. A connection to a network which is not used for any other purpose.

Direct Hit A system used in the HOTBOT search engine which checks how relevant the results of the searches made by a SEARCH ENGINE are. It works by monitoring the CLICKS made on the results of a search by the user.

directory 1. A named collection of files administered by an operating system. The Windows and Macintosh version of this term is FOLDER.

2. Any collection of data which is used by another program. For example, directories are used to contain information about the devices which are attached to a network.

3. A collection of data about the resources in a DISTRIBUTED SYSTEM. *See* DIRECTORY SERVICE. Some SEARCH ENGINES such as YAHOO use directories which have been compiled by human indexers.

Directory Access Protocol A DIRECTORY SERVICE keeps details of all the resources in a CLIENT SERVER COMPUTING system in a database which can be accessed by programs written for the system. This database is replicated over a number of DIRECTORY SERVERS. When a program requires some details of a resource that is available, say a printer, it communicates with one of the directory servers using a protocol known as the Directory Access Protocol. This was defined as part of the x500 directory standard developed by the International Standards Organization. *See also* DIRECTORY SYSTEM PROTOCOL.

directory agent An AGENT which moves around a network gathering information about the resources on that network, which may be hardware resources such as printers or software resources such as programs.

directory search engine Search engines which use human indexers rather than SPIDERS. When a site is submitted to such a search engine it is read by an indexer who decides whether to list it and, if so, indexes it in a DIRECTORY structure. The best-known search engine in this category is YAHOO.

directory server A SERVER which dispenses data about the resources in a CLIENT SERVER COMPUTING system; it provides a DIRECTORY SERVICE which is a key component of a networked system. If a directory server fails, then the whole network fails: as a consequence there are usually a number of directory servers found in a network, each using DATA REPLICATION schemes to ensure that if a server malfunctions an up-to-date database of resources is available for any backup server.

directory service A CLIENT SERVER COMPUTING system consists of a large number of different resources including clients, servers, networks, printers, transmission lines, mass storage devices, and even the users of the system. Programs which execute on such a system will often need to know details about the state of a resource. For example, a program may need to know whether a printer is busy with a long printing job and, if so, where an alternative printer can be found. A directory service provides information on these resources. For example, it might keep data on the name of a server, its physical location, and its current utilization. Such a service relies on a database of resource details which is continually changing and which is replicated. It is replicated because if the computer on which it is stored malfunctions the whole of a network ceases functioning. Directory services are based on the x500 standard; however, the protocol which this standard is based on (the OPEN SYSTEMS INTERCONNECTION communications PROTOCOL) has been replaced by TCP-IP. Programmers communicate with a directory service using an APPLICATION PROGRAMMING INTERFACE. *See also* DIRECTORY ACCESS PROTOCOL, LIGHTWEIGHT DIRECTORY ACCESS PROTOCOL, and NAME SERVICE.

Directory Service Markup Language A MARKUP LANGUAGE which allows applications that use XML to share data over a wide variety of DIRECTORY services with differing formats.

directory site A WEB SITE which contains information usually found in large book-based directories such as phone books.

Directory System Protocol One of the most important components found in a CLIENT SERVER COMPUTING system is the DIRECTORY SERVICE. This keeps details of all the computing resources in such a system. The data which details the resources is contained in a database that is replicated over a number of DIRECTORY SERVERS. The protocol which the individual servers use to communicate with each other is known as the Directory System Protocol. It is defined as part of the x500 standard for directory services.

dirty connection 1. A slow connection to the Internet. This could occur for a variety of reasons, the main one being heavy traffic.
2. A connection which generates a lot of noise.

DISA *See* DATA INTERCHANGE STANDARDS ASSOCIATION.

disambiguate To clarify.

discussion group A group of users who employ Internet technology such as NEWSGROUPS or EMAIL to discuss some topic. *See* WEBLOG.

disintermediation The process of removing the middle man in a business transaction. For example, Web-based insurance sites are gradually removing the need for an insurance broker.

disk dancer An Internet user who take advantage of the initial free period provided by INTERNET SERVICE PROVIDERS and then moves to another service provider to use their free period: in this way they never have to pay to access the Internet. With the advent of free services this is a dying breed. The term is derived from the CD that is provided by most Internet service providers to new users.

dispersion What happens to light pulses as they are sent down a fibre optic transmission line. As they progress they expand and become more narrowly focused, the degree of dispersion depending on the wavelength. This is a major problem and much research is being carried out to reduce this effect. *See* SOLITON.

distance learning The use of educational materials such as television programmes, books, and tapes to study a course at a distant educational establishment. Increasingly Internet technology such as the WORLD WIDE WEB, CONFERENCING, and EMAIL is being used to supplement and even replace some of these traditional media.

Distance Vector Multicast Routing Protocol A ROUTING ALGORITHM which is based on DISTANCE VECTOR ROUTING and which is used to send data round the collection of networks and computers that form the multimedia network which lies on top of the Internet and which is known as the MULTICAST BACKBONE.

distance vector routing A form of ADAPTIVE ROUTING ALGORITHM which uses information about the 'length' between computers in a network to determine which computer to send a PACKET of data to. This length could be expressed in a number of ways: by the length of queues of data waiting for transmission, by the delay experienced, or by the number of HOPS.

Distributed Component Object Model® A DISTRIBUTED OBJECT technology developed by Microsoft. It is currently the main competitor to the COMMON OBJECT REQUEST BROKER ARCHITECTURE. It is often abbreviated to DCOM.

Distributed Computing Environment A highly flexible NETWORK OPERATING SYSTEM developed by the OPEN SOFTWARE FOUNDATION. It contains all the services expected in such an operating system including a DISTRIBUTED FILE SYSTEM, a NAME SERVICE, and a DISTRIBUTED TIME SERVICE. It is able to administer and maintain a DISTRIBUTED SYSTEM comprising hardware and OPERATING SYSTEMS from a number of vendors.

distributed database A database that is spread over a number of DATABASE SERVERS in a network. The main reason for distribution is that this allows parts of the database to be close to those users who have a frequent need for that data and hence reduces the transmission time that would be experienced if the data was held on a geographically remote server. There is a wide variety of sophisticated software available for such databases: one of the main characteristics of such software is that it ensures that the user is unaware that parts of the database might be spread around a network, effectively giving the impression that the data is stored on the CLIENT computer that is accessing it.

distributed deadlock This event occurs when two programs residing on separate computers are DEADLOCKED.

distributed file system The software and hardware architecture which allows users spread over a number of computers in a network to access FILES in the network without there being a need to know about the location of the files. Use of such files in a distributed file system should be as easy as the use of files in a stand-alone computer: for example, files should use the same naming conventions as normal files with no indication of their location being included in their name.

distributed object An OBJECT which resides on a computer in a distributed system to which messages can easily be sent by programs executing on other computers. Such messages abstract away much of the programming details required to send data over a network, thus reducing the programming effort needed. The three main distributed object technologies are COMMON OBJECT REQUEST BROKER ARCHITECTURE, REMOTE METHOD INVOCATION, and DISTRIBUTED COMPONENT OBJECT MODEL.

distributed operating system An OPERATING SYSTEM which manages a number of computers and hardware devices which make up a DISTRIBUTED SYSTEM. Such an operating system has a number of functions: it manages the communication between entities on the system, it imposes a security policy on the users of the system, it manages a DISTRIBUTED FILE SYSTEM, it monitors problems with hardware and software, it manages the connections between application programs and itself, and it allocates resources such as file storage to the individual users of the system. A good distributed operating system should give the user the impression that they are interacting with a single computer.

Distributed Queue Dual Bus A transmission standard which has been proposed for METROPOLITAN AREA NETWORKS. It consists of two cables to which all the computers in the network are connected. One of the major features of this standard is the fact that since two cables are used the design of networks is greatly simplified compared with other network technologies, since signals which are going in opposite directions are separated rather than having to traverse the same communications line.

distributed system A system which contains a number of hardware elements such as computers and ROUTERS which are connected by some transmission technology. Such systems consist of a number of executing programs which interact with each other via transmission lines. Many of the computers in a distributed system act as CLIENTS to computers known as SERVERS. There are many reasons for implementing a system in a distributed fashion: the first is to ensure that processing power is as close to the users as possible; the second is to ensure a high degree of robustness, for example via the use of DATA REPLICATION; and the third is to enable hardware to be easily added as the resource demands of the applications running on the distributed system start increasing. There are many problems facing the designer of a distributed system including predicting the performance of a particular design, keeping all the clocks in the system synchronized, and ensuring that if a hardware element of the system malfunctions users are, at best, only affected in a minimal way. Distributed systems have been in existence since the 1970s; but they were mainly closed systems confined to a physical location such as a building. The rise of the Internet has meant that many distributed systems are open to the world. This has given rise to a major problem: ensuring that such systems are secure. The best-known distributed system is the comparatively simple WORLD WIDE WEB which consists of a very large number of clients running BROWSERS and a large number of WEB SERVERS.

distributed time service In a DISTRIBUTED SYSTEM there are a number of servers, each of which has its own clock. Often, such clocks are out of synchronization. A distributed time service periodically synchronizes the clocks and, in the time period between each synchronization, provides CLIENTS and SERVERS with information about the current time inaccuracy of the servers. Such a service is vital in a system where closely spaced transactions have to be carried out in some temporal order.

distributed transaction A transaction that involves a number of SERVERS: for example, a banking transaction which requires account details to be updated at a server located at the bank's headquarters and a server at one of the bank's branches. There are potentially a number of problems with such transactions. For example, the time at one server may be different from the time at another server, and some parts of the transaction may need to be carried out before other parts. Also one or more of the servers may fail to carry out its part in the transaction so that the transaction may have to be returned to its initial state. The management and administration of transactions is carried out using a program known as a TRANSACTION PROCESSING MONITOR.

distributed transaction coordinator A program found in a DISTRIBUTED SYSTEM which coordinates the execution of a series of DISTRIBUTED TRANSACTIONS. For example, it ensures that one TRANSACTION does not interfere with the data currently being processed by another transaction.

disusering The act of removing a user from a network when he or she has violated the AUTHORIZED USE POLICY of an INTERNET SERVICE PROVIDER.

dithering The use of existing colours to approximate another colour which was not contained in the palette of the graphics program used to create a picture. The approximation is achieved by drawing adjacent pixels in different colours. One of the problems with dithering is that if it is used in a GRAPHICS INTERCHANGE FORMAT-based graphic it reduces the compression efficiency, since the LOSSLESS COMPRESSION SCHEME used for such graphics performs relatively poorly when adjacent pixels are of different colours.

DLTM Abbreviation for Don't Lie To Me used in EMAILS and NEWSGROUPS.

DMZ *See* DEMILITARIZED ZONE.

DNS *See* DOMAIN NAME SYSTEM.

DNSSEC *See* DOMAIN NAME SYSTEM SECURITY STANDARD.

Document Object Model A standard developed by the WORLD WIDE WEB CONSORTIUM which defines how BROWSERS can access details of a WEB PAGE in order to carry out processes such as executing ROLLOVERS.

document type definition Text which describes the structure of a document expressed in the XML MARKUP LANGUAGE. For example, it defines the TAGS that can appear, their order, and which tags can appear within other tags. A PARSER processes the document type definition and checks any document that claims to conform to the definition. Usually abbreviated to DTD.

dog food Usually employed as a verb. It describes the process whereby a software product developed by a manufacturer is tested out on the manufacturer's staff before being released. For example, 'Let's dog food this browser before we let it loose.'

dogpile What happens when a large number of participants to a NEWSGROUP or MAILING LIST respond very unfavourably to a POSTING or a message. The participants are said to have dogpiled the sender. It is also the name of a successful METASEARCH ENGINE.

domain A collection of computers on the Internet. For example, the domain name uk stands for those computers registered with organizations associated with the United Kingdom and open.ac.uk is the collection of computers associated with the Open University which forms part of the United Kingdom academic domain.

domain dipping The process of using a BROWSER to open and investigate WEB SITES created by typing in random words between the www. and .com parts of a URL.

domain dropping Similar to name dropping but involves introducing the name of the trendy DOMAIN that forms part of your EMAIL ADDRESS into a conversation, POSTING, or EMAIL.

domainism Prejudice based on how highly the DOMAIN part of an EMAIL ADDRESS is regarded.

domain name A symbolic name used to identify a collection of resources on the Internet. Resources are identified by a series of domain names separated by dots, with the right-hand name being known as the TOP-LEVEL DOMAIN. Domain names are read from right to left and become progressively more specific as you proceed leftwards. There are a series of top-level domain names each of which categorizes the domain: for example, edu stands for an educational establishment in the United States, mil stands for a military establishment, and net is used for a major network support centre. There are also a number of top-level domains associated with countries: for example, uk refers to the United Kingdom and fr refers to France. Internet users come into contact with domains in accessing the WORLD WIDE WEB and sending EMAIL. Symbolic addresses of Web resources, expressed as a URL, include the name of the organization which hosts the resource. For example, the URL http://www.open.ac.uk/Students/hm refers to an HTML file held on the computer www at the educational institution identified by open in the United Kingdom academic domain. Email addresses also contain domain names: for example, the email address D.K.Lombard@Firefly.com refers to the user D. K. Lombard at the organization Firefly which is an organization registered as a company.

domain name deactivation The process whereby a DOMAIN NAME is removed from the INTERNET DOMAIN NAME SERVICE. Any client wishing to look up this name is informed that it is no longer available. The name is not removed from the DATABASES used for the service. When it is finally moved it is subject to the process of DOMAIN NAME DELETION.

domain name deletion The process whereby a DOMAIN NAME is removed from the databases used for the INTERNET DOMAIN NAME SERVICE. Any client wishing to look up this name is informed that it is no longer available and has been deleted.

It is also known as domain name deactivation.

domain name dispute This occurs when someone registers a DOMAIN NAME which is similar to a trademark or trading name of a third party. There have been a number of court cases which have been in favour of the third party. *See* CYBERSQUATTING.

domain name registrar A company that has been authorized by ICANN to register DOMAIN NAMES on behalf of individuals, companies, and organizations.

domain name registration The process whereby an individual, organization or business registers a DOMAIN NAME. This is usually carried out via a third party known as a DOMAIN NAME REGISTRAR. Most registrars offer a Web-based service and all that is necessary to register a domain name is to supply technical and contact information through the site. Each registrar sets a charge for this process. From January 2000 registrars are allowed to offer an initial registration period and renewal periods which are no longer than ten years in total.

domain name server A SERVER which contains IP ADDRESS data about DOMAINS on the Internet and their locations. Such a server implements a DOMAIN NAME SERVICE. There are a large number of these servers spread about the Internet; they cooperate together in order to discover the IP address of a particular domain. Each domain has at least one domain name server which is able to discover addresses within that domain. However, if an address falls outside the domain the server queries other domain name servers. To do this it keeps a database of server addresses.

domain name service A service which is provided by a DOMAIN NAME SERVER. Programs such as EMAIL READERS work with symbolic names of domains and require the physical details of these domains (for example, the IP ADDRESS) in order to send an email. A domain name service provides them. The best example of a domain name service is the INTERNET DOMAIN NAME SERVICE.

Domain Name System The most famous NAME SERVICE and the one most frequently used. It converts a DOMAIN NAME into the corresponding IP ADDRESS of the domain. It is used by a very large number of utilities which access the Internet. For example, when an EMAIL ADDRESS such as D.Ince@MagicIsp.com is typed in the email program used looks up the IP address of MagicIsp.com in order to discover its address before sending an email. The domain name system is implemented by a large number of DOMAIN NAME SERVERS physically spread over the Internet, and linked together so that they can collaborate on discovering the address of a particular name. In most documents it is referred to as the Domain Name System or the DOMAIN NAME SERVICE, but its full name is the INTERNET DOMAIN NAME SERVICE. *See also* PRIMARY SERVER and SECONDARY SERVER. Often the term is abbreviated to DNS.

Domain Name System Security Standard A security standard which attempts to bring some form of security to the DOMAIN NAME SYSTEM of the Internet in which PUBLIC KEYS are assigned to a DOMAIN. Users of a domain which uses software employing this technology will have a high degree of assurance that they are, in fact, interacting with the domain. Often abbreviated to DNSSEC.

domain trafficking The process of selling DOMAIN NAMES which have already been registered.

domestic grade security Until the end of the 1990s the US government imposed tight restrictions on cryptographic technology and specified what could or could not be exported to other countries. The US government partitioned security products into two categories: EXPORT GRADE SECURITY and domestic grade security. Domestic grade security technology could not be exported and is characterized by software which can resist the most powerful attacks by intruders. At the beginning of the twenty-first century the restrictions were relaxed and only a small number of countries were prevented from accessing export grade security.

dongle A protection device which has to be plugged into a computer before the software it is associated with can be used.

doorstop A term used to describe an obsolete computer or piece of equipment such as a printer.

doorway page Another name for a GATEWAY PAGE: a WEB PAGE constructed in such a way that a SPIDER associated with a SEARCH ENGINE catalogues it so that the page always appears in a prominent position in a search.

dormant account An ACCOUNT on a networked system which has not been used for some time. The two most common reasons for this are that the user who owns the account has left the organization that runs the system, or that the user cannot use the account, for example during a period of hospitalization. Dormant accounts are often targeted by intruders who can use them as a springboard into a networked system. They are particularly attractive to the intruder since the user associated with the account is unaware of any unusual activity associated with the account such as the creation of new FILES.

DoS *See* DENIAL OF SERVICE ATTACK.

DoS attack *See* DENIAL OF SERVICE ATTACK.

dot address An Internet address expressed in DOTTED QUAD NOTATION: for example, 70.100.99.12.

dot com Used to describe an ecommerce company. Derived from the fact that the Internet address of the company usually finishes with .com.

dot comify The practice of transforming a word or phrase by adding .com. For example goforit.com.

dot commerce A very occasionally used alternative to the term ECOMMERCE.

dotted decimal notation An alternative name for DOTTED QUAD NOTATION.

dot gone An Internet company that has disappeared, usually because of bankruptcy. A play on the term Dot Com.

dotted quad notation A notation used to represent the unique IP ADDRESSES of computers on a TCP-IP network. It consists of four integers separated by three dots. Each integer is less than or equal to 255. For example, 122.34.45.1 is an example of an IP address expressed in this notation. It is sometimes referred to as DOTTED DECIMAL NOTATION. This notation is only rarely used since symbolic DOMAIN NAMES allow meaningful names to be used for computers on a network. The INTERNET DOMAIN NAME SERVICE converts from domain names to dotted quad form.

Double DES A version of the DATA ENCRYPTION STANDARD encryption algorithm (DES) which applies the algorithm twice to the PLAIN TEXT with a different key each time. It does not lead to a major increase in security. *See* MEET IN THE MIDDLE ATTACK. A much more secure way of improving DES is via TRIPLE DES.

double reverse lookup A security technique in which the INTERNET PROTOCOL ADDRESS of a CLIENT computer is retrieved from the DOMAIN NAME SERVICE and then the domain name service is consulted again to check that the Internet protocol address matches the original address of the client. It is an attempt to ensure that a valid computer has connected to a SERVER.

double transposition cipher Used to describe the double application of a TRANSPOSITION CIPHER to a PLAIN TEXT.

download The copying of a file or collection of files from one computer to another. One of the main technologies used for this purpose is the FILE TRANSFER PROTOCOL. *See also* UPLOAD.

download manager A sophisticated program which carries out the download of data or software from an FTP SERVER. It carries out sophisticated functions such as recovering from download errors, resuming a download that has failed, and scheduling of downloads.

download site A WEB SITE which is devoted to the downloading of software or files. It contains either HYPERLINKS to commercial sites or FTP links to resources subscribed by users and which the site

administers. Such sites can be devoted to a specialized topic such as Shakespearean texts or a specific software product, or is general. For example, a site might be devoted to downloading Web software. There are a number of download sites associated with FREEWARE and SHAREWARE.

downtime The time that a SERVER is not operating: this is usually due to a hardware error or routine maintenance. It is an important factor in judging an INTERNET SERVICE PROVIDER'S performance.

DPLT *See* DIGITAL POWER LINE TECHNOLOGY.

DPRL *See* DIGITAL PROPERTY RIGHTS LANGUAGE.

DQDB *See* DISTRIBUTED QUEUE DUAL BUS.

DQMOT Abbreviation for Don't Quote Me On This used in EMAILS and NEWSGROUPS.

draft standard A document which is originated by the INTERNET ENGINEERING TASK FORCE and which represents the penultimate stage in the process of developing an Internet standard. The draft standard source document is the PROPOSED STANDARD. The proposed standard will have been tested against two implementations and will have been modified to form the draft standard. The draft standard will need to be extant for at least four months for many more implementations of the standard to be created. Any problems with these implementations will give rise to modifications. The document which is formed by modifying the draft standard is the final Internet standard and is known as the OFFICIAL STANDARD.

drawer attack An attack on a computer network which relies on data that can be physically discovered rather than electronically discovered: for example, the use of a PASSWORD stored in a document held in an unlocked drawer. Such attacks are often much easier to perpetrate than technological attacks such as KEY SEARCH ATTACKS: companies may have very sophisticated electronic anti-attack measures yet have very few physical security controls. *See also* WHITE BOARD ATTACK.

dread question mark disease The strange characters that were introduced by Microsoft Word when documents written using that word processor were copied into an HTML document, such characters being displayed as question marks.

drill down The act of navigating a set of deeper and deeper HYPERLINKS in a WEB SITE in order to find more and more detailed information. It is also used as jargon to indicate a search for deeper issues in a text or conversations: for example, 'I'm interested in your idea about co-ownership, let's drill down on that.'

drop cable In an ETHERNET network this is the cable that connects a device to the network.

drop shadow The shadow drawn around a GRAPHIC IMAGE which is implemented by drawing a shadow which is offset in the horizontal and vertical directions.

dry line A transmission line that has not been modified by inserting electrical elements such as resistors and inductors in order to change its electrical characteristics.

DSA See DIGITAL SIGNATURE ALGORITHM.

DSL See DIGITAL SUBSCRIBER LINE.

DSML See DIRECTORY SERVICE MARKUP LANGUAGE.

DSO See DATA SOURCE OBJECT.

DSP See DIRECTORY SYSTEM PROTOCOL.

DSS See DECISION SUPPORT SYSTEM.

DSW Abbreviation for DICK SIZE WAR used in EMAILS and NEWSGROUPS.

DTD See DOCUMENT TYPE DEFINITION.

DTRT Abbreviation for Do The Right Thing used in CHAT ROOMS, EMAILS, and NEWSGROUPS.

dumb terminal A monitor-based input/output device that has no processing associated with it. This means that all functions, such as displaying a graphical interface, are carried out by the computer to which it is currently connected. Normally such terminals are associated with

MAINFRAME COMPUTERS. Much of the power of CLIENT SERVER COMPUTING arises from the fact that a large amount of processing can now be transferred to the personal computers and workstations which have replaced dumb terminals.

dumpster diving The act of rummaging through a waste container in order to retrieve hard copy of important files. Surprisingly this is one of the most successful ways of obtaining computer-based information, as there has been a history of companies investing in high-technology security devices and ignoring physical security.

duplex communication The transmission of data in a network where the signals are allowed to travel in both directions simultaneously: for example, the communication that occurs between a CLIENT and a SERVER.

durability A property of a DISTRIBUTED TRANSACTION. It describes the fact that such a transaction must have been stored in some permanent medium such as a FILE or a DATABASE. This is an important property of a distributed transaction along with ATOMICITY, CONSISTENCY, and ISOLATION. See also ACID.

dustbuster An EMAIL message sent to someone who has not received a message from the sender for some time. Such a message is used to check that a connection is still established, since EMAIL ADDRESSES can be deleted or changed over short periods of time. Normally such messages consist of a minimal amount of text.

DVMRP See DISTANCE VECTOR MULTICAST ROUTING PROTOCOL.

DWB Abbreviation for Don't Write Back used in EMAILS, usually used to indicate that the sender regards the discussion as terminated.

DWDM See DENSE WAVELENGTH DIVISION MULTIPLEXING.

dweeb A user of the Internet who misuses its facilities, for example by sending PASTE BOMBS. Unlike CRACKERS they are regarded as a nuisance rather than a danger. There are a range of abusive terms for certain types of Internet user, for example GEEK and NERD. Usage of such terms has not yet established any hierarchy in terms of abusiveness.

DYJHIW Abbreviation for Don't You Just Hate It When used in EMAILS and NEWS-GROUPS. For example: 'DYJHIW when a browser manufacturer issues a release which is bug-free, only for an update to follow the next day.'

dynamic adaptive routing The process of routing messages through a network in such a way that they reach their destination as quickly as possible. Dynamic adaptive routing relies on analysing traffic condition information in order to send data along communication lines which are not heavily loaded.

dynamic content CONTENT in a WEB SITE that changes frequently. A good example of this is the content of a Web site devoted to providing current stocks and shares prices or a Web site which provides breaking news.

dynamic font The term that the Netscape Corporation gave to a WEB FONT.

Dynamic Hypertext Markup Language The combination of HTML, style sheets implemented using CASCADING STYLE SHEETS, and scripting languages such as JAVASCRIPT or VBSCRIPT. This combination enables dynamic behaviour to be incorporated into a WEB PAGE. Typical behaviours include: those associated with ROLLOVERS; the transfer to another Web page after a page has been displayed for a short time; and the display and hiding of portions of a HTML FORM, depending on the user who is employing the BROWSER. Dynamic HTML is closely integrated with the DOCUMENT OBJECT MODEL developed by the WORLD WIDE WEB CONSORTIUM. It is usually abbreviated to DHTML.

dynamic page A WEB PAGE that is dynamically modified before being sent to the BROWSER that requested it. Normally such pages are associated with rapidly changing information such as a share price or the number of items in stock in a warehouse. There are a number of technologies used to implement dynamic pages: the most popular currently are ACTIVE SERVER PAGES® and JAVA SERVER PAGES®. Dynamic pages are built ON THE FLY.

dynamic rotation The process of delivering BANNER ADVERTS to a WEB PAGE on a rotating basis. An AD SERVER continually places such adverts on a Web page that is registered with it; the duration, selection and display time is determined by the server. This is in contrast to HARD-WIRED ADVERTS which are found permanently on a Web page.

dynamic web page 1. A WEB PAGE that contains DYNAMIC CONTENT, such as video clips.
2. A page implemented using DYNAMIC PAGE technology that changes rapidly over a period of time: for example, a page which delivers stock and shares prices to the user.

E

E2E Abbreviation for Email to Email used in CHAT ROOMS and NEWSGROUPS. For example, a participant in a chat room might say 'Can we continue this discussion E2E?'

EARN *See* EUROPEAN ACADEMIC AND RESEARCH NETWORK.

Easter egg A secret message hidden in the object code of a program. Increasingly it is being used in the context of an EASTER EGG HUNT. It can also be used to describe some hidden feature such as an animation contained in a WEB SITE. The term has also been used to describe hidden text in a message: for example, the message formed by extracting out every tenth character in a text. *See* STEGANOGRAPHY.

Easter egg hunt A project set by a teacher in a higher education establishment which asks students to find some information that has been hidden on the WORLD WIDE WEB. Such an activity provides training in the use of SEARCH ENGINES.

eavesdropping The act of capturing data which is flowing through the communications media used by a computer network. There are a variety of methods used to eavesdrop ranging from gaining access to a system by pretending to be a SYSTEM ADMINISTRATOR to physically implanting hardware into a system which can monitor traffic down a communication line. The main technology used to counteract eavesdropping is ENCRYPTION.

ebay effect The large rise in the price of a company's stock after it has announced that it is to start working in the ONLINE AUCTION area. Named after eBay, one of the first online auction companies.

EBCDIC *See* EXTENDED BINARY CODED DECIMAL INTERCHANGE CODE.

Ebone One of the main European BACKBONE networks, it mainly connects organizations such as INTERNET SERVICE PROVIDERS within Western Europe although it has started expanding into Eastern Europe.

ebook A book that is stored on a WEB SITE and can be downloaded to a CLIENT, printed and read. Currently such books are out of copyright and are supplied free. However, there are some sites which sell ebooks in a computer readable form. *See* PROJECT GUTENBERG and BOOK SITE.

ebook reader A hardware device which is posited to replace the conventional book. The ideal ebook reader contains a screen which is as clear as a normal book and weighs about the same as a paperback. The user of such a book would download copies of texts from BOOK SITES on the WORLD WIDE WEB.

ECA *See* ELECTRONIC COMMERCE AGENT.

ecard An electronic greetings card which can be sent by email. There are a large number of Web sites which allow you to choose from a variety of general or occasion-specific greetings cards.

ecash 1. Those technologies used to implement small monetary transactions for ECOMMERCE organizations. **2.** The name of a proprietary technology developed by a company known as Digi-Cash.

ecatalog A catalogue of products which is held on line and is accessible to users. Such catalogues may form part of an ECOMMERCE system which supports the sale of products to the general public or may form part of a BUSINESS-TO-BUSINESS system where purchases are made between companies.

ECC *See* ELLIPTIC CURVE CRYPTOGRAPHY.

ECDTF *See* ELECTRONIC COMMERCE DOMAIN TASK FORCE.

echo port A DEDICATED PORT on a computer which echoes any message sent to it.

This port is often used to receive test messages from other computers and is often configured to reject any echo response.

ECMA *See* EUROPEAN COMPUTER MANUFACTURERS' ASSOCIATION.

ECMAScript A standardized version of the JAVASCRIPT language,

ecommerce Sometimes written as e-commerce. *See* ELECTRONIC COMMERCE.

ecommerce site builder A program which is normally based on a WIZARD that takes an unsophisticated user through the process of setting up an ECOMMERCE Web site. There are a number of processes that such a program steps through, including: the setting up of pages containing basic details of a business, the construction of a catalogue, the creation of a SHOPPING CART facility, the insertion of BANNER ADVERTS, the insertion of HIT COUNTERS and programs which monitor the number of hits, the establishment of security controls including the process of obtaining a DIGITAL CERTIFICATE, the development of links to other software such as a spreadsheet, the downloading of the site to a WEB SERVER, and the registration of the site with a number of SEARCH ENGINES.

ecruiting The recruiting of staff via the Internet, normally by using specialized sites on the WORLD WIDE WEB. The late 1990s saw a major explosion of such sites.

EDI *See* ELECTRONIC DATA INTERCHANGE.

EDI service provider A company that provides facilities and expertise required by organizations who wish to use EDI to transport data over the Internet. Such companies provide legal advice and advice on network security and they often provide tailored software which can quickly enable trading partners to set up EDI connections with each other.

EDI translator A program which converts stored data in a DATABASE into a ELECTRONIC DATA INTERCHANGE (EDI) format. The term is also used to describe programs which convert from one EDI format to another.

edit detection A synonym for CHANGE DETECTION.

editor A program which is used to modify text files: for example, the text files which contain the source of a computer program.

editor software *See* EDITOR.

edu An Internet DOMAIN associated with educational institutions such as colleges and universities: for example, BramCollege.edu.

edutainment Interactive media, a combination of education and entertainment, which is implemented via software and delivered by a cable network or the Internet. The term is a broad one and is used to describe anything from a computer game to sophisticated MULTIUSER DIMENSION games.

EFTPOS *See* ELECTRONIC FUNDS TRANSFER AT POINT OF SALE.

EG 1. An abbreviation for Evil Grin used in CHAT ROOMS, EMAILS, and NEWSGROUPS. **2**. Also the COUNTRY CODE for Egypt.

egosurfing The process of searching the Internet for references to yourself. For example, an academic might egosurf the WORLD WIDE WEB using a SEARCH ENGINE for favourable references to his or her work or egosurf the reviews of books that he or she has written at an online book store.

EGP *See* EXTERIOR GATEWAY PROTOCOL.

EIGRP or Enhanced Interior Gateway Routing Protocol An improved version of the Interior Gateway Protocol for very large networks.

EIS *See* EXECUTIVE INFORMATION SYSTEM.

EJ An announcer for audio programmes which are broadcast over the Internet. The Internet version of a disc jockey.

ejournal A journal, academic in nature, which is published using the WORLD WIDE WEB. Such a journal usually uses Internet technology such as CONFERENCING to carry out associated activities such as the refereeing of papers. Many ejournals pride themselves on rapid refereeing and consequent rapid publication.

elancer A freelance employee who mainly operates via the Internet: for example, a Web designer who engages in TELEWORKING or a CYBRARIAN.

electronic brokerage The provision of stocks and shares buying facilities using the WORLD WIDE WEB. Such services are taken advantage of by users who carry out DAY TRADING.

electronic business An umbrella term which describes the use of network technology within business; it covers both ELECTRONIC COMMERCE and business processes which occur between companies: for example, those associated with SUPPLY CHAIN management. *See also* B2B and B2C.

electronic cheque A form of payment used in ECOMMERCE. An electronic cheque functions in the same way as a paper cheque: it acts as a message to a bank to transfer funds to a third party; however, it has a number of security advantages over conventional cheques since the account number can be encrypted, a DIGITAL SIGNATURE can be employed, and DIGITAL CERTIFICATES can be used to validate the payer, the payer's bank, and the account. There are a number of schemes for electronic cheques which have been developed including one from the FSTC, a consortium of US banks and clearing houses.

electronic commerce The use of network technology, more specifically Internet technology, to carry out business functions remotely. It was only in the late 1990s that electronic commerce took off, although the Internet has been used for commercial activities since the 1980s when pornographers used FTP SERVERS to sell salacious images. The huge expansion of ECOMMERCE, as it is often known, occurred in the late 1990s because of the huge increase in availability of access to the Internet. The typical ecommerce venture sells a product such as books or CDs over the Internet using credit cards as the payment medium. However, the term has a much wider use including ventures such as ONLINE AUCTIONS, GAME SITES, the use of Internet technology for SUPPLY CHAIN management and INTERNET ADVERTISING, together with the use of the Internet for applications such as ELECTRONIC DATA INTERCHANGE. Increasingly the term 'electronic commerce' has been applied to on-line sales ventures with the term ELECTRONIC BUSINESS being applied as an umbrella term to describe any use of network technology in business.

electronic commerce agent A category of AGENT which carries out a function associated with ECOMMERCE. For example, a typical electronic commerce agent would look for the best price of a particular commodity that the user of the agent wishes to buy.

Electronic Commerce Domain Task Force A group set up by the OBJECT MANAGEMENT GROUP which has been given the task of developing a standard for ECOMMERCE with particular reference to OBJECT-ORIENTED TECHNOLOGY.

electronic data interchange A generic term used to describe the interchange of data between companies across a network or a number of networks. The data may contain a variety of information including: financial information such as cheque-clearing data, purchasing information such as purchase orders, or securities information such as the prices of futures and derivatives. It is usually abbreviated to EDI.

Electronic Frontier Foundation A US organization which champions the rights of the Internet user. It deals with issues such as copyright, privacy, pornography, and libel.

electronic funds transfer at point of sale The initiation of a transfer of funds between a buyer using a charge card, credit card, or cash and a vendor, which is carried out at the vendor's premises or point of sale. Hardware used for this form of payment is found at supermarkets and other retailers and is usually integrated with the normal cash tills. This technology is often referred to as EFTPOS.

electronic journal An academic journal which is only published on the WORLD WIDE WEB. It carries out all its activities including peer review and publishing using net technologies such as CONFERENCING, EMAIL, and the use of WEB SITES.

Such journals pride themselves on the rapid publication of articles and are often referred to as ejournals.

electronic library A WEB SITE which makes free copies of books available to visitors. Normally these books are classics which have no copyright restrictions. The term 'library' is not used in its strict sense, as once a book has been DOWNLOADed it is not returned.

electronic mall A WEB SITE which contains a number of vendors who maintain WEB PAGES on the site. Such malls can resemble real malls with a wide variety of ECOMMERCE companies selling products or services or they can be specialized operations where the vendors concentrate on one particular area such as sports goods or cosmetics. Occasionally the term is used to describe a collection of Web-based service providers rather than product vendors.

electronic paper A technology which attempts to mimic normal paper. The best example of this is the PORTABLE DOCUMENT FORMAT (PDF) popularized by Adobe, which enables a wide variety of documents to be converted to PDF and reproduced on a screen by PDF viewers. The term was frequently used in the late 1980s to describe other technologies which are now defunct.

Electronic Privacy Information Center A research-based public interest centre which focuses on general privacy issues; however, it has increasingly become interested in online privacy issues.

electronic publishing The process of publishing some CONTENT using the WORLD WIDE WEB. Anyone who adds a WEB SITE to the World Wide Web is theoretically 'publishing'. However, the term is normally used to describe the process of presenting magazine or newspaper material on the Web.

electronic storefront The first pages that you meet when you visit the WEB SITE of an ONLINE RETAILER. Usually these pages are highly designed and often present some of the products which the retailer is selling.

electronic text Texts stored on the WORLD WIDE WEB and usually freely available to anyone who accesses the WEB SITE in which they are held. Often such texts are out of copyright. The forerunner of all electronic text projects was PROJECT GUTENBERG.

electronic token A form of electronic cash which is used for small transactions. *See* TOKEN.

element The basic building block of a document written using the HYPERTEXT MARKUP LANGUAGE. An example of such an element is an ANCHOR.

ELF *See* EXTENDED LOGFILE FORMAT.

Eliza effect The impression of interacting with a human when using a computer program. Named after the 1960s computer program Eliza which exhibited semi-intelligent responses. The programs that carry out this function are sometimes referred to as RESPONSE BOTS. *See also* CHATTERBOT.

elliptic curve cryptography A competitor to the RSA ENCRYPTION system. In order to crack a CIPHER TEXT constructed using this system the CRACKER has to solve a very difficult and time-consuming mathematical problem known as the elliptic curve discrete logarithm problem. This is in contrast to RSA where the cracker has to factor very large numbers.

email One of the most important and primitive technologies employed by Internet users. It is a form of electronic messaging where a user creates a text message which may have a number of ATTACHMENTS and sends it to a recipient. The program that is used to carry out the sending is known as an EMAIL PROGRAM. In order to send an email to someone it is necessary to know their EMAIL ADDRESS. Emails are processed by an EMAIL SERVER which carries out the process of delivering email to recipients. It is possible to send a copy of an email to other recipients using a CARBON COPY or a BLIND CARBON COPY. EMAIL LISTS are collections of email addresses, used to send emails to groups of users who have a common interest. Email can be made secure by means of technologies such as CRYPTOGRAPHY: *see*, for example, PRIVACY

ENHANCED MAIL. Email can also be abused. The most prevalent abuse is the use of SPAM, although an increasingly common form of abuse is the use of email by CYBER-STALKERS and the spreading of VIRUSES by means of attachments. There are a number of protocols used for sending email: two examples are the POST OFFICE PROTOCOL and the SIMPLE MAIL TRANSFER PROTOCOL.

email address An email address consists of two components: the name of the re-cipient and the DOMAIN with which they are associated. The name must be a unique name within the domain and the two components are separated by an @ charac-ter. So, for example, the email address d.king@flyhigh.co.uk refers to the user d.king who is registered at the domain flyhigh.co.uk.

email bot A BOT which carries out some task associated with EMAIL such as finding the name of a user, given his or her EMAIL ADDRESS, or creating an EMAIL LIST. An example of this type of bot is an ADDRESS HARVESTER.

email directory A directory of the email addresses of Internet users. Many email directories are confidential and cannot be accessed over the Internet.

email filter A program which prevents certain EMAILS from being read. A major use for such software is for the identifica-tion and disposal of SPAM. It can also be used for screening off harmful emails from children. An email filter rejects emails using a large number of criteria, including the length of the email, key-words in the header of the email, the sender of the email, the size of the email, and the occurrence of certain words in the body of the text. There are many email filters, ranging from the simple ones found in the major email programs to so-phisticated stand-alone utilities. *See also* ANTI-SPAM SOFTWARE and BOZO LIST.

email flooding The process of sending large quantities of emails, often with large ATTACHMENTS, in order to disable a net-work or part of a network such as a MAIL SERVER. This is an example of a DENIAL OF SERVICE ATTACK. Such attacks increased in the 1990s, both in terms of frequency and in terms of severity. *See also* LIST LINKING.

email forwarding A service, often offered by INTERNET SERVICE PROVIDERS, that enables a user with multiple EMAIL accounts to have all emails sent to these accounts directed to a single MAILBOX.

email harassment The act of harassing a user of the Internet using EMAIL, usually by sending salacious, abusive, or intrusive messages. This is a form of harassment carried out by CYBERSTALKERS which is il-legal in both the United States and Europe. There are a number of solutions to this problem, including the use of an ANONYM-OUS REMAILER SERVICE or a FREE EMAIL address which is only used for sending messages.

email link A HYPERLINK found on a WEB PAGE which, when clicked, starts a dia-logue that prompts the user with a window containing a blank EMAIL form. This form can then be used to send an email to the user specified in the link. Such links should be used with caution as they can be used for EMAIL HARASSMENT or captured by ADDRESS HARVESTERS and used to send SPAM.

email list A collection of EMAIL AD-DRESSES which are stored in a FILE. Such lists can be used by EMAIL programs for the bulk delivery of email to the members of the list.

email program A program which is used to send, receive, and administer EMAIL. Such programs can range from primitive SHAREWARE utilities to large, complex and expensive programs which also carry out other functions such as diary management.

email reader An alternative name for an EMAIL PROGRAM.

email search The process of searching for the EMAIL ADDRESS of an Internet user. The main way of doing this via one of the search engines such as YAHOO, DE-JANEWS, or BIGFOOT, although there are also specialized WEB SITES dedicated to ad-dress finding. *See also* PEOPLE FINDING.

email server A specialized program which receives EMAILS from users of the

Internet and then forwards them to the recipients. Such servers can also carry out other functions such as detecting email which is potentially SPAM mail.

email tennis What occurs when two users are on line simultaneously and they engage in an EMAIL dialogue which happens in real time.

email volley What happens when two EMAIL users send a number of messages to each other with each new message added to the end of a previous message. *See also* EMAIL TENNIS.

emanations Radiation which is produced by devices that are attached to a network. Typically they are produced by monitors or other visual display units. Such radiation can be monitored by CRACKERS and important information such as PASSWORDS discovered and used for illegal access to a network. *See* TEMPEST.

emaul The act of sending an EMAIL message which criticizes some other message or a POSTING in a NEWSGROUP.

Embedded Font® The term used by the Microsoft Corporation to describe a font which is embedded into a WEB PAGE.

embedded hyperlink A HYPERLINK which is found embedded in a line of text rather than in a graphic image. Usually such links are underlined, although increasingly designers are using the advanced facilities of the HYPERTEXT MARKUP LANGUAGE to eliminate this and to display them in some colour.

embedded plug-in A PLUG-IN which processes material such as a VIDEO CLIP which is displayed on a Web page along with the remainder of the page. This type of plug-in is in contrast to a FULL-PAGE PLUG-IN where a new browser window is opened to accommodate the material that is being displayed by the plug-in.

embossing A technique which when applied to a GRAPHIC IMAGE gives the impression that the image has been carved out of some base material such as stone.

EMFBI Abbreviation for Excuse Me For Butting In used in CHAT ROOMS and NEWS-GROUPS. It is usually used sarcastically

when a long, seemingly interminable argument is being carried out on a news-group.

EML Abbreviation for Evil Manic Laugh used in EMAILS and NEWSGROUPS.

emotag Pseudo HTML TAGS used in WEB PAGES and EMAILS. For example, if someone wanted to compliment another email user they might enclose the compliment in the tags <COMPLIMENT> ... </COMPLIMENT>. Emotags are often used to indicate something that would be conveyed by a facial expression or vocal nuance in a face-to-face conversation. *See also* EMOTICON, ASSICON, and PARALAN-GUAGE.

emoticon A series of typed characters usually used in EMAIL messages which indicate some mood or state that is normally conveyed in a face-to-face conversation but which cannot be conveyed in an email. For example, the emoticon : D means that the writer is laughing. Emoticons usually have to be read sideways and are often referred to as smileys. *See also* EMOTAG, ASSICON, and PARALANGUAGE. This dictionary contains a list of emoticons in appendix 2.

employment site A WEB SITE which posts details of jobs that are available in a particular employment sector. The first of these sites concentrated on posts in the IT industry, but the late 1990s saw an explosion in other sectors. A number of the sites ask users to fill in a questionnaire about themselves before accessing their database of vacancies. *See also* ECRUITING.

empty element A TAG in the HYPERTEXT MARKUP LANGUAGE which is not associated with an END TAG. The tag <HR> which introduces a horizontal line in a WEB PAGE is an example of an empty element.

EMSG Abbreviation for Email MeSsaGe used in EMAILS and NEWSGROUPS.

EMUL A HAKSPEK abbreviation for EMail you Later used in CHAT ROOMS, EMAILS, and NEWSGROUPS.

e-nally retentive Used to describe an EMAIL user who writes perfectly formed, syntactically correct messages.

encryption The process of transforming some text known as the PLAIN TEXT into a form which cannot be read by anyone who does not have knowledge of the mechanisms used to carry out the encryption. The transformed text is known as the CIPHER TEXT. There are a wide variety of ALGORITHMS available to carry out this process.

encryption algorithm This is an ALGORITHM that is used to change a PLAIN TEXT into an unreadable CIPHER TEXT using ENCRYPTION. There are a wide variety of algorithms that can be used, ranging from simple ones which provide limited facilities to very complex and resource-intensive ones which are used for the highest security materials. *See also* SYMMETRIC KEY ENCRYPTION, and PUBLIC KEY ENCRYPTION.

end office The telephone exchange which lies closest to the telephone. It is also known as a LOCAL EXCHANGE or LOCAL CENTRAL OFFICE.

end system A jargon term used to describe a computing system which lies behind a Web facade. A stock control system used by an online bookseller is an example of an end system.

end tag Some of the TAGS in the HYPERTEXT MARKUP LANGUAGE are associated with end tags formed by prefacing their name with a FORWARD SLASH symbol: for example, the <TITLE> tag is associated with the end tag </TITLE>. Tags and end tags delineate text that is associated with the tag: for example, the text associated with the <TITLE> tag </TITLE> end tag is the title of the HTML document.

Enterprise JavaBeans® A component architecture which is built on top of the JAVA programming language. It enables software developers to produce business components such as bank ledgers and slot them into SERVERS which are part of an overall ECOMMERCE system. The major advantage of this technology is that it takes care of many of the programming problems that arise when implementing TRANSACTIONS. Another advantage is the fact that the components can be moved easily from one server to another.

enterprise server A server, usually a web server, which addresses the needs of a whole company or enterprise rather than the needs of a small part of the whole.

enterprise system A collection of hardware and software which implements an ECOMMERCE application: for example, the software and hardware used by an ONLINE RETAILER.

entity A networking term which describes some active element associated with a LAYER. This element can be some software or a piece of hardware.

entreprenerd A technology-oriented entrepreneur who starts up an Internet business. Bill Gates of Microsoft is often referred to as the archetype of the entreprenerd.

entropy coding Techniques used to achieve data compression which do not take account of the semantics of the data: that is, they do not depend on whether the data is from a video file, audio file, or some laboratory experiment. The two main techniques which are described by this term are STATISTICAL ENCODING, where the statistical properties of the data are used to guide compression, and REPETITIVE SEQUENCE SUPPRESSION, where repetitive data is replaced by a character or sequence of characters which is shorter than the sequence.

entry tunnel A short sequence of WEB PAGES which are encountered by a visitor to a WEB SITE as they access the site through a HOME PAGE. They provide a taster for the site and build up a sense of anticipation for the main part of the site. Normally entry tunnels are used for consumer sites. Opinion is divided on their effectiveness.

environment variable A variable used to describe some property of a system. Such variables are accessible by programming languages which can change them, or base the execution of their programs on their value. For example, the COMMON GATEWAY INTERFACE (CGI) has a number of environment variables which can be used by PERL or SERVLET programmers when carrying out CGI PROGRAMMING. A typical example of a CGI environment variable is SERVER_SOFTWARE which describes the name and version of the server software that is processing a Web CLIENT request.

EOD Abbreviation for End Of Day used in emails and newsgroups.

EOM Abbreviation for End Of Message used in CHAT ROOMS, EMAILS, and NEWS-GROUPS. Usually used to stress the text which appears before EOM.

EOT Abbreviation for End Of THREAD used in NEWSGROUPS.

EPIC Acronym for ELECTRONIC PRIVACY INFORMATION CENTER.

e-purse A term used in ELECTRONIC COM-MERCE to denote an electronic financial transaction. So, for example, if you have ordered a series of books from an online bookshop and are using a credit card, the cost of the transaction is associated with an e-purse. It is also called an E-WALLET.

error correcting code A way of using extra data in a collection of data to detect whether there is an error in the collection, pinpoint where that error is, and then correct it. *See also* ERROR DETECTING CODE.

error detecting code A way of using redundant data in a signal in order to detect whether there is an error in the data. For example, a set of integers might be accompanied by another integer which represents their sum. If the sum does not match the sum of the integers after transmission then an error in transmission has occurred.

error trapping The process of recognizing an error in a system and starting the process of responding to it. For example, a number of programming languages such as JAVA feature facilities which enable them to carry out error trapping. In such languages a typical error that would be trapped might occur when a connection is attempted to a SERVER which is malfunctioning.

escrow The safe keeping of an entity which two or more parties have an interest in. For example, an ESCROW SERVICE associated with an ONLINE AUCTION provides for an intermediary temporarily taking care of an item until both parties, the vendor and the buyer, agree that the

transaction should proceed. A KEY ESCROW service keeps KEYS used in CRYPTOGRAPHY-based communication.

escrow service A service provided by an intermediary who stands between someone selling a product on the Internet and someone buying it. Instead of the buyer sending payment to the seller and the seller sending the product to the buyer, they both send these items to the escrow service. The service then checks that the product matches its description and the payment sent is adequate: if so, then they are sent to the participants. If anyone backs out of the deal then the payment is sent back to the buyer and the product to the vendor. An escrow service usually charges a fee for this process. Increasingly the term is being used to describe any service which requires some safe keeping by a third party, such as the safe keeping of PASSWORDS used in ENCRYPTION.

etailing The sale of goods and products over the Internet.

etherhose Slang term used to describe the collection of ETHERNET cabling used in a computer network.

ethernet A LOCAL AREA NETWORK technology which uses CSMA-CD and which was originally developed by the Xerox Corporation, Intel, and the now defunct Digital Equipment Corporation. It is a highly flexible form of networking which can employ a variety of cable types and a variety of network topologies including bus and tree topologies. It can also use a variety of transmission technologies ranging from UNSHIELDED TWISTED PAIR CABLES to FIBRE OPTIC CABLES.

ethernet address A 48-bit address which uniquely identifies a NETWORK INTERFACE CARD on an ETHERNET.

ethernet meltdown A slang term which describes the situation that occurs when an ETHERNET becomes saturated with data. Usually this happens because of a misrouted or invalid PACKET.

ETLA Abbreviation for Extended Three Letter Acronym used in EMAILS and NEWS-GROUPS.

European Academic and Research Network A European network which contains computers associated with research laboratories and universities. It is the European equivalent of BITNET. Usually known as EARN.

European Computer Manufacturers' Association A European body which was set up to develop IT standards.

Euroseek A SEARCH ENGINE which concentrates on European material.

event manager This is a term employed in connection with programming languages which have facilities for developing Windows interfaces. The event manager is the software that is associated with user events such as a mouse being clicked or a MENU being pulled down. The event manager usually calls upon other software to implement the processing associated with the event.

evil empire In the past this was a pejorative term that HACKERS used to describe IBM. During the 1990s it was transferred to Microsoft.

e-wallet An alternative name for an E-PURSE.

Excite A SEARCH ENGINE which was one of the first to offer the user the facility to express queries using natural language rather than a formal QUERY LANGUAGE. It is one of the largest search engines in the Internet.

exe A FILE EXTENSION used in Windows and DOS systems for executable programs.

executable content A program embedded within a WEB PAGE. The program may carry out a variety of functions including ANIMATION and FORMS PROCESSING. The three main technologies used for the implementation of executable content are APPLETS, JAVASCRIPT, and ACTIVE X.

executable virus A VIRUS which is resident on a computer and which is executed in order to carry out its purpose. This is in contrast to a DATA VIRUS which just infects a data file and is usually deleted.

executive information system A system which offers an interface to a DATA WAREHOUSE. It enables the user to discover a wide variety of information from the data that is stored. Typically the user of such a system associated with, say, a travel agency, could discover information about the most popular holiday, the number of complaints made about certain holiday firms, and the age profile of the customers of the company. Increasingly such systems are also becoming capable of combining searches of a company data warehouse with searches of the WORLD WIDE WEB.

exit page A WEB PAGE that is displayed when a visitor to a WEB SITE decides to leave the site. There are a number of ways of using this type of page; probably the most common is to inform the visitor of future content changes or additions which are due to occur in the near future. Another use is to ask visitors to sign up for a MAILING LIST. Opinion is divided about the effectiveness of exit pages.

exit tunnel A series of WEB PAGES which are traversed by the user of a BROWSER when they inform the site that they are leaving it. Typically it contains material which thanks the user for visiting, asks whether they want to sign up for any special offers, and alerts them of any exciting new CONTENT. Opinion is divided on the usefulness of exit tunnels.

Exon Used after 1996 to denote an obscenity, it is based on the name of Senator John Exon, the main author of the COMMUNICATIONS DECENCY ACT. It is occasionally used in NEWSGROUPS as in 'I am tired of all the Exons that are being said in this newsgroup.'

export grade security The US government had tight restrictions on the export of cryptographic technology until the end of the 1990s and specified what could or could not be exported to other countries. A rough and ready guide partitioned this technology into two categories: export grade security and DOMESTIC GRADE SECURITY. Export grade security technology could be exported and is characterized by software which can resist casual eavesdropping but which cannot resist a determined attack by an intruder. The situation changed drastically in the year 2000 when restrictions were lifted for all but a few countries.

exposure Used in WEB ADVERTISING to describe the number of times a visitor to a WEB SITE is exposed to a particular BANNER ADVERT.

Extended Binary Coded Decimal Interchange Code An alternative to the AMERICAN STANDARD CODE FOR INFORMATION INTERCHANGE (ASCII). It was used extensively in IBM computers, but is rapidly disappearing in use.

Extended Logfile Format A format for WEB LOG FILES which has been developed by the WORLD WIDE WEB CONSORTIUM. It extends existing log file formats and has the aim of making LOG FILE ANALYSIS by WEB LOGGING TOOLS easier. *See also* COMMON LOGFILE FORMAT.

Extensible Business Reporting Language A language based on XML which has been defined for presenting financial information such as balance sheets and accounts. It was developed by a consortium of companies including Oracle, Microsoft, and Deloitte and Touche. Usually abbreviated to XBRL.

Extensible Forms Description Language A language used for creating legally binding documents expressed in the EXTENSIBLE MARKUP LANGUAGE.

Extensible Hypertext Markup Language The next version of the HYPERTEXT MARKUP LANGUAGE. It is touted by the WORLD WIDE WEB CONSORTIUM as being its successor. It is usually referred to as XHTML.

Extensible Log Format A standard which defines the format of WEB LOG FILES. This format is based on XML. The project that defined it had, as one of its main aims, the standardization of all Web log file formats around a common XML-based standard. Such a standardization would, for example, eliminate the large number of non-compatible tools for log file processing that are currently extant.

Extensible Markup Language Usually referred to as XML. This is an example of a MARKUP LANGUAGE that was developed in order to overcome some of the major problems with HTML. One problem is that HTML is not easy to extend so, for example, a mathematician or scientist looking for a markup language to display mathematics would find huge difficulties using HTML and extending it. When companies have extended it, for example the main browser vendors, there have been problems with displaying documents expressed in a browser dialect of HTML that was intended for another browser. Another problem with HTML is the fact that it does not contain facilities for indicating the structure of a document. For example, many ECOMMERCE companies publish catalogues of products on the Web; unfortunately, HTML is unable to specify whether an entry in such a catalogue is the serial number of a product, the number in stock, or the price. XML was developed in order to overcome these and other problems. It was developed as a subset of the SGML markup language and, in 1998, became the final recommendation of the WORLD WIDE WEB CONSORTIUM. XML is not strictly a markup language, but a language which can be used to define both general and special-purpose markup languages. It is a language that separates content from structure. The structure is defined in a DOCUMENT TYPE DEFINITION, often referred to as a DTD. This is a document that defines the structure of an document: what TAGS to expect, in what order they are found, and what tags can be found within other tags. Thus a company that wishes to define a markup language would develop a DTD that could be used by anyone who employs the language. The correctness of an XML document is checked using a parser. There are two types of XML parsers: VALIDATING XML PARSERS and NON-VALIDATING XML PARSERS. The former check the XML source against the DTD; the latter carry out a rudimentary validation which, for example, checks that tags are accompanied by their end tags. When a document expressed in an XML-based markup language is displayed on a browsing device the way it is displayed can be varied according to the device. For example, the display of a fragment of such a language on an electronic organizer would be different from that on a conventional browser.

There have been a number of languages defined using XML: for example, the language MATHML has been developed for displaying mathematics in a browser; the World Wide Web's Platform for Privacy Preferences Activity has defined a language which users can employ to define the degree to which personal details can be published to others on the Web; and the EXTENSIBLE LOG FORMAT language has been developed for defining a standard format for WEB LOG FILES.

Extensible Style Language A language based on STYLE SHEETS and the EXTENSIBLE MARKUP LANGUAGE which is supported by the two main BROWSERS INTERNET EXPLORER and NETSCAPE NAVIGATOR. It is often abbreviated to XSL.

Extensible Style Language Transformation A language which transforms documents written in the EXTENSIBLE MARKUP LANGUAGE (XML) into documents expressed in some other format. For example, an ECOMMERCE developer may have a number of documents expressed in XML which need to be read using a word processor. The Extensible Style Language Transformation provides an easy way to convert an XML document into this format. It is often abbreviated to XSLT.

Exterior Gateway Protocol A PROTOCOL which is used for GATEWAYS to communicate data such as ROUTING information. This type of protocol is used when an organization has a number of physically separated networks and uses the Internet to communicate between them. This type of protocol is in contrast to the INTERIOR GATEWAY PROTOCOL.

extranet An INTRANET which is also available to users outside the organization that owns it. A typical extranet application is where a manufacturer integrates its database with databases from its component suppliers so that production planning can be carried out more easily. This EDI application requires two intranets to be joined together to form an extranet which can then be accessed by selected staff from the manufacturing organization and its suppliers. The late 1990s saw a large increase in companies sharing information with other companies and customers; consequently there has been a major increase in the deployment of intranet and extranet technology.

eyeballs A slang term for the users of a WEB SITE.

eye candy Visually attractive material: for example, a well-designed WEB SITE. The opposite of EYE TRASH, BLENDO PAGE and ANGRY FRUIT SALAD. *See also* BEST OF THE WEB.

eye trash Often used to refer to BANNER ADVERTS. Sometimes it is applied to WEB PAGES with intrusive content such as inappropriate video clips and animations. *See also* ANGRY FRUIT SALAD, WORST OF THE WEB, and BLENDO PAGE.

ezine A name for a magazine which is Web-based. Such magazines are also known as WEBZINES or ZINES.

F

F2F Abbreviation for Face to Face used in CHAT ROOMS, EMAILS, and NEWSGROUPS. An example of its use is 'I'm tired of using email. We live close together so let's go F2F.'

facemail Used to describe a face-to-face meeting. *See also* FACE TIME *and* FACE TO FACE.

face time Time spent meeting someone face to face rather than communicating using a computer. *See also* F2F, FACEMAIL, *and* FACE TO FACE.

face to face Used to describe contact which does not occur on line, usually abbreviated to F2F. *See also* FACEMAIL.

failure transparency The property of a well-designed DISTRIBUTED SYSTEM: it should shield the user from any failures that affect the network in which the system is situated. It must, for example, ensure that when a SERVER fails only a degradation in performance is experienced, not a complete withdrawal of service.

fake copy listing A criminal activity which involves stealing some WEB PAGES and placing them on your site in order for the site to be placed in a prominent position when a search using a SEARCH ENGINE is carried out. *See* COPYCAT PAGE.

fake user interface BANNER ADVERTS which look like windows with visible entities such as BUTTONS and MENUS; they are designed to tempt the user to click on the advert and hence visit the advertiser's WEB SITE. Since such banner adverts are usually paid for on a per-click basis, it benefits the owner of the site containing the adverts.

fall back Occurs when two MODEMS experience data corruption due to noise on the transmission line used to connect them. In order to eliminate the noise the modems negotiate with each other to

send data at a speed lower than the one they are currently using.

fall forward When two connected modems experience noise they negotiate a lower transmission speed in an attempt to eliminate it. This is known as FALL BACK; fall forward is where they return to their original speed.

fall over A term synonymous with CRASH: for example, 'I must complete my session with the server as the system administrator has just told me that it is about to fall over.'

false drop A page that has been retrieved by a SEARCH ENGINE which is not relevant to the SEARCH QUERY that has been used.

FAP *See* FORMAT AND PROTOCOLS.

FAQ *See* FREQUENTLY ASKED QUESTION.

FAQ archive A file of FREQUENTLY ASKED QUESTIONS which have usually arisen as part of the postings to a NEWSGROUP. Such an archive can be readily consulted by new contributors to the newsgroup before they pose a question and potentially waste the time of other contributors. *See* FAQ *and* RTFAQ. Such files are usually administered by the MODERATOR of the newsgroup.

FAQL *See* FREQUENTLY ASKED QUESTION LIST.

FAQ page A WEB PAGE which contains FREQUENTLY ASKED QUESTIONS about the WEB SITE in which it is embedded and the answers to these questions.

fasgrolia A term often used to describe the language of ABBREVIATIONS and acronyms found on the Internet. It is short for 'the fast growing language of initialisms and acronyms'.

FastCGI One of the problems with SERVER APIS is that, since they are closely integrated with a WEB SERVER, security can be a problem. FastCGI is an approach to CGI programming developed by a company called Open Market, which overcomes this problem and also addresses the inefficiency overheads normally associated with CGI PROGRAMMING. A number of popular Web servers, including APACHE, now support this technology.

Fast Ethernet A version of the ETHERNET protocol which supports high speeds up to 100 Mbps. It requires non-standard and expensive hardware such as CONCENTRATORS and NETWORK INTERFACE CARDS. It also requires high-speed UNSHIELDED TWISTED PAIR CABLES, SHIELDED TWISTED PAIR CABLES, or FIBRE OPTIC CABLE.

fast infector A VIRUS which is copied into memory and then infects other programs on the computer when it is executed. See also SLOW INFECTOR.

Fast Local Internet Protocol A protocol developed at the University of Vrije and modelled on the INTERNET PROTOCOL. It attempts to overcome some of the problems with the Internet protocol concerned with security and network management.

fat client A client computer which contains the bulk of a CLIENT SERVER COMPUTING application. A good example of such an application is a DECISION SUPPORT SYSTEM where the bulk of the functionality resides in the client code and where the server might provide only basic code for sending large amounts of data to the clients. The advantage of having a fat client system is that the functionality of the application can be easily extended by the users of the system; the disadvantage is that software changes to the system have to be communicated to what could be a large number of client computers. Fat clients are associated with THIN SERVERS.

fat server A server which runs an application where most of the program code resides on it rather than on the CLIENT computers. A good example of this type of server is a WEB SERVER, where the code for responding to requests from a BROWSER resides on the server. Fat servers are normally associated with THIN CLIENTS. Fat servers and thin clients have the advantage that software updates to the service are easy to carry out: all that needs to

be changed is the code on the server, not the code on the many clients that might access the server.

fault management A sub-discipline of NETWORK MANAGEMENT. It consists of detecting a network error such as a malfunctioning ROUTER, rectifying the error, and retesting the network to check that the modification made to eliminate the error has been correctly carried out.

fault-tolerant system A system where a fault, be it a hardware or software fault, does not immediately lead to total failure. A fault-tolerant system either degrades gracefully when some fault is detected or carries on with the fault hidden from users. There are a number of techniques used to implement fault-tolerant DISTRIBUTED SYSTEMS. The most common is replication. Hardware replication involves constructing a system with a number of computers with each carrying out the same function; when one of these computers malfunctions its processing is taken over by one of the other computers. Another technique is DATA REPLICATION where an important database resides on a number of computers. If one of these computers malfunctions then this would not be a disaster, as another computer would be available to take part in any processes involving the database.

FAX A form of transmission over communication lines which involves the conversion of pages of documents into electronic form, which is then decoded at a FAX receiver and reproduced on paper. FAX has been an important technology for sending documents quickly but with the rise of EMAIL its use is decreasing.

FAX modem A MODEM which has been designed for the sending of FAXes, such modems are also capable of being used in connection with DIAL-UP ACCESS although, they have normally been optimized for FAX use.

FAX over IP The transmission of FAX messages over a network using the TCP-IP protocol.

FAX to email service A service which enables FAX messages to be diverted to an EMAIL system. This is often provided free.

All a subscriber has to do is register with the service, which then provides a personal telephone number to which FAXes can be sent and then diverted. The provider of this service usually makes a profit by taking a percentage of the telephone charges. *See also* UNIVERSAL MESSAGING SERVICE.

FBC Abbreviation for Fully Buzzword Compliant used in EMAILS and NEWSGROUPS.

FC Abbreviation for Fingers Crossed used in EMAILS and NEWSGROUPS.

FDDI *See* FIBRE DISTRIBUTED DATA INTERFACE.

feathering A technique used to blur the edges of a graphic image giving the impression that it gradually blends into the background.

FedCIRC *See* FEDERAL COMPUTER INCIDENT RESPONSE CAPABILITY.

Federal Computer Incident Response Capability A US organization that provides security-related services to federal civilian agencies. Often abbreviated to FedCIRC.

Federal Information Exchange A connection point between the Internet and a number of US government networks.

Federal Networking Council A group of large US governmental agencies involved in the use of Internet technology.

Federal Trade Commission A US government body which monitors fraudulent business practices. Its WEB SITE contains up-to-date material on commercial Internet crime.

federated naming The process of identifying a resource in a network which forms part of a CLIENT SERVER COMPUTING system. It is akin to the use of country codes in telephone systems.

FEDI *See* FINANCIAL EDI.

female connection A hardware connection (effectively a socket) which consists of a recessed hole in a metal holder.

fewest hops routing A form of ROUTING which attempts to send messages in a network from a source computer to a destination computer in a way that minimizes the number of intermediate computers that the messages have to travel through. *See* HOP.

FGK algorithm An alternative name for ADAPTIVE HUFFMAN CODING the F, G, and K stand for the names of the researchers who devised the algorithm: Faller, Gallager, and Knuth.

Fibre Distributed Data Interface A protocol used to connect two LOCAL AREA NETWORKS using FIBRE OPTIC CABLE. It provides speeds of up to 100 Mbps. Usually known as FDDI.

fibre media A term used for paper-based material such as business letters. *See also* PMAIL, PAPER MAIL, PAPER NET, and DEAD TREE.

fibre optic cable Cabling that consists of a glass core which is surrounded by a number of layers of protective materials. It is a light conducting medium which, consequently, does not suffer from electrical interference. It is normally used in environments where electrical interference is high; it is also used to connect buildings together because it is highly resistant to external weather conditions. Fibre optic cable is faster than other cabling such as COAXIAL CABLE and is often used for high bandwidth applications such as VIDEO CONFERENCING. The principle of operation of such cabling is simple: light is generated at one end and is pulsed in binary signals down the glass towards a detector at the end of the cable which converts the light pulses to digital signals. Fibre optic transmission lines where the light continually bounces off the central core is known as MULTI-MODE FIBRE; if it travels in a straight line then it is known as SINGLE-MODE FIBRE.

fibre to the curb Used to describe the process of replacing much of the LOCAL LOOP with fibre optic cabling connected to a junction box. Each home would then be connected to this junction box using copper cabling. This is a cheaper solution to BANDWIDTH problems than FIBRE TO THE HOME.

fibre to the home Used by technologists concerned with the problems of upgrading the BANDWIDTH of a communications network in order to provide an infrastructure which enables applications such as VIDEO ON DEMAND to be delivered to homes and offices. It involves totally replacing the LOCAL LOOP with fibre optic cable.

FidoNet A large network of hobbyist computers which is mainly devoted to EMAIL, NEWSGROUPS, and BULLETIN BOARDS.

file A collection of BYTES held on a mass storage device. The collection might be data, a GRAPHIC IMAGE, a VIDEO CLIP, an AUDIO CLIP, the source code of a program, or the binary code of a program, etc. Data stored in files is much slower to access than data stored in a computer's main memory.

file attachment An attachment to an EMAIL. Such attachments are increasingly being used to spread VIRUSES.

file compression The process of using a COMPRESSION algorithm in order to reduce the size of a file, usually as a prelude to sending the file over a network or archiving it on a slow storage device.

file extension The letters following the full stop in a file name. The file extension usually identifies the type of data found in the file. For example, the extension htm or html indicates a file that contains code expressed in the HYPERTEXT MARKUP LANGUAGE and the extension txt indicates a file containing textual data.

file format The way that data is structured and organized in a FILE. A file format is normally associated with a particular application.

file infector A form of VIRUS which attaches itself to or replaces a program resident in a computer. When the program is executed the virus carries out some malicious act such as deleting important files.

file server A SERVER which enables CLIENT computers on a network to access a central store of files. Usually these files are too large to store permanently on the clients. A WEB SERVER is a good example of a special type of file server, since it dispenses a wide variety of files to client computers which are executing BROWSERS. There are, however, other uses for file servers: for example one might be used in a drawing office for dispensing the large files used by electronic draughtsmen.

file signature Data, usually fairly short in length, which describes a FILE and which is calculated from the contents of the file. It has the property that if the file is altered and the data recomputed there is a very high probability that the new data is different from its previous value. It is similar to a MESSAGE DIGEST. File signatures are used to check whether a file has been altered by, say, a VIRUS or some malicious intruder. Periodically, special-purpose software processes sensitive files in a system checking the value of each file's signature against the previous value. If it has changed then these files are flagged as having a high probability of having been changed.

File Transfer Protocol This is a STATEFUL PROTOCOL, more often referred to as FTP, which forms part of TCP-IP and which is used for the transfer of data held in FILES stored in an FTP SERVER. This transfer is often known as ANONYMOUS FTP since the FTP client that carries out the transfer does not usually have to identify itself using an account number or password. There are a variety of utilities available which allow a user to interact with a FTP server and DOWNLOAD files.

filler app An application which acts as a bridge between a base version of a piece of software and a much more enhanced version which has not yet been released. Filler apps usually contain code that rectifies errors in previous versions and implements minor functional enhancements. *See also* KILLER APP.

fill-out form A form, often seen on the WORLD WIDE WEB, which mimics a paper form and asks for details such as name, geographical address, EMAIL ADDRESS, services required, and gender. The form contains visual objects such as BUTTONS and TEXT BOXES.

filter A general term used to describe software which examines some content and prevents it from reaching its destination, based on a number of rules stored in a SCRIPT or a PROFILE. Internet-based applications of filters include those for EMAIL programs which detect SPAM and reject it, and those which prevent children from accessing adult WEB SITES.

filtering router A ROUTER which examines PACKETS of data and filters those packets which a system administrator has determined should not reach certain destinations. A good example of the use of a filtering router is in implementing a FIREWALL using a PROXY SERVER.

financial EDI EDI which is used within the finance industry. This includes banks, loan companies, building societies, insurance companies, and stockbrokers. Financial EDI is concerned with the transfer of monetary information such as clearing data, cross-payments, debits, and credits across a network. In the past FEDI was confined to organizations which had private networks and which would communicate with similar organizations using DEDICATED LINES. However, there have been a number of experiments of FEDI using the Internet. *See also* ELECTRONIC DATA INTERCHANGE.

Finger Originally a program used by a SYSTEM ADMINISTRATOR which displayed the identities of all the users who were logged in to a network. It was based on the Finger program used in UNIX. However, the term has been extended to describe any utility which looks up user details such as their name, given an email address. The information provided by a Finger utility is usually taken from the member details held by an INTERNET SERVICE PROVIDER. There are a large number of Web-based interfaces to Finger systems.

finger of death The removal of a user from a network facility for antisocial behaviour. It was originally used to describe the ejection of players from MULTI USER DUNGEON games.

fingerprint The sequence of activities that a particular CRACKER carries out when attempting to make an illegal intrusion into a network. While such a sequence does not have the uniqueness of fingerprints it is clear that certain crackers can be identified by their sequence of attempts to enter a network.

firefighter A member of a NEWSGROUP who attempts to dowse a FLAME WAR. Often they are highly abused by those who are engaged in the war.

firehose syndrome What happens when a large number of packets of data are received by a server which is unable handle the load. It is derived from the saying that drinking from a firehose is a good way to rip your lips off.

firewall A combination of hardware and software which surrounds a CLOSED NETWORK and which prevents access to that network. *See* FIREWALL ROUTER, PROXY SERVER, BASTION HOST, and SCREENED HOST FIREWALL. It is a term that is increasingly being used in non-computing contexts: for example, 'He is so self-reliant nothing gets past his firewall.'

firewall router A FILTERING ROUTER which checks packets of data which are destined for a closed network such as an INTRANET. If the data is directly allowed into the network then it passes through. If it is not allowed to pass through, two conditions may hold. The first is that the packet may be destined for a PROXY SERVER; in this case the packet is sent to that computer and processed there. The second is that the packet has been sent by a user who is not allowed access to the network; in this case it is rejected. Firewall routers are also known as PACKET FILTERING GATEWAYS or SCREENING ROUTERS. *See also* BASTION HOST.

firewall server A SERVER that provides a FIREWALL which ensures that a system is secure.

fireworks mode A computer that it is in the process of CRASHING. The term is derived from the fact that the computer often issues large amounts of spurious characters which are received by any computers that are connected to it.

firm In 1997 the Internet Ad Hoc committee proposed a number of new names for

DOMAINS. firm is one of these; it represents businesses.

FIRST *See* FORUM OF INCIDENT RESPONSE AND SECURITY TEAMS.

first-generation Web site WEB SITES which emerged just after WORLD WIDE WEB technology such as MOSAIC started being made generally available. Such sites are characterized by large amounts of text in a single FONT, few if any graphics, no animation, and no FORMS PROCESSING. Effectively the pages found on a first-generation Web site looked very much like their paper equivalents.

first in still here Used to describe the state of messages or TRANSACTIONS in a network where one or more of the computers in the network have CRASHED and where this has led to a suspension of traffic.

FISH *See* FIRST IN STILL HERE.

fishbowl The area of a computer system where an intruder is sent for its behaviour to be observed. *See also* WEB TRAP and MIRROR WORLD.

fish food Inducements to visit a WEB SITE or to browse further than the HOME PAGE. These include free games, competitions, and promotions.

FISH queue A network whose response time is very slow or non-existent. *See* FIRST IN STILL HERE.

FIX *See* FEDERAL INFORMATION EXCHANGE.

flaky An adjective used to describe a system or piece of software which is barely working. For example, it often crashes or has a very poor response time.

flame An insulting or provocative POSTING on a NEWSGROUP or in an EMAIL. *See also* FLAME WAR. A posting to a newsgroup devoted to the UNIX operating system extolling the virtues of Microsoft operating systems is an example of a flame.

flame bait A POSTING to a NEWSGROUP which is deliberately intended to start a FLAME WAR.

flame off When the user of a NEWSGROUP wishes to indicate the end of some text in a POSTING which represents a FLAME, then he or she terminates the message with the words 'flame off'. *See also* FLAME ON.

flame on When the user of a NEWSGROUP wishes to indicate some text in a POSTING which represents a FLAME, he or she precedes the message with the text 'flame on'. *See also* FLAME OFF.

flame war What occurs when a large number of users send FLAME messages to each other, usually within a NEWSGROUP. Such incidents are often sparked by TROLLS and often take some time to calm down. *See also* FIREFIGHTER.

flapping router A ROUTER which transmits updates via a number of different routes.

flash A form of DENIAL OF SERVICE ATTACK where a monitor or VDU is flooded with text.

Flash A proprietary graphics product from the company Macromedia Inc. which uses vector graphic animation technology. To use Flash a PLUG-IN to your BROWSER is necessary. Flash was previously known as FutureSplash.

flash crowd A large number of users who suddenly appear on a network and then disappear. A good example of this was the large number of Web users who suddenly accessed the WEB SITE holding the newly released Starr report which detailed President Clinton's indiscretions. Used in the same sense as flash flood. Flash crowds usually give rise to short-lived, severe response-time problems.

flat file A FILE that holds data which contains no structural information.

flat page A WEB PAGE which does not change during the process of being retrieved by a WEB SERVER and sent to a BROWSER. This is in contrast to DYNAMIC PAGES, created using technologies such as ACTIVE SERVER PAGES or JAVA SERVER PAGES which are altered before being sent, for example by including dynamic data from a database.

FLIP *See* FAST LOCAL INTERNET PROTOCOL.

flood bot A BOT which intrudes into a CHAT ROOM and floods it with a large amount of text. This text appears on the screens of all the participants at the same time. This type of bot effectively carries out a DENIAL OF SERVICE ATTACK. It is more of a nuisance than a security risk.

floodgater An EMAIL user who sends many further irrelevant messages to a recipient who has initially replied favourably.

flooding 1. A NON-ADAPTIVE ROUTING ALGORITHM which is used for ROUTING data stored in PACKETS. This algorithm involves a computer sending the packet out on every transmission line that it is connected to, apart from the line it emerged from. In this way a packet is guaranteed to traverse the current shortest path in a network. When such a packet arrives, all the duplicate packets are then discarded. This is an expensive form of routing as it can increase network TRAFFIC considerably. However, it has its uses: for example, in a military network where robustness and reliability are required. A more efficient version of flooding is known as SELECTIVE FLOODING.
2. Used to describe a DENIAL OF SERVICE ATTACK, when a computer is bombarded with messages. *See*, for example, SYN FLOODING.

flow-based routing A form of ROUTING which uses ADAPTIVE ROUTING ALGORITHMS that base their decisions on the traffic conditions between one computer and all the other computers it is connected to. It makes the decision about which computer to send a PACKET to, based on the TRAFFIC within a SUBNETWORK.

flyspeck 3 Jargon used to describe any FONT that is so small that it renders the text unreadable. It is derived from the fact that fonts are usually identified by their name followed by their point size; for example, Courier 10.

flytrap Jargon term used to describe a computer employed in a FIREWALL. Also used to describe a computer to which a CRACKER is diverted in order for his or her behaviour to be examined. *See also* WEB TRAP and FISHBOWL.

FMTYEWTK Abbreviation for Far More Than You Ever Wanted To Know used in EMAILS and NEWSGROUPS. Usually used to describe voluminous POSTINGS or emails.

FOAF Abbreviation for Friend Of A Friend used in CHAT ROOMS, EMAILS, and NEWSGROUPS. Usually refers to some non-existent person.

FOC Abbreviation for Free Of Charge used in EMAILS and NEWSGROUPS.

FOD *See* FINGER OF DEATH.

folder A collection of FILES administered by an operating system which uses some form of desktop metaphor. The term derives from the fact that the image of a folder is used to identify the collection of files. It is equivalent to the term DIRECTORY.

FOLDOC *See* FREE ONLINE DICTIONARY OF COMPUTING.

follow me service As telecommunications systems have got more sophisticated it has meant that the services offered by telephone companies have become more sophisticated. A conventional follow me service enables a subscriber to use a telephone number to which calls to their mobile, home telephone, or office telephone can be diverted when they are away from them. Such conventional services have now been supplemented by the ability to divert phone calls and FAXES to an EMAIL account: these can then be displayed or replayed on a PC. This type of service is an example of a general trend: the gradual integration of conventional communications services with computer and Internet technology. *See also* FAX TO EMAIL SERVICE.

follow-up A POSTING in a NEWSGROUP that responds to an existing posting. The posting is known as the PARENT MESSAGE.

FOMCL Abbreviation for Falling Off My Chair Laughing used in EMAILS and NEWSGROUPS.

font A collection of alphabetic and other characters which are displayed in a certain style. There are thousands of fonts in existence, ranging from those such as Baskerville which have been in existence for two centuries to more modern fonts such as Futura. One of the problems that WEB DESIGNERS face when developing WEB PAGES is the limited number of fonts that are available to the BROWSERS that access the pages. There are a number of solutions to this problem, the most promising being the use of WEB FONTS.

font and background spoof The process of setting the colour of the background of a WEB PAGE and the font colour to be the same. The text on the page contains keywords which are used to improve the page's chances of being catalogued by a SEARCH ENGINE in such a way that it is prominently positioned when a search occurs. The hope is that search engine staff will not be able to spot this attempt at SPAMDEXING.

font description Text placed in a WEB PAGE which describes a WEB FONT that has been embedded into that page. It includes the name of the font and the location on a SERVER where the font can be found if it is not installed on the BROWSER that is used to display the page.

font site A WEB SITE which contains FONTS that can be DOWNLOADED. Some sites dispense SHAREWARE and others are purely commercial. A few sites dispense free fonts.

font substitution The process that occurs when a document using a particular set of fonts is displayed on a computer on which one or more of the fonts are not installed. The software that is carrying out the display, for example a BROWSER, substitutes a font that looks most like the missing font. This can lead to the design of the document being compromised. *See* WEB FONT for a possible solution to this problem.

fool file A mythical FILE of very stupid remarks issued by the users of the Internet. An example of this would be when one user wishes to lambaste another POSTING to a newsgroup, saying that it deserves to be placed in the fool file.

fork bomb Another name for a LOGIC BOMB.

form A collection of visual objects which enable a user to communicate a request to a computer. For example, when users log into a Windows-based network they are almost invariably faced with a form which contains space for their name and password. A form can consist of a number of diverse elements including boxes into which text can be entered; RADIO BUTTONS which can indicate an option to be taken; MENUS which allow the user the choice of a number of options; and BUTTONS which, when clicked, initiate some process. Forms can form part of a window: for example, an HTML FORM can reside on part of a WEB PAGE, or can occupy the whole of a window.

Format and Protocols The format of the SQL messages sent from a client to an SQL SERVER and the associated HANDSHAKE that occurs. Often abbreviated to FAP.

forms processing The process of reading and processing the contents of a form. FORMS on a WEB PAGE are normally sent to a server where a program written for the COMMON GATEWAY INTERFACE reads the data in the form and carries out an action such as querying or updating a database. Sometimes, when a form is implemented using APPLETS or a SCRIPTING LANGUAGE, all or some of the processing can occur at the client. *See also* BACK END PROCESS.

fortune cookie A wise or pithy saying that often greets users of certain networked systems, usually those administered by the UNIX operating system. Collections of these sayings are stored in a COOKIE FILE and randomly extracted for display to a user.

forum An entity that is similar to a CHAT ROOM but less transient. Discussions in chat rooms are deleted fairly quickly after they occur; in a forum the discussions stay around for a long time. Forums are usually associated with a WEB SITE: for example, a webzine site might have a forum devoted to a particular newsworthy and long-running topic such as Microsoft's influence on the Internet. The term is often used to describe discussion groups on BULLETIN BOARD systems. *See also* WEBLOG.

Forum of Incident Response and Security Teams A collection of organizations, many of them national organizations, modelled on the COMPUTER EMERGENCY RESPONSE TEAM idea. It is a voluntary umbrella organization that mainly offers help to systems administrators who find their systems under attack from intruders.

forward error correction A collection of techniques used for detecting and correcting errors in a one-way communication system. All the techniques rely on extra data being sent with the data that is to be checked.

forward slash The character '/'.

Four11 This is one of the best-known SEARCH ENGINES for locating users of the Internet. *See also* PEOPLE FINDING.

four horsemen of the apocalypse-gram A mythical PACKET of data which would cripple every computer on a NETWORK. It is the electronic version of the holy grail to many CRACKERS.

fourth-generation Web site A WEB SITE which contains a diverse number of media including VIDEO CLIPS, SOUND CLIPS and EXECUTABLE CONTENT. Such sites are highly structured, often featuring ENTRY TUNNELS and EXIT TUNNELS.

four zero four A derogatory term used to describe someone who is not particularly intelligent. It is derived from the error message that occurs when the user of a BROWSER attempts to transfer to a WEB PAGE which does not exist. The error code that is returned by a WEB SERVER when this happens is '404 Not Found'. *See* HTTP STATUS CODE.

four zero four compliant A term used to describe a WEB SITE that has been deleted. It is based on the 404 status code error that occurs when a BROWSER attempts to access a WEB PAGE which does not exist. *See* HTTP STATUS CODE. Also used as a term of abuse: *see* FOUR ZERO FOUR.

FPING A version of the PING utility which carries out the process of sending test messages to a number of computers. It processes a list of computers and sends the messages to them in parallel. In essence it is a faster version of the PING utility.

FPS Abbreviation for FRAMES PER SECOND.

FQDN *See* FULLY QUALIFIED DOMAIN NAME.

fragmentation When a DATAGRAM is too large for a network or for the software that processes it, then it is split up into smaller pieces. This process is known as fragmentation.

frame 1. A scrollable PANE which forms part of a BROWSER window. It can be scrolled independently of other frames in the window. A collection of frames in a WEB PAGE is referred to as a FRAMESET. One popular use of a frame is to hold an INDEX PAGE.
2. A term used to describe a DATAGRAM which is ready to be sent over a network. Normally the term is used when discussing ETHERNETS.
3. A single picture in an ANIMATION or VIDEO CLIP.

frame rate The rate at which the individual images which make up a video signal are displayed; the faster the frame rate the smoother the image seems to be.

frame relay One of the most popular PACKET SWITCHING technologies used for WIDE AREA NETWORKS. It is quite an old technology in Internet terms having been introduced in 1992. It is capable of sending variable length packets over existing equipment at speeds in excess of those found with T1 CARRIER technology. It does not provide for error detection or correction.

frameset A collection of FRAMES in a browser window which can be scrolled independently of each other. Framesets are normally used to facilitate navigation where, for example, one of the frames is used as an index to material contained in other frames. Developing framesets in HTML is quite a difficult task; happily both HTML EDITORS and WYSIWYG EDITORS provide semi-automatic means for carrying this out. Current Web design opinion is that frames should be discouraged.

frames per second The metric used to describe the speed at which ANIMATIONS or VIDEO CLIPS are displayed. Such technology splits the content into a series of frames and the metric quantifies the speed at which these frames are displayed. It is usually abbreviated to fps. The faster the fps the smoother the moving image will seem to be.

Frankenedit One of the problems of writing books about a particular piece of Internet technology is that the technology changes very fast. This has meant that publishers have had to shorten their publication cycles. A Frankenedit is one of the less appealing results of this rush to publication. It is a term used to describe some text produced by an author which has been hurriedly edited to the point where it is in a worse condition than the original version of the text.

frednet Used in connection with some arcane protocol. For example, a PROTOCOL engineer, in attempting to develop some software to interface to a little known protocol, might state that he or she has a 'frednet problem'. Surprisingly, given the ubiquity of the Internet, this is still a major problem for communications companies.

free email During the 1990s people either possessed an EMAIL account by virtue of the fact that they worked for an organization that had the capability of administering this form of communication or they paid a fee to an INTERNET SERVICE PROVIDER. While this is still the case with the majority of email users, there are an increasing number who use free email services. The advance of Web technology has meant that it is quite easy to develop a site which offers free email. Such sites offer registration, email construction, and sending and receiving facilities. They usually make money via BANNER ADVERTS or via other services such as the administration of MAILING LISTS. The facilities that they offer tend to be less comprehensive than those offered by conventional EMAIL READER software.

free Internet service provider The first INTERNET SERVICE PROVIDERS made profits from charging subscribers a fee for access to the Internet. The late 1990s saw an increasing number of so-called free Internet service providers. Such companies make profits in a number of ways: by taking a proportion of the phone bill of the number a subscriber uses, by charging premium telephone rates for their support lines, by insisting that subscribers change their phone company to one for which the service provider receives an introduction fee, or by interrupting subscribers' access to the Internet with adverts paid for by other companies.

freely distributable software Software for which the user pays no charge at all. It is a comparatively recent phenomenon. There are two reasons for individuals or companies developing such software: one is altruistic and the other is for commercial gain. The altruistic reason is that an individual may feel that there is a major demand for a particular program and that, as part of a community, he or she does not want to charge for it. Almost certainly the best example of this is the LINUX operating system, a variant of UNIX, which can be run on a PC and which is maintained by a network of unpaid volunteers. The other reason for developing such software is for commercial gain: a company provides a version of a system or some core software, from which they can profit by offering services, selling computers, or selling add-on software. The best example of this is JAVA, much of which is available at no cost. *See also* FREE SOFTWARE FOUNDATION.

free net A network facility which offers free access to members of a local community through entities such as public libraries.

Free Online Dictionary Of Computing A WEB SITE which contains definitions of many computing terms ranging from academic terms to jargon. It is maintained by volunteers. Entries are posted to the dictionary by users who mainly work in higher education, so the content is quite eclectic. It is often abbreviated to FOLDOC.

Free Software Foundation A charity which is dedicated to distributing free software. It was started in the belief that software should be free. It mainly distributes UNIX software.

freeware Software which can be downloaded and which is free. The practice of providing free software has become increasingly common over the last five years. Both large software companies and individuals offer freeware: the former do it in order to sell peripheral services, premium versions of the software, or components that can be added on to the free product; the latter often do it out of altruism or a strong feeling that all software should be free.

frequency The number of oscillations per second made by an electromagnetic wave. It is measured in HERTZ.

frequency modulation The dispatch of DIGITAL SIGNALS over a TRANSMISSION LINE by changing the frequency of a sine wave.

frequency shift keying An alternative term for FREQUENCY MODULATION.

frequently asked question A question about a particular topic that many users of the Internet may have asked before: for example, 'Where can I download the current version of Internet Explorer?' It is often abbreviated to FAQ. NEWSGROUPS maintain lists of frequently asked questions about the topics which the newsgroup discusses in order to save time in posting copies of the same answer to a question. WEB SITES also maintain FAQ PAGES which fulfil the same function. A question posted to a newsgroup which is a frequently asked question often evinces the response RTFAQ.

frequently asked question list A collection of FREQUENTLY ASKED QUESTIONS stored in a DIRECTORY or FILE. Often known as a FAQ ARCHIVE.

fried Adjective used to describe a computer that has CRASHed. Similar in usage to TOAST.

friends and family virus A VIRUS that works by examining an EMAIL address book and sending multiple emails to all the addresses it finds there. Some variants also send multiple messages to anyone who emails a particular email address. Often such viruses infect not only the address book of the initial recipient but those of other recipients.

fritterware Software which contains FUNCTIONS that serve little if any purpose,

and which consumes a large amount of computer resources.

front end A computer that acts as a slave to another computer, carrying out some dedicated task before passing control and data to the second computer. For example, a PC might be used as a communications handler to a WORKSTATION or a MAINFRAME COMPUTER.

frowny face This is one of the most commonly occurring EMOTICONS. It indicates displeasure or unhappiness and is written as :-(This dictionary contains a list of such emoticons in Appendix 2.

FSK See FREQUENCY SHIFT KEYING.

FTBOMH Abbreviation for From The Bottom Of My Heart used in EMAILS and NEWSGROUPS to indicate total belief in some proposition. It is occasionally used in an amorous context in a chat room.

FTC See FEDERAL TRADE COMMISSION.

FTP See FILE TRANSFER PROTOCOL.

FTP link A HYPERLINK found on a WEB PAGE which, when clicked, starts a dialogue that eventually results in the storage of the FTP file referenced in the link on the CLIENT computer.

FTP server A computer which stores large collections of files which can be DOWNLOADed to users. Normally such servers are isolated from the computer network they are part of because of their vulnerability to attack by CRACKERS. See also WAREZ.

FTP software In the early days of the Internet, if a user wanted to download an FTP file from another computer then it was achieved using a simple COMMAND LANGUAGE, often the one associated with the UNIX operating system. Currently there are two means of downloading FTP files. The first is by clicking an FTP link on a BROWSER. When this happens the user is taken through a dialogue which eventually results in the software being stored on his or her computer. The second way of downloading FTP files is by using a specialized tool. Such tools are WINDOWS-based and allow the user to examine the structure of the FTP directories that are being accessed. In effect FTP software tools enable the user to treat an FTP site as if it is a folder on his or her computer. A good FTP tool provides many functions including Windows-based access, a quick connection to computers holding FTP files, bookmarks to individual FTP sites and FTP files, the facility to have files passed to other applications, and the facility to interrupt and resume the copying of FTP files.

FTTC *See* FIBRE TO THE CURB.

FTTH *See* FIBRE TO THE HOME.

FUD Abbreviation for Fear, Uncertainty and Disinformation used in EMAILS and NEWSGROUPS.

FUI *See* FAKE USER INTERFACE.

full duplex communication This is where transmission occurs in two directions between two hardware entities such as two computers or a computer and a satellite and where the same BANDWIDTH is available in both directions at the same time.

full-page plug-in A PLUG-IN which gives rise to material that is displayed on a full page of a browser window. This is in contrast to an EMBEDDED PLUG-IN where the media displayed occupies part of a page, with material defined by the enclosing HTML surrounding it. When the full page has been browsed a user usually collapses the window in which it is contained and returns to reading the HTML PAGE that gave rise to the displayed material.

full-text index An INDEX used by a SEARCH ENGINE which contains every significant word in the documents that the search engine has catalogued.

fully qualified domain name This is a domain name which starts with the name of a computer and terminates with a TOP-LEVEL DOMAIN. www.open.ac.uk is an example of a fully qualified domain name. Occasionally it is abbreviated to FQDN.

fun bot A BOT or intelligent agent designed for recreational use including games, virtual environments, and virtual reality characters.

function A task that a software product is designed to carry out. For example, one of the (optional) functions of a word processor is to format text so that it has a right-hand margin that is in alignment.

funeral attack An attack on a computer installation which uses old data. For example, an intruder may use an old PASSWORD to enter a system: perhaps a password which was initially allocated to a SYSTEM ADMINISTRATOR.

funnelling The process of attracting visitors to a particular WEB PAGE which, for example, offers free software or contains some inducement, in order to send them on to other pages which have some commercial intent such as advertising a product or a service. *See also* FISH FOOD.

furrfu Used to indicate disbelief and disgust. It is usually found in response to a naive POSTING to a NEWSGROUP. Its derivation is unclear.

furvert Someone who uses the alt.fan. furry NEWSGROUP. This is a newsgroup devoted to users who enjoy emulating fantasy animals. It is worth pointing out that this is not a site about bestiality, just a site catering for users who wish to fantasize on line about possible life as an animal.

fuzzball The name given to a small computer connected to the supercomputers found on the precursor network to NSFNET. It was one of the first computers to communicate using the TCP-IP protocol, but is now only of historical interest.

FWIW Abbreviation for For What It's Worth used in EMAILS and NEWSGROUPS. Used to indicate some degree of defensiveness.

FYA Abbreviation for For Your Amusement used in EMAILS and NEWSGROUPS. Usually it is followed by some text taken from a WEB PAGE, POSTING or EMAIL.

FYE Abbreviation for For Your Entertainment used in EMAILS and NEWSGROUPS. Similar in intent to FYA.

FYI Abbreviation for For Your Information used in EMAILS and NEWSGROUPS. Usually it is followed by some text taken from a WEB PAGE, POSTING or EMAIL which the poster thinks will be useful.

G

G5 Messaging Protocol A proposed standard which would enable FAX and EMAIL messages to be encoded in the same way. This would have the major advantage that software for processing these technologies could be integrated into a single application.

GA 1. Abbreviation for Go Ahead used in CHAT ROOMS, EMAILS, and NEWSGROUPS. **2**. The COUNTRY CODE for Gabon.

gadaboutag A tag which causes an error when the web page in which it is contained is viewed.

GAL Abbreviation for Get A Life used in EMAILS and NEWSGROUPS. Usually used to address someone who is either obsessed with a particular topic or someone whose life totally revolves around the Internet and its associated technologies.

game site A WEB SITE which hosts a number of computer-based games. These games may be online versions of the single-user computer games that are normally supplied on CDs or may be electronic versions of conventional, multi-player games such as bridge or chess where a SERVER mediates a game between a number of players. Often the larger game sites provide CHAT ROOMS and online FORUMS which enable game players to communicate with each other about their interests. The sites make money in a variety of ways: by taking a proportion of the phone charges, by charging a flat-rate subscription fee, or by charging a per-game fee. Many sites offer free games as an inducement to sample games for which a charge is made.

gang FAQ The process whereby a number of Internet users—usually members of a NEWSGROUP—send a copy of an FAQ to someone who has posted an old question to the newsgroup. This is a forceful way of making the recipient realise that he or she should look in an FAQ ARCHIVE before POSTING a question.

gateway A computer which acts as a router on the Internet. It processes DATAGRAMS flowing through the network, determines which SUBNETWORK they are destined for and sends them on to their destination. If the destination is a subnetwork connected to the gateway then it sends the data to that network. A gateway can also convert from one PROTOCOL to another: say from TCP-IP to a proprietary protocol used by a subnetwork.

gateway page A WEB PAGE constructed in such a way that a SPIDER associated with a SEARCH ENGINE catalogues it so that the page always appears in a prominent position in a search. Often such a page is hidden from the user and the spider is diverted to it via a technique known as AGENT NAME DELIVERY. It is also known as a BRIDGE PAGE.

Gateway-to-Gateway Protocol A PROTOCOL which enables GATEWAYS to communicate with other gateways. Typically a gateway-to-gateway protocol is used to inform other gateways about data which can be used for routing messages within a network. Ideally, TCP-IP should be used as a gateway-to-gateway protocol, but for the sake of efficiency special-purpose protocols are used.

Gbps Abbreviation for GIGABITS per second, a measure of transmission speed.

GDS *See* GLOBAL DIRECTORY SERVICE.

geek Someone who is very proficient in modern computer technology. It can refer to someone who has a huge indepth knowledge of some piece of software or someone who has a good broad knowledge of a variety of software. Not normally used as a derogatory term. However, it can be used derogatorily in a social context, as in the term GEEK OUT. *See also* ALPHA GEEK and TECHIE.

geek code Occasionally used to describe programs written by someone who has an advanced knowledge of the technology used for developing the code or the technical application area.

geek out The process of talking about technical computing matters in a social context such as a party.

gender bender An alternative to GENDER MENDER. It describes a hardware connection between two MALE CONNECTIONS or two FEMALE CONNECTIONS.

gender blender Sometimes used as an alternative to GENDER MENDER or GENDER BENDER.

gender mender A cable connector which is used to correct mismatches between two sockets which either have two MALE CONNECTIONS or two FEMALE CONNECTIONS.

genealogy The process of researching information about ancestors. The WORLD WIDE WEB contains a large number of genealogical databases and has provided a huge fillip to what was once an activity that was carried out by a very small number of people. There is a large variety of genealogy sites, tools for displaying family trees as WEB PAGES, and a number of different FORUMS.

general public license A software licence promoted by the FREE SOFTWARE FOUNDATION which allows the individual customer to use software for non-commercial purposes. Sometimes abbreviated to GPL.

generic font A FONT which can be expected to reside on any computer that accesses a WEB PAGE. A typical generic font is Times New Roman.

get a life An expression used in connection with someone who has had their life taken over by the Internet: for example, someone who is an addicted user of NEWSGROUPS. Often abbreviated to GAL.

GFN Abbreviation for Gone For Now used in CHAT ROOMS. It usually indicates that a participant has taken leave of the chat room for an extended period.

GFR *See* GRIM FILE REAPER.

ghost The image of text typed by the user of a CHAT ROOM after the user has disconnected from the chat room.

ghost imaging The process of copying the whole of the hard disk of a computer to another computer. The second computer then behaves exactly like the first computer when it is started up.

GIF *See* GRAPHICS INTERCHANGE FORMAT.

GIF89A The latest version of the GRAPHICS INTERCHANGE FORMAT for graphical images. It has improved on previous versions of the standard in two respects. The first is that it allows for TRANSPARENT GIFs; the second is that it enables GIF ANIMATIONS to be developed.

GIF animation A simple form of animation which was very popular on the Web in its early days and is still frequently seen. It consists of drawing a number of GIF graphics which differ slightly from each other and displaying them sequentially. For example, a simple animation which consisted of a dog walking across a BANNER ADVERT would be created by drawing separate pictures of the dog in slightly different positions along the path that it walks, and then displaying each picture for a short period of time. This form of animation is just the electronic equivalent of the flick books which have been used by children down the ages. Writing a program to carry out simple GIF animations is straightforward. There are, however, a number of tools which enable you to implement animations without carrying out any programming. Some of these tools are SHAREWARE. *See also* GIF ANIMATION TOOL.

GIF animation tool A program which takes a series of graphics expressed in the GRAPHICS INTERCHANGE FORMAT. Each image represents one frame of an animation which differs slightly from the previous frame and from the next frame. The tool takes each frame, displays it for a short period, and then displays the next frame. There are a large number of utilities which enable the WEB DESIGNER to produce GIF ANIMATIONS including SHAREWARE programs. Increasingly tools for developing WEB PAGES contain facilities for creating the animations and embedding them in Web pages.

gigabit A unit of measurement which is 1,073,741,824 BITS. It is used to measure transmission speed in a network.

gigabyte A unit of storage equivalent to 1,073,741,824 BYTES.

gigalapse What happens when a SERVER is unable to respond adequately to CLIENTS when an excessive demand occurs. The users of the clients experience a poor RESPONSE TIME.

GIGO Abbreviation for Garbage In Garbage Out used in EMAILS and NEWSGROUPS. It refers to the fact that if a program is well constructed, but receives erroneous data, it will produce erroneous results. However, its use has expanded considerably outside this narrow interpretation and now, for example, encompasses the idea that a faulty conclusion is reached from faulty premises.

GII See GLOBAL INFORMATION INFRASTRUCTURE.

GILC See GLOBAL INTERNET LIBERTY CAMPAIGN.

GIWIST Abbreviation for Gee I Wish I'd Said That used in NEWSGROUPS.

GL Abbreviation for Good Luck used in CHAT ROOMS, EMAILS and NEWSGROUPS.

glass wire Jargon for a FIBRE OPTIC CABLE.

glassroots campaign A campaign conducted over the Internet. A recent example of such a campaign is the one against the Microsoft implementation of the JAVA programming language.

global directory service A DIRECTORY SERVICE which administers the resources in a number of networks, many of which could use disparate technologies and PROTOCOLS. The industry standard for global directory services is x500.

Global Information Infrastructure A term coined by the Clinton administration in the United States for the collection of computers, computer NETWORKS, and transmission lines that make up the INFORMATION SUPERHIGHWAY.

Global Internet Liberty Campaign An organization which has been set up to promote free speech and personal liberty on the Internet.

global name service A NAME SERVICE which is used by a number of networks. Almost certainly the best example of a global naming service is the INTERNET DOMAIN NAME SERVICE which administers the names of resources over the whole of the Internet.

global namespace The collection of names that is administered by a GLOBAL NAME SERVICE: for example, the DOMAIN NAMES administered by the INTERNET DOMAIN NAME SERVICE.

Global Positioning System A system which determines position on the earth. It works by sampling signals from up to six navigational satellites which are fixed in the earth's orbit. Usually abbreviated to GPS.

Global System for Mobile Communications A major standard for mobile phone services which has been adopted by the majority of countries outside the USA. For example, it is the standard for mobile communications within Europe, with commentators predicting that the adoption of this standard will give European countries a head start over the United States in MOBILE COMPUTING. Usually abbreviated to GSM.

global variable A term that is sometimes used as an alternative to ENVIRONMENT VARIABLE.

glowing The process of making a GRAPHIC IMAGE glow by placing a highly coloured diffuse background behind it.

glue Any hardware or software which is used to connect two software or hardware entities: for example, software which enables a WEB SERVER to communicate with some non-standard software such as an arcane DATABASE MANAGEMENT SYSTEM. It is often used to describe hardware or software converters which mediate between two PROTOCOLS.

glyph The visual representation of a character in a FONT when displayed on an output device such as a monitor or printer.

GMAB Abbreviation for Give Me A Break used in EMAILS and NEWSGROUPS. Often employed by a user who is being heavily criticized by others.

GMTA Abbreviation for Great Minds Think Alike used in EMAILS and NEWS-GROUPS.

Godwin's law A law that states that as the length of a THREAD proceeds on a NEWSGROUP the probability of a comparison with Hitler or the Nazis approaches one. A number of groups have the tradition that when this happens the discussion is regarded as over. *See* HITLER.

godzillagram A network message that, in theory, could be sent to every computer on the Internet. This is an example of an INTERNET HOLY GRAIL.

going down 1. What happens when, because of either a hardware or a software fault, a computer becomes unavailable for use. The term is normally used to describe computers found on a network. **2**. A term synonymous with DRILL DOWN which refers to the process of navigating deeper and deeper HYPERLINKS in a WEB SITE.

going postal Used to describe the process of being highly stressed. It is derived from the fact that many postal workers in the United States have become stressed and, as a result, gone on the rampage with a gun. Used in NEWSGROUPS and in EMAILS.

gonk Unacceptably exaggerating or embellishing the truth. For example 'John, you're gonking again. You cannot have built a supercomputer from your two PCs and your pocket calculator.'

Google A SEARCH ENGINE which has rapidly become one of the most popular search engines on the Internet. During a period when most search engines have transmuted into PORTALS, Google has remained a pure search engine with a very simple interface.

Gopher A precursor to the WORLD WIDE WEB developed by the University of Minnesota in order to make distributed information easy to access. Gopher sites are rapidly decreasing in number although there are still quite a few that exist because the effort of converting them to WEB SITES is too large. Gopher sites can be accessed via GOPHER LINKS embedded into WEB PAGES as ANCHORS.

Gopher link A link to a GOPHER site embedded into a WEB PAGE via a URL. When the text associated with the link is clicked in a BROWSER the user is taken to the Gopher site. Such links can often be found in FIRST-GENERATION WEB SITES, but with the rapid demise of Gopher services they are now something of a historical curiosity.

Gopherspace The area of the Internet searchable by GOPHER.

gossip architecture A software architecture used to implement DATA REPLICATION. The SERVERS which contain replicated data, exchange messages called gossip messages in order to inform each other that they have changed and the nature of the change that has taken place.

gossip replication A technique used to support DATA REPLICATION where servers storing replicated data exchange messages in order to keep each other up to date and in synchronization with each other. The messages are known as gossip messages.

gov A type of Internet DOMAIN associated with governmental institutions: for example, www.FedForum.gov.

government bot A BOT which carries out some task that is related to government, such as accessing planning data, retrieving census data, or finding tax details.

government gigabit In 1989 the US government decided to fund a number of experimental networks which were planned to work at a transmission rate of 1 GIGABIT. In some of these networks the data transmission rate was smaller, approximately 600 megabits per second, although if you counted the speed in both directions then the gigabit target could be said to have been achieved. A number of cynical computer scientists decided to call the 600 megabit speed a government giga-bit after the US government had claimed that the funded networks had met their speed targets.

GPL *See* GENERAL PUBLIC LICENSE.

GPS *See* GLOBAL POSITIONING SYSTEM.

GRAD Abbreviation for Grinning Running And Ducking used in EMAILS and NEWSGROUPS. Usually used by someone who has perpetrated a practical joke or written something in semi-seriousness that he or she knows will attract criticism.

gradient The gradual transition from one colour to another colour in a graphic image, usually a background colour.

gramify The tendency for hackers to add the ending 'gram' to words and phrases. *See, for example,* FOUR HORSEMEN OF THE APOCALYPSEGRAM and NASTYGRAM.

grammar flame A FLAME which refers to a POSTING to a NEWSGROUP and which criticizes the poor grammar in the posting. Often the flame does not respond to any of the points made in the original posting.

graphical user interface A term used to describe a collection of visual objects such as BUTTONS, WINDOWS, TEXT BOXES, and MENUS which make up the interface to a computer program. It is usually abbreviated to GUI.

graphic anchor A graphic image embedded in a WEB PAGE which, when clicked by the user of a BROWSER, displays the page which is referenced by the URL associated with the anchor. Graphical anchors can be bullets, icons, or advertisements. *See also* TEXT ANCHOR, IMAGE MAP, and BANNER ADVERT.

graphic file format The way that the data representing a GRAPHIC IMAGE is stored in a FILE. For example, it describes the meaning of the data that describes individual PIXELS in the graphic. There are a number of these formats, including GRAPHICS INTERCHANGE FORMAT, JOINT PHOTOGRAPHIC EXPERTS GROUP, and PORTABLE NETWORK GRAPHIC.

graphic format A term synonymous with GRAPHIC FILE FORMAT.

graphic image The visual instantiation of a file which stores a drawing or illustration. The transition from FIRST-GENERATION WEB SITES to SECOND-GENERATION WEB SITES was partly marked by the ability to display graphic images in a number of formats such as the GRAPHICS INTERCHANGE FORMAT.

Graphics Interchange Format A GRAPHIC FORMAT standard used for images and an example of a BITMAPPED GRAPHIC format. It is the most popular image format currently being employed on the World Wide Web. It uses a compression scheme for transmission over the Internet known as LEMPEL ZIV WELSH CODING which is a LOSSLESS COMPRESSION SCHEME that results in no information being lost when the graphic is compressed. GIF supports 256 colours and is used on a Web page when colour depth is not important, or if there are a limited number of colours in an image. The current GIF format is GIF89A which has a number of additional features over earlier versions such as transparency. GIF ANIMATION is a popular technique used for developing simple animations suitable for Web pages. This format is supported by virtually all graphics programs.

greater than The symbol > used to identify the end of a TAG in the HYPERTEXT MARKUP LANGUAGE.

great runes Text rendered only in upper case. *See also* SHOUTING.

great worm Sometimes used to describe the INTERNET WORM. A VIRUS which, in the late 1980s, paralysed a large part of the embryonic Internet.

greek The process of laying out text in an abstract way using simple lines or dots in order to gain a feel of how it would look on a page, either a textual page or a WEB PAGE. It can also describe the process of displaying a page using random words which have been cut and pasted and then replicated. The term is used in the printing trade and has been adopted by WEB DESIGNERS. It is sometimes used as a verb. *See also* LOREM IPSUM.

grey bar land The almost hallucinogenic state a computer user is in when staring at the grey bar display that accompanies long computer processes such as downloading a very large WEB PAGE. It is occasionally used in day-to-day speech to indicate that someone is not paying full attention to something. For example, 'he didn't respond to my suggestion. I think he was in grey bar land.'

grey matter Older business staff (30+) hired by young start-up Internet companies in order to provide a veneer of being established and wise. Often a funding agency such as a venture capitalist insists on a particular proportion of grey matter employees to younger employees.

grim file reaper A program which deletes FILES stored on a computer. Often these programs only delete certain files: for example, those with a particular FILE EXTENSION. The types of files to be deleted are specified in a script read by the program. Sometimes these programs are used to devastating effect when they are captured and used by VIRUSES which have been illegally introduced into a computer system.

Gripenet An internal IBM network that has been used to carry criticisms of IBM and its policies.

gronking A verb used to describe a malfunctioning computer.

group account An ACCOUNT associated with a group of users. Group accounts can be used to associate a series of ACCESS CONTROLS with a group of users: for example, ensuring that the group can only read or write to specific FILES in a computer system. Group accounts are also used for day-to-day accounting purposes, such as keeping project-based data on computer use which can then be used for billing purposes.

groupware The software that is employed to organize and coordinate the activities of a group of people. This group may be static—for example, they may all form part of a department within a company—or may be transitory—for example they may be assigned to a fixed-term project. Typical groupware administers EMAIL, runs diaries, fixes the date of

meetings, acts as a FILE SERVER, dispenses documents required for meetings, coordinates staff activities, issues reminders, reports on a project's day-to-day status, and produces high-level reports on the progress of a project.

groupware server A SERVER which manages the interaction between a number of users of a GROUPWARE system. It receives messages such as requests for diary dates, sends messages such as reminders of meetings that are to occur in the near future, and maintains files which contain entities such as personal schedules, diaries, versions of documents and MAILING LISTS. Such servers hold data which supports groupware software and will often act as a MAIL SERVER, CALENDAR SERVER, and FILE SERVER.

GSM *See* GLOBAL SYSTEM FOR MOBILE COMMUNICATIONS.

GTGB Abbreviation for Got To Go Bye used in CHAT ROOMS.

GTRM Abbreviation for Going To Read Mail used in CHAT ROOMS.

GTSY Abbreviation for Glad To See You used in CHAT ROOMS.

Guardian An AUTHORIZATION and AUTHENTICATION scheme developed by the INTERNIC which provided for the secure storage of DOMAIN NAME records.

gubbish A portmanteau word made from the words garbage and rubbish used in POSTINGS to NEWSGROUPS and EMAIL messages. *See also* RUBBAGE. It is used as a higher form of abuse than its component words.

guest book A FORM filled in by a visitor when accessing a WEB SITE. Often these forms ask for basic information such as your name, EMAIL address, and phone number. They are sometimes used for legitimate purposes: for example, for the notification of Web site updates. However, guest books are often used by MAILING LIST compilers who sell the lists to users who carry out SPAMMING. WEB DESIGNERS use guest books with discretion: often, asking a visitor to a Web site to fill in a guest book results in their leaving the site.

GUI *See* GRAPHICAL USER INTERFACE.

guiltware SHAREWARE for which the programmer asks payment as a donation to charity. *See also* CHARITYWARE and CARE-WARE. It has also been used to describe software which is adorned with some message in a device such as a SPLASH SCREEN telling the user how hard the programmer who has developed the software has worked and how he or she needs money.

Gulliver The SPIDER used by the Northern Light SEARCH ENGINE.

guru site A WEB SITE which has been put together by someone who is very knowledgeable about a particular topic. Such a site contains myriads of links to Web sites which are relevant to that topic and also a commentary associated with each of the links. *See also* PORTAL and LINK FARM.

GYPO Abbreviation for Get Your Pants Off used in CHAT ROOMS. Often used amorously.

gz A FILE EXTENSION for files condensed using the ZIP algorithm on UNIX systems.

H

hack The use of a facility in a language, usually a programming language or a MARKUP LANGUAGE, for which it is not intended. A hack is normally used to overcome a weakness in the language. The term is also used to describe some use of a language which is in opposition to its philosophy. Probably the best example of a hack relevant to this dictionary is the use of the TABLE feature in HTML to provide more accurate layout control than the original features of the language would allow. The table feature was originally used to provide tabular layout of figures and text; however, the original inadequacies of HTML led many designers to use tables for the precise positioning of graphics and chunks of text. *See also* SINGLE-PIXEL GIF and SHIM. The word can also be used as a verb.

hacker 1. Someone who uses a high degree of computer skill to carry out unauthorized acts within a network: for example, a hacker might have no access rights to a network, yet might bypass all the access controls and carry out some act such as leaving a file in a public directory which describes what they have done. The action of hackers can range from relatively harmless ones to malicious acts where system resources are incapacitated.
2. Someone who is possessed of a high degree of computer skills and who employs them in a conventional, non-criminal way. Because of this duality of meaning, hackers who are in the second category use the word CRACKER to describe those in the first category. The second meaning predates the first.

HAGN Abbreviation for Have A Good Night used in CHAT ROOMS.

hakspek A form of speedwriting or shorthand employed by users of NEWS-GROUPS or BULLETIN BOARD systems. It involves replacing syllables and whole words by single letters or digits. For example the hakspek 'c u 2day' stands for 'See you today'.

half bridge An OBJECT REQUEST BROKER that is described as being CORBA compliant must either implement the INTERNET INTER-ORB PROTOCOL or provide a connection to this PROTOCOL. The connection is known as a half bridge.

half duplex communication Used to describe transmission in a network where data can travel in both directions but not simultaneously.

half smiley face One of the most commonly occurring EMOTICONS. It indicates some form of knowingness and is written as ;-) Appendix 2 details the main emoticons.

Hand-Held Device Markup Language A MARKUP LANGUAGE used to define the documents which are displayed on hand-held devices such as cellular phones, pagers, and personal digital assistants. The language allows access to the WORLD WIDE WEB via such devices. It is often abbreviated to HDML.

handle A pseudonym used to hide a contributor to a NEWSGROUP or someone who has sent an EMAIL. It is derived from citizen's band culture. *See also* SOCK PUPPET.

handshake The process whereby two entities on the Internet start the process of transferring data to and from each other. The handshake acts as a coordination point for such transfers. Usually the two entities swap information about themselves during the handshake. This information is needed when they start passing data: for example, the format of the data expected. *See* HANDSHAKE PROTOCOL.

handshake protocol 1. PROTOCOL that is used to establish a connection between two entities on a computer network. The protocol establishes the link and usually passes information about each entity to the other.

2. Within the SECURE SOCKETS LAYER a handshake protocol is used to establish an encrypted link between a SERVER and a CLIENT and is used to exchange information such as the ENCRYPTION ALGORITHM used.

hang The event that occurs when software or hardware has stopped functioning waiting for an event which will never happen. For example, a SERVER in a network hangs if no CLIENTS can connect to it. It is also used to describe what happens to software which stops processing because it contains a programming error. Hanging is usually due to a software error or hardware error.

haque An elegant variant spelling of HACK.

hard address Synonym for a PHYSICAL ADDRESS.

hard boot Synonym for BOOT.

hardware address Synonym for PHYSICAL ADDRESS.

hardware replication The process of constructing a system out of a number of similar computers in order to achieve a high reliability. There are a number of ways of arranging for these replica computers to operate. One way is to execute them in parallel and continually check their answers; if one disagrees then it must be malfunctioning. Once this happens the malfunctioning computer is stopped and often replaced by a spare computer. A cheaper way of using hardware replication is to keep one computer running and monitor its operations; when it malfunctions work is immediately transferred to a spare computer, a technique known as HOT SWAPPING. *See also* DATA REPLICATION and FAULT-TOLERANT SYSTEM.

hardwired advert An advert on a WEB PAGE which stays on the page until it is physically moved. This is in contrast to the DYNAMIC ROTATION of adverts where an ADVERT SERVER periodically replaces BANNER ADVERTS in a page.

hash function Synonymous with MESSAGE DIGEST.

hash sign The symbol #.

Hashed Message Authentication Code A technique which uses a KEY and a MESSAGE DIGEST to strengthen an existing message digest.

hate site A web site which has been set up by users who are dissatisfied with the products or services of another company, usually a major company. Often the name of the company is incorporated in the name of the site with words such as 'suck' or 'useless' appended. Also known as a suck site.

HCI *See* HUMAN COMPUTER INTERFACE.

HDML *See* HAND-HELD DEVICE MARKUP LANGUAGE.

HDSL *See* HIGH BIT RATE DIGITAL SUBSCRIBER LINE.

headend A central distribution point in a CABLE TELEVISION network which sends data to subscribers.

header The text that appears before the main body of an EMAIL message. It contains information such as the date of origin of the message, the EMAIL ADDRESS of the sender, and the subject of the message.

heartbeat A signal periodically emitted by software or hardware, often for synchronization purposes. For example, a program may emit heartbeats in order to tell another program that it is still waiting for some data and has not terminated.

heat index A measure of the amount of animated discussion of a topic in a NEWSGROUP.

heavy client Synonym for THICK CLIENT.

Hello Protocol An example of an INTERIOR GATEWAY PROTOCOL: a PROTOCOL that is used to communicate data to and from GATEWAYS inside a network rather than from one network to another. It is a much less popular protocol than the ROUTING INFORMATION PROTOCOL.

help page A WEB PAGE which contains information that helps a user access the site in which the page is embedded. For example, it might provide details on the QUERY LANGUAGE used for searching the site.

helper application A program which adds some functionality to another program. The best-known helper applications are PLUG-INS which provide extra functionality to BROWSERS. Often such applications are susceptible to VIRUS attack.

hertz The unit used to measure FREQUENCY, named after the German physicist Heinrich Hertz. It is usually abbreviated to Hz.

heterogeneous network A computer network which uses a variety of PROTOCOLS. Occasionally the term is used to describe a network which has a number of different computers running different PLATFORMS connected to it. A typical heterogeneous network uses a proprietary protocol for communication within the network and TCP-IP for connection with other networks.

heuristic analysis A process used by ANTI-VIRUS SOFTWARE which detects viruses by monitoring behaviour rather than looking for physical signs such as the existence of a strange FILE.

HHIS Abbreviation for Hanging Head In Shame used in EMAILS and NEWS-GROUPS.

hidden URL A UNIFORM RESOURCE LOCA-TOR which references a WEB PAGE that is not referenced by any other Web page. Such a URL is given to a restricted set of users so that they can access the page in a semi-private fashion.

hierarchical naming The naming of resources in a system which splits the name into a number of areas and subareas: for example, if network A consisted of two SUBNETWORKS B and C, and B contained the computer named Server1 then a way of naming Server1 would be A.B.Server1. If there was a computer known as Server1 on subnetwork C then this would be named A.C.Server1. A hierarchic naming convention such as this ensures that duplication of individual names can be achieved, yet ensures that individual resources associated with a name can be uniquely identified. The best-known example of hierarchic naming is the INTERNET DOMAIN NAME SERVICE.

hierarchical routing This is a form of ROUTING where a network is divided into a number of SUBNETWORKS called regions. Each region contains details that are used for routing within the region but does not contain information about other regions. This does not lead to an optimal routing solution but it does reduce network overhead.

hierarchic caching The organization of CACHES into a hierarchy of levels. A typical two-level cache used for dispensing WEB PAGES might have local caches associated with a cluster of computers connected via a LOCAL AREA NETWORK and a regional cache which serves all the computers in all these networks. If a BROWSER resident on the local network asks for a Web page which is not in the local cache for its network, then the regional cache is consulted. If the page requested is found there, it is returned via the local cache to the browser that asked for it. If it is not found, it is retrieved from the server on which it resides. *See also* CACHING, CACHING POLICY and CACHING PROXY SERVER.

Hierarchic JPEG A variant of the JOINT PHOTOGRAPHIC EXPERTS GROUP (JPEG) image format which stores a graphic in a number of increasingly high resolution versions. As the image is transferred to an application or a BROWSER the lowest resolution image is displayed first and displayed quickly; after this, increasingly high resolution versions of the graphic are displayed. In this way a low-resolution version of the graphic is displayed quickly with the final high resolution image being eventually displayed. The intent of this format is the same as an INTERLACED GIF graphic although the method used is different.

HIG Abbreviation for How's It Going used in CHAT ROOMS, EMAILS, and NEWSGROUPS.

High Bit Rate Digital Subscriber Line A form of DIGITAL SUBSCRIBER LINE technology which allocates BANDWIDTH symmetrically and can act as a replacement for T1 CARRIER communication circuits. It is often abbreviated to HDSL.

high ping A connection to the Internet which is slow. It is derived from the PING utility which sends a test packet of data to a computer which then sends it back. The utility checks out a connection and produces some timing information.

hit The act of reading a WEB PAGE using a browser. Sometimes it is used to describe a visit to a whole WEB SITE. The hits that occur when visitors enter a Web site can be found in a WEB LOG FILE. Information about hits is used by WEBMASTERS to optimize a Web site and by ecommerce companies to gauge the effectiveness of their Web marketing. *See also* VISIT and CLICKSTREAM.

hit and run mailing The process of acquiring an account with an INTERNET SERVICE PROVIDER which includes a mail account, using that account for SPAMMING and then moving to another account before the recipients of the spam have had time to complain.

hit counter A graphic which is embedded on a WEB PAGE that displays the number of visitors to that page. Hit counters have two functions: first, they enable a company to see how successful a particular page on a WEB SITE is in attracting customers and, second, they are often used as a form of bragging by WEBMASTERS. Hugely visible hit counters are rapidly becoming the electronic version of the furry dice found hanging from the back windows of cars. To program a hit counter requires a little skill in CGI PROGRAMMING; however, most INTERNET SERVICE PROVIDERS are able to supply such counters ready programmed for inclusion in their customer's Web pages. WEB DESIGNERS tend to frown on the visible use of hit counters. *See also* COUNTER SCRIPT and HIT SLUT.

hit slut A WEBMASTER who is obsessed by the number of HITS that his or her WEB SITE gets. This obsession can get to the point where it dominates important activities such as keeping the site up to date, checking for invalid links, and finding ORPHAN LINKS.

Hitler The termination of a THREAD, usually by a MODERATOR, within a newsgroup. Usually it is used as a verb. *See* GODWIN'S LAW for the derivation.

HMAC *See* HASHED MESSAGE AUTHENTICATION CODE.

hoax email An EMAIL which attempts to garner some money from the recipient. This may range from emails which ask for a postcard to be sent to a dying child to fake VIRUS warnings.

holised A term used to describe an employee who has been forbidden to post any material that is company-related on a NEWSGROUP or any other similar forum. This is something that is increasingly becoming a specific clause in the contracts of information technology workers.

hollywired The MEDIA CONVERGENCE between film, television, and networking evidenced both by the development of technology to interface or combine these technologies or the merger of companies which have expertise in the areas.

holy war Popular NEWSGROUP discussions which recur time and time again with participants often taking very pro and anti stances. Holy wars often generate FLAME WARS. Typical examples of holy wars are the discussions about the merits of the Windows series of operating systems as compared to UNIX or whether Microsoft is a positive influence for the Internet industry.

home box The computer used by industrial software developers at home.

home page The first page that a visitor to a WEB SITE encounters. It has to fulfil two functions: first it has to give the visitor some indication of the content and purpose of the Web site; second it has to provide the visitor with an incentive to continue the visit so that they view lower-level pages in the site. Designing a WEB PAGE so that both these functions are satisfied and, at the same time, ensuring that the page does not occupy too much memory and leads to a fast DOWNLOAD time, requires the highest design skills.

home page directory A directory of home pages maintained by an INTERNET SERVICE PROVIDER. Such directories are often accessible to non-customers of the service provider.

homosexual adaptor Used as an alternative to GENDER MENDER for a hardware adaptor which connects two MALE CONNECTIONS.

honey pot Part of a computer system which looks attractive to an intruder but which is heavily monitored by security software. Such honey pots are used to divert intruders into a computer system in order that they can be caught.

honeypot Another name for a TEERGRUBE or FLYTRAP.

hop When data is sent across a NETWORK it proceeds via a number of computers in the network. The transfer from one computer to another is called a hop. A number of ROUTING methods attempt to minimize the number of hops.

hose Used to describe the fact that a program has used so much hardware resource that it has seriously degraded the performance of a computer or a network. It is also used to describe any thick cabling used to connect devices together in a network.

hosery Slang term for the collection of cabling used in a computer network.

host The name used to describe a computer connected to a network—usually the Internet. The term END SYSTEM is also occasionally used. A host on the Internet has an INTERNET PROTOCOL ADDRESS.

hostmaster The name of an EMAIL account which is concerned with receiving messages associated with network administration. Therefore, if there is a problem with network administration at domain open.ac.uk it is necessary to send an email to hostmaster@open.ac.uk.

host name The name given to a computer attached to a network. If the network uses TCP-IP as its communication medium the host name will consist of a symbolic name followed by the domain name. For example, www.open.ac.uk refers to the server www (usually a WEB SERVER) found at the domain open.ac.uk.

hot desking Working for a company which does not give you a permanent office or even a desk. When you arrive at work you normally plug your mobile computer into the first available network connection and work from the desk associated with that connection. This is a form of working adopted by companies whose staff are often found on other premises: for example, staff employed by a computer consultancy company or a sales company. *See also* HOTELLING, TELECOTTAGING, and TELEWORKING.

hotelling A way of organizing an office which has been made possible by DISTRIBUTED SYSTEM technology. The term arises from the fact that office location and assignment is carried out in the same way as rooms are assigned in a hotel: when a worker arrives he or she is assigned an office for a few hours or a day rather than being assigned a permanent office. Hotelling is usually carried out in conjunction with TELEWORKING. It is best suited to companies where there are a high proportion of staff out of the office: for example, sales staff visiting clients. The word was first invented by up-market prostitutes to describe the way they work. Se also HOT DESKING.

HotJava One of the design aims of the JAVA programming language was that it would be capable of developing snippets of program code known as APPLETS which would be incorporated into WEB PAGES. In the early period of Java's life the only browser that could properly process applets was HotJava. This was a BROWSER developed by Sun Microsystems. A few months after the launch of Java, PLUG-INS allowed the more popular browsers to accept applets. Eventually, even plug-ins became redundant, since the mainstream browsers had applet support built in. This has meant that the HotJava browser has become marginalized, although it still has a life as a testbed for new Java ideas.

hot list A collection of URLs which identify those WEB SITES which have superior content and organization. Often these are embedded as HYPERLINKs within a WEB PAGE. There are a number of Web sites which feature hot lists, some of which are general and others which are specific to a particular topic. The term was originally used by the developers of the MOSAIC browser to describe URLs which had been saved by the user for future use. *See also* BEST OF THE WEB and COOL SITE OF THE DAY.

hot site A WEB SITE which is very popular. Its popularity might have been achieved by excellent CONTENT and good design or because it contains material that is in demand for other reasons: for example, the fact that the site contains the first specifications of a particularly sought-after piece of hardware or text linked to a major news story. Hot sites which achieve their status because of superior design and content are often featured in HOT SITE OF THE DAY sites and BEST OF THE WEB sites. *See also* COOL.

hot site of the day A WEB SITE which regularly features other sites that are superior because of their excellent CONTENT and good design. *See also* HOT LIST and BEST OF THE WEB.

hot spot A part of a system which is heavily used or executed. For example, programs have hot spots that are regions of code which are frequently executed; networks also have hotspots (known as CHOKE POINTS) where traffic is at its heaviest.

hot swapping The process of immediately using a spare computer as soon as a computer in a network malfunctions. *See also* HARDWARE REPLICATION and FAULT-TOLERANT SYSTEM.

Hotbot One of the largest SEARCH ENGINES indexing over 100 million WEB PAGES.

hourglass mode The process of waiting for some lengthy event to occur. It refers to the hourglass icon associated with the Windows operating system. This icon appears when a process occurs which is destined to take a long time. Hourglass mode is occasionally used in normal conversation to describe the state of someone who is not paying full attention to what is being said by another person: for example, 'Ignore her, she's in hourglass mode.' *See also* GREY BAR LAND.

hqx A FILE EXTENSION for files which are associated with the Macintosh OPERATING SYSTEM which can be safely transferred over the Internet.

HTH Abbreviation for Hope This Helps used in EMAILS and NEWSGROUPS.

htm One of the FILE EXTENSIONS for FILES containing HTML code. The other is html.

html One of the FILE EXTENSIONS for FILES containing the HTML code. The other is htm.

HTML Acronym for HYPERTEXT MARKUP LANGUAGE.

HTML author Synonym for HTML EDITOR.

HTML checker A tool which examines the HTML for a WEB PAGE and checks that it is syntactically correct and that BROWSERS will have no problems displaying it. *See also* HTML VALIDATION SITE.

HTML editor A program which provides a wealth of facilities for developing WEB PAGES. The most sophisticated provide facilities for the automatic insertion of TAGS, HYPERLINKS, and GRAPHIC IMAGES, the checking of HTML for adherence to a particular BROWSER, the previewing of a page that has been constructed, the construction of ANIMATIONS, the copying of Web pages to a WEB SERVER using the FILE TRANSFER PROTOCOL, the laying out of text on a page using precise positioning, and the formatting of text. The aim of an HTML editor is to isolate the user from the concrete details of the HYPERTEXT MARKUP LANGUAGE. HTML editors are sometimes known as HTML AUTHORS.

HTML form A set of WIDGETs which implements a FORM, which is embedded in an HTML PAGE, and which is defined using the HYPERTEXT MARKUP LANGUAGE. It contains all the visual objects that you would normally associate with forms such as BUTTONS and TEXT BOXES. When a user employs a form, for example a form which implements a GUEST BOOK, the data that is contained on the form is sent to the WEB SERVER that stores the page in which the form is displayed. A Web server then often employs CGI SCRIPTS to process the form: for example, storing the data provided by the user in a database and sending an HTML page back acknowledging the data. Forms can also be found on Web pages embedded in APPLETS or in ACTIVE X CONTROLS. The rise of JAVA and

JAVASCRIPT has meant that much form processing can be carried out by a Web CLIENT.

HTML level A number which represents a version of the HYPERTEXT MARKUP LANGUAGE: for example, HTML 4 designates level 4 of the language. Successive levels build upon previous levels and include further more advanced and sophisticated facilities. For example HTML 4 included a new TAG <COLGROUP> which allowed the HTML developer finer control over TABLES. When a new version of HTML emerges some tags become DEPRECATED TAGS whose use is frowned on and others become OBSOLETE TAGS.

HTML page A subdivison of a WEB SITE that is stored in a single file and which normally has the FILE EXTENSION htm or html. The term 'page' is somewhat confusing since the size of an HTML page can be very much larger than a book page. There are a number of categories of Web pages including HOME PAGE and HELP PAGE. Normally the designer of a Web site ensures that a particular page contains only information that is relevant to the content of the page. If the page needs to reference different information then this is achieved via HYPERLINKS.

HTML tag A tag is a device which notifies a browser that some formatting of a WEB PAGE is required at the point where the tag has been inserted; for example, the <P> tag tells the browser to insert a new paragraph and the <TABLE> tag informs the browser that formatting associated with a TABLE is about to start. In HTML tags are delineated by the < and > brackets. Many tags are associated with end tags; for example, the tag <TABLE> which introduces a table is associated with </TABLE> which marks the end of the table. There are other uses for tags over and above formatting: *see, for example,* METATAG. *See also* BROKET.

HTML template A chunk of HTML code which provides the skeleton structure for a page. It can be reused time and time again with the detail added for each page that is based on it. An example of an HTML template is a catalogue page which is used for an ECOMMERCE site that sells some products via a catalogue. A template would define each page and contain space for the name of the product, details of the product including the price, and an image of the product. This template would be reused again and again with the specific details of each product being inserted into a copy of the template, thus ensuring a consistent look and feel across all the pages of the catalogue. A number of modern HTML EDITORS provide a facility for the development of HTML templates and their repeated use.

HTML validation site A WEB SITE that either checks individual WEB PAGES or a whole Web site. Usually such a site spellchecks the document, checks that the syntax of HTML has not been violated, verifies that the HYPERLINKS on the page are to valid sites, and provides some display of the structure of the page in terms of the HTML facilities that are used. *See also* LINK CHECKING SITE.

HTML Writers' Guild A collection of Web developers who have as their aim the improvement of the art of developing WEB PAGES.

HTTP *See* HYPERTEXT TRANSFER PROTOCOL.

HTTPD *See* HYPERTEXT TRANSFER PROTOCOL DAEMON.

HTTP daemon A DAEMON, often referred to as HTTPD, which executes on a WEB SERVER and carries out the process of waiting for an HTTP REQUEST, decoding the request, obtaining any information required by the request such as data held in a database, carrying out the request, initiating an HTTP RESPONSE, closing the network connection with the client that made the request, and then idling, waiting for the next request. It is the HTTP daemon which instigates all the main functions of a Web server.

HTTP request A request by a BROWSER running on a CLIENT to a WEB SERVER. The request is made using the HYPERTEXT TRANSFER PROTOCOL. Most requests are for the return of a WEB PAGE.

HTTP response The reply made by a WEB SERVER in response to an HTTP REQUEST. The response consists of three elements: a status line which indicates whether the request has been successful or not; a description of the information in the response (whether, for example it is text or a graphic); and the information requested. This is normally a WEB PAGE. The status line includes the HTTP STATUS CODE. The information contained in the response will be displayed in a BROWSER.

HTTPS *See* HYPERTEXT TRANSFER PROTOCOL SECURE.

HTTP status code The code used by the HTTP protocol to indicate the result of a request made by a BROWSER. It consists of a three digit-number which can indicate anything from total success in providing a service such as returning a WEB PAGE, to total failure when, for example, a Web page has not been found. The most frequent error status code returned to a browser is 404. This indicates that the Web page that the browser requires cannot be found. *See also* FOUR ZERO FOUR COMPLIANT.

hub There are two uses for this term. The first use is hardware-oriented and refers to a common connection point for devices in a network. The second use is software-oriented and refers to a WEB SITE which either contains a number of PORTAL sites or is linked to a number of portal sites via HYPERLINKS.

hub network A network which uses a cable called a BACKPLANE. A series of hardware ports are connected to this cable to which devices such as computers can be connected.

Huffman coding An ENTROPY CODING method used to achieve data COMPRESSION. It uses the frequency of characters in a file to determine the amount of memory to represent each character. This is a static method where the transformation of characters into their compressed form is fixed before the data is compressed. A dynamic version of this method is known as ADAPTIVE HUFFMAN CODING.

huge pipe Jargon term used to refer to a large BANDWIDTH connection to the Internet.

human computer interface A collection of visual objects such as BUTTONS, WINDOWS, TEXT BOXES, and MENUS which make up the interface to a computer program. It was a term popular in the 1980s and early 1990s but is now being superseded by the term GRAPHICAL USER INTERFACE.

hyperlink An area in a HYPERMEDIA document which normally points to either another part of the document or to another, separate, document. Navigation between hypermedia documents is normally achieved by clicking a hyperlink with a mouse. Hyperlinks can also point to other entities: for example, an FTP LINK points to a site where file transfers can be achieved using the FILE TRANSFER PROTOCOL. Clicking on this type of link takes the user to the site.

hypermedia Documents which can be read non-linearly by following links known as HYPERLINKS embedded in the document. This term has superseded the term 'hypertext': the latter implies that such documents are purely textual when many technologies using hyperlinks now contain mixed media. The best-known example of hypermedia is the WORLD WIDE WEB.

hypertext Any medium that can be accessed non-linearly. A hypertext document contains links known as HYPERLINKS which allow the reader to navigate through the document using a number of paths. Hypertext is not just a Web-based phenomenon but has existed in conceptual form since 1945 when the American information scientist Vanevar Bush described it in a seminal paper, and in implementations described in the 1960s. However, the use of hypertext ideas within the HTML language used to describe WORLD WIDE WEB documents has meant that something that was an academic curiosity up to the early 1990s has become the main information medium on the Internet. The term 'hypertext' gives the impression of links solely occurring in plain text documents; the term HYPERMEDIA has superseded it since links in Web documents can be embedded in both text and graphics.

Hypertext Markup Language The language used to develop documents which are to be placed on the WORLD WIDE WEB. It is usually known as HTML. As the name suggests it is a MARKUP LANGUAGE. It contains a number of TAGS which indicate what facility is required by the writer: for example, the tag <P> inserts a paragraph at the place where it occurs in a WEB PAGE. The language consists of facilities for a large number of textual features including paragraphs, headings, lists, and images. It also contains facilities for changing the look of particular elements of a Web page: for example, the colour of a section of text. An important part of HTML are the features in the language which enable HYPERLINKS to be embedded in it. In the past WEB PAGES were constructed by hand using simple program editors. However, there are now a wide variety of HTML EDITORS available which relieve the user of the tedium of writing HTML. Versions of HTML are each identified by an HTML LEVEL. A number of tools and HTML VALIDATION SITES are available for carrying out processes such as checking links for ORPHAN LINKS. When a document expressed in HTML is processed by a BROWSER, it interprets the tags in the document and displays it according to the meaning of the tags.

Hypertext Transfer Protocol This protocol, commonly known as HTTP, is one of the most important PROTOCOLS used on the Internet. It is used when a BROWSER communicates with a WEB SERVER. For example, when the user of a browser clicks a mouse on a HYPERLINK in a WEB PAGE the browser sends a message to the Web server which contains the file referenced in the link to ask for the file to be retrieved. A typical message would be GET/findpage.html HTTP/1.0. This informs the server that the client browser would like to retrieve the file findpage.html in order to display it, and that the version of HTML that the client currently understands is 1.0. This is an example of one of the most popular commands in the HTTP protocol, the GET command; there are a number of others which, for example, are concerned with FORMS processing. The server also uses commands from the repertoire of commands within the HTTP protocol to send messages back to the browser. For example, the first line of a response from a server to a request from a browser might be HTTP/1.1 200 OK. This tells the browser that its request (usually a request for a Web page to be sent) has been correctly processed and that the server is using version 1.1 of HTTP. The number 200 is an example of an HTTP STATUS CODE which gives an indication of the status of the request; 200 indicates that the request was communicated successfully. HTTP is a stateless protocol: a protocol where each command has no knowledge of any previous command. There are currently two version of HTTP: 1.0 and 1.1. The vast majority of browsers now support version 1.1. *See also* COOKIE, WEB SERVER, and COMMON GATEWAY INTERFACE.

Hypertext Transfer Protocol Daemon A DAEMON which is always active in a WEB SERVER. It waits for an HTTP REQUEST and then carries out the processes required to respond to the request. For example, it might retrieve a WEB PAGE and then send that page back to the BROWSER that made the request. Usually abbreviated to HTTPD.

Hypertext Transfer Protocol Secure Software which enables a SERVER to process secure TRANSACTIONS. A UNIFORM RESOURCE LOCATOR which contains the protocol designator HTTPS indicates that a server is running this software.

hz An abbreviation for HERTZ, the unit used to measure FREQUENCY.

IAB *See* INTERNET ARCHITECTURE BOARD.

IAE Abbreviation for In Any Event used in CHAT ROOMS, EMAILS, and NEWSGROUPS.

IANA *See* INTERNET ASSIGNED NUMBER AUTHORITY.

IANAL Abbreviation for I Am Not A Lawyer used in EMAILS and NEWSGROUPS. It is usually followed by the word 'but' and some semi-legal or legal opinion.

I-bahn A shortened version of INFOBAHN.

IC Abbreviation for In Character used in EMAILS and NEWSGROUPS. It is also used as a HAKSPEK abbreviation for 'I see'.

ICANN *See* INTERNET CORPORATION FOR ASSIGNED NAMES AND NUMBERS.

ICC *See* INTERNET COMMERCE COMMISSION.

ICCB *See* INTERNET CONFIGURATION CONTROL BOARD.

ICMP *See* INTERNET CONTROL MESSAGE PROTOCOL.

icon A small image usually found on a WEB PAGE representing a piece of information. The image is normally associated with a HYPERLINK. A typical icon is a graphic question mark which points at an FAQ PAGE or HELP PAGE in a WEB SITE.

ICRA *See* INTERNET CONTENT RATING ASSOCIATION.

IDEA *See* INTERNATIONAL DATA ENCRYPTION ALGORITHM.

identification 1. The process of telling a computer or a network who the user is. This is usually via a set of characters known as a USER NAME or ACCOUNT NAME. This has to be followed by AUTHENTICATION, a process which proves to the system the user is who they claim to be. This is normally achieved via a PASSWORD.
2. The term used to refer to the identification of computers on a network via schemes such as an IP ADDRESS.

identifying certificate A DIGITAL CERTIFICATE which provides some identification of the person associated with the certificate.

identity hacking 1. Using a NEWSGROUP or BULLETIN BOARD with a false identity or pseudonym.
2. EMAILing others using a false identity. There are a number of reasons for identity hacking ranging from criminal reasons such as being a CYBERSTALKER to sensible reasons such as avoiding SPAM.

identity theft A crime which many computer industry observers are predicting will be a major problem in the early twenty first century. It involves the theft of personal identification information such as DIGITAL CERTIFICATES, PASSWORDS, and PINs in order to use them for some criminal purpose. There is an extensive amount of research being carried out on BIOMETRIC IDENTIFICATION SYSTEMS which aim to provide virtually foolproof identification schemes.

IDF *See* IMAGE MAP DEFINITION FILE.

IDKY Abbreviation for I Don't Know You used in CHAT ROOMS.

IDL *See* INTERFACE DEFINITION LANGUAGE.

IDST Abbreviation I Didn't Say That used in EMAILS and NEWSGROUPS. Usually used when someone has misinterpreted a remark.

IDTS Abbreviation for I Don't Think So used in EMAILS and NEWSGROUPS.

IDU *See* INTERFACE DATA UNIT.

IEE *See* INSTITUTION OF ELECTRICAL ENGINEERS.

IEEE *See* INSTITUTE OF ELECTRICAL AND ELECTRONIC ENGINEERS.

IEPG *See* INTERNET ENGINEERING AND PLANNING GROUP.

IESG *See* INTERNET ENGINEERING STEERING GROUP.

IETF *See* INTERNET ENGINEERING TASK FORCE.

IGP *See* INTERIOR GATEWAY PROTOCOL.

IIOP *See* INTERNET INTER-ORB PROTOCOL.

IIS *See* INTERNET INFORMATION SERVER®.

IIS Standard Log File Format A format used by Microsoft to describe each entry in the WEB LOG FILES produced by their popular IIS WEB SERVER.

image A graphical entity which can be displayed in a document or a WEB PAGE. There are a number of formats used for storing images. On the WORLD WIDE WEB the two most popular are the GRAPHICS INTERCHANGE FORMAT and the JOINT PHOTOGRAPHIC EXPERTS GROUP format.

image format A specification which is used to describe how a graphic element is stored. There are a large number of formats in existence. Two of the most popular are the GRAPHICS INTERCHANGE FORMAT and the JOINT PHOTOGRAPHIC EXPERTS GROUP format. *See also* FILE FORMAT.

image map A graphic which is found on a WEB PAGE and which contains HYPERLINKS to other Web pages. For example, a company which is based in the United Sates might keep a separate WEB PAGE for its branches in each of the states. A good way of accessing these pages would be through an image map in a graphic showing a map of the United States, where hyperlinks are embedded in each state. Clicking on each state would result in the page for that state being loaded into a BROWSER for viewing. In the early days of the Web, producing image maps was a complicated and tedious process. However, there are now many tools which can provide a high degree of automation and, increasingly, HTML EDITORS and WYSIWYG EDITORS are providing this facility. There are two types of image map: CLIENT SIDE IMAGE MAPS and SERVER SIDE IMAGE MAPS. The latter is the oldest type of image map. When a user clicks on this type of map the browser sends the information to the server which then decides on the Web page to send back. The former is a more up-to-date technique, where all the processing of the clicking of the image map is carried out by the client computer on which the browser is being used.

image map definition file A file that is stored on a WEB SERVER and is associated with an IMAGE MAP that occurs on a WEB PAGE which is maintained by the server. The file contains details of the shape of entities on the image map: whether, for example, they are circles or rectangles, the dimensions of the entity, and the URL associated with the entity to which control is transferred when it is clicked in a browser window. There are two formats for such files: the CERN IMAGE MAP FORMAT and the NCSA IMAGE MAP FORMAT. They are structurally similar, the only difference between them being the format of the data they contain. Creating such files manually is very tedious; they are normally created by specialized tools which, for example, allow you to draw image map regions over existing graphics.

IMAO Abbreviation for In My Arrogant Opinion used in EMAILS and NEWSGROUPS. Usually used as a reaction to IMHO.

IMAP *See* INTERNET MESSAGE ACCESS PROTOCOL.

IMCO Abbreviation for In My Considered Opinion used in CHAT ROOMS, EMAILS, and NEWSGROUPS. One of a whole range of opinion abbreviations including IMHO and IMAO.

IME Abbreviation for In My Experience used in EMAILS and NEWSGROUPS.

IMHO Abbreviation for In My Humble Opinion used in EMAILS and NEWSGROUPS.

iMing The process of chatting in a CHAT ROOM and carrying out some other activity at the same time, such as writing an EMAIL.

immediate response EDI The transfer of data, usually commercial data, which is to be responded to in real time. For example, transactions from a dealing room to a stock exchange SERVER are categorized as immediate response EDI.

IMNSHO Abbreviation for In My Not So Humble Opinion used in EMAILS and NEWSGROUPS. Used as a reaction to IMHO.

One of a number of opinion abbreviations including IMAO.

IMO Abbreviation for In My Opinion used in EMAILS and NEWSGROUPS. One of a number of opinion abbreviations including IMHO and IMAO.

IMP *See* INTERNET MESSAGE PROCESSOR.

impression 1. Used in connection with ECOMMERCE. It refers to the number of times a BANNER ADVERT is downloaded to a WEB SITE and displayed to users of that Web site.
2. Synonym for AD VIEW.

inappropriate fidelity Occurs when a document is copied and some content is found within the document which is relevant to the original version but not to the copied version. For example, a document may exist in its original form with some text indicating that it is printed on recycled paper and yet it has been photocopied onto paper which has not been recycled.

inbound link A HYPERLINK to a WEB PAGE from another site.

include war A set of POSTINGS on a topic, usually abusive, many of which contain INCLUSIONS. Often the postings consist of inclusions which themselves contain inclusions and so on. This eventually leads to postings which are unreadable.

inclusion Text which is cut and pasted into an EMAIL or POSTING to a newsgroup from another email or posting in order to reply to it or to FOLLOW-UP some aspect of the message. This is a practice which is quite extensive and is often overdone, leading to unreadable messages with large amounts of inappropriate text included in them.

index 1. A document which contains references to other documents or to sections of itself. Most WEB SITES contain pages which function as an index, sometimes the HOME PAGE, sometimes a special INDEX PAGE which is embedded in a FRAME.
2. A term to describe the collection of FILES which are used by a SEARCH ENGINE. An index contains a collection of words and

the UNIFORM RESOURCE LOCATOR for the documents that each word is contained in.

index page A WEB PAGE which contains links to the pages which make up a WEB SITE. Very occasionally you find the HOME PAGE of a Web site referred to as the index page and it is often stored in a file index.htm or index.html.

index spamming The submission of WEB PAGES to a SEARCH ENGINE which contain a large amount of descriptive information or the swamping of a search engine with a large number of pages. Both of these are intended to ensure that the site submitted is placed near the top of the list of retrieved sites when a user of the search engine sends a query. It is similar to SPAMMING, but the recipient is a search engine rather than an EMAIL account. The companies which provide search engines frown on this activity and will remove sites which carry out index spamming from their databases. The term SPAMDEX is also used to describe this activity.

inflate The process of decompressing a file which has undergone COMPRESSION.

info In 2000 seven new DOMAIN NAMES were created. info was one of these. It is intended for general use.

Infobahn A term which, curiously, is used more by English-speaking users than German ones; it describes the INFORMATION SUPERHIGHWAY.

infobot A BOT which is used in a CHAT ROOM to respond to queries from participants about topics covered in the room. Often these queries are framed in terms of keywords, although some infobots are able to extract the keywords from natural language queries.

information gridlock The traffic jams on the Internet which occasionally occur when some site becomes popular, or access to a number of sites has been restricted to a small number of routes. This usually results in a severely degraded RESPONSE TIME.

information island A collection of data which would be useful to a large number of users but which is not networked.

Information Superhighway A term which is used to describe the Internet. It was coined by Al Gore, vice president of the USA, in a speech which dealt with the deregulation of the Internet.

InfoSeek One of the largest SEARCH ENGINES in the WORLD WIDE WEB. It provides everything that is expected of a sophisticated search engine including personalization services and the ability to search all the main forums on the Internet.

infospace The totality of the Internet including the WORLD WIDE WEB and NEWSGROUPS.

infowarrior Someone who attempts to subvert an adversary's means to wage war by attacking communication and computer infrastructures. This can be carried out by conventional means such as bombing communications centres or by technological means such as inserting VIRUSES into a computer system.

initialization string The series of characters which, when received by a MODEM, starts it processing data.

Inktomi A large database which is used by some SEARCH ENGINES including HOTBOT.

inline image A graphic image which is embedded in a WEB PAGE.

innocent bysender A MAIL SERVER that has been used to send SPAM mail without the mail administrator associated with the server knowing about it.

insecure host A computer on a network which is not protected from attack by technologies such as ENCRYPTION, FIREWALLS, or DIGITAL CERTIFICATES.

insert your favourite ethnic group Used in jokes found on NEWSGROUPS and BULLETIN BOARD systems. The phrase is inserted so that the creator of the joke does not have to mention any specific ethnic group and hence anger members of that group. Usually regarded as an inadequate response to a criticism that the perpetrator is reinforcing racial or sexual stereotypes.

install To place a program or set of programs on a computer so that it can be run by a user.

instant messaging The generic name of a technology which enables PRIVATE CHAT to take place. When the user of this technology logs in to the Internet he or she will be informed which of their friends are on line. They also receive any messages their friends have left for them and any friends who are on line are informed of their presence. They can then interact with their friends using ONLINE CHAT.

Institute of Electrical and Electronic Engineers A professional society of engineers in the USA equivalent to other bodies such as the British Computer Society. It proposes and administers a large number of standards, many of which are relevant to computer networks: for example, standard IEEE 802.5 governs the physical transfer of data on an ETHERNET.

Institution of Electrical Engineers The British equivalent of the INSTITUTE OF ELECTRICAL AND ELECTRONIC ENGINEERS.

int A type of Internet DOMAIN associated with an international organization.

Integrated Digital Subscriber Line A variant of ASYMMETRICAL DIGITAL SUBSCRIBER LINES technology which runs on the same media that ISDN can be used on.

Integrated Services Digital Network A digital telephony technology which enables the high-speed transfer of both voice and data across conventional telephone lines. It does this by creating two 64 kbits/s channels for data and voice. ISDN, as it is more commonly known, can offer speeds of around 128 kbits/s. It currently exists in two variants: BASIC RATE INTERFACE and the much less common PRIMARY RATE INTERFACE.

integrity checker A form of VIRUS DETECTION SOFTWARE. It keeps data similar to a MESSAGE DIGEST for each file on a computer. Periodically it checks that files have not been interfered with by a VIRUS by recomputing the message digest and comparing it with its old value. If the values differ then there is a very good chance that a virus has infected the file. These programs are usually executed frequently.

intel The term used to describe any useful information found when SURFING the WORLD WIDE WEB.

Intel A major manufacturer of computer chips.

intelligent agent An alternative name for a DELIBERATIVE AGENT.

intelligent bot A BOT which carries out some task based on a knowledge of a narrow domain such as online shopping for CDs.

interactive voice response A technology used by companies to filter queries and demands for service using the telephone system. The user who phones in to the company is presented with a number of spoken options. The user responds either by pressing a key on the telephone or by speaking a simple word such as 'yes' or 'no.' Such systems are usually connected into a network containing large databases. A typical use for this type of system is for dealing with simple banking enquiries or providing a help facility for a computer manufacturer.

interexchange carrier A company whose business is the transport of long-distance phone calls.

interface data unit When two layers in a network LAYERED ARCHITECTURE communicate, they have to have an agreed way of doing so. This is achieved by means of an interface data unit. The term is often abbreviated to IDU.

interface definition language A language which is similar to a programming language. However, it is restricted to specifying a collection of data and functions which are implemented on a remote computer contained in a network. For example, the COMMON OBJECT REQUEST BROKER ARCHITECTURE has an interface definition language which defines the data and executable code associated with DISTRIBUTED OBJECTS defined by this architecture. Such languages are not confined to distributed object schemes; they are also associated with more conventional

software technologies such as REMOTE PROCEDURE CALL. Such languages are processed by programs which convert them into program code that is used when the entities described by the language are deployed: for example, if the language describes a distributed object the program produces the code required to communicate with it. Often abbreviated to IDL.

Interior Gateway Protocol A PROTOCOL that enables GATEWAYS in a SUBNETWORK to communicate with each other, for example two subnetworks which are assigned to two departments in the same company. The main use of such a protocol is for ROUTING.

interlaced GIF A GIF image in which the individual pixels are represented in blocks stored out of order: for example, a block may consist of ninety pixels with ten pixels per block, and is stored in the order block1, block4, block7,..., block2, block5, block8,..., block3, block6, block9,... When such a GIF image is transferred to the browser the image is built up in the order that the blocks are stored; hence the user is given the impression of a graphic gradually being built up from a rather foggy image to the point where the final image is displayed. Such graphics enable the BROWSER user to gain a quick idea of what is in an image before deciding whether they are going to transfer to another WEB PAGE or stay with the page that they are browsing. An interlaced GIF occupies slightly more memory space than a normal GIF image. It is not recommended for TEXT GIFs as such images are not really clear until they have all been transferred to the browser. *See also* THUMBNAIL IMAGE.

interlaced image This is an image which is gradually displayed, at first in a fuzzy way but gradually becoming sharper. It has the advantage that the user is able to discern what the image contains well before it fully arrives and can decide whether or not they want to view it. The best-known interlaced image is the INTERLACED GIF found in WEB PAGES.

intermediate system An alternative name for a ROUTER.

intermercial Jargon for an advert which is published on the Internet, typically a BANNER ADVERT.

internal navigation aid The graphical devices and HYPERLINKS embedded in a WEB PAGE that provides the visitor to a WEB SITE with the means whereby he or she can navigate through the site. *See also* NAVIGATION BAR.

International Atomic Time The most accurate time that is available to computers in a DISTRIBUTED SYSTEM. Clocks which adhere to this standard are accurate to one part in 10,000,000,000,000. Such clocks are often used to coordinate the individual computer clocks in a DISTRIBUTED SYSTEM which process TRANSACTIONS that are highly time-dependent.

International Data Encryption Algorithm A very effective algorithm used for the ENCRYPTION of data across the communication media used in a network. The algorithm, more commonly known as IDEA, is a BLOCK CIPHER. It is used in the PRETTY GOOD PRIVACY system.

International Standards Organization The main world standards organization. It specifies many standards which are relevant to communications and networking—for example, the OPEN SYSTEMS INTERCONNECTION standards—along with myriad other standards ranging from those which describe mechanical devices to those which describe programming languages. The organization is divided into area subcommittees which are further divided into working groups. Each working group has a wide international membership.

International Telecommunications Union A world standards-making body which concerns itself with standards for telecommunications. Often abbreviated to ITU. It was formerly known as the CONSULTATIVE COMMITTEE FOR INTERNATIONAL TELEPHONE AND TELEGRAPH.

International Trading in Arms Regulations The US regulations that prevented highly secure cryptographic technology from being exported from the United States. It categorized cryptography software as an armament. Condi-

tions have relaxed on export since the early part of 2000 with only a handful of countries being prevented from receiving cryptography technology. *See* EXPORT GRADE SECURITY and DOMESTIC GRADE SECURITY.

internaut An expert user of the Internet.

internesia The state an Internet user is in when he or she cannot remember the location of a piece of information on the net.

Internet The Internet is a network which consists of a number of other networks connected together using the TCP-IP set of PROTOCOLS. A major part of the Internet is the WORLD WIDE WEB: a collection of documents interlinked by means of HYPERLINKS. The most popular technologies used in the Internet are EMAIL, the FILE TRANSFER PROTOCOL, and the World Wide Web. *See also* INTERNET HISTORY, INTERNET STATISTICS, INTERNET STANDARD, INTERNET LAYERED ARCHITECTURE, INTERNET SOCIETY, INTERNET SERVICE PROVIDER, and INTERNET LAYER.

Internet access provider Synonymous with INTERNET SERVICE PROVIDER. Gradually the term is being used less and less in this context and is being used to describe companies who sell high-speed Internet access as a wholesaler to both Internet service providers and other organizations such as companies. Often abbreviated to IAP.

Internet Activities Board The previous name of the INTERNET ARCHITECTURE BOARD, a body which is charged with maintaining the openness of the Internet.

Internet advertising The process whereby a product or service is made visible to users of the Internet, usually via BANNER ADVERTS placed on WEB PAGES. Such adverts are often negotiated by an INTERNET ADVERTISING BUREAU or may form part of an ADVERT AUCTION. The Web site on which the adverts are placed is normally paid a fixed amount when a visitor either clicks on the banner advert to take them to the advertiser's site, or when a purchase is made after the banner advert has been clicked; the amount paid for the former is usually very small. The monitoring of the use of banner adverts and the payment process is often carried out by an intermediary company known as a PURCHASE INTERMEDIARY or a CLICK INTERMEDIARY. There are other forms of advertising on the Internet: for example, the use of SPAM or NEWSGROUPS devoted to commercial announcements. However, the bulk of the advertising associated with the Internet is that associated with banner adverts.

Internet advertising bureau A company that negotiates the placing of BANNER ADVERTS on WEB PAGES. In functional terms they differ little from their print and other media equivalents although, in technical terms, where negotiations involve many thousands more adverts which are rotated for a few seconds over a variety of WEB SITES, the processes they are involved in are more complex.

Internet agent An AGENT that carries out some task associated with the Internet: for example, storing UNIFORM RESOURCE LOCATORS and periodically checking that they still exist.

Internet applicance A consumer electronics product which allows access to the WORLD WIDE WEB but which does not contain an OPERATING SYSTEM and hence cannot function as a conventional computer. An example of this is a television set which has a facility for sending and receiving EMAIL.

Internet Architecture Board A board set up by the INTERNET SOCIETY which is charged with maintaining the openness of the Internet. It carries out a number of functions including appointing a chair of the INTERNET ENGINEERING TASK FORCE, overseeing Internet protocols, external liaison with other standards bodies such as the INTERNATIONAL STANDARDS ORGANIZATION, editing and overseeing the RFC documents concerned with the Internet, and acting as a source of advice to the INTERNET SOCIETY. It was previously known as the Internet Activities Board.

Internet Assigned Number Authority A non-profit-making organization set up to define and store the numbers and parameters which are responsible for the standard working of the Internet. For example, it defines the numbers of DEDICATED PORTS and oversees the DOMAIN NAME system. It was reorganized in 1999 and renamed the INTERNET CORPORATION FOR ASSIGNED NAMES AND NUMBERS, although many documents still refer to it by its original name.

Internet backbone A very high-speed transmission line to which many other Internet media are connected. *See* BACKBONE.

Internet books There are a huge number of books written on Internet subjects ranging from those addressed to the complete beginner to those which describe specific technologies such as SERVLETS and BROWSERS in minute detail. Internet book publishing was the fastest growing area of publishing in the 1990s.

internet café Another name for a CYBERCAFÉ.

Internet channel enabled threat The process of monitoring and capturing data from a user's computer as they access the WORLD WIDE WEB. Often abbreviated to ICE-T.

Internet chat *See* INTERNET RELAY CHAT.

Internet Commerce Commission A private consumer protection agency which concerns itself with Web-related commercial fraud. For example, it provides information about how to avoid being the victim of an Internet scam.

Internet Configuration Control Board In 1980 when the DEFENSE ADVANCED RESEARCH PROJECTS AGENCY set up a group to define Internet standards it was called the Internet Configuration Control Board. It was reorganized into the INTERNET ACTIVITIES BOARD in 1983.

Internet Content Rating Association An association of large companies including British Telecom, Microsoft, and AOL which is developing a CONTENT RATING scheme based on the RSACI content rating system.

Internet Control Message Protocol A PROTOCOL which forms part of TCP-IP.

It is responsible for monitoring and checking the status of computers on a network.

Internet copyright One of the features of the Internet is the ease with which a user can borrow media: for example, it is relatively easy to copy a graphic from a WEB SITE and place it in your own Web site, or CUT AND PASTE some text from a document attached to a Web site. Laws on copyright and plagiarism are no more openly flouted than on the WORLD WIDE WEB. The law, however, is fairly clear that any material, irrespective of whether it resides in print media or on the Internet, is the property of the originator and that no registration is required, although it is usually a good idea to do this. If you want to use some text or other media found on the Internet it is a very good idea to gain permission first. This would avoid, at best, embarrassment or, at worst, litigation. Given this fairly clear definition of the law it is worth pointing out that there are some issues which are specific to the Internet which have not yet been fully worked out within the law: for example, the copyright position of someone who makes a DEEP LINK to an existing site. *See also* BANDWIDTH THEFT.

Internet Corporation for Assigned Names and Numbers A non-profit-making corporation that was formed to take over responsibility for IP ADDRESS space allocation, protocol parameter assignment, domain name system management, and ROOT SERVER system management, all of which was previously carried out by the INTERNET ASSIGNED NUMBER AUTHORITY.

Internet crime Crime involving computer networks has always been in existence. However, the fact that the Internet is a public network which has been constructed from components whose structure and specification are publicly available has meant that the amount of computer-related crime has increased substantially since the mid-1980s. This crime ranges from nuisance activities such as sending unsolicited EMAILS, known as SPAM, advertising services or products for sale, to CHAIN LETTER SCAMS which ask

recipients of an email to send it on to a friend and deliver some money. There are also a number of crimes which are just electronic versions of existing ones: for example, PONZI SCHEMES, PYRAMID SCHEMES, and SHARE RAMPING. However, the Internet has made such crimes easier to carry out in terms of the number of potential victims and the speed of delivery of documents associated with the crime. The most serious crimes are perpetrated by CRACKERS and involve intrusion into a private network. Since many of these networks have interfaces to the Internet it is now easier to enter them, although well-established techniques such as those involving the use of PASSWORD SNIFFERS and DUMPSTER DIVING are still frequently used. Typical crimes include the SALAMI ATTACK in which very small amounts of money are taken from a financial account and added to the perpetrator's account, and the DENIAL OF SERVICE ATTACK which ties up an important computer resource such as a processor and denies access to users of a network.

Internet Domain Name Service A NAME SERVICE which associates DOMAIN NAMES with IP ADDRESSES. It replaced an original scheme in which this information was held in a central database and downloaded to computers using the FILE TRANSFER PROTOCOL. It is set up as a number of NAME SERVERS spread throughout the Internet partitioned into zones. Each server receives requests for addresses and either resolves them when the information required can be found on its database or sends a request on to another server administering a different zone. This service is one of the most frequently used on the Internet, as whenever a symbolic domain name is employed, for example in an email address, the service needs to be consulted.

Internet draft An Internet standards document originated by the INTERNET ENGINEERING TASK FORCE and produced when a REQUEST FOR COMMENT has had valid comments incorporated in it. This draft is again distributed and further comments sought from interested parties. The document is quite close to a formal Internet standard, but has to be further transformed into a PROPOSED STANDARD, DRAFT STANDARD, and OFFICIAL STANDARD.

Internet Engineering and Planning Group The part of the INTERNET SOCIETY which concerns itself with the operation of the Internet. It takes no part in the standards-making process. It is often abbreviated to IEPG.

Internet Engineering Steering Group The operational management arm of the INTERNET ENGINEERING TASK FORCE.

Internet Engineering Task Force A voluntary organization responsible for the administration of working groups which deal with short-term and operational questions about the functioning of the Internet. These working groups issue reports and recommendations which can be split up into two categories: those which are advice and which organizations connected to the Internet can adopt voluntarily, and those which are sent to the INTERNET ARCHITECTURE BOARD for more formal adoption. While the description above makes the task force seem fairly weak, an organization which did not abide by its decisions would soon have to leave the Internet because of technological incompatibility.

Internet Explorer® The BROWSER marketed by the Microsoft Corporation. It was developed as a response to the success of similar products launched by competitors. It is now the most popular browser. During the 1990s there was a BROWSER WAR between Microsoft and the Netscape Corporation who marketed a browser known as NETSCAPE NAVIGATOR. This lead to accusations of Microsoft taking advantage of their monopoly position in order to force a competitor out of the browser market.

Internet game There are now a huge number of games on the Internet. These range from simple games found on BANNER ADVERTS to very sophisticated games similar to those found on game consoles. The vast majority of Internet games are now found on Internet GAME SITES which have a number of charging mechanisms ranging from payment per game played to subscription. Sometimes these sites allow the visitor to play a small number of games for no charge as an inducement to carry on and play games that have to be paid for.

Internet history In the mid-1960s the US Department of Defense decided that they wanted a command and control system that could survive attack by nuclear weapons. In order to do this they asked their research arm the ADVANCED RESEARCH PROJECTS AGENCY to initiate a number of projects which looked at the possibility of using packet switching as a mechanism to connect a number of computers together. This led to the development of a network known as ARPANET which connected a number of universities, research organizations, and defence organizations. The early experiments with ARPANET indicated that the original protocols devised for the network were not adequate and this led to the development of TCP-IP. In order to encourage the use of these protocols a number of development contracts were awarded by ARPA to integrate them into a number of versions of the UNIX operating system. By 1983 there were hundreds of computers connected to ARPANET and the TCP-IP protocol set had become stable. In the late 1970s the US National Science Foundation, the major funding agency for research in the United States, decided to develop their own network which would connect US universities and research establishments. This network, named NSFNET, used the TCP-IP protocol from the start. It was a huge success and was immediately overloaded. In 1991 the US congress passed a bill authorizing the NREN network. This was a successor to NSFNET and was intended to be its GIGABIT successor. The major growth in the Internet started when ARPANET and NSFNET were connected together. Much of the growth has come from the fact that whole networks, for example the massive internal IBM network, joined the Internet, connecting thousands of computers at one fell swoop. The exponential growth of the Internet meant that the old, ad hoc methods of running it were not really adequate and the INTERNET SOCIETY was born. Commercial involvement in the Internet came in 1990 when a consortium of companies known as ANS took over NFSNET. Since then, a network which was previously mainly confined to researchers and academics has been rapidly commercialized to the point where the vast majority of users are commercial users or home-based users accessing the Internet via INTERNET SERVICE PROVIDERS. There were a number of other developments which accelerated the growth of the Internet. Almost certainly the most influential was the development of the WORLD WIDE WEB by Tim Berners-Lee at CERN and the development of the first BROWSER called MOSAIC.

Internet holy grail An ultimate task or product which, in practice, can never be achieved. A GODZILLAGRAM is an example of a holy grail: a packet of data which could, theoretically, reach every computer on the Internet.

Internet Information Server ® One of the most popular WEB SERVERS; it is marketed by the Microsoft Corporation.

Internet Inter-ORB Protocol A PROTOCOL that enables OBJECT REQUEST BROKERS to communicate with each other. This means that DISTRIBUTED OBJECTS which are defined by the COMMON OBJECT REQUEST BROKER ARCHITECTURE (CORBA) and implemented by different vendors are able to communicate with each other. In the early days of CORBA this protocol was not defined, which meant that CORBA objects produced by software from different vendors were incapable of communicating with each other. Often abbreviated to IIOP.

Internet layer A layer in the INTERNET LAYERED ARCHITECTURE which is equivalent to the OSI NETWORK LAYER: it carries out the process of routing data from one computer to another. To do this it examines possible routes and determines an optimal or near optimal route for PACKETS of data to travel over.

Internet layered architecture A layered architecture which describes the components of the Internet. It consists of a number of layers including the APPLICATION LAYER, the TRANSPORT LAYER, the INTERNET LAYER, and the NETWORK LAYER.

Internet Message Access Protocol A PROTOCOL that is used for sending EMAIL across the Internet. It is distinguished from the other well-known protocol POP3 by the fact that it stores messages on the MAIL SERVER rather than DOWNLOADing them to a mailing program on a client computer. Often abbreviated to IMAP.

Internet Message Processor A switching computer used on ARPANET. It was usually abbreviated to IMP.

Internet Multicast Backbone A VIRTUAL network which sits on top of the Internet and which supports the routing of data that has been subject to MULTICASTING.

Internet Open Trading Protocol A specification of a PROTOCOL which attempts to improve on existing trading protocols for ECOMMERCE. It has been defined by the INTERNET ENGINEERING TASK FORCE and makes extensive use of EXTENSIBLE MARKUP LANGUAGE technology. It describes the processes that make up a typical electronic trading transaction involving activities such as the transmission of the payment for a product, the checking of the payment, and the delivery of a receipt.

Internet organizations There are a huge number of organizations which have been formed with the Internet as their focus. They range from political organizations resisting the commercialization of the Internet to trade associations which promote the Internet.

Internet Packet Exchange A look-alike proprietary PROTOCOL similar to the INTERNET PROTOCOL which has been developed by the US company Novell. It is often abbreviated to IPX.

Internet PCA Registration Authority An organization operated by the INTERNET SOCIETY which administers the granting of certificates to various bodies known as a POLICY CERTIFICATION AUTHORITY. These authorities, in turn, issue security certificates to individual organizations which are known as a CERTIFICATE AUTHORITY. Hence the Internet PCA Registration Authority lies at the top of the pyramid which is concerned with the granting of SECURITY CERTIFICATES.

Internet piracy The theft and reuse of entities found on the Internet. These include VIDEO CLIPS, GRAPHIC IMAGES, and text. It is also the term that is used to describe the wholesale theft of WEB SITES where an illicit organization copies an existing site and places a new HOME PAGE for the site as part of a criminal enterprise. In general the unauthorized use of Internet media is as much a crime as the unauthorized use of any other media. *See* INTERNET COPYRIGHT.

Internet pornography The storage and sale of pornographic still and moving images on the Internet, usually on the WORLD WIDE WEB. Internet pornography was the first ECOMMERCE application that was a financial success. Even as early as the 1980s, when the Internet was only populated by a relatively small number of academics, government staff, pornographers, and their customers, there were a number of thriving FILE TRANSFER PROTOCOL sites which sold pornographic images. Internet pornography businesses have always been in the forefront in terms of employing new technology such as VIDEO STREAMING and new businesses models; indeed many commentators have ascribed the success of advanced technologies to the demands placed on them by pornographers.

Internet Protocol A protocol which forms part of TCP-IP. Its function is to carry out the transport of data packets collected together by the TRANSMISSION CONTROL PROTOCOL (TCP) to a destination computer. It also carries out this function for data collected together by the UNRELIABLE DATAGRAM PROTOCOL. It is usually abbreviated to IP.

Internet Protocol Address Often known as the IP address. This is a unique 32-bit address which identifies a computer and the SUBNETWORK in which it resides. Most users see this address as a series of four integers separated by full stops, a notation known as DOTTED QUAD NOTATION.

The address is used by the TCP-IP protocols to correctly send a collection of DATAGRAMS to a destination computer identified by its Internet Protocol address. There are four formats for this address according to the size of the SUBNETWORK involved and whether MULTICASTING is used. *See also* INTERNET PROTOCOL VERSION 6.

Internet Protocol datagram header Data that is placed in a DATAGRAM which provides important information used by the protocols that make up TCP-IP: for example, the header contains the sending address of the computer that initiated the datagram and the destination computer which is due to receive the datagram.

Internet Protocol next generation The next generation of INTERNET PROTOCOLs which will include increased space for more INTERNET PROTOCOL ADDRESSES and improved security. *See also* INTERNET PROTOCOL VERSION 6.

Internet Protocol Version 6 One of the future problems that the Internet will face is that the number of computers connected to it will reach the point where the 32-bit format used in the INTERNET PROTOCOL to store INTERNET PROTOCOL ADDRESSES will not be big enough. Internet Protocol Version 6 is an attempt to overcome this problem. It involves extending the address range to 128 bits. It will also support authentication and encryption of data. Often referred to as IPv6.

Internet radio station *See* RADIO SITE.

Internet Relay Chat This was the first real ONLINE CHAT service on the Internet and is still the most popular. It is free: all a potential participant needs to do is to obtain easily available CHAT CLIENT software which enables them to participate in CHAT ROOMS.

Internet Research Task Force This is the part of the INTERNET ARCHITECTURE BOARD which deals with the long-term issues that will face the Internet. Often abbreviated to IRTF.

Internet Server Application Programming Interface An API developed by Microsoft which enables developers to integrate a SERVER with application programs; in this case programs written for the Windows operating system. For example, it would allow access to DATA-BASE MANAGEMENT SYSTEMS and enable BACK END PROCESSes.

Internet service provider A company which provides access to the Internet. Usually abbreviated to ISP and sometimes known as INTERNET ACCESS PROVIDERS. Such companies provide connection to the WORLD WIDE WEB, provide customers with some space on a WEB SERVER for their own WEB SITE, provide EMAIL ADDRESSES and DOMAIN NAMES, act as intermediaries in ECOMMERCE, and offer other technical assistance. Many companies also offer more specialized services such as Web design and WEB SITE PROMOTION. In the past Internet service providers charged a fee for their service; increasingly such providers are now charging indirectly by taking a proportion of the telephone charges that a user incurs when accessing services via the provider. Many service providers who charge a fee usually provide a large amount of CONTENT or a service such as free technical advice. There are a small number of totally free Internet service providers. However, the majority of them currently receive funds indirectly by asking their customers to switch to another phone company who then pays them an introduction fee.

Internet Society An umbrella group of organizations which was set up to oversee the growth of the Internet. It is responsible for the work of two further important working groups: the INTERNET AR-CHITECTURE BOARD and the INTERNET ENGINEERING TASK FORCE. The former deals with open standards for the Internet, while the latter deals with short-term and operational issues.

Internet standard A standard sanctioned and recognized as an official standard by the INTERNET SOCIETY. Standards exist for virtually every base technology used on the Internet including the HYPER-TEXT MARKUP LANGUAGE, CASCADING STYLE SHEETS, and DIGITAL SIGNATURES. An Internet standard starts life as a REQUEST FOR COMMENT issued by the INTERNET ENGIN-EERING TASK FORCE. This then goes through a process of refinement where it moves from being a request for comment to being an INTERNET DRAFT, PROPOSED STANDARD, DRAFT STANDARD, and finally an OFFICIAL STANDARD.

Internet statistics There are mounds of statistics about the Internet, all of them involving huge numbers. These include the number of Internet users, the number of INTERNET SERVICE PROVIDERS, the number of SERVERS, the number of DOMAINS registered, and so on. In a printed book such as this one it would be futile to quote numbers: this is best left to the WEB SITES containing up-to-date statistics. These should be consulted in preference to books and printed reports which tend to become out of date very quickly.

Internet telephony The use of the Internet to send telephone calls, often at little or no charge. This is a promising technology which, however, is still in its infancy. It has huge potential since the Internet has a higher BANDWIDTH than normal telephone lines and enables a much greater volume of calls to be placed. However, the quality of service experienced by current users of Internet telephony is much lower than that provided by telephone companies.

Internet time The CYCLE TIME of products developed using Internet technology. This is often a very short time indeed because many products are subject to continuous change and product investment. *See also* WEB YEAR.

Internet transaction broker An alternative term for a CYBERMEDIARY.

Internet worm A VIRUS which was developed by a young student Robert Morris in 1988. It was the first real large-scale attack on the Internet and resulted in a large proportion of the computers on the Internet having to be closed down in order to eliminate the virus from their memories. Morris used a well-known bug in the UNIX operating system to spread the worm from one computer on the Internet to other computers.

internetwork Two or more networks connected by ROUTERS and BRIDGES. The largest Internetwork is the Internet.

InterNIC A cooperative effort between the US government and the company Network Solutions Inc. which managed the registration and maintenance of COM, NET, and ORG, TOP-LEVEL DOMAIN names. In 1998 the US government liberalized the process of registration and set up the INTERNET CORPORATION FOR ASSIGNED NAMES AND NUMBERS that administers REGISTRAR companies which have been set up to carry out the registration process.

internot Someone who has a negative relationship with the Internet: for example, a non-user of the Internet or someone who is opposed to it. *See also* IN-TERNAUT.

interoperability The ability of entities in a network to connect with each other and carry out their functions: for example, the ability of a Novell Netware network to operate properly as a part of the Internet.

interpreted programming language A programming language which is directly executed rather than being converted into a basic form such as machine code for execution as with a COMPILED PROGRAMMING LANGUAGE. The vast majority of interpreted languages are converted into an intermediate form which is then executed.

interpreter A program which takes another program written in some language and then executes it directly. Sometimes the interpreter converts the program to an intermediate form which is easier to execute. Interpreters are different from COMPILERS which convert the code to machine code which is then directly executed by a computer. Occasionally the term is also used to describe any processor which carries out execution based on the content of a FILE, for example a program which forbids certain categories of user from accessing parts of the WORLD WIDE WEB based on some SCRIPT.

intersecting ring network A network that consists of two or more SUBNETS which are RING NETWORKS and which share some common computers.

intersig Sometimes users of a NEWS-GROUP place a phrase between their first name and surname: for example Darrel, 'I did that before' Ince. The phrase is known as an intersig.

interstit An abbreviation for INTERSTITIAL ADVERT.

interstitial advert An advert encountered when browsing a WEB SITE which appears after you have clicked on a HYPERLINK, but before your browser displays the page associated with the URL referenced in the hyperlink. Such adverts usually appear on a WEB PAGE for a relatively short period.

in the wild Applied to a VIRUS which has been found on computers that are in real use, rather than viruses which have been artificially constructed by researchers. *See also* IN THE ZOO.

in the zoo Used to describe an experimental VIRUS which has been created by researchers to check out an OPERATING SYSTEM and which cannot be found on an external network such as the Internet. *See also* IN THE WILD.

intranet A network which has been set up by an organization that is not accessible to users outside the organization. Intranets use the TCP-IP protocol rather than proprietary protocols for communication between computers. They are proving popular for a number of reasons. First, they are based on free or freely available software such as BROWSERS. Second, there is often a need for internal networks to connect to other intranets and to the Internet and hence a requirement for some standardized protocol to be used. An intranet is an example of CLIENT SERVER COMPUTING in action. *See also* EXTRANET.

intrusion detection software Software that can detect when an unauthorized access has been made to a network. There are a number of types of intrusion detection software. The first is based on the processing of LOG FILES; software in this category examine these files looking for unusual activity on a network, for example a repeated attempt to LOG-IN to the network at an unusual time. This type of software only detects intrusion after it has occurred. The second type of software attempts to detect intrusion in REAL TIME by monitoring traffic in the network looking for unusual PACKETS of data.

intrusive virus A VIRUS which infects a computer by overwriting some of the program code found on the computer.

invisible page A WEB PAGE which is invisible to someone browsing a WEB SITE, because the site does not contain any HYPERLINKS to the page. Access to it is usually only granted to users who are sent the UNIFORM RESOURCE LOCATOR of the page.

invitation bot A malicious BOT which intrudes into a CHAT ROOM and issues an invitation to the participants to join some other chat topic which does not exist.

IO An abbreviation for Input/Output, the processes and devices used to communicate with a computer system.

IOH Abbreviation for I'm Outa Here used in CHAT ROOMS.

IOTP See INTERNET OPEN TRADING PROTOCOL.

IOW Abbreviation for In Other Words used in CHAT ROOMS, EMAILS, and NEWSGROUPS.

IP See INTERNET PROTOCOL.

IP address An abbreviation for INTERNET PROTOCOL ADDRESS.

IPCA See INTERNET PCA REGISTRATION AUTHORITY.

IP multicast The broadcasting of a message using MULTICASTING to a number of computers on the Internet using TCP-IP. Each of these computers has subscribed to a MULTICAST GROUP which is identified in the destination part of the message.

IP-SEC A standard developed by the INTERNET ENGINEERING TASK FORCE for secure communication between FIREWALL servers.

IPng See INTERNET PROTOCOL NEXT GENERATION.

ippie An early user of the Internet who had his or her own INTERNET PROTOCOL ADDRESS and who was among the first users of fast communications technologies such as T1 CARRIER.

IP spoofing Some networked systems allow access only to hosts which have a particular INTERNET PROTOCOL ADDRESS. IP spoofing involves an unauthorized entry into one of these systems. It is carried out by modifying PACKETS of data that are sent to a network so that they look as if they have originated from a computer whose address indicates that it is allowed access into the network.

IP switching The processes involved in moving a packet of data round the Internet from one computer to another.

IP telephony The use of the Internet to carry voice communications, thus bypassing expensive telephone company charges. There are still major problems with this form of communication such as voice degradation at peak loading time. The companies who provide this service are known as IP TELEPHONY SERVICE PROVIDERS.

IP telephony service provider A company that provides services that enable an Internet user to carry out phone-like conversations over the Internet.

IPv6 See INTERNET PROTOCOL VERSION 6.

IPX See INTERNET PACKET EXCHANGE.

IRC See INTERNET RELAY CHAT.

IRCOP Someone who has been granted major privileges on an INTERNET RELAY CHAT network. For example, they are able to disconnect or suspend a user of such a service. Normally an IRCOP is someone who is in charge of a server used for Internet relay chat.

IREDI See IMMEDIATE RESPONSE EDI.

IRL Abbreviation for In Real Life used in CHAT ROOMS, EMAILS, and NEWSGROUPS. See also FACE TO FACE.

iron Usually used in a derogatory way to describe the large mainframe computers that were common until the mid-1980s. Normally used in the phrase 'big iron'.

iron age Used to describe the period prior to the current Internet period when early technology such as card readers and ferrite core memories were employed.

iron box A computer or set of computers that has been specially configured in order to trap a CRACKER who has infiltrated a computer system. *See also* FLYTRAP and WEB TRAP.

irregular network A network which does not conform to any one of the standard architectures such as RING NETWORK, STAR NETWORK, TREE NETWORK or COMPLETE NETWORK. The Internet is the largest and best-known irregular network.

IRTF *See* INTERNET RESEARCH TASK FORCE.

ISAPI *See* INTERNET SERVER APPLICATION PROGRAMMING INTERFACE.

ISDN *See* INTEGRATED SERVICES DIGITAL NETWORK.

ISO Acronym for the INTERNATIONAL STANDARDS ORGANIZATION.

isochronous Adjective used to describe a form of data transfer that ensures a guaranteed minimum TRANSMISSION RATE. This is particularly important for data such as audio data where the signal degrades to the point where it cannot be understood if the transmission rate falls below a certain figure. *See also* QUALITY OF SERVICE.

isochronous network A high-speed network for which the LATENCY can be easily predicted. Such networks are used for applications such as VIDEO ON DEMAND.

isolation A property that a DISTRIBUTED TRANSACTION must have. It means that a transaction must not be interfered with by another transaction. For example, a banking transaction which credits a series of accounts must not be interfered with by another transaction which debits the accounts leaving the database of accounts in an inconsistent state. This is an important property of a distributed transaction; the others are ATOMICITY, CONSISTENCY, and DURABILITY. *See also* ACID.

ISP *See* INTERNET SERVICE PROVIDER.

ISTM Abbreviation for It Seems To Me used in CHAT ROOMS, EMAILS, and NEWSGROUPS.

ISTR Abbreviation for I Seem To Recall used in EMAILS and NEWSGROUPS.

IT An abbreviation for Information Technology.

ITIGBS Abbreviation for I Think I Am Going To Be Sick used in EMAILS and NEWSGROUPS.

ITRO Abbreviation for In The Region Of used in CHAT ROOMS, EMAILS, and NEWSGROUPS. Usually used to indicate some approximation: for example, 'I think there were ITRO 200 users of this newsgroup last year.'

ITSP *See* IP TELEPHONY SERVICE PROVIDER.

ITU *See* INTERNATIONAL TELECOMMUNICATIONS UNION.

ITU-R The part of the INTERNATIONAL TELECOMMUNICATIONS UNION that deals with radio communications.

ITU-T The part of the INTERNATIONAL TELECOMMUNICATIONS UNION that deals with telecommunications standardization.

IVR *See* INTERACTIVE VOICE RESPONSE.

I-way A short version of INFORMATION SUPERHIGHWAY.

IWBNI Abbreviation for It Would Be Nice If used in EMAILS and NEWSGROUPS.

IXC Acronym for INTEREXCHANGE CARRIER.

IYFEG *See* INSERT YOUR FAVOURITE ETHNIC GROUP.

IYSS Abbreviation for If You Say So used in CHAT ROOMS, EMAILS, and NEWSGROUPS.

IYSWIM Abbreviation for If You See What I Mean used in EMAILS and NEWSGROUPS.

J

jabber The transmission of erroneous data across a network, for example by a malfunctioning NETWORK INTERFACE CARD. It is also used to refer to the users of CHAT facilities who make meaningless contributions.

jacking in The process of logging in to some VIRTUAL REALITY system such as a MULTI USER DUNGEON.

jacking out The process of logging out from some VIRTUAL REALITY system such as a MULTI USER DUNGEON.

jaggies The small 'steps' appearing on a sloping line on a bitmapped graphic display, caused by the use of PIXELS to approximate a line.

Jakarta A project which forms part of the APACHE project. It has the aim to develop servers that are integrated with the JAVA programming language. One part of the project is TOMCAT.

JAM Abbreviation for Just A Minute used in CHAT ROOMS. For example, 'JAM, are you sure that's right?'

jamming Attacking a computer network by preventing traffic flowing to one or more computers in the network. Jamming can be achieved by a DENIAL OF SERVICE ATTACK on a number of key computers in a network through which a large amount of traffic flows.

JANET The network for the education and research community within the United Kingdom. It is managed by the United Kingdom Education and Research Networking Association.

JAR *See* JAVA ARCHIVE.

JAR file A file that contains either files used by a Java APPLET or JAVA BEANS. Such files use a form of file COMPRESSION.

Jargon File An online dictionary of computer definitions, many of which are written in an amusing way. The paper edition of this dictionary is published by MIT Press. The dictionary contains a fair number of Internet terms but most of them are either jargon or computer science terms.

jarjar Verb used to describe the addition of superfluous features to a software product, usually in order to secure upgrade sales. Often these features render the product marginally more unusable.

JARS *See* JAVA APPLET RATING SERVICE.

Java A programming language which was developed by Sun Microsystems. It has a number of features which make it an excellent medium for developing programs for the Internet. The first is the fact that it contains a large number of facilities for carrying out tasks such as connecting to another computer on the Internet and sending data to it. Before the development of Java this type of processing was carried out in programming languages such as C and C++ and required some very arcane programming. The facilities in Java for carrying out tasks such as communicating with a computer using TCP-IP has meant that programs which were hundreds of lines in length have been reduced to tens of lines. The other feature which almost certainly attracted much of the hype that revolved around Java in 1996 and 1997 was the fact that it enabled programming code to be embedded within a WEB PAGE. Up until that time most WEB SITES were, at best, SECOND-GENERATION WEB SITES and, for example, included very little animation or interactivity. One of the main features of Java is its ability to develop programs known as APPLETS. These are programs that can be embedded in a Web page and which can be executed via a BROWSER. Applets can implement a diverse number of functions: for example, they can be used to embed forms in a page, to produce animations, and to interact with databases which are stored on the SERVER where the Web page originated. A third feature of Java which is not directly connected with the Internet, but which has attracted a huge amount of attention is the fact that Java programs are claimed to be portable across a wide variety of computer operating systems. The compiler for the Java programming language produces code known as byte code. This code is a computer-independent low-level language. It can be executed on any operating system which contains a piece of software known as an INTERPRETER. Because this interpreter can easily be implemented on a computer system this means that, in theory, Java programs written for one operating system, say Windows 98, can be transferred to another system such as UNIX just by moving the file containing the byte code without recompiling the program. There has been a major debate raging in the late 1990s about this portability issue; what can be said is that the original Sun aim of total portability is gradually being achieved. This portability has given rise to a major disagreement between Sun and Microsoft, the company which developed the Windows operating systems and other software products, over the licensing of the original Java system produced by Sun, and has led to a number of legal cases. Java resembles the programming language C++—indeed it is a superset of the language which is known as an OBJECT-ORIENTED PROGRAMMING LANGUAGE and hence is somewhat more difficult to learn than earlier languages such as C. Java should not be regarded solely as a programming language but more as a technology. For example, it has given rise to a software reuse model known as JAVA BEANS, a new way of programming servers using programs called SERVLETS, and a model of interconnectivity known as JINI which enables a diverse number of hardware devices including computers, FAX machines, intelligent overhead projectors, and electronic notebooks to be easily connected together. *See also* JAVA APPLET RATING SERVICE.

Java Applet Rating Service One of the best software sites for JAVA code. It is a repository of Java APPLETs which have been rated by their users. This site is normally the first stop for developers looking for applets.

Java archive An archive format used to store FILES containing JAVA code. Usually abbreviated to JAR.

Java Bean A component technology associated with the JAVA programming language. It enables the developer to produce a component such as a small spreadsheet and reuse it time and time again in a variety of systems.

Java Database Connectivity A collection of software which allows JAVA programs to interface to a RELATIONAL DATABASE. The technology allows companies to provide access to their existing databases. The software allows a programmer to connect to a database, send a QUERY expressed in SQL to the database, and receive the results of the query. It is often abbreviated to JDBC.

Java Development Kit A collection of software freely distributed by Sun Microsystems which enables users to write, execute, debug, and document programs written in the JAVA programming language. It is usually abbreviated to JDK.

Java Electronic Commerce Framework A series of code libraries associated with the JAVA programming language which provide facilities for the implementers of ECOMMERCE systems. Typically it includes facilities for WALLETS, electronic payments, and security. Combined with software such as the JAVA DATABASE CONNECTIVITY it enables developers who use Java to produce ENTERPRISE SYSTEMS.

Java Native Interface An APPLICATION PROGRAMMING INTERFACE to the JAVA programming language which enables programmers to interface Java code to code which is specific to some PLATFORM or to another programming language. Often abbreviated to JNI.

javant garde Sometimes used to describe someone who evangelizes on the superiority of Internet technology such as the WORLD WIDE WEB and JAVA over 'old' technologies such as books. More often than not it is used to describe those who proselytize Java technology.

JavaScript A programming language which bears some resemblance to C++.

JavaScript programs are inserted into the HTML of a WEB PAGE and are executed by a BROWSER. JavaScript contains facilities which include allowing interaction with a user's environment, changing the look of a page, and responding to events such as a mouse being clicked. A typical example of a JavaScript application is changing a graphic when it is clicked. The JavaScript code that does this is attached to the behaviour of mouse clicking: when a mouse clicks, the browser checks where it occurred and if it was within the graphic then the graphic is changed. This is a technique used when developing ROLL-OVERS, where the appearance of a graphic changes when a mouse passes over it. Contrary to its name, JavaScript bears only a fragmentary resemblance to the JAVA programming language.

Java Server Pages The JAVA equivalent of ACTIVE SERVER PAGES. It is a technology that allows the programmer to vary the content of WEB PAGES which are sent back to a browser. For example, it enables rapidly changing pages to be developed for a financial reporting system, where changes to the underlying data occur every few seconds. Often abbreviated to JSP.

Java stripping The process of removing all references to JAVA code within a WEB PAGE. This is done in highly secure environments in order to prevent hostile AP-PLETS from executing on a computer within the environment.

Java Virtual Machine An idealized computer for which the JAVA programming language was designed. When implementing Java on a new computer the first step to be carried out is to implement a simulation of this computer using software that is resident on the target computer. The Java virtual machine enables developers to implement a Java system very easily.

J code The rudimentary language to which JAVA programs are converted when they are compiled. The vast majority of OPERATING SYSTEMS have software installed which is capable of executing programs expressed in this code. This has ensured that Java is a highly portable programming language. However, the cost of this portability is a degree of slowness.

JDBC *See* JAVA DATABASE CONNECTIVITY.

JDK *See* JAVA DEVELOPMENT KIT.

JECF *See* JAVA ELECTRONIC COMMERCE FRAMEWORK.

jello A POSTING which has been excessively CROSS-POSTED to a number of NEWS-GROUPS irrespective of the topic of the posting.

JEPI *See* JOINT ELECTRONIC PAYMENTS INITIATIVE.

JIC Abbreviation for Just In Case used in CHAT ROOMS, EMAILS, and NEWSGROUPS.

jiffy Jargon used to describe the period of one clock tick on a computer.

Jigsaw The experimental server which has been developed by the WORLD WIDE WEB CONSORTIUM. Its main use has been to evaluate new Web technologies such as SERVLETS, version 1.1 of the HTTP protocol, and further extensions to this version of the protocol. It is the server equivalent of the AMAYA browser.

JINI A technology developed as part of the Java program. It enables a wide variety of devices not normally associated with DISTRIBUTED SYSTEMS to be networked, such as smoke detectors, televisions, and burglar alarms. Its developers and proponents hope this technology will bring about applications associated with MEDIA CONVERGENCE.

jitter 1. What happens on a twisted pair ETHERNET when signals become out of phase with each other.
2. What happens when a signal which has a regular time period starts to diverge from the period.

JK Abbreviation for Just Kidding used in CHAT ROOMS, EMAILS, and NEWSGROUPS.

JMHO Abbreviation for Just My Humble Opinion used in EMAILS and NEWSGROUPS. One of a number of opinion abbreviations including IMHO and IMAO.

JMO Abbreviation for Just My Opinion used in EMAILS and NEWSGROUPS.

JNI Acronym for JAVA NATIVE INTERFACE.

jock An expert in a particular computing field. The word is usually preceded by the particular field in which the expert deploys his or her expertise: for example BROWSER Jock. *See also* GEEK, TECHIE, and ALPHA GEEK.

joe An ACCOUNT which has the same password and ACCOUNT NAME. Such accounts are easy to break into since a CRACKER can easily discover the account name.

Joint Electronic Payments Initiative A standard for secure electronic payments over the net which is being developed by the WORLD WIDE WEB CONSORTIUM. For the buyer it enables a variety of payment protocols to be used; for the merchant it acts as a secure messenger, passing payment details to a protocol such as the HYPERTEXT TRANSFER PROTOCOL. *See also* SECURED ELECTRONIC TRANSACTION STANDARD. It is often abbreviated to JEPI.

Joint Photographic Experts Group A popular format for BITMAPPED GRAPHICS frequently found on the WORLD WIDE WEB. It is usually abbreviated to JPEG. It is a graphic format which can describe images that can contain over 16.7 million colours. Consequently it is used when an image is a complex one with large number of colours and colour effects such as shading. Photographs are usually displayed on WEB PAGES using this format. A major advantage of the JPEG format is that it can be compressed, using a LOSSY COMPRESSION SCHEME, by a factor of up to 20 to 1 without any discernible degradation in the image.

JPEG *See* JOINT PHOTOGRAPHIC EXPERTS GROUP.

JPG Acronym that is occasionally used for JOINT PHOTOGRAPHIC EXPERTS GROUP. In a lower case form it is also used as a FILE EXTENSION for files holding JPEG images.

JPIG An Internet user who lobbies for the removal of pornographic images from the net. Usually written using capitals as a play on JPEG.

J Random Equivalent to John Doe or the man on the Clapham omnibus. Used in NEWSGROUPS, CHAT ROOMS, and EMAIL messages it is often suffixed with a noun to indicate some category of person: for example, 'Would you let J Random NEWBIE loose with this software package?'

JScript A shortened version of JAVASCRIPT.

JSP *See* JAVA SERVER PAGES.

JTLYK Abbreviation for Just To Let You Know used in EMAILS and NEWSGROUPS.

Jumpstation One of the first SEARCH ENGINES to use a BOT. It is now only of historical interest.

junk email The EMAIL equivalent of junk mail. It is more commonly known as SPAM.

junk mailer A name for an Internet user who carries out SPAMMING. Junk mailers normally buy EMAIL ADDRESSES from companies who collect them using ADDRESS HARVESTERS. They then use these addresses to send mail which usually contains some inducement to buy a product or service.

JVM *See* JAVA VIRTUAL MACHINE.

K

k A letter used to denote either a thousand or 1,024. For example kbytes stands for 1,024 bytes.

KA9Q An implementation of TCP-IP for amateur radio networks. The name is derived from the call sign of the radio amateur who first implemented the PROTOCOL.

kamikaze packet Another name for a CHRISTMAS TREE PACKET.

kb An abbreviation for KILOBYTE: 1,024 BYTES.

kbps An abbreviation for KILOBITS per second, a measure of transmission speed.

Ken A user who frequently initiates FLAMES. The derivation of the term is unclear, but the most probable is that it was the first name of an early flamer.

Kerberos A widely used security protocol which uses a SERVER known as an AUTHENTICATION SERVER to authenticate passwords and administer ENCRYPTION schemes. It has been widely employed on computers which run the UNIX operating system.

Kermit A popular PROTOCOL for transferring text files and binary files over a variety of transmission media. There are implementations of this protocol for a large number of PLATFORMS.

kerning The term used to describe the process of moving letters closer together for better visual effect.

kevork A verb taken from the name of Dr Jack Kervorkian, the American doctor who has been accused of assisting the death of the terminally ill. It is used to describe the process of terminating a program: for example, killing the downloading of a WEB PAGE when you see that it contains uninteresting material or killing a program because it is demonstrating undesirable features such as looping interminably doing nothing.

key 1. A set of characters used in the ENCRYPTION of a message. The key is used to vary the ALGORITHM used to transform the message into a form in which it cannot be read by an unauthorized person. For example, a very simple use of a key would be a sequence of character pairs where, when the first character in a pair is encountered in a text, it is replaced by the second character. Once a message has been encrypted it is sent to its recipient who then uses the key for DECRYPTION, returning the message to its original form. *See also* PUBLIC KEY, PRIVATE KEY, and SYMMETRIC KEY ENCRYPTION.
2. A unique set of characters that identify a record in a FILE. For example, in a file containing employee records, each employee is associated with a unique works number which acts as a key.

keyboard plaque The dirt and dust that builds up on a keyboard after considerable use.

keyboard sniffer A program which reads the keystrokes made by a user and transmits them to someone else. Such programs are usually used by intruders into computer systems in order to capture important information such as PASSWORDS.

key escrow A technique claimed to be a good compromise between the needs of law enforcement agencies to access messages sent over a network and the requirements of personal privacy. A key escrow scheme involves the user of an ENCRYPTION ALGORITHM depositing the KEY used in the algorithm with a trusted third party, such as a bank. If a law enforcement agency requires the key then it is made available to them by the third party only after a warrant has been issued. There is also a very practical rationale for such a service: if the holder of a key loses it or it is destroyed then all the data associated with the key can be lost; having the key held by a third party guards against this. The third party is often known as a TRUSTED THIRD PARTY.

key file A FILE which contains the KEYS used for activities such as sending or accessing secure WEB SITES. Usually these files are strongly encrypted and a PASSWORD or PASSPHRASE is required to enter them.

key library A set of KEYS used for ENCRYPTION shared by a group of users. To access the library requires the use of another key.

key management In a network there are many users who have different KEYS that allow them different levels of ACCESS to the network. Key management is the process of generating, certifying, distributing, and revoking these keys. It is one of the most difficult of all security tasks.

key manager A key manager is a software tool which allows users to manage KEYS and DIGITAL CERTIFICATES. Typically such a tool enables a user to list certificates, acquire and delete them, view them and verify them for authenticity. With the increasing use of such security devices in the Internet and the need for users to possess a number of keys and interact with a number of digital certificate authorities, such software is becoming more and more popular.

key pal The Internet equivalent of a pen pal.

key recovery encryption system Passwords used for ENCRYPTION can be very long and not very memorable. A key recovery encryption system is one which allows for the safe storage and recovery of such keys.

key ring The PUBLIC KEY and PRIVATE KEY used in PUBLIC KEY ENCRYPTION.

key search attack A form of BRUTE FORCE ATTACK where the key used for the ENCRYPTION of messages is found by decrypting messages that have been encrypted with every possible key that could have been used. The longer the key the longer it takes to find it. As computers become more powerful such attacks become more and more feasible and considerable research has to be carried out by cryptographers to devise more and more powerful encryption technology.

keyspace The collection of all possible values for a KEY used in ENCRYPTION. The larger the keyspace the more difficult it is to break the encryption method. *See also* COST OF CRACKING ADJUSTMENT.

keyword A word used in a QUERY, For example the keywords 'Java' and 'compiler' might be used in a SEARCH ENGINE query which looks for COMPILERS that process the JAVA programming language.

keyword advert A BANNER ADVERT which appears on a WEB PAGE when the reader of that page types a KEYWORD into a form. Such adverts are usually related to the search being carried out and are retrieved and displayed by the SEARCH ENGINE. *See* KEYWORD PURCHASING.

keyword density A metric which quantifies how close together in a WEB PAGE keywords used in a KEYWORD SEARCH are. It is one of the metrics used by a number of SEARCH ENGINES to determine the order in which the results of a search are presented to the user.

keyword purchasing The purchase of a KEYWORD by companies from SEARCH ENGINE providers so that when a particular keyword is used in a search a BANNER ADVERT for that company is displayed on the WEB PAGES that are returned by the search engine.

keyword search A search of WEB PAGES, an application database, or the database used by a SEARCH ENGINE for documents that contain a number of KEYWORDS. These keywords are often written with BOOLEAN CONNECTIVES separating them. For example, the keyword search 'Java AND compiler' looks for all those documents or records which contain the keywords 'Java' and 'compiler'.

keyword stuffing The process of inserting a large number of keywords into a WEB PAGE in order to ensure that it has a prominent place in the list of pages returned by a SEARCH ENGINE. A practice also known as SPAMDEXING.

KIBO Abbreviation for Knowledge In Bullshit Out. The term describes what happens when valuable data is communicated to an organization or person and ignored or only partially understood. It is an enhancement of the common saying 'garbage in garbage out'. *See also* GIGO.

kiboze Used to describe the frequent scanning of NEWSGROUPS by a user, often using a software tool, in order to detect certain keywords in a POSTING. Usually the user issues a further posting in response. So, for example, a user who has strong views about the Microsoft Corporation may scan a large number of newsgroups in order to respond to any posting mentioning that company, often not keeping to the main point of the posting.

kill To end a particular event or action violently. For example, if a program is misbehaving it can be killed by pressing some keys on a keyboard, or if a THREAD in a NEWSGROUP is deviating from the aims of the newsgroup then the MODERATOR may kill it. *See* TOPIC DRIFT.

killer app Short for killer application: a program which is so successful that it drives a huge demand for hardware to support it and peripheral software to interact with it. Probably the best recent example of this was NETSCAPE NAVIGATOR. *See also* FILLER APP.

kill file A FILE that contains information which enables the user of a NEWSGROUP to FILTER any POSTINGS on a particular topic or from particular users. *See also* BOZO FILTER.

kill list Another name for a B LIST.

kilobit A unit of transmission speed equivalent to 1,024 BITS.

kilobyte A unit of storage equivalent to 1,024 BYTES.

Kilroy page A WEB PAGE which has been developed by a company or a single user whose sole aim is to announce the company or person's presence.

KIS *See* KNOWBOT INFORMATION SERVICE.

KIT Abbreviation for Keep In Touch used in CHAT ROOMS, EMAILS, and NEWSGROUPS.

KLB *See* KNOWN LAZY BASTARD.

knowbot 1. A BOT which wanders the WORLD WIDE WEB looking for specific information, such as new product announcements.
2. Used in a derogatory way to refer to an arrogant user who claims extensive knowledge about a particular topic.

Knowbot Information Service A service which provides an interface to a variety of Internet DIRECTORY SERVICES such as WHOIS and FINGER. It is also known as NETADDRESS.

known lazy bastard A user who instead of reading a manual asks others, often via a NEWSGROUP, for information and advice. Often abbreviated to KLB.

known plaintext attack An attack on a text to which ENCRYPTION has been applied. In this attack the intruder knows the contents of the text and, using this information, attempts to discover the cryptographic KEY used to encrypt the text. Once the key has been determined the intruder can decrypt other texts.

known text attack Alternative term for KNOWN PLAINTEXT ATTACK.

Kobrigram A letter threatening litigation in response to some defamatory material published on the Internet. Named after Helena Kobrin, a lawyer for the Church of Scientology, who has threatened copyright lawsuits against users who have posted documents originated by the church.

KOC Abbreviation for Kiss On Cheek used in CHAT ROOMS, EMAILS, and NEWSGROUPS.

KOL Abbreviation for Kiss On Lips used in CHAT ROOMS, EMAILS, and NEWSGROUPS.

KOTC Abbreviation for Kiss On The Cheek used in CHAT ROOMS, EMAILS, and NEWSGROUPS.

KUTGW Abbreviation for Keep Up The Good Work used in CHAT ROOMS, EMAILS, and NEWSGROUPS.

KWIM Abbreviation for Know What I Mean used in EMAILS and NEWSGROUPS.

KYPO Abbreviation for Keep Your Pants On used in CHAT ROOMS, EMAILS, and NEWSGROUPS.

L2TP *See* LAYER TWO TUNNELING PROTOCOL.

L8R A HAKSPEK abbreviation for Later used in CHAT ROOMS, EMAILS, and NEWS-GROUPS.

lag A period of time during which nothing happens: for example, the time that it takes for a FILE to be DOWNLOADED. It is also called a HANG.

lamer A derogatory term for a user whose behaviour is the result of a lack of knowledge of the Internet. A much more derogatory version of NEWBIE.

LAN *See* LOCAL AREA NETWORK.

LAN bridge A BRIDGE that connects two SEGMENTS of a LOCAL AREA NETWORK.

LAN ignorant program A program designed to operate as a stand-alone program. It contains no facilities which enable it to be used in a network.

lase To print a document or graphic using a laser printer. For example, 'Can you lase me that document as soon as possible?'

last mile The cabling that connects a user to the Internet and which uses standard telephone PROTOCOLS. At the time of writing this is mainly copper-based cabling which has been laid by the telephone companies. Most phone companies now have plans to migrate to fibre-based technologies or other technologies such as ISDN.

last mile problem A term used to describe the fact that many home telephone systems are still connected to the Internet via slow media. There is a major BAND-WIDTH mismatch between this type of connection and the high-speed technologies that are gradually being deployed, such as ASYNCHRONOUS TRANSFER MODE.

LATA *See* LOCAL ACCESS AND TRANSPORT AREA.

latency The time required to send an empty message from one computer to another on a network. It measures the time taken to access the network at both the sender and receiver end and those delays which occur inside the network.

launch 1. To start a computer program. For example, it is necessary to launch a BROWSER before SURFING the WORLD WIDE WEB.
2. To release a WEB SITE on its first day.

layer Many computer systems are defined in terms of a layered architecture. For example, the INTERNET LAYERED ARCHITECTURE is based on a five-layer model and the OSI REFERENCE MODEL is based on a seven-layer architecture. Each layer provides functionally distinct services to the other layers: for example, one layer may be responsible for checking correct transmission of data, with the top layer providing a service to programs that use the architecture. Each layer draws on services provided by the next layer down.

layered architecture A way of structuring a system in which each component is implemented as a LAYER which draws upon services made available by a lower layer. The INTERNET LAYERED ARCHITECTURE is a good example of this.

Layer Two Tunnelling Protocol An open PROTOCOL standard which is used for the development of VIRTUAL PRIVATE NETWORKS.

LDAP *See* LIGHTWEIGHT DIRECTORY ACCESS PROTOCOL.

LDR Abbreviation for Long Distance Relationship used in CHAT ROOMS, EMAILS, and NEWSGROUPS: a relationship that is carried on using technologies such as EMAIL.

lead generation site A WEB SITE which helps you find products at the lowest price. You inform the site what you want to buy and it finds a number of suppliers who contact you and offer to sell the product at a competitive price.

leading The space between the lines of text in a printed document or a document displayed on some visual output device. The term was originally used in conventional printing and was derived from the lead strips used to separate lines of text.

leaf page A WEB PAGE in a WEB SITE which contains no HYPERLINKS to other pages. It represents a dead end.

leaf site A computer solely devoted to reading and originating NEWSGROUP postings and mail.

leapfrog attack The use of an illegally obtained PASSWORD to access a computer or computer network. The password may have been obtained by a variety of means ranging from a WHITE BOARD ATTACK to the use of a PASSWORD SNIFFER.

learning bridge A BRIDGE which has intelligence built into it. It can monitor the traffic state of a network and then determine how to route data efficiently through it.

leased line A telecommunications line, usually a phone line, which is rented exclusively to establish a permanent connection to a network or to connect two networks together.

least privilege A principle adhered to by the designers of security systems for networks: that every user of the network should have just enough, but no more privileges to enable them to carry out their jobs. For example, users should not be allowed to access files that they do not need.

LEC *See* LOCAL EXCHANGE CARRIER.

legal disclaimer Now that the use of the Internet is increasing dramatically, companies and employees are using legal disclaimers more and more. For example, EMAILS often contain some text in their SIGNATURE FILE which states that the contents are the opinions and views of the author rather than the company. Another example is the legal disclaimer placed on software DOWNLOADED from the Internet. A third example is the practice of companies placing legal notices on WEB SITES to which access is restricted:

this is done in order to make the prosecution of CRACKERS who enter the site easier.

Lempel Ziv Welsh coding A class of ALGORITHMS which carries out data COMPRESSION using a dictionary containing frequently found combinations of symbols: for example, the combination 'the' found in natural language texts. The algorithms replace these frequently occurring combinations of symbols by smaller combinations of symbols. The dictionary used in this method contains fixed length entries which occupy the same number of bits. A variant known as ADAPTIVE LEMPEL ZIV WELSH CODING uses a variable length dictionary.

less than The symbol < used to identify the beginning of a TAG in the HYPERTEXT MARKUP LANGUAGE. *See also* GREATER THAN.

letter bomb An EMAIL message containing an ATTACHMENT which carries out a malicious act such as deleting the recipient's files. This is an increasingly common way of spreading a VIRUS. *See also* TROJAN HORSE and FRIENDS AND FAMILY VIRUS.

lexical analysis The process of automatically examining the text passing down a TRANSMISSION LINE to detect certain words or phrases. One use of this form of monitoring is to detect employees who are accessing undesirable sites. For example, the occurrence of words such as 'sex' and phrases such as 'big girls' travelling on a transmission line to a BROWSER would indicate an interest in non-work-related activities.

LHM Abbreviation for Lord Help Me used in CHAT ROOMS, EMAILS, and NEWSGROUPS.

LHO Abbreviation for Laughing Head Off used in CHAT ROOMS, EMAILS, and NEWSGROUPS.

LHU Abbreviation for Lord Help Us used in CHAT ROOMS, EMAILS, and NEWSGROUPS.

light client A term synonymous with THIN CLIENT.

Lightweight Directory Access Protocol A cut-down version of the DIRECTORY ACCESS PROTOCOL defined in the x500 standard for DIRECTORY SERVICES.

It is supported by a number of large companies including Netscape, IBM, Microsoft, and Novell. Usually abbreviated to LDAP.

line conditioning The insertion of hardware elements into a transmission line in order to modify its electrical characteristics: for example, inserting micro amplifiers in a transmission line in order to boost a signal.

line noise The spurious characters which travel down a transmission line because of a hardware fault or electrical interference.

link checker A software tool which checks the correctness of HYPERLINKS in a WEB SITE. One of the major problems faced by WEBMASTERS who have to administer large sites is that the links in their Web documents become corrupted as the site grows and is modified. For example, a link may point to an external page in a site which has disappeared or to an internal page that has been deleted. Another problem is the reverse of this: that of pages, known as ORPHAN PAGES, which are not linked to any other page. A link checker is a software utility which examines links and pages and provides a report on the extent of these problems. Such utilities can be stand-alone or can be incorporated into an existing tool such as an HTML EDITOR. Link checkers are an example of a generic type of software known as SITE ADMINISTRATION SOFTWARE. *See also* LINK CHECKING SITE and LINK ROT.

link checking site A WEB SITE which checks the links on another site. Using such a commercial service is straightforward: all that has to be provided is the URL of a Web site. When this has been done the service provides periodic reports on the state of the site and identifies when one of its HYPERLINKS has been broken. The service offered by INTERNET SERVICE PROVIDERS is becoming more and more sophisticated, with facilities including notification via pagers of any problems with a site. *See also* LINK CHECKER, HTML VALIDATION SITE and WEB ROT.

link farm 1. A WEB SITE devoted to storing and making available a large collection of HYPERLINKS associated with a particular subject or group of subjects: for example, links to material on a particular computer operating system. Link farms lack the authority of GURU SITES: they are often just a collection of links found by an enthusiast with little surrounding editorial text. Nevertheless, they can be an excellent resource and a starting point for searching a particular topic area.
2. A DIRECTORY containing links to files in other directories.

link rot The process whereby the HYPERLINKS in a Web document become obsolete. Such links disappear because WEB SITES close down or are moved to new locations and the owner of the site does not provide automatic REDIRECTION for a visitor.

link segment A cable which connects a computer to some interconnecting device such as ROUTER, or connects one interconnecting device to a second interconnecting device.

link state packet A PACKET of data which contains information that is used by ADAPTIVE ROUTING ALGORITHMS to determine the route of a packet through a network.

link swapping The process whereby the owners of two WEB SITES agree to include HYPERLINKS to each other's sites. The sites are often commercial and offer complementary products or services or deal with different aspects of a topic.

Linux A version of UNIX for PCs which came into prominence in the early 1990s since it was distributed at no cost. The late 1990s saw a big expansion of interest in this operating system, which was seen by many of the opponents of the Microsoft operating systems as a viable competitor. A large number of individuals and some organizations including the Chinese government use Linux in conjunction with the APACHE server to host WEB SITES.

list linking Attacking an individual user of the Internet by subscribing him or her to a large number of MAILING LISTS. This results in the user being deluged by a large quantity of EMAIL. Often the emails have large FILE ATTACHMENTS and hence can hugely inconvenience those who have been attacked in this way.

Listserv Most MAILING LISTS are passive: the administrator of the list sends messages to the members. A mailing list which allows the members to post messages is known as a listserv mailing list. It is named after a mailing list server developed for BITNET.

lite An adjective used to describe a software product which has been disabled by removing many of its functions. Such products are usually distributed free in order to tempt the user to buy the fully functioning version. Normally the products are just about viable but their continued use serves as a constant reminder of the missing functions.

little endian Someone who supports the placing of the smallest digit first in a numeric encoding scheme. This is in contrast to a BIG ENDIAN. The Internet has seen a number of heated discussions between both groups; these arguments provides an example of a HOLY WAR.

LiveAudio An important PLUG-IN which allows a BROWSER to play sound files in a number of different formats.

live newsgroup A system which acts as a real-time CHAT ROOM.

live object A software entity embedded into a WEB PAGE which adds an animation facility to it. APPLETS are a good example of live objects.

living in hypertext Used to describe an individual who has a lot to hide.

LLTA Abbreviation for Lots and Lots of Thunderous Applause used in CHAT ROOMS, EMAILS, and NEWSGROUPS.

LMAO Abbreviation for Laughing My Ass Off used in CHAT ROOMS, EMAILS, and NEWSGROUPS.

load 1. To place a computer program into memory in order to execute it. It is now often used to describe the process whereby a WEB PAGE and INLINE IMAGES are placed in a BROWSER ready for display. **2.** The amount of work being asked of a computer system: for example, 'The response of the main server was sluggish. It was really heavily loaded.'

load balancing Administering a network so that the traffic across it is spread as evenly as possible across the transmission lines. One of the most difficult tasks that a NETWORK ADMINISTRATOR has to carry out.

loaded line A transmission line which has had electrical elements such a resistors inserted into it in order to change its electrical characteristics.

load shedding The process whereby a SYSTEM ADMINISTRATOR specifies that whenever a SERVER load exceeds a certain number it processes no more requests for its service, and that such requests are either sent to another server, queued, or rejected.

load time The time it takes to load a WEB PAGE in a BROWSER so that all the elements of the page can be viewed. The time depends on a number of factors including the number of words on the page, the amount of network TRAFFIC, and the amount of video, audio, graphic, and animation technology on the page. *See also* WORLD WIDE WAIT.

local access and transport area An American term used to describe a geographic area that has been assigned to a telephone company. Often abbreviated to LATA.

local area network A small network situated within a single building or a small number of buildings. It is often abbreviated to LAN. Such networks are used to connect computers, printers, and mass storage devices together and to share information. Typically they transmit data at speeds which range from 10 Mbits/s to hundreds of Mbits/s. Local area networks are usually organized around a single transmission line and hence can be regarded as BROADCAST NETWORKS. The two most popular configurations for a LAN are as an ETHERNET network or as a token ring network.

local central office The telephone exchange which lies closest to the telephone. It is also known as a LOCAL EXCHANGE or END OFFICE.

local exchange The telephone exchange which lies closet to the telephone set. It is also known as an END OFFICE or LOCAL CENTRAL OFFICE.

local exchange carrier A US company that holds a virtual monopoly of conventional telephone services within a LOCAL ACCESS AND TRANSPORT AREA.

local loop The connection to the main telephone trunk routes from offices and homes. This is the slowest part of the telephone system which usually relies on slow, outdated analogue technology. It gives rise to the LAST MILE PROBLEM.

locals Used to distinguish the users of a local network such as an ETHERNET from users who are associated with the Internet. For example, 'I am going to have to do something about the loading on the LAN. The locals are getting restless.'

location transparency One of the features of a true DISTRIBUTED SYSTEM: that when the user of the system requests a resource they should not have to provide any information about where the resource is located on the system. For example, when a user wants to read a file and if location transparency is ensured, then all the user need do is quote the name of the FILE. It is then up to the NETWORK OPERATING SYSTEM to discover where it is on the distributed system and retrieve it.

locking The condition that occurs when a TRANSACTION or group of transactions has access to a particular resource in a DISTRIBUTED SYSTEM and other transactions do not. For example, part of a file may be locked while a transaction updates it. If a transaction wants access to a resource that is locked, then it normally has to wait until the resource is released—usually when the transaction that is using it has completed the process it was carrying out.

log file A FILE containing details of activities occurring in a system. For example, a security log file may contain entries which detail any attempted accesses to a PASSWORD FILE. *See* WEB LOG FILE.

log file analysis A number of activities in a distributed system generate FILES describing the details of each activity, known as log files. For example, the process of logging in to a computer generates entries in a log file which monitor activities that could threaten a system security. The process of analysing a log file involves producing summary listings and any exception reports about unusual activities: for example, a user LOGGING in at the dead of night. There are other uses of log file analysis over and above those associated with system and network administration. For example, a WEB SERVER generates information about the HITS that are made on WEB PAGES in a WEB LOG FILE; this is commercially useful in that it provides data on who is visiting a WEB SITE and what pages are popular and enables the WEBMASTER to structure the Web pages so as to maximize the number of visitors.

logging Writing details about an event of interest to a LOG FILE: for example, the start and finish time of a user session with a computer.

logical clock A device invented by the American computer scientist Leslie Lamport which enables time-dependent TRANSACTIONS in a DISTRIBUTED SYSTEM to be properly synchronized. Although it is called a clock there is no reason for it to track the real time; all it does is to function as a counter.

logical time Is the time that is associated with a LOGICAL CLOCK. It is the time used to identify TRANSACTIONS in a DISTRIBUTED SYSTEM.

logic bomb A program that is usually introduced in a computer system via a TROJAN HORSE. The logic bomb carries out a destructive act such as destroying key files. It is programmed to do this at a certain time or when certain conditions occur, such as the perpetrator's name being removed from the personnel files of the company that he or she works for. Logic bombs are usually purely malicious, and there have been examples of them being used as a blackmail device.

log-in To identify yourself to a CLOSED NETWORK. This normally requires the use of an ACCOUNT NAME and a PASSWORD. For example, the process of identifying yourself to a WEB SITE which requires some form of identification.

log-off To terminate a session with a computer. It is the opposite of LOG-IN. It is very occasionally used in everyday speech to describe the termination of some relationship; such as 'I logged off from Jane yesterday.'

log-on transparency A property of a DISTRIBUTED SYSTEM which enables users to employ the same PASSWORD and account name for any of the computers contained in the network that makes up the distributed system.

log out To terminate an interaction with a computer, usually by issuing a shut down or using some command in an operating system such as BYE. It is synonymous with LOG-OFF.

LOL Abbreviation for several phrases such as Laughing Out Loud, Lots Of Love or Lots Of Luck used in CHAT ROOMS, EMAILS, and NEWSGROUPS.

long distance carrier A telephone company which provides service over a large geographic area such as a country.

LookSmart A medium-sized SEARCH ENGINE which is based on directories.

loopback address A distributed system consists of many programs executing on a number of computers communicating with each other using some transmission medium. It is very difficult to test such systems, since programs would be running on a number of physically separated computers. The loopback address is used when distributed programs are brought together on the same computer and tested. It is an IP ADDRESS which ensures that when it is used in a program communication occurs with a program running on the same computer. The loopback address is an IP address with a value 127.0.0.1 with the address expressed in DOTTED QUAD NOTATION. A whole distributed system can be executed on the same computer connected through loopback addresses. The term is derived from the fact that when a message is sent to the loopback address it loops back to the original computer.

lorem ipsum A piece of Latin text (now slightly scrambled) that is used to test the layout of a document or WEB PAGE. The text starts 'Lorem ipsum dolor sit amet, consectetaur adipisicing elit, sed do eiusmod tempor incididunt ut labore et dolore magna aliqua. Ut enim ad minim veniam' and continues for many more words. It is used because it contains the average number of words and letters found in a typical document. The text started out as part of Cicero's *De Finibus et Malorum*.

lossage The loss of some data as a result of a software error or hardware fault. For example, a faulty ROUTER might cause lossage, in that data intended for a destination computer never reaches it.

lossless compression scheme A process which, when applied to a file, compresses it in size but does not result in any loss of contents. *See* GIF for an example of a graphic format which uses a lossless compression scheme.

lossy compression scheme A process which, when applied to a file, compresses it in size but results in the loss of some of the contents. Such a scheme is used when the application which uses the file is one where a small loss of data can be tolerated. For example, complicated graphics can be compressed and some of the picture lost in a way that is indiscernible. For an example of a lossy compression scheme in action *see* JOINT PHOTOGRAPHIC EXPERTS GROUP format.

lost in the noise What happens when the size of a signal traversing a communication line is so small that it cannot be extracted from the underlying noise that occurs on the line.

lost URL service A service used to identify when a UNIFORM RESOURCE LOCATOR no longer exists. Normally the user provides a file of URLs for the service and is sent an EMAIL when one becomes defunct. At the heart of such a service is a fairly simple piece of software which periodically tries connecting to the WEB SITE identified by the URLs and makes a note of those which do not respond.

lots of MIPS but no IO Used to describe someone who has a brilliant mind but is very poor at communication. MIPS is one measure of the power of a computer and IO is an abbreviation for Input Output.

low ping Used to describe a connection to the Internet which is very fast. It is derived from the PING utility which sends a test packet of data to a computer which then sends it back. The utility checks out a connection and produces some timing information.

LTA Abbreviation for Later used in CHAT ROOMS, EMAILS, and NEWSGROUPS.

LTM Abbreviation for Laugh To Myself used in EMAILS and NEWSGROUPS.

LTNS Abbreviation for Long Time No See used in CHAT ROOMS and NEWSGROUPS.

LTS Abbreviation for Laughing To Self used in CHAT ROOMS and NEWSGROUPS.

Luhn formula A mathematical formula used to determine whether a credit card number is valid. It is one of the checks that a credit card company makes before accepting an online TRANSACTION.

LULAB Abbreviation for Love You Like A Brother used in CHAT ROOMS, EMAILS, and NEWSGROUPS.

LULAS Abbreviation for Love You Like A Sister used in CHAT ROOMS, EMAILS, and NEWSGROUPS.

lurking The process of reading the POSTINGS on a NEWSGROUP without initiating any. The term is not normally used in a derogatory sense. *See also* DELURKING.

luser A derogatory term used to describe a naive or untrained computer user. It is a very much more derogatory term than NEWBIE.

Lycos One of the largest SEARCH ENGINES on the Internet. In the late 1990s it migrated towards becoming a PORTAL in which its SEARCH ENGINE functions became embedded.

Lynx A text-only BROWSER which does not display any graphics. Because of this it is much faster than conventional browsers.

LZ77 The first algorithm to use the LEMPEL ZIV WELSH CODING.

LZW *See* LEMPEL ZIV WELSH CODING.

MAC *See* MESSAGE AUTHENTICATION CODE.

machine code The basic instructions of a computer which are executed when a program is run.

macro A chunk of program code which can be repeatedly used by a programmer. Macros implement common functions required in applications such as interest rate calculations in spreadsheets. They are normally associated with packages such as spreadsheets and word processors although they were mainly used within programming languages up to the 1980s.

macro virus A VIRUS which attaches itself to a MACRO and which is executed when the macro is invoked. For example, Microsoft Word has a facility for macros and it is also a very popular word processing package; hence it has been the favourite target of CRACKERS who want to spread viruses.

MAE *See* METROPOLITAN AREA EXCHANGE.

magalog A magazine, often found on the Web, which masquerades as a magazine but is really a catalogue.

magic cookie A term for a collection of data that is passed from one program to another. For example, one program may produce data while the second displays it, with the data being held in the magic cookie. This is an old-fashioned term for a COOKIE; it was first used in connection with the UNIX operating system.

mail bomb The mailing of a large number of EMAIL messages to a recipient who has annoyed others, usually carried out by a number of users. *See also* GANG FAQ and PASTE BOMB.

mailbox A FILE on a computer in which mail is stored. This file is usually found on a MAIL SERVER.

mail bridge A GATEWAY that forwards EMAIL messages from one network to another.

mail delivery agent A program which retrieves messages from a remote EMAIL SERVER and copies them to a user's MAIL PROGRAM. The term is sometimes abbreviated to MDA.

mail exploder The part of an EMAIL system which takes an email addressed to a group of users, usually those on a MAILING LIST, and creates a number of identical emails addressed to the each of the members of the list.

mail filter A program which examines incoming EMAILS and rejects those which the user has indicated that he or she is not interested in. There are a number of criteria for rejecting an email, ranging from the name of the sender to the occurrence of certain words in the HEADER or body of the email. For example, a mail filter for SPAM includes words such as dollar, offer, make, and money. Mail filters can be found as part of a sophisticated mail reader or can be stand-alone programs. *See also* BOZO LIST.

mailing list A list of users who have expressed an interest in a particular topic and who wish to receive regular news via EMAIL about the topic. A mailing list can also contain users who are related to each other in some way: for example, technical staff who are UNIX systems administrators. Mailing lists can be private to a network—for example a mailing list for a business may be one which includes senior staff responsible for marketing; or it could be public—for example a mailing list for users of the Internet who are interested in woodworking. To subscribe to a mailing list is usually very easy. Often all that is required is to send an email to a MAILING LIST SERVER with a simple message such as 'Subscribe' in it. Web-based mailing lists often make use of forms. Increasingly mailing lists are being used by ECOMMERCE enterprises to keep in contact with their customers. A mailing list where the subscribers can contribute is known as a LISTSERV.

mailing list server A server which carries out three functions: first to send EMAIL messages to users who are registered on any of the MAILING LISTS administered by the server; second to respond to users who wish to subscribe to a mailing list or to delete their names from a mailing list; and third to identify and report on any users of a mailing list who cannot be sent email messages and whose messages BOUNCE, usually because their email account has been deleted.

mailing list service A service which allows users to construct a MAILING LIST and send messages to those on the list. There are a number of WEB SITES which provide this service.

mailing list software Software which administers the process of creating and maintaining a MAILING LIST. Such software allows a mailing list administrator to set up a mailing list; permits the administrator to add recipients to the list and delete others; sends emails to the members of a list; allows users to EMAIL requests to register and deregister; and provides summary facilities for a mailing list administrator, such as the identity of members of a list who have had bounced email messages. Mailing list software can also function with little input from an administrator: for example, LISTSERV software allows individual subscribers to add their names to or delete their names from a mailing list. Mailing list software can range from the very simple which allows the maintenance of single lists to sophisticated software which administers hierarchic collections of lists.

mail management software Software which manages a large collection of EMAILS. Typical functions that such software can carry out include categorizing email according to a set of keywords, filing emails, and retrieving a single email or set of emails based on criteria expressed in a QUERY LANGUAGE: for example, selecting emails which contain certain keywords which were sent after a particular date. Such software used to consist of stand-alone programs but the functions of mail management software are gradually being integrated into email software.

mail merge The process of merging a set of addresses and other personalised information into a word-processed document, so that a whole series of versions of the document are produced, each of which is personalized to the recipient.

mail program A program which retrieves and sends EMAILS to and from a MAIL SERVER and carries out a number of functions associated with the storage, reading, and writing of email. These include constructing an email, constructing a MAILING LIST, sending an email, storing an email, and retrieving emails which match a specific set of criteria.

mail reflector A program that sends out files or EMAILS in response to a command embedded in an email. For example, a mail reflector may administer a DATABASE of software manuals and might respond to an email containing the command 'manual' followed by the name of the manual by sending the designated manual as an attachment.

mail server A SERVER which receives and sends EMAIL.

mail storm The receipt of a large number of EMAIL messages after a period when no emails were received due to a hardware fault such as a malfunctioning MAIL SERVER.

mail thread A series of EMAILS dealing with the same issue. Such threads often contain emails which include text from previous emails. They then turn out to be the email equivalent of the INCLUDE WAR.

mail transfer agent A program executed on a server that transfers mail from an email CLIENT to a MAIL SERVER. It is often abbreviated to MTA.

mail user agent An alternative name for a MAIL PROGRAM. It is sometimes abbreviated to MUA.

mainframe computer A large computer situated in its own air-conditioned room. It normally contains at least one very powerful processor and many times more memory than a personal computer. Such computers were the main workhorses of computing up to the late 1980s.

Since then their dominance has been challenged by CLIENT SERVER COMPUTING in which the processing power and storage associated with an enterprise's applications is distributed among a large number of smaller computers connected by some networking technology. Mainframe computers are still found in companies, but many commentators have predicted their demise in the first decade of the twenty-first century.

male connection A hardware connection which consists of one or more pieces of protruding metal.

malicious applet An APPLET which is downloaded to a client computer via a WEB PAGE and which carries out a malicious act such as hogging a processor by carrying out a computationally heavy process. *See also* VIRUS and BLACK WIDOW. Usually such applets are involved in DENIAL OF SERVICE ATTACKS. *See also* CRAPPLET.

malicious code Program code which has been added to or inserted into existing program code in order to carry out a criminal action. VIRUSES are examples of malicious code.

malware A generic term used to describe software such as VIRUSES which have been developed for malicious intent.

MAN *See* METROPOLITAN AREA NETWORK.

management information base The collection of data used by the SIMPLE NETWORK MANAGEMENT PROTOCOL to manage the devices connected to a TCP-IP network. It is often abbreviated to MIB.

management support system A generic term used to describe software which provides help to a manager in carrying out his or her job. It can describe anything from a sophisticated DECISION SUPPORT SYSTEM to a simple program which simulates a Filofax.

mandatory access control The collection of policies and procedures which enforce a company's policy about the sharing of data, both between its employees and between employees and the public. Occasionally abbreviated to MAC.

man in the middle attack An attack on a computer system whereby the attacker intercepts messages between two entities on a network, for example a SERVER and a CLIENT, and makes each one think it is communicating with the other. This form of attack can be addressed by means of ENCRYPTION and technologies such as the SECURE SOCKETS LAYER.

mapping An ECOMMERCE term which means targeting an audience, as in the sentence 'The Web site is mapping senior managers.'

markup language A text-processing language which embeds commands into the text that is to be processed. These commands then instruct a display device or a printer to carry out some formatting. For example, the command <BR> found in HTML instructs a BROWSER to issue a line break. Markup languages have a long history and were the main medium for word and document processing in the 1970s and 1980s. However, they were eclipsed by more sophisticated word processors in the late 1980s. There is now a renaissance of such languages due to the fact that the main tool for developing Web pages is the HYPERTEXT MARKUP LANGUAGE which is an archetypal markup language. Other important markup languages which are associated with the Internet are the EXTENSIBLE MARKUP LANGUAGE and the STANDARDIZED GENERAL MARKUP LANGUAGE.

Marquee 1. A BANNER which contains text that usually scrolls in a westward direction in a WEB PAGE. Marquees are normally used as advertising or for displaying breaking content such as news headlines. **2**. A synonym for SPLASH SCREEN.

marshalling The process of collecting together data from some data structure and converting it into a form that is capable of being sent over a network. For example, objects produced by a program written in an OBJECT-ORIENTED PROGRAMMING LANGUAGE such as JAVA need to be marshalled before they are sent to another computer.

martian A strange occurrence on a network for which there is no explanation:

for example, a SERVER malfunctioning then CRASHing but quickly returning to normal operation.

martian mail EMAIL messages which, because of systems errors, find their way to the wrong destination.

masquerading 1. Pretending to be another user, usually in order to make an illegal access to a computer network. **2**. Used to describe the process whereby a piece of hardware such as a telephone or a CLIENT computer is configured to appear as a different telephone or client.

mass customization Another name for MASS INDIVIDUALIZATION: a term used in ECOMMERCE circles to describe the large-scale development of products which are customized to individual buyers.

mass individualization A term used in ECOMMERCE to describe the large-scale development of products which are customized to buyers. The concept predates the Internet; however, network technology has provided the infrastructure for a major expansion in companies offering mass individualization. It can be applied to anything from services such as financial investment packages to manufactured products such as computers. It is also known as MASS CUSTOMIZATION.

MathML A MARKUP LANGUAGE based on XML which was designed for displaying mathematics on the Web using a BROWSER. Some mathematical packages use this notation and a subset of the language is supported by the WORLD WIDE WEB CONSORTIUM's test browser AMAYA.

maven The strict definition of the term is an expert or connoisseur. However, when used on the Internet it is generally someone who is expert in some aspect of Internet technology such as MARKUP LANGUAGES.

maximum transmission unit The largest PACKET of data that can be sent through a PACKET SWITCHED NETWORK. Often abbreviated to MTU.

Mb An abbreviation for MEGABYTE.

MBONE *See* MULTICAST BACKBONE.

Mbps An abbreviation for MEGABITS per second, a measure of transmission speed.

MCSE *See* MICROSOFT CERTIFIED SYSTEMS ENGINEER.

MD2 *See* MESSAGE DIGEST 2.

MD5 *See* MESSAGE DIGEST 5.

MDA *See* MAIL DELIVERY AGENT.

meat space Employed by some users of the Internet to denote the physical world, as distinct from the electronic world of the Internet. *See also* CYBERSPACE.

media convergence The rapid convergence of Internet technology, computing, and other technologies such as television. Such a convergence gives rise to many applications ranging from intelligent fire alarm systems which page the owner of a house when smoke is detected to WEB TV.

meet in the middle attack A theoretical attack on the DATA ENCRYPTION STANDARD (DES) encryption algorithm which involves using DES to encrypt and decrypt messages. This theoretical attack was used to demonstrate that the DOUBLE DES algorithm has not led to a major improvement in security over the DES algorithm.

megabit A unit of transmission speed equivalent to 1,024 KILOBITS.

megabyte A unit of storage equivalent to 1,024 KILOBYTES. Usually abbreviated to Mb.

meltdown What happens when a network becomes saturated. It is usually caused by ROUTING problems or some event such as a WEB SERVER attracting a large number of users. It results in poor service to a user in terms of response time, usually for a relatively short period.

member directory The store of names, addresses, and EMAIL ADDRESSes of the customers of a particular INTERNET SERVICE PROVIDER.

menu A list of options that is presented to the user of a computer program. The generic name of the options is usually placed at the top of a WINDOW and when this name is clicked the options are displayed

The user selects one by clicking on it with the mouse.

merchant account The paperwork required for a company to be able to take credit card orders using the WORLD WIDE WEB.

merchant fee The fee that a customer pays to a credit card company for the use of its facilities. The way the fee is calculated differs from one credit card company to another, but it is often based on a fixed cost and a per-transaction cost.

message A set of characters which are passed from one entity on a network to another. For example, SERVERS which hold identical databases in a highly reliable DISTRIBUTED SYSTEM communicate via messages in order to ensure that their databases are in synchronization.

Message Authentication Code A version of a MESSAGE DIGEST which also includes a PASSWORD. The user of a message authentication code cannot recreate the number associated with the message digest unless they also know the password. This represents an attempt to strengthen the security of basic message digest schemes.

message box A window that appears during the operation of a program which informs the user that an error has occurred or a problem has been encountered. The user often has to carry out some action such as clicking a BUTTON in the box before it disappears.

message digest A technique used to establish whether text sent over a network has been tampered with. It consists of a mathematical rule which, when applied to a piece of text, generates a relatively short number, usually between 128 and 512 bits. This number is then sent with the text to a recipient who reapplies the mathematical rule to the text and compares the result with the original number. If they are the same then there is a very high probability that the message has not been tampered with during the sending process; if it does differ it is virtually certain that the message has been tampered with. *See* MESSAGE DIGEST 5, HASH FUNCTION, and MESSAGE DIGEST 2.

Message Digest 2 An algorithm used to generate MESSAGE DIGESTS. It was used for PRIVACY ENHANCED MAIL but is now regarded as being obsolete.

Message Digest 5 An algorithm used to generate MESSAGE DIGESTS. It was developed by the American computer scientist Ronald Rivest and is used in a number of commercial products.

message flooding A DENIAL OF SERVICE ATTACK. It involves the perpetrator flooding the computer to be attacked with thousands of messages. These messages might be comparatively simple, such as messages which access the ECHO PORT, but if there are enough of them, it can lead to the computer being severely disabled. *See* PING FLOODING.

message header Text which precedes the body of an EMAIL. It contains information about the sender of the email, the route the email travelled through the Internet, and the format of the message that has been sent.

message of the day A message associated with a computing system which is updated daily. The message might contain some important system information, a technical tip, or just a pithy saying. *See also* FORTUNE COOKIE.

message-oriented middleware Software which resides between a CLIENT and a SERVER. It stores messages awaiting dispatch to both of these entities, usually in some form of queue structure. Often abbreviated to MOM.

message passing In a DISTRIBUTED SYSTEM the individual SERVERS and CLIENTS need to communicate with each other: for example, a WEB SERVER may need to communicate with a DATABASE SERVER in order to retrieve some data which is to be displayed in a WEB PAGE. When the communication occurs via textual messages passed over some transmission medium, this is known as message passing.

messaging A generic term used to describe any form of communication over a network ranging from EMAIL and FAX to the use of integrated media such as the use of email to send paging messages and technologies such as FAX TO EMAIL SERVICE.

meta A prefix placed before a word in order to describe properties about the original word. For example a metafile is a file which contains data about files, metadata is data about data.

MetaComputing The use of a number of personal computers and the Internet to collaboratively solve some problem which requires very large processing power. Metacomputing takes advantage of the fact that a personal computer is idle for much of its time, with, for example, the user doing little else but staring at the screen. Typical problems that have been attacked using metacomputing include breaking code systems and factoring large numbers.

metacontent The name given to the content of a WEB PAGE which is associated with METATAGS. There are a variety of uses for such content, the main one being to embed information such as KEYWORDS which can be used by a SPIDER employed by a SEARCH ENGINE to index a site.

MetaCrawler This was one of the earliest METASEARCH ENGINES. It still appears in the top six of surveys of metasearch engines. It provides the ability for users to select the search engines to be used for any particular search.

metadata Data which describes other data. For example, a description of a DATABASE in terms of its structure and the relationship between the entities in the database is an example of metadata.

metadictionary An online dictionary which combines the power of a number of existing online dictionaries. For example, a metadictionary on computing would look for the definition of a word provided by a user in a number of specialized dictionaries.

Metafind One of the best known METASEARCH ENGINES.

metasearch engine Each SEARCH ENGINE has strengths and weaknesses and one search engine may have indexed WEB SITES that another has not. Metasearch engines have been developed to overcome this problem. When presented with a search query they submit it to a variety of engines and display the combined results. Three of the most famous metasearch engines are SAVVYSEARCH, DOGPILE, and META-CRAWLER. Many of these search engines now allow the option of nominating which combination of search engine to use for a particular search. Metasearch engines were very controversial when they were first developed as they did not retrieve the BANNER ADVERTISING that individual search engine developers used to raise revenue.

metatag The metatag <META> is an HTML tag which provides ancillary information about an WEB PAGE. For example, a metatag can be used to transfer control to another WEB SITE after a specified number of seconds if the site has been moved. The main use for such tags is to provide information about a page or a site which can be used by a search engine for indexing it. *See also* WEB SITE PROMOTION.

metatag generator A software tool that helps WEB DESIGNERS insert METATAGS into a WEB PAGE. The main use for such a tool is to remind the Web designer about each TAG.

metatag scanner A software tool which examines the use of METATAGS in a WEB SITE and reports how they can be used more effectively for optimizing site retrieval by a SEARCH ENGINE.

metaverse A slang term used to describe a virtual representation of reality implemented by means of VIRTUAL REALITY software.

metropolitan area exchange A NETWORK ACCESS POINT where INTERNET SERVICE PROVIDERS can establish connections with each other's systems. Sometimes it is abbreviated to MAE.

metropolitan area network A metropolitan area network, often abbreviated to MAN, is an IEEE-approved network that serves a metropolitan area such as a city or a town, although it is not restricted to such uses. For example, the term has been used to describe a network connecting a number of local universities and colleges.

MHEG *See* MULTIMEDIA AND HYPERMEDIA INFORMATION CODING EXPERT GROUP.

MHOTY Abbreviation for My Hat's Off To You used in CHAT ROOMS, EMAILS, and NEWSGROUP.

MIB *See* MANAGEMENT INFORMATION BASE.

Micro$oft A mildly derogatory reference to the Microsoft Corporation found in NEWSGROUPS and BULLETIN BOARD systems. *See also* COF$.

microcash Many transactions on the Internet have a low monetary value: for example, the preparation of a weather report, or the downloading of a chapter of a book or of a font may only cost a fraction of a pound or of a dollar. Such transactions would usually attract commission charges from a bank or credit card company much larger than the amount involved; hence it becomes financially infeasible to use conventional payment means to handle them. Microcash is the term used to describe the low-value monies involved. A number of schemes to solve this problem have been proposed. Many involve a purchaser receiving an injection of DIGITAL CASH via a bank and then spending it in very small amounts, very much like the schemes which operate for pre-paid mobile telephones. *See also* MICROMERCHANT and TOKEN.

micromerchant An ECOMMERCE organization which is prepared to sell goods or services for DIGITAL CASH. At present there seems no inclination for Internet users to use digital cash, so currently there are very few organizations that can be described by this term.

micropayment A monetary transaction that is so small that it is not economically feasible to process it using conventional means such as bank clearing. Many of the financial transactions within the Internet are micropayments involving no more than a few cents or pence. The difficulty in charging for them has led to a number of token-based or account-based payment systems using technologies such as MONDEX and DIGITAL CASH.

Microsoft Certified Systems Engineer A program run by the Microsoft corporation which certifies SYSTEM ADMINISTRATORS and NETWORK ADMINISTRATORS. It has become the IT industry's leading training qualification.

Microsoft Internet Security Framework A collection of security technologies developed by Microsoft targeted at Internet security.

microtransaction A financial transaction on the Internet so small that if it is carried out using a conventional payment method such as a credit card, the processing of the transaction costs more than the transaction itself. A number of ways of overcoming this problem have been proposed including DIGITAL CASH.

middleware A very general term used to describe software which mediates between CLIENTS and SERVERS. A good example of middleware is the software that mediates between a BROWSER making requests using the HYPERTEXT TRANSFER PROTOCOL and a WEB SERVER. Another good example of middleware is the software that implements the SECURE SOCKETS LAYER and which carries out the ENCRYPTION and DECRYPTION of data as it passes from a client to a server and back.

MIDI *See* MUSICAL INSTRUMENT DIGITAL INTERFACE.

Military Network A network that was originally part of ARPANET. It is now used by those organisations which require secure network services. It is often abbreviated to MILNET.

MILNET *See* MILITARY NETWORK.

MIME *See* MULTIPURPOSE INTERNET MAIL EXTENSIONS.

MIME type The type of a document which is described by the MULTIPURPOSE INTERNET MAIL EXTENSIONS standard. Some examples of MIME types are text/plain, which is plain text that is unformatted; text/html, which is HTML formatted text; and image/jpeg, which is an image that conforms to the JOINT PHOTOGRAPHIC EXPERTS GROUP format. When a WEB PAGE is sent from a SERVER to a client, part of the header contains details of the MIME type so that the browser can properly interpret the file.

mimicking An alternative term for SPOOFING.

Mining Company A large directory-based SEARCH ENGINE whose directories are spread over a number of different sites.

mirror The process of keeping duplicate data on a network. *See, for example,* MIRROR SITE. *See also* DATA REPLICATION.

mirroring tool A software tool which ensures that WEB SITES which are MIRROR SITES of an original site are kept up to date even when the updates to the main site are not automatically applied to the other sites.

mirror site A WEB SITE which is a copy of an existing site. The reason for this duplication is efficiency: for example, a United Kingdom mirror site of a WEB SERVER which is located in the United States provides a faster service to European users than the original site because PACKETS do not have to travel as far from the mirror site as packets from the American site.

mirror world A WEB SITE constructed to trap attackers and to monitor their activities in order to detect their identities. *See also* WEB TRAP and FLYTRAP.

misc This abbreviation designates those NEWSGROUPS which discuss matters not covered by any other newsgroup.

MISF *See* MICROSOFT INTERNET SECURITY FRAMEWORK.

MJPEG *See* MOVING JPEG.

MMF Abbreviation for Make Money Fast, usually applied to commercial SPAMS, PONZI SCHEMES, and CHAIN LETTER SCAMS.

mobile agent An AGENT which carries out some task for a user and, in doing so, visits a number of computers in a network. It achieves this by its code being copied to a remote computer and then executed. For example, a mobile agent might be used by someone who wants to order a series of books on a particular subject and yet wants to make sure that his or her cost is minimized in terms of the purchase price of the books and the shipping rates charged by the online bookshops.

One of the major advantages of mobile agent technology is that it can minimize the communication time that might normally be involved in such a search. A mobile agent does not have to communicate with the user while carrying out the search: the only time that any bandwidth is used is when the agent returns from the search and issues its results.

mobile client A client that is not fixed in one position: for example, a portable computer which is using a mobile phone to communicate with a SERVER or a mobile phone using a protocol such as the WIRELESS APPLICATION PROTOCOL to connect into a WEB SERVER. Mobile computing is a major expansion area; although it poses large challenges to developers. For example, there are more factors which reduce reliability in mobile computing than there are in normal DISTRIBUTED SYSTEMS.

mobile code Program code which can migrate from one computer to another in a network. APPLETS are a good example of mobile code technology. Mobile code is often used to develop AGENTS that can roam a network looking for information such as the best price for an airline ticket.

mobile computing The use of DISTRIBUTED SYSTEM technology to enable users who are not fixed in a single physical position to communicate with computers which form part of a network; more often than not these computers act as some form of SERVER. This is one of the major development areas in distributed computing, with many manufacturers attempting to embed the same functions found in a normal computer into handheld devices such as mobile phones.

mobile server Used in automotive circles to describe the use of powerful computers within cars. Such a computer would carry out functions such as accessing the Internet, communicating with navigation systems and diagnosing the performance of a car.

mockingbird A program which imitates a computer during a log-in and reads account names and PASSWORDS in order to gain access to a network or a user's FILES.

This is a particular example of a TROJAN HORSE attack on a system.

modem An electronic device which converts digital signals used within a computer system to signals which can be processed by a telephone system and vice versa.

modem optimizer Programs which optimize the speed of a MODEM. They do this using a variety of means, including changing the default settings for the TCP-IP connection.

modem ready A term found on the label of some MODEMS meaning that the modem has been switched on and is ready to receive or transmit data.

moderated An adjective used to describe any process which is controlled by a human being, rather than by a computer or not being controlled at all. For example, a MODERATED NEWSGROUP is administered by a moderator who decides which POSTINGS to publish in the NEWSGROUP.

moderated newsgroup A NEWSGROUP which is mediated by one or more of its members. POSTINGS are read by these moderators and are accepted or rejected depending on a number of criteria, including relevance to the topic discussed by the newsgroup, the amount of abuse, and whether the posting is SPAM.

moderator A member of a NEWSGROUP who censors or rejects the postings to a MODERATED NEWSGROUP. A variety of criteria are used to decide on whether to allow a posting. These include whether the POSTING is libellous, whether it represents an attempt at SPAMMING, or whether it is relevant to the topic that the newsgroup was set up to discuss. The term is also used to describe someone who carries out the same functions in a CHAT ROOM.

modulation The process of adding a signal to an existing signal (known as the CARRIER). There are two main forms of modulation used: AMPLITUDE MODULATION and FREQUENCY MODULATION. The process of recovering the signal is known as DEMODULATION.

MOM *See* MESSAGE-ORIENTED MIDDLEWARE.

Mondex A SMART CARD system which allows the owner of a card to spend cash without a vendor carrying out authentication.

Mongolian hordes technique Originally used to describe the process of carrying out large software projects by hiring huge numbers of programmers. It is now occasionally used to describe BRUTE FORCE ATTACKS on computer networks.

MOO *See* MUD OBJECT-ORIENTED.

MorF Abbreviation for Male or Female? used in CHAT ROOMS. The reply to this question cannot be totally relied on, as a number of Internet users enjoy role playing.

morphing A technique normally used in ANIMATION in which one object is gradually changed into another by incrementally introducing features of the second object into the first. For example, a Dr Jekyll figure might be morphed to a Mr Hyde figure. *See also* TWEENING.

Morris worm A name occasionally used for the INTERNET WORM. Robert Morris was the author of this particular item of MALICIOUS CODE.

mortuary site A WEB SITE which has not been updated for a long time. Also referred to as a COBWEB SITE.

Mosaic One of the first BROWSERS. It was developed at the NATIONAL CENTER FOR SUPERCOMPUTING APPLICATIONS. It is historically important because it was the first browser with a common interface that was available for a number of PLATFORMS. It has been superseded by other browsers including NETSCAPE NAVIGATOR and INTERNET EXPLORER, both of which can trace their ancestry back to Mosaic.

MOSS Or MOTSS. Abbreviation for Member Of the Same Sex? used in in CHAT ROOMS, EMAILS, and NEWSGROUPS. The answer, or even the question, cannot be totally relied on since a number of Internet users enjoy role playing which involves taking on the identity of a member of the opposite sex.

MOTOS Abbreviation for Member Of The Opposite Sex? used in CHAT ROOMS.

The answer, or even the question, cannot be totally relied on since a number of Internet users enjoy role playing which involves taking on the identity of a member of the opposite sex.

mouse around Synonymous with SURFING but used very much less frequently.

mouse droppings 1. PIXELS which are not immediately restored to their original colour when a mouse cursor passes over them; this gives the impression that something has been deposited on the screen following the path of the mouse.
2. The INTERNET PROTOCOL ADDRESS of a user in a WEB LOG FILE.

mouse elbow A physical injury akin to tennis elbow caused by excessive use of a mouse.

mouse potato The Internet version of a couch potato: someone who does very little but sit at a computer SURFING the Internet.

moved to Atlanta When a HYPERLINK is clicked on a WEB PAGE, and an error message is displayed indicating that the page cannot be found, the page is said to have moved to Atlanta. The term is derived from the fact that the HTTP STATUS CODE for this event is 404 which is the telephone area code for Atlanta.

Moving JPEG A compression technique for video images which applies the JPEG compression algorithm to each still image making up the video clip that is to be compressed.

Moving Picture Experts Group More commonly known as MPEG, it is a compression method which is applied to video images. There are two versions of this technology: MPEG1 which is used for Internet-based video and MPEG2 which is used for broadcast applications.

Moving Picture Experts Group Audio Layer 3 File A format for the distribution of music files over the Internet which is fast becoming a de facto standard. It enables files of recorded music to be compressed to the point where it becomes feasible for an Internet user to download a recording from a music sales site. MP3, as it is more commonly known, is being touted as a replacement for other media including CDs: there are already a number of electronic devices for playing music in this format, including portable players. The development of MP3 holds out the promise that a bulky collection of CDs will be replaced by MP3 files stored on a player that contains a disk drive similar to that found on current PCs. At present the size of the MP3 market is small, although it is expected to expand hugely. At present it is mainly used as a medium for distributing music from aspiring musicians and segments of larger works from well-known artists for promotional purposes.

Mozilla 1. The original name for the NETSCAPE NAVIGATOR browser. Computing myth has it that the name was formed from a contraction of MOSAIC and Godzilla. **2**. The name of an open source project set up by the Netscape Corporation to support their development of software for the browser.

MP3 See MOVING PICTURE EXPERTS GROUP AUDIO LAYER 3 FILE.

MPEG See MOVING PICTURE EXPERTS GROUP.

MPEG1 A version of the MOVING PICTURE EXPERTS GROUP standard for video which is targeted at Internet-based video.

MPEG2 A version of the MOVING PICTURE EXPERTS GROUP standard for video which is targeted at commercial broadcast applications.

mpg A FILE EXTENSION for video files defined by the MPEG standard.

MR See MODEM READY.

MSDOS® An early Microsoft OPERATING SYSTEM in which the user communicated with the system using a simple COMMAND LANGUAGE rather than a graphic interface.

MTA See MAIL TRANSFER AGENT.

MTF Abbreviation for More To Follow used in EMAILS and NEWSGROUPS. It usually announces that the rest of a message or a POSTING is to follow separately.

MTU See MAXIMUM TRANSMISSION UNIT.

MUA *See* MAIL USER AGENT.

MUD *See* MULTI USER DUNGEON or MULTI USER DIMENSION.

muddie A derogatory term for someone who is obsessed by MULTI-USER DUNGEON games. *See also* MUD HEAD.

MUD head A frequent user of MULTI USER DUNGEONS; usually someone who is addicted to the technology.

MUD Object-Oriented One of an increasingly large number of multiuser, role-playing virtual environments. Participants use an OBJECT-ORIENTED PROGRAMMING LANGUAGE to construct characters and interact with their environment. Usually abbreviated to MOO.

multicast address An IP ADDRESS which is used in IPv6, the partial replacement for TCP-IP. It enables a group of computers to receive the same message.

Multicast Backbone Often abbreviated to MBONE. A MULTICASTING network which overlays the Internet and which is used for the transmission of digital multimedia. In effect it is a form of television and radio broadcasting network which employs Internet technology.

multicast group A group of computers in a network that have been designated as the destination for MULTICASTING messages.

multicasting A limited form of broadcasting where a network supports the sending of PACKETs to a subset of the computers on the network. Networks which support this form of data transmission organize the computers in the network into MULTICAST GROUPS which can all be addressed together and to which multicasting data can be sent.

multicomputer A computer which is made up of a number of individual computers connected via buses which are physically close to each computer. This type of computer configuration represents a half-way house between DATA FLOW COMPUTERS and computers in a CLIENT SERVER COMPUTING system. Typically multicomputers are situated within a metre of each other.

multihomed host A computer which is connected to more than one network.

Multilink Point-to-Point Protocol A standard which defines the connections between an INTERNET SERVICE PROVIDER and an INTEGRATED SERVICES DIGITAL NETWORK terminal adapter.

Multilink PPP A short version of MULTILINK POINT-TO-POINT PROTOCOL.

multimedia A generic term used to describe the different types of media that can be processed by a computer. Examples of multimedia include sound, graphics, video images, animations, and text.

Multimedia and Hypermedia Information Coding Expert Group A standard developed by the INTERNATIONAL STANDARDS ORGANIZATION for the representation of HYPERMEDIA and MULTIMEDIA content. The standard was developed to facilitate the exchange of such media. Often abbreviated to MHEG.

multimode fibre Fibre optic cabling where many different rays of light bounce around the cable at different angles of incidence. This is in contrast to SINGLE-MODE FIBRE.

multipartite virus A VIRUS which infects both FILES and the BOOT SECTOR of a computer. *See also* BOOT VIRUS.

multipath fading The undesirable phenomenon which occurs when buildings and other solid objects interfere with the transmission of microwaves resulting in some waves arriving out of phase.

multiple search engine submission There are now a very large number of SEARCH ENGINES. Submitting a site for indexing to all of them is a time-consuming and tedious process. Multiple site submission is the process of submitting a WEB SITE to a number of sites for indexing by accessing only a single WEB PAGE. Such a Web page is maintained by companies who offer multiple submission services. They often charge for this service, but there are a number of free services available. Sometimes payment involves accepting a BANNER ADVERT on the site. *See also* ALL IN ONE SEARCH ENGINE.

multiplexing The transmission of a number of signals simultaneously over a single channel. This is implemented by splitting up the signals into discrete chunks and sending each chunk over a network. The receiver then reassembles the signals that were transmitted. The hardware that carries out this process is known as a MULTIPLEXOR.

multiplexor A device which sends a number of signals over a transmission medium using MULTIPLEXING.

multipoint video conferencing VIDEO CONFERENCING which involves more than two participants.

Multipurpose Internet Mail Extensions Usually referred to as MIME. Each block of data sent to a BROWSER using the HYPERTEXT TRANSFER PROTOCOL is preceded by a text block which describes what type of data it is: whether, for example, it is a graphic or a sound clip, or plain text. Each block is known as a MIME TYPE. The standard which is used to construct such identifying blocks is the Multimedia Internet Mail Extensions standard. It enables the browser to work out which data it is about to receive and how to display it. Some examples of MIME types are text/plain which is plain text that is unformatted, text/html which is HTML formatted text, and image/jpeg which is an image that conforms to the JOINT PHOTOGRAPHIC EXPERTS GROUP format.

multisearch engine A term that is occasionally used to describe a METASEARCH ENGINE.

multi user dimension See MULTI USER DUNGEON.

multi user dungeon A special type of CHAT ROOM where participants engage in a role-playing game. For example, they may take on the role of travellers in a strange country looking for some highly prized object such as a soothsayer's stone. Early multiuser dungeons featured simple text input, but these have been superseded by graphics-enhanced systems where players are represented by AVATARS and where each player can construct their own char-acter and influence the environment of the game by deploying a special-purpose programming language. Sometimes multi user dungeons are known as multi user dimensions. See also MUD OBJECT-ORIENTED. Usually abbreviated to MUD.

multi user shared illusion A form of MULTI USER DUNGEON game where the users can augment the current world they are playing in. Often abbreviated to MUSH.

mumble A word used in a public forum such as a NEWSGROUP when the user wishes to hide some details which are secret. For example, 'I know of one company mumble where they have threatened their workers with dismissal if they contribute to this newsgroup.'

mumble mode 1. The state of a program, computer, or networked system when it produces totally inappropriate responses to the data it is given. For example, a BROWSER is in mumble mode if instead of displaying normal WEB PAGES it displays flashing blank colours.
2. Sometimes used to describe users who are incapable of communicating: for example, 'I could not understand any of John's postings to the newsgroup. He always seems to be in mumble mode.'

munching Taking advantage of the security holes in a computer system in order to enter the system illegally. Often such an intrusion is carried out for non-criminal reasons such as gaining a vicarious thrill or annoying a SYSTEM ADMINISTRATOR.

munging The insertion of some text into an EMAIL ADDRESS in order to fool the automated ADDRESS HARVESTERS that SPAMMERS use to collect email addresses. For example, writing an address as D.C.Ince at email address nowfree.co.uk should defeat most harvesters. The text representing the modified email address is known as a SPAMBLOCK.

museum In 2000 seven new DOMAIN NAMES were created. Museum was one of these. It is intended for use by museums.

MUSH See MULTIUSER SHARED ILLUSION.

Musical Instrument Digital Interface A standard which allows musical instruments and recording devices to be connected together via computers. The standard describes the files and the interface hardware used to connect a musical instrument to a computer. Usually abbreviated to MIDI.

MUSM Abbreviation for Miss U So Much used in CHAT ROOMS and EMAILS.

nagling coalescence A method of improving TRANSMISSION RATE of messages transmitted using TCP-IP. It consists of marshalling small PACKETS of data and merging them into a larger packet.

nagware SHAREWARE which displays a screen either before it is used or when it finishes asking the user to register and pay a fee if they are intending to continue to use the software. This feature is normally disabled after the user has registered.

nak attack A form of attack on a computer which takes advantage of the fact that the OPERATING SYSTEM is in a vulnerable state after an interrupt has occurred.

name In 2000 seven new DOMAIN NAMES were created. Name was one of these. It is intended for use by individuals.

Named Pipes A technology that provides a very reliable two-way communication between CLIENTS and a SERVER. Programming for Named Pipes is very much like the simple programming that is involved when reading and writing to files. The technology is supported by the Microsoft Windows operating systems and by UNIX.

name resolution The process of discovering some physical information about a resource identified by a name. Discovering the IP ADDRESS of a computer by using the INTERNET DOMAIN NAME SERVICE is an example of name resolution.

name server A server used for NAME RESOLUTION: a CLIENT provides the symbolic name of a resource and the server responds with some physical information such as an address. The INTERNET DOMAIN NAME SERVICE which consists of a number of communicating name servers which provide the IP ADDRESS of a computer, given its name, is an example of the use of a name server.

name service A service provided by a NAME SERVER in a DISTRIBUTED SYSTEM.

In such a system there are a large number of shared resources: computers, files, programs, and databases. Each of these has a unique address: for example, a computer on a TCP-IP network is identified by its IP ADDRESS. Usually the addresses used to identify a resource are difficult to remember. For example, addresses expressed in the DOTTED QUAD NOTATION used for identifying computers on the Internet consist of four integers. A name service stores easily remembered details of the resources in a distributed system. Each resource entry consists of a symbolic name and the actual address of the resource. When a user is required to identify a resource by the program he or she is interacting with, they use the symbolic name; the program then consults a name service to find out its location before carrying out any processing using that resource. There is a second reason for name services: resources in a distributed system have a tendency to move around the system. For example, a frequently used file might be moved to a server which is optimized for file access. A name service means that the many users of such a resource do not need to be told of the change in address: only the NAME SERVER that implements the service needs to be informed of it. The most famous name service is the INTERNET DOMAIN NAME SERVICE found on the Internet; this maps domain names into Internet addresses.

namespace transparency The property of a DISTRIBUTED SYSTEM which enables users to employ the same naming conventions to access resources on the network in which the system resides. For example, a file stored in one part of a distributed system should ideally be referred to using the same naming convention as a file stored on another part of the system.

NAP *See* NETWORK ACCESS POINT.

Napster A system created by the teenage hacker Shawn Fanning which allows users of the Internet to register MP3 files in such a way that the user of a BROWSER is able to copy any file that has been registered from another personal computer. The Recording Industry Association of America has attempted to sue Fanning for copyright infringement.

narrowcasting The broadcasting of video-based material to a relatively small niche audience using a combination of television and Web-based technology: for example, the broadcasting of video material to insurance professionals containing information about trends in their profession.

NAS *See* NETWORK ACCESS SERVER.

nastygram 1. A PACKET which takes advantage of a security flaw in a system to cause havoc on that system.
2. A disapproving EMAIL; and third,
3. An error message delivered by email from a DAEMON.

National Center For Supercomputing Applications This centre was very active in the early days of the Internet. For example, the original MOSAIC browser was developed there. The centre is still active in areas such as high-performance computer architectures. It is often abbreviated to NCSA.

National Fraud Information Center A clearing house for information on commercial criminal schemes on the Internet. Its WEB SITE contains a host of information on commercial Internet crime.

National Information Infrastructure Used by the Clinton administration in the United States to describe the electronic network of the future; it envisages linking government, companies, and the citizen via high-speed, high-BANDWIDTH connections utilizing home phones, mobile phones, and televisions.

National Research And Education Network A US government-funded initiative to combine a number of governmental networks together into one high-capacity, high-speed network. This was the successor to the NSFNET network. It is usually referred to as NREN.

National Science Foundation A US governmental body charged with the fostering and support of American research. It played a very important part in the development of the Internet in the 1980s when it started its Supercomputer Center Program. It is usually abbreviated to NSF. An early decision made by the NSF was to make supercomputing power available to as many American researchers as possible. In order to do this they networked the small number of supercomputers using Internet technology such as the TRANSMISSION CONTROL PROTOCOL. The network that was developed was known as NSFNET and was the core of the Internet until the mid-1990s when it was retired and replaced by the NATIONAL RESEARCH AND EDUCATION NETWORK.

National Security Agency A US government agency charged with carrying out technical activities which support the US government's intelligence agencies. It is often abbreviated to NSA.

nav bar Abbreviation for NAVIGATION BAR.

navigate To travel around the WORLD WIDE WEB by following HYPERLINKS.

navigation bar A set of images and text embedded in a WEB PAGE which help users NAVIGATE around the WEB SITE in which the page is embedded. Navigation bars are usually found at the top, bottom, or side of a page.

NBIF Abbreviation for No Basis In Fact used in EMAILS and NEWSGROUPS.

NCSA *See* NATIONAL CENTER FOR SUPERCOMPUTING APPLICATIONS.

NCSA Image Map Format One of the two IMAGE MAP formats used for SERVER SIDE IMAGE MAPS. It describes the data that should be contained in the WEB SERVER file which is consulted when an image map is clicked in a BROWSER. The other format is the CERN IMAGE MAP FORMAT.

NDA Abbreviation for Non Disclosure Agreement used in emails and newsgroups.

NDMP *See* NETWORK DATA MANAGEMENT PROTOCOL.

near-line storage Used to describe large-scale storage devices such as DAT tapes and CD ROMs. Such devices offer massive storage capacity at the expense of slow retrieval times.

near video on demand A primitive form of VIDEO ON DEMAND where the provider runs a number of copies of a video over a network, with each video being played over a channel with a delayed starting time. The technological requirements for this form of video on demand are much lower than for pure video on demand, where the user is effectively associated with their own copy of the video. However, some functions associated with pure video on demand are lost, such as the ability to rewind a video.

neep Someone who is fascinated by computers to the exclusion of almost anything else in their life.

nerd Someone who has a passionate and thoughtful interest in computers, networks, and their use. Often this interest dominates their lives to the point where their social skills suffer. When the term is used in non-computing circles it is meant in a derogatory fashion. However, the growth of large, successful Internet companies set up by nerds has meant that its use as a derogatory term has decreased. *See also* ENTREPRENERD and NERD PRIDE.

Nerd Pride A movement set up by two MIT professors, Gerald Sussman and Hal Abelson, and modelled on the Gay Pride movement. The aim of the movement is to stress to children the more positive aspects of being a nerd, such as an inclination to direct thought rather than anti-intellectual disdain.

Net.god Someone who is a veteran of the Internet and whose words are taken very seriously by other users.

net 1. A type of Internet DOMAIN associated with organizations and institutions closely connected with the Internet. **2**. A short version of Internet, as in 'I surfed the net yesterday.'

Netaddress Another name for KNOWBOT INFORMATION SERVICE.

net dot A prefix used to denote people, states of mind, events or products associated with the Internet: for example, net dot guru, net dot god, and net dot tiredness. The word 'dot' is often replaced by a full stop.

net god Someone who has had a prominent presence on the Internet for some time. For example the MODERATOR of a large, well-known NEWSGROUP might be regarded as a net god. Often this term is written as net.god.

net lag Occurs when some part of a network becomes overloaded and users are made aware of this by poor response times and the delivery of data in discrete bursts. This is a fairly common occurrence with the WORLD WIDE WEB.

net personality Someone who has gained a reputation for their contributions to NEWSGROUPS, often a bad reputation: for example, someone who persistently FLAMES other users. The term is often written as net.personality.

net police Internet users, normally found in NEWSGROUPS, who feel it necessary to FLAME any POSTING they find objectionable. Usually used as a pejorative term, it has also been used to vilify those who advocate censorship on the Internet.

netary public An organization or person connected with the copyrighting of Web documents. They keep details of Web pages, including the date on which they were created. A play on the term 'notary public'.

netcasting The broadcasting of data and information to users using PUSH TECHNOLOGY. *See also* MULTICASTING and BROADCASTING.

Netfind The default SEARCH ENGINE for the huge American INTERNET SERVICE PROVIDER America Online.

netiquette The series of informal rules which users of the Internet are often urged to follow in order not to provoke others into acts such as sending FLAMES. Typical rules include: check with an FAQ list before asking a question, don't betray confidences, use EMOTICONS to indicate subtleties, and stick to the subject you are writing about.

netizen A word formed by combining 'Net' and 'Citizen'. It is used to describe a habitual or keen user of the Internet.

netopath An Internet user who engages in extreme forms of net abuse such as stalking.

Netscape Navigator One of the most popular BROWSERS. It was originally developed by the Netscape Corporation and was based on the MOZILLA browser. In the late 1990s there was a BROWSER WAR between its makers and the Microsoft Corporation who marketed the other popular browser INTERNET EXPLORER.

Netscape Server Application Programming Interface A SERVER API which was designed as an efficient alternative to CGI PROGRAMMING and intended for servers originally developed by the Netscape Corporation. Combined with CGI, JAVA, and a JavaScript-based server API, it makes up Netscape's Internet Application Framework. Usually abbreviated to NSAPI.

NetShepperd One of a number of CONTENT RATING SYSTEMS which allow Web developers to categorize the content of their WEB SITES. *See also* RASCI.

Netstat A WEB SITE which allows visitors to look at the current performance of a number of American networks.

netter Someone who has an IP ADDRESS or is a regular poster to NEWSGROUPS.

nettie A regular user of NEWSGROUPS, occasionally used in a pejorative sense.

nettop An abbreviation for NETWORK OPERATIONS MANAGER.

network A collection of computers connected by transmission media ranging from physical wiring to satellite links. The Internet is a network. However, it contains other networks known as SUBNETWORKS which, in turn, contain other networks. Although the Internet is the best-known network there are many other networks in existence ranging from small LOCAL AREA NETWORKS which are physically situated in a single building

to private networks which are maintained by large companies or government organizations. A network that contains a number of connected computers that carry out processing is known as a DISTRIBUTED SYSTEM. Networks suffer from a number of problems which do not affect individual computers, the main one being LATENCY: the fact that data from one computer often has to pass through a number of slow transmission lines and intermediate computers before it reaches its destination.

Network Access Point A term given to the points in the NSFNET to which network operators had to connect. This meant that operators who had to deliver a backbone service were forced to compete on price and performance. The term was often abbreviated to NAP.

network access server A hardware device which enables users to gain temporary access to a network. The term is often used to describe computer hardware which supports DIAL-UP ACCESS.

network administrator A member of staff or group of staff who have the responsibility for the smooth functioning of a large network. They carry out a number of functions: defining and enforcing security policies, specifying ROUTING policies, accounting for system resources on the network and ensuring that they are efficiently used, responding to hardware and systems errors, and administering any connections to external networks such as the Internet. Sometimes the term SYSTEM ADMINISTRATOR is used to describe a network administrator although this may be someone who administers a small network where many of the network functions tend to be trivial.

network analyser A hardware device which can read the PACKETS of data travelling around a network. It is mainly used for the diagnosis of system problems such as a malfunctioning NETWORK INTERFACE CARD. However, it is also a potent tool in the hands of a CRACKER who wishes to access data illegally.

network architecture The term given to the model of a network expressed in terms of LAYERS and PROTOCOLS, where each layer communicates with PEERS using one of the protocols and draws upon services provided by lower level layers. Two examples of network architectures are the INTERNET LAYERED ARCHITECTURE and the OSI REFERENCE MODEL.

network computer A concept which emerged in the late 1990s and was pioneered by Sun Microsystems. A network computer is a PC which, apart from input/output facilities such as a keyboard and a monitor, has very few other peripherals such as a hard drive. A network computer is connected to a CLIENT SERVER COMPUTING system where all the services, such as file access, which would normally be expected to reside on the CLIENT are provided by SERVERS. There are a number of advantages to this form of networking: for example, it eliminates problems with different clients using different versions of a software package such as a word processor: each network computer communicates with the same package which is delivered to them from a server. As yet the idea of a network computer has to reach commercial fruition.

Network Data Management Protocol A PROTOCOL which enables a number of different servers from a number of manufacturers to carry out the BACKING UP of the files found on the servers. NDMP, as it is often known, is an open standard protocol supported by a number of software companies and server vendors.

network file server A synonym for FILE SERVER.

Network File System A set of PROTOCOLs which use TCP-IP to provide a DISTRIBUTED FILE SYSTEM. Such protocols are common in large organizations which use the UNIX operating system. It is usually abbreviated to NFS.

network information centre The name given to a repository of Internet information such as REQUEST FOR COMMENTS, PROPOSED STANDARDS, and FREQUENTLY ASKED QUESTION LISTS.

Network Information Service A PROTOCOL used in a network for accessing a distributed DIRECTORY SERVICE.

network interface card An electronic board which fits into the back of a computer and which handles the basic connection from the computer to a network. It is often abbreviated to NIC.

network layer 1. Layer in the OSI REFERENCE MODEL. It carries out the process of routing data from one computer to another. To do this it examines possible routes and determines an optimal or near optimal route for PACKETS of data to travel.
2. A layer in the INTERNET LAYERED ARCHITECTURE which corresponds to the DATA LINK LAYER and the PHYSICAL LAYER in the OSI REFERENCE MODEL.

network management The process of managing a computer network in order to maximize the overall performance of the network in terms of metrics such as its data throughput and its reliability. *See* NETWORK ADMINISTRATOR and QUALITY OF SERVICE.

network meltdown The process whereby a network goes into overload when, for example, a heavy burst of user activity occurs. It usually results in a degradation of response time for users who are unfortunate enough to be logged on to the network when it happens.

network modem A MODEM attached to a LOCAL AREA NETWORK which can be employed for sending signals by any computer attached to the network.

Network News Transfer Protocol A PROTOCOL which handles the sending, retrieval, and POSTING of items to NEWSGROUPS. It is often abbreviated to NNTP. Software which reads and makes POSTINGS to a newsgroup has to employ this protocol.

network operating system An OPERATING SYSTEM which administers a number of interconnected computers. It carries out a number of functions over and above those found in conventional operating systems such as providing a facade which gives the user the impression that he or she is interacting with a simple computer, managing data spread out over a number of DISTRIBUTED DATABASES, providing monitoring information which can be used in PERFORMANCE MAN-AGEMENT, monitoring hardware faults and reconfiguring the network in order to bypass hardware that is malfunctioning, and isolating the user from system-dependent features such as addresses expressed in DOTTED QUAD NOTATION which the user does not have to know about.

network operations centre An office responsible for the operation of a network. It is staffed by a NETWORK ADMINISTRATOR.

network operations manager Another name for NETWORK ADMINISTRATOR.

network scanning tool A generic term used to describe those tools which check for vulnerabilities which intruders might take advantage of in order to enter a network. For example a network scanning tool might detect a communication path which does not employ ENCRYPTION.

network service provider A company which sells access to very high transmission speed lines to INTERNET SERVICE PROVIDERS. A typical network service provider is MCI.

Network Time Protocol A protocol, often known as NTP, which was developed in 1991 for synchronizing the clocks in a DISTRIBUTED SYSTEM. It has a number of aims: to enable computers in a network to be synchronized to COORDINATED UNIVERSAL TIME; to provide a reliable service in the presence of faults in a network; to provide a resynchronization service which can be used frequently; and to provide protection against malicious tampering with time signals. It is now used extensively in the Internet.

network topology See TOPOLOGY.

network transparency The property of a NETWORK OPERATING SYSTEM which enables the user of a network to be unaware that he or she is interacting with a network of computers. For example, the operating system should allow the user to refer to files by a symbolic name which does not contain information about which computer that file is currently stored on. Effectively network transparency should give the user the impression that they are interacting with a single computer.

network weaving A term synonymous with CONNECTION LAUNDERING.

newbie A user who is new to the Internet. It is a common term that is not used derogatorily like, say, LAMER or LUSER.

news An abbreviation that designates those NEWSGROUPS which discuss events on the Internet.

news bot A BOT which carries out some function associated with online newspapers, such as searching for specified classified adverts.

news feed A source of the daily POSTINGS to NEWSGROUPS. News feeds are normally supplied to INTERNET SERVICE PROVIDERS or large organizations since each daily set of postings can occupy many megabytes of storage.

newsgropes A pejorative term used to describe NEWSGROUPS which deal with sexual matters. Usually these groups are found in the ALT category.

newsgroup A collection of Internet users who discuss a topic. This topic could be a broad one such as parenting, or it could be quite narrow, such as a technical facet of an OPERATING SYSTEM. Contributors to a newsgroup use an item of software known as a NEWSREADER. This enables them to make a contribution to the newsgroup (a POSTING) and read the contributions from others. Newsgroups adopt a HIERARCHICAL NAMING convention. For example, the newsgroup comp.infrsystems.www.announce is a newsgroup dedicated to making announcements about new WEB SITES and forms part of the hierarchy which is rooted in comp. The first word in the hierarchy signifies the type of newsgroup: for example, COMP is usually associated with newsgroups which have a technical computing content and ALT is associated with alternative topics, often of an adult nature. Newsgroups can be moderated or unmoderated; the former have a human administrator who reads postings before they appear and rejects those which are not directly relevant; in the latter type of newsgroup any posting appears.

newsgroup bot A BOT which carries out some function associated with newsgroups. For example, a newsgroup bot might examine postings to specific newsgroups for a particular topic.

newsgroup link A HYPERLINK found on a WEB PAGE which, when clicked, starts a dialogue that executes a NEWSREADER, to allow the user to participate in one or more NEWSGROUPS: for example, reading POSTINGS from a particular newsgroup.

newsgroup search The process of searching the POSTINGS of a newsgroup for specific topics or for the names and email addresses of those who post to the newsgroup. The best way of carrying out such a search is via a specialized SEARCH ENGINE such as DEJANEWS.

newsgroup server A SERVER which provides access to a NEWSGROUP.

newsgroup site A WEB SITE which receives NEWSGROUP articles from a NEWS FEED. Users of the Internet who wish to contribute to a newsgroup normally do so via such sites.

newsgroup war An interchange of POSTINGS or EMAIL messages, often acerbic, as to whether a new newsgroup should be formed or a moribund one deleted.

newsreader A program that enables users to access NEWSGROUPS. A good newsreader should offer a number of facilities to the user. First, it should enable the FILTERing of postings to a newsgroup: much of what is posted to the various groups is, at best, peripheral to the intent of the newsgroup and a newsreader should provide facilities for finding relevant POSTINGS. Second, a good newsreader should be able to filter off postings based on criteria such as the time a posting was made, who made it, and its length. Third, a newsreader should have a multi-PANE interface which, as a minimum, shows newsgroups in one pane, postings in another pane, and the content of postings in another. Fourth, it should enable the user to follow a THREAD easily. Fifth, it should

provide facilities whereby a user can connect in to a newsgroup, download postings of interest, and then work OFF LINE with them. Sixth, it should offer facilities for searching for postings, either by content or via METADATA, such as the name of the poster, the date of posting, and the topic posted. Seventh, a newsgroup reader should be able to allow the user to access a variety of NEWSGROUP SERVERS. Newsreaders can be stand-alone, part of a BROWSER, or can be delivered as part of a browser package. Accessing a newsgroup via a newsreader is not the only way to read postings. Another way is to use a WEB-BASED NEWSGROUP SERVICE which reads archived postings.

news site A WEB SITE which provides news CONTENT. This can range from current affairs to specialized news on different topics such as music. This content may be provided on an almost REAL TIME basis or may be updated on an hour-by-hour basis. This has been one of the fastest growing areas of the WORLD WIDE WEB.

news ticker A constantly updated line of text which displays breaking news headlines. Tickers are available as FREEWARE and SHAREWARE and can easily be added to a WEB SITE.

NFS *See* NETWORK FILE SERVER or NETWORK FILE SYSTEM.

NFS attack The NETWORK FILE SYSTEM (NFS) allows users to share files across a network. NFS-based systems are vulnerable to attack if they are not surrounded by a FIREWALL. Such an attack, known as an NFS attack, can result in important files being stolen or deleted.

NIS *See* NETWORK INFORMATION SERVICE.

NNTP *See* NETWORK NEWS TRANSFER PROTOCOL.

NOC *See* NETWORK OPERATIONS CENTRE.

node A device attached to a network. The device could be a computer or a hardware entity such as a ROUTER or BRIDGE.

noise The electrical energy in a TRANSMISSION LINE which does not form part of the signal transmitted. There are a number of sources of noise: inductive effects between wires in close proximity, electromagnetic radiation from other devices, and the random movements of electrons in a physical transmission line are just some of these.

nom In 1997 the Internet Ad Hoc committee proposed a number of new names for DOMAINS. nom is one of these. It represents individuals.

NOMEX underwear Flame-retarding underwear mainly bought by racing drivers. The term is usually used in POST-INGS to NEWSGROUPS to indicate that a FLAME is going to occur: for example, 'Before responding to David I am going to slip into some NOMEX underwear' or 'I would say that if you carry on along that line of argument you will need to get out your NOMEX underwear.'

non-adaptive routing algorithm When a ROUTER uses a non-adaptive routing algorithm it consults a static table in order to determine to which computer it should send a PACKET of data. This is in contrast to an ADAPTIVE ROUTING ALGO-RITHM, which bases its decisions on data which reflects current traffic conditions.

nonce A jargon term for a TIME STAMP.

non-optimal solution Used in NEWS-GROUPS to sarcastically describe a solution which is useless, crass, or unimplementable.

non-repudiation The process of establishing electronic receipts which prove that a particular user has sent a message such as an instruction to buy an item in an ONLINE AUCTION.

non-reusable password A PASSWORD which is only used once and is then discarded. When a user is granted access to a computer network they may be provided with a series of such passwords, but once they use one of the passwords it is crossed off the list and they then have to employ the next one. This is a highly secure way of accessing a computer network which is impervious to normal password attacks. However, it relies on the user keeping the list of passwords physically secure.

non-validating XML parser A program that makes a rudimentary check on the source of a document developed using the EXTENSIBLE MARKUP LANGUAGE. It does not consult the DOCUMENT TYPE DEFIN-ITION which describes the source, but carries out simple checks, such as ensuring that each TAG is associated with its END TAG.

nooksurfer A user who limits their access to the Internet to a small part of the network. For example, a nooksurfer might often carry out LURKING on one or two NEWSGROUPS.

Northern Light One of the most highly regarded SEARCH ENGINES.

NOS *See* NETWORK OPERATING SYSTEM.

notwork A slang term for a NETWORK that is currently not working.

Novell Netware One of the most popular networking systems for PCs. It is based on a five-layer model drawn from the XNS network system developed by the Xerox Corporation. The two lowest layers in this model are the physical layer and the data link layer. These can be chosen from a number of standards including the ETHER-NET standard.

NP 1. Abbreviation for No Problem used in CHAT ROOMS, EMAILS, and NEWSGROUPS. **2**. The designated COUNTRY CODE for Nepal.

NREN *See* NATIONAL RESEARCH AND EDU-CATION NETWORK.

NRG A HAKSPEK abbreviation for Energy used in CHAT ROOMS, EMAILS, and NEWS-GROUPS.

NRN Abbreviation for No Reply Necessary used in EMAILS.

NSA *See* NATIONAL SECURITY AGENCY.

NSA Line Eater A program reputedly developed by the NATIONAL SECURITY AGENCY which eavesdrops on traffic on the Internet looking for subversive EMAILS or POSTINGS. It is not quite clear whether this program exists, although it is firmly established in HACKER mythology.

NSAPI *See* NETSCAPE SERVER APPLICATION PROGRAMMING INTERFACE.

NSF *See* NATIONAL SCIENCE FOUNDATION.

NSFNet A network which linked a number of supercomputers together in the 1980s. It formed the core of the Internet until its retirement in the mid-1990s.

NSP *See* NETWORK SERVICE PROVIDER.

NTA Abbreviation for Non Technical Acronym used in EMAILS and NEWSGROUPS.

NTP *See* NETWORK TIME PROTOCOL.

nut cluster A group of MUD users, usually in a university, who take over a room of computers for playing a MULTI USER DUNGEON game.

nyetwork A malfunctioning network, usually one which is not accepting any data or commands from a user. Derived from the Russian for 'no': nyet.

nym A SERVER which carries out an ANONYMOUS REMAILER SERVICE. Formed from the fourth to sixth letters of anonymous. Also known as a NYM SERVER.

nym server A more formal name for a NYM.

nymrod An individual who insists on turning multiple words into acronyms. The term is formed from the last three letters of 'acronym'.

OBI *See* OPEN BUYING ON THE INTERNET.

object A discrete chunk of data and functionality which can be queried or altered by sending messages to it. *See* OBJECT-ORIENTED TECHNOLOGY and OBJECT-ORIENTED PROGRAMMING LANGUAGE.

Object Management Group A group of companies and organizations responsible for the development of the COMMON OBJECT REQUEST BROKER ARCHITECTURE.

object-oriented programming language A programming language that provides facilities for the definition and manipulation of objects, an object being a collection of data which can be sent messages that change the values of its components. For example, a typical object in a stock control system is a product which is stored in a warehouse. A product object contains data that is relevant to the use which is made of it, for example its name, the quantity in stock, and the level below which it has to be reordered. Typical messages which such an object would receive include a message which reduces its stock level, increases its stock level, and which returns with the name of the supplier of the product. Object-oriented languages are not new: they date from the late 1960s. However, in the 1990s they have achieved increasing prominence: first through the use of C++ in conventional applications and then through the use of JAVA in Internet applications. If current trends continue, Java and C++, together with the programming language PERL, will dominate software development for the Internet in the coming years.

object-oriented technology A general term which describes tools, processes, and programming languages concerned with the development of systems that consist of chunks of data known as objects. This technology is not new: it can be traced to a programming language SIMULA which was invented in Norway in the late 1960s. However, since 1990 there has been a rapid growth in the use of the technology, fired by the promise of software reuse that it offers and the increasing availability of commercial OBJECT-ORIENTED PROGRAMMING LANGUAGES such as JAVA and C++. Many commentators have predicted that much of the future development of Internet applications will be carried out using this technology.

object request broker A key component of the COMMON OBJECT REQUEST BROKER ARCHITECTURE more commonly known as CORBA. This is a DISTRIBUTED OBJECT technology which enables objects resident on a number of physically remote computers to interact with each other via messages. An object request broker is a program which sits in the middle of these objects directing messages to their destination along with any replies from objects. Object request brokers also implement a NAME SERVICE so that distributed objects can be identified; they also implement security services. Usually abbreviated to ORB.

obsolete tag A TAG whose use has been made redundant by a new version of the HYPERTEXT MARKUP LANGUAGE: for example, the tag <LISTING> was made obsolete by HTML 4. While BROWSERS support obsolete tags there is no guarantee that their developers will support them in the future. *See also* HTML LEVEL and DEPRECATED TAG.

off hook A term used to describe a lamp on a MODEM which, when lit, indicates that the phone line to which the modem is connected is ready for data.

official standard A document which has been recognized by the INTERNET SOCIETY as a final Internet standard. Such a standard will have been under the aegis of the INTERNET ENGINEERING TASK FORCE from the point where it first saw the light of day as a REQUEST FOR COMMENT.

It will then have gone through a number of documentation stages during which it will have been transformed into an INTER-NET DRAFT, a PROPOSED STANDARD, and a DRAFT STANDARD.

off line Used to describe the state of a computer when it is disconnected from a network. The term is also employed by users to describe the fact that they are not currently interacting with a network, usually the Internet: for example, 'I'm going to the baseball game tonight. I'm really looking forward to being off line.'

offline browser A utility which copies the whole of a WEB SITE to the local computer disk so that it can be accessed without using slow, external communication lines. There are a variety of such utilities available. A typical, sophisticated offline browser enables the periodic automatic copying of sites; disallows copying of specified pages, such as pages which are of no interest to the user; stops the copying at a certain level, say after two links have been followed; and fetches only those pages which have changed.

offline world A jargon term for the world outside the Internet. *See also* MEAT SPACE.

off the grid A period of time when an Internet user has not had access to a network, for example during a holiday.

off the trolley Used to describe a program or a computer which is malfunctioning but has not stopped or CRASHed.

OFX *See* OPEN FINANCIAL EXCHANGE.

OH *See* OFF HOOK.

OIC A HAKSPEK abbreviation for Oh I See used in CHAT ROOMS, EMAILS, and NEWS-GROUPS.

OLAP *See* ONLINE ANALYTICAL PROCESSING.

OLTP *See* ONLINE TRANSACTION PROCESS-ING.

OMG *See* OBJECT MANAGEMENT GROUP.

one-phase commit protocol A TRANS-ACTION may consist of a number of individual transactions which carry out processes such as reading and writing to a DATABASE. When the transaction is com-pleted all the individual transactions must have successfully carried out their tasks. A one-phase commit PROTOCOL involves a coordinator periodically communicating with the SERVERS that are carrying out each individual transaction in order to inform them whether to commit the transaction or abort it. *See also* TWO-PHASE COMMIT PROTOCOL.

one-time pad An alternative name for a CODE BOOK.

one-time password A password that is used only once. Such passwords provide a high degree of security. A number of schemes have been adopted for one-time passwords including low-tech printed lists, TOKEN CARDS, and special-purpose computer programs.

on line When a computer or a user is directly connected into a network and is capable of interacting with it, for example by querying the contents of a DATABASE.

online Adjective used to describe something which is on line: for example ON-LINE CHAT.

online analytical processing A syno-nym, used for advertising purposes, employed by vendors to differentiate their products from executive informa-tion systems, although here are no dis-cernible differences between the two types of system.

online auction An auction organized via a WEB SITE. The company organizing the auction places an item for auction on their site with a low starting price. Visitors to the site then bid for the item as in a normal auction, the only difference being that there is often an advertised time when the auction is deemed to have finished. This time might be expressed as a specific date or a certain number of days after the last bid has been received. Some-times the auctions are organized in REAL TIME; in this case they closely mimic their conventional, non-electronic, counter-parts.

online broker A broker who provides standard brokerage services on the Inter-net, for example by selling securities or advising on financial portfolios. Rates vary from dealer to dealer, but they usually charge a specific rate on the first few thousand pounds of a transaction, with smaller percentages for additional amounts. They also frequently specify a minimum charge.

online catalogue A catalogue of products stored at a WEB SITE, with details of each product on a separate WEB PAGE.

online chat The process whereby users of the Internet engage in REAL TIME conversations using their computers. Online chat consists of these users exchanging text messages. In order to engage in online chat a CHAT CLIENT must LOG-IN to a CHAT CHANNEL and contact a CHAT SERVER. There are a large number of chat channels, ranging from those which support general conversations to those which are devoted to a specific topic. *See also* INTERNET RELAY CHAT, INSTANT MESSAGING, and PRIVATE CHAT.

online community Another name for a VIRTUAL COMMUNITY.

online content provider Originally an online content provider was an INTERNET SERVICE PROVIDER that offered exclusive access to their content to their subscribers. This content was very large including CHAT ROOMS, INTERNET GAMES, news, sport, consumer information, and so on. Many charge customers for their Internet service as compared with FREE INTERNET SERVICE PROVIDERS who often have less content but offer free access. The term has also spread to describe any company that provides content, including newspapers and magazines.

online dictionary In effect a conventional dictionary transferred to the Web. However, such dictionaries are often supplemented by interactive search facilities and cross referencing to other dictionary entries. *See also* METADICTIONARY.

online magazine An electronic version of a conventional magazine. Typically the content of an online magazine is the same as its conventional counterpart. However, it is often supplemented by devices such as MAILING LISTS, ONLINE CHAT, and DYNAMIC CONTENT. Such magazines are often known as EZINES.

online mall The collection of a number of Internet stores linked in a WEB SITE. Often such malls centralize expensive technical functions such as product ordering and credit card processing. The malls usually consist of stores which are complementary: for example, they may all sell items which can be given as gifts.

online newspaper The electronic version of a newspaper stored at a WEB SITE. Usually the newspaper consists of content found in a conventional newspaper supplemented by devices such as MAILING LISTS, EMAIL, DYNAMIC CONTENT, interactive competitions, and BANNER ADVERTS. Many conventional news organizations maintain Web sites which are almost exact replicas of their daily paper-based newspapers.

online news service A WEB SITE which provides news on a basis which is close to REAL TIME. A good news site updates its content every few minutes and provides a ticker tape service that displays a summary of news which is in the process of breaking.

online profile A description of a user of a network or the customer of an INTERNET SERVICE PROVIDER. This contains a lot more detail than the basic information found in a MEMBER DIRECTORY.

online retailer An ECOMMERCE company that sells products such as CDs, clothes, or books.

online service provider A company that offers customers access to its private network. Such private networks are not part of the Internet. Many online service providers are increasingly migrating to the Internet and offering the same services as INTERNET SERVICE PROVIDERS.

online transaction processing Used in a system where clients store and interrogate data which is important to an organization's business. Typical applications include stock control, airline seat reservation, and share dealing. Such applications require secure data and guaranteed response times for TRANSACTIONS. They were once only found on MAINFRAME COMPUTER systems but they are increasingly being found on CLIENT SERVER

COMPUTING systems. Online transaction processing systems which are DISTRIBUTED SYSTEMS provide major technical challenges in terms of response time, security and reliability.

on the fly Used to describe the process of building DYNAMIC PAGES. These are WEB PAGES which change over a period of time; for example, pages which detail the price of stocks and shares. There are a number of technologies used for developing on the fly pages, the two main ones being JAVA SERVER PAGES and ACTIVE SERVER PAGES.

OOTB Abbreviation for Out Of The Box or Out Of The Blue used in EMAILS and NEWSGROUPS.

Op See SYSTEM OPERATOR.

open To make a FILE ready for reading or writing or to start the execution of a program.

Open Buying on the Internet A standard for BUSINESS TO BUSINESS transactions developed by a consortium of organizations numbering over 50 members. It is intended for high-volume, low-value transactions. Often abbreviated to OBI.

open collar worker Someone who works at home using MOBILE COMPUTING technology. See also TELECOTTAGING, TELECOMMUTING, and TELEWORKING.

Open EDI A future standard for Electronic Data Interchange (EDI) which is targeted at the interchange of data over public networks such as the Internet.

Open Financial Exchange A standard developed by Microsoft, Intuit, and a company known as CheckFree which specifies how financial data such as accounts information, credit card information, and bill payments are to be shared between financial institutions. It is based on the XML language.

open network A network which provides open access to its users with little, if any, authentication being applied. The best example of an open network is the Internet.

open shirt worker A term often used to refer to workers in Silicon Valley where dress codes are laissez-faire or non-existent. It is also applied to users of the Internet who engage in TELEWORKING. See also OPEN COLLAR WORKER.

open shortest path first A basic routing policy used in networks. It uses a variety of criteria including route speed, reliability, and traffic conditions to determine the route that DATAGRAMS take in the Internet.

Open Software Description A technology which has been developed by the Microsoft Corporation and a company called Marimba; it enables the latest versions of software to be downloaded onto a user's computer using PUSH TECHNOLOGY. It has been submitted to the WORLD WIDE WEB CONSORTIUM for standardization.

Open Software Foundation A consortium of companies which promote standards and specifications for software that is intended to run on the UNIX operating system.

open source The process of releasing the program code of a software product in order to encourage companies to build on the original product. The archetypal open source product is LINUX, but there are an increasing number of companies, for example Netscape with their MOZILLA project, releasing the code for their products. See also OPEN SOURCE MOVEMENT.

open source movement A movement characterized by a body such as the OPEN SOFTWARE FOUNDATION which believes that, as a minimum, the code of software systems should be available to all so that individuals can tailor a system or provide add-on software or support software for it. The more extreme members of this movement advocate the removing of copyright and patent laws from software so that products become a free commodity. The open source movement is best exemplified by the community that has grown up around the LINUX operating system. This OPERATING SYSTEM, a clone of UNIX, is freely available in source form to any developer in the world. See also MOZILLA.

Open Systems Interconnection A seven-layered architecture specification which was developed by the INTER-

NATIONAL STANDARDS ORGANIZATION. The standard, as the name suggests, defines the facilities required for a number of networked systems to be connected to each other. Although the INTERNET LAYERED ARCHITECTURE has five layers there are a number of similarities between them. The model is now only of historic interest.

Open Trading Protocol A project aimed at defining an open protocol which can be used by ECOMMERCE companies to carry out processes such as the transfer of goods and services, delivery of products, and the expedition of multiple methods of payment and offers for sale. The protocol is based on XML.

operating system A collection of software which administers, maintains and provides access to the resources of a computer system. For example an operating system maintains a FILE STORE which contains files that have been created by users. It limits access to the files to authorized users and associates symbolic names to files. Increasingly operating systems are providing more and more facilities for networking: in the past technologies such as TCP-IP were regarded as add-ons, but now they are regarded as a vital component of an operating system. See also NETWORK OPERATING SYSTEM.

optical repeater A hardware device which amplifies light signals that travel down a fibre optic communication line. The active repeater receives a light signal, increases its strength, and then retransmits it. This is in contrast to an ACTIVE REPEATER which has to convert the signal to an electrical one before amplification and then has to reconvert it to a light signal.

ORA See ORGANIZATIONAL REGISTRATION AUTHORITY.

orange badge A temporary Microsoft employee such as an agency worker, derived from the orange identification badge worn. See also BLUE BADGE and TURNING BLUE.

Orange Book The name frequently used for the US Defense Department's TRUSTED COMPUTER SECURITY EVALUATION CRITERIA.

ORB See OBJECT REQUEST BROKER.

org A type of Internet DOMAIN associated with an organizational grouping of enterprises set up to promote some topic or idea.

organizational registration authority An organization which registers users with a CERTIFICATE AUTHORITY.

originate mode The state of a MODEM when it is sending a signal to a computer system.

orphan Annie See ANNIE: a WEB PAGE that has not been changed for a considerable time.

orphan link A link in a WEB PAGE which contains a URL to a page that no longer exists. When the user of a browser clicks this link an error message is displayed. See FOUR ZERO FOUR COMPLIANT.

orphan page A WEB PAGE in a WEB SITE that is linked to no other page. This is normally a useless page which no BROWSER user can reach without explicit knowledge of its existence. However, orphan pages are also used as INVISIBLE PAGES which only a subset of visitors is able to read.

OS See OPERATING SYSTEM.

OSF See OPEN SOFTWARE FOUNDATION.

OSI See OPEN SYSTEMS INTERCONNECTION.

OSI Reference Model A major reference standard for networks. Most network standards have either been inspired by or can be discussed with respect to this model. For example, the architecture of TCP-IP is very similar to the OSI model, apart from the fact that it combines some of the functions of the layers into a single layer. The OSI Reference Model is partitioned into seven layers. These are the APPLICATION LAYER, PRESENTATION LAYER, SESSION LAYER, TRANSPORT LAYER, NETWORK LAYER, DATA LINK LAYER, and PHYSICAL LAYER. The application layer is where applications such as EMAIL reside. The presentation layer converts data generated by an application into a common format that other layers can understand. The session layer controls the flow of data between applications. The transport layer supervises the transport of data from one computer on a network to another and checks that data sent is received. The network layer handles the routing of data from one computer to another and determines the path that it takes. The data link layer detects and handles any errors which occur because of poor transmission: for example, errors that are caused by electrical interference. Finally, the physical layer is responsible for the transmission of data at the hardware level: the sending of packets of binary data from one computer to another.

OSP *See* ONLINE SERVICE PROVIDER.

OSPF *See* OPEN SHORTEST PATH FIRST.

OTOH Abbreviation for On The Other Hand used in EMAILS and NEWSGROUPS.

OTTOMH Abbreviation for Off The Top Of My Head used in EMAILS and NEWSGROUPS.

out of band A jargon term used to describe any communication which is not email-based, such as written letters or the use of a mobile phone.

over the wire A term synonymous with ON LINE.

overload attack A DENIAL OF SERVICE ATTACK where an important resource in a computer system is overloaded. For example, an intruder may create thousands of programs which hog the processor of a computer to the extent that other users experience very slow response times for their programs, or may create so many FILES that other users cannot store any data.

P2P An abbreviation for Person to Person or Peer to Peer. It describes activities where users of the Internet cooperate with one another, such as in sharing files. Probably the best example of P2P is NAPSTER which allows Internet users to share music files.

packet A collection of data which is sent through a network to a destination computer. As well as data the packet contains subsidiary information such as the IP ADDRESS of the computer which sent the packet and the IP address of the destination computer. A transfer of information normally involves the splitting of the information to be sent into packets. Each of the packets may be sent over a number of different routes, the routes being determined by ROUTERS found on the network. Transport of data and programs across the Internet is based on packets.

packet filtering The process used to pass data packets which only satisfy certain criteria through a hardware device such as a ROUTER: for example, only allowing packets which access a WEB SERVER or an EMAIL SERVER.

packet filtering gateway A synonym for FIREWALL ROUTER.

Packet Internet Groper A utility, commonly known as PING, which is used to query another computer on a TCP-IP network in order to check that there is a connection to it. The user of this utility executes it with the name of the computer or its IP ADDRESS, and it then sends out a set of messages which ask the remote computer to reply and produce a short report on whether the connection was achieved. Most operating systems contain a simple PING utility; there are also many commercial and shareware versions available. It is sometimes referred to as the Packet INternet Gopher.

packet radio The use of amateur radio equipment for networking and

supporting such technologies as EMAIL and BULLETIN BOARDS.

packet routing filter Another name for a FIREWALL ROUTER.

packet sniffing The process of illegally reading PACKETS of data that travel through a network. There are a number of ways in which this can be done, ranging from pretending to be a SYSTEM ADMINISTRATOR and using restricted tools or attaching hardware devices to the media used to transmit packets. This is normally a criminal activity aimed at gaining unauthorized access to a network.

packet switched network Another name for a POINT-TO-POINT NETWORK.

packet switching The process whereby data that is to be sent around a network is partitioned into discrete chunks known as PACKETS and sent independently around a network, intermingled with packets from other data. Each packet contains the address of its destination. This is the technique used in the Internet, which employs the PROTOCOL known as TCP-IP to carry out packet switching.

packet switching node An alternative name for a ROUTER.

padded cell Software that limits the facilities that a user is able to employ on a computer or a network. Usually ensures that novice users do not cause problems that could adversely affect a system. *See also* SANDBOX.

paddle The electronic identity given to a participant in an ONLINE AUCTION. It is derived from the name given to the piece of cardboard given to potential bidders at conventional auctions.

page A shortened version of WEB PAGE.

page information request A more formal name for a CLICK THROUGH.

page jacking Where a WEB SITE makes its pages look like those of a famous or popular site. The owners of such sites will also SPAMDEX a SEARCH ENGINE with KEY-WORDS relevant to the copied site so that it will attract large numbers of visitors. Such sites are often used to sell pornographic material or to initiate some financial scam.

page popularity A measure of how popular a WEB PAGE is, calculated by counting the number of links to the page from pages in other WEB SITES. It is used by a number of SEARCH ENGINES when ordering the results of a SEARCH QUERY made by a user.

page positioning The process of designing a WEB PAGE so that it takes advantage of the perceived POSITIONING ALGORITHM that is used by a SEARCH ENGINE. Since these algorithms are secret and the only information that can be gained about them concerns their behaviour this process can be quite a hit and miss affair, especially since many search engines change their strategies from time to time.

page request A unit which represents the number of times a WEB PAGE is requested from a WEB SERVER by users. It is used for estimating Web server traffic and gauging the popularity of WEB SITES.

page view Another name for a PAGE RE-QUEST.

paid link placement A practice adopted by some SEARCH ENGINE companies where they accept payment from companies who want their WEB SITES presented prominently when a query is submitted to a search engine. The practice is controversial: its opponents point out that it often distorts the results returned from a query. The proponents point out that most search engines cannot rely on just advertising for revenue and in order to maintain a search engine on the Internet, commercial services such as paid link placement have to be employed.

painting the screen The practice of conspiring to artificially inflate the price of a share by spreading rumours and buying tranches of the share. When the share price rises the shares are sold at a profit. *See* SHARE RAMPING. The term comes from the term 'painting the tape,'

used to describe the same process applied to a ticker tape and used in pre-Internet times.

palette The selection of colours available to the user of a graphics program.

palm computing The use of small, hand-held computing devices such as PER-SONAL DIGITAL ASSISTANTS.

PAN *See* PERSONAL AREA NETWORK.

pane A subdivison of a WINDOW. Normally a window using panes contains a number of panes showing related information: for example, the popular Windows Explorer tool uses panes to show directories and the contents of directories. In HTML a pane is known as a FRAME.

PANS Abbreviation for Pretty Awesome New Stuff used in CHAT ROOMS, EMAILS, and NEWSGROUPS. It is usually used to describe new computer hardware or software.

PAP *See* PASSWORD AUTHENTICATION PROTOCOL.

paper mail A term used for postage-based mail. *See also* PMAIL and SNAIL MAIL.

paper net Used to describe the postal system. *See also* PMAIL and SNAIL MAIL.

paralanguage A collection of symbols, icons, or words used to provide additions to a written text as substitutes for facial or vocal cues. EMOTICONS are a good example of a paralanguage. There is a large debate about whether such devices are needed for communication media such as EMAILS, with opponents putting forward the view that they are only a crutch for poor writers who, if they improved their communication skills, could provide the cues using text.

parallel port A port on a computer to which devices such as printers are connected. *See also* SERIAL PORT.

parent message A POSTING that generates a FOLLOW-UP. For example, a message announcing a new software product would be the parent message of postings which describe users' early experiences with that product.

parse The process of checking the correctness of text and then splitting it up into its constituent components. For example, when a SEARCH ENGINE processes a SEARCH QUERY it splits the query into the individual words to be searched for and the BOOLEAN CONNECTIVES between each word.

parser A computer program which checks a file for adherence to a set of rules. For example, programming languages are processed by a parser to check that the programmer has adhered to the syntax of the language. The EXTENSIBLE MARKUP LANGUAGE (XML) is also associated with a number of parsers which check documents expressed in XML for adherence to their DOCUMENT TYPE DEFINITION.

partial URL A UNIFORM RESOURCE LOCATOR in a HYPERLINK which refers to a WEB PAGE relative to the page which contains the hyperlink. If the address of the page containing the hyperlink is *x* and the relative address is *y* then the link is designated by *x/y*. A link which is expressed in such a way is known as a RELATIVE LINK. A document expressed in terms of relative links is much easier to move around on a computer than one in which the whole URL is specified.

passive attack An intrusion into a computer network which reads the data passing along some of the TRANSMISSION LINES without modifying it. *See also* ACTIVE ATTACK.

passive star A form of STAR NETWORK architecture which is used for fibre optic networks.

passphrase A set of characters used to identify a user to a computer system. It is similar to a PASSWORD but a passphrase is much longer.

password A series of characters typed into a computer in order to gain access to the network. It is important not to use any words such as your name for a password, as an intruder would be able to guess it. There is a wide variety of software available for password processing, including software for managing a database of passwords, software enabling someone to retrieve a forgotten password if they know

roughly what it is, and software which provides a password which is easy to memorize but difficult to guess.

password adviser A program which advises a user whether the PASSWORD they want to use is weak and hence could be discovered by an intruder: for example, a short password with no non-alphabetic characters.

Password Authentication Protocol An AUTHENTICATION protocol that is used when connecting to an INTERNET SERVICE PROVIDER. *See also* CHALLENGE HANDSHAKE AUTHENTICATION PROTOCOL. It is often abbreviated to PAP. It is less secure than the CHALLENGE HANDSHAKE AUTHENTICATION PROTOCOL because the PASSWORD that is passed to a server is sent as plain text.

password constraint The rules which constrain the form of a PASSWORD. Some passwords are quite easy for an intruder to guess. For example, short passwords containing only alphabetic characters can be cracked very easily. Password constraint is the process of rejecting passwords based on criteria specified by a system administrator or a security administrator. Users may be prevented from creating short passwords, passwords which have the user's name contained in it, or passwords which do not include at least one non-alphabetic or numeric character. The rejection of a password is normally carried out by an OPERATING SYSTEM or software tool when a user attempts to create a new password or change an existing password.

password cracker A program which generates a large number of easily crackable passwords that might be employed by the users of a computer network. These programs are usually used by a SYSTEM ADMINISTRATOR to check that no user has a password that can be easily cracked by an intruder. These programs can, of course, be used by intruders to gain unauthorized access into a network.

password dispenser A program which generates passwords. One of the main security problems with network access is the fact that many users choose very simple PASSWORDS. Typical of these are the first name of the user, the surname of the user, the user's car registration, or the name of the user's pet. Such passwords are easily guessed by a potential intruder. A password dispenser is a software utility which generates a password that is not obvious but can be remembered: for example, the password R2eesie7.

password file A file used to store the individual passwords of the users of a system, sometimes referred to as a COOKIE JAR by CRACKERS.

password modem A MODEM which requires a PASSWORD from a user before it can be used to connect into a computer on a network.

password protection The process of limiting access to a program or file by means of a PASSWORD. Anyone who tries to open a program or file which is password-protected is asked for the password before they are allowed to proceed.

password sniffer An unauthorized program which monitors the traffic down a transmission line and captures the first hundred or so bytes of data that are emitted when a network connection is established. Within this data is the password employed by the user to gain access. The password is extracted and an intruder then uses it to gain unauthorized access to the network.

paste bomb A chunk of text, usually long and irrelevant, that has been pasted in a NEWSGROUP posting or into an EMAIL message. Occasionally it is done in order to irritate and annoy others.

patch A small change to a program which usually eradicates an error. Patches are normally sent out by software companies in between launching new versions of the software. For example, when a company is notified of a security problem with some software, it sends out a patch to eradicate the problem. Reputedly the popular server APACHE was given its name because of the large numbers of patches which were applied to it during its initial release period.

path name A set of DIRECTORY names which identify a particular FILE or directory on a computer. Each directory is separated by a PATH NAME SEPARATOR.

path name separator The character that is used to separate each DIRECTORY that forms part of a PATH NAME. In UNIFORM RESOURCE LOCATORS the path name separator is the FORWARD SLASH character '/'.

pay-by-click model A way of earning revenue by being an affiliate in an ASSOCIATE PROGRAM. Each affiliate links to the WEB SITE of a trader and is paid for every visitor arriving at the site via the affiliate's site. *See also* PAY-BY-PURCHASE MODEL.

pay-by-purchase model A way of earning revenue by being an affiliate in an ASSOCIATE PROGRAM. Each affiliate links to the WEB SITE of a trader and is paid for every visitor making a purchase at the site via the affiliate's site. The payment is a commission, which usually ranges between 5 and 15 per cent. *See also* PAY-BY-CLICK MODEL.

payment protocol A PROTOCOL which governs and mediates the online payment made by a customer to a vendor. Such a protocol has security and reliability as its top two aims. The two main protocols currently in use are the Secure Electronic Payment Protocol and the SECURED ELECTRONIC TRANSACTION STANDARD.

payware Software that is commercially sold, in contrast to SHAREWARE or FREEWARE.

PC card A small device, a little smaller than a credit card which plugs into a computer—usually a portable computer—and can provide extra memory or the facilities found in a FAX MODEM or normal MODEM. Such cards conform to the PCMCIA standard.

PCA *See* POLICY CERTIFICATION AUTHORITY.

PCI *See* PERIPHERAL COMPONENT INTERCONNECT.

PCMCIA 1. Abbreviation for PERSONAL COMPUTER MEMORY CARD INTERNATIONAL ASSOCIATION.
2. Abbreviation for People Can't Master Computer Industry Acronyms used in EMAILS and NEWSGROUPS.

PD Abbreviation for Public Domain used in EMAILS and NEWSGROUPS. It is usually used to describe software that is available at no charge.

PDA **1**. Abbreviation for PERSONAL DIGITAL ASSISTANT.
2. Abbreviation for Public Display Of Affection used in CHAT ROOMS.

PDF See PORTABLE DOCUMENT FORMAT.

PDS Abbreviation for Please Don't Shoot used in EMAILS and NEWSGROUPS. Usually used to precede some controversial message.

PDU See PROTOCOL DATA UNIT.

PeaceNet An international network which supports peace, justice, and human rights.

PEBCAK Abbreviation for Problem Exists Between Computer And Keyboard used in EMAILS and NEWSGROUPS. Used to indicate that the person who is using the computer is at fault.

peer The name given to the LAYERS which communicate with each other in a network. For example, if layer n in one network communicates with layer m in another then these layers are known as peers.

peer entity A networking term referring to an ENTITY that resides on the same LAYER as another entity in a network, but on different computers.

Peer to Peer An Internet activity where users collaborate without the use of any intervening SERVERS. The best example of this is the sound-file sharing system known as NAPSTER. Usually abbreviated to P2P and sometimes referred to as person to person.

peer-to-peer network A network which consists of a series of devices with no central coordinating or service computers: every computer has an equal status. This is in contrast to a CLIENT SERVER COMPUTING system where the CLIENTS take a subservient role to the SERVERS.

PEM See PRIVACY ENHANCED MAIL.

penetration testing The legal intrusion into a computer system by HACKERS

in order to test the security mechanisms in the system. See TIGER TEAM.

penis size war A quantitative argument carried out on a NEWSGROUP, such as an argument over processor speed. Usually such arguments generate a lot of heat and FLAMES. Also known as a DICK SIZE WAR.

peon A user with no special privileges on a computer system.

people finding The process of finding the addresses or EMAIL addresses of users of the Internet. There are a number of ways of doing this. If the person has submitted at least one POSTING to a NEWSGROUP then the DEJANEWS search engine can be used. Another location is the FOUR11 search engine which is dedicated to people searches.

performance management A subdiscipline of NETWORK MANAGEMENT. It consists of two tasks. The first is monitoring the performance of a network in terms of throughput rates and identifying bottlenecks (known as CHOKE POINTS) in the network. The second is modifying the configuration of a network in order to improve throughput and eliminate bottlenecks.

performance monitoring The process of checking the performance of a network in terms of the response time that a user of that network achieves. There are a number of performance tools available which simulate a typical mix of activities and monitor the response time of the network to these activities.

Peripheral Component Interconnect® A local bus standard developed by the INTEL corporation.

Perl A programming language which is included in this dictionary because it has become the main language of programmers who carry out CGI PROGRAMMING. The language manipulates strings (sequences of characters) and contains facilities for searching for particular sequences of characters in a string, replacing parts of strings and creating new strings from other strings. It can also manipulate numbers and OBJECTS. It is currently being challenged by JAVA. See also SERVLET.

permatemp An employee who has been working for a company for some time but has not yet achieved permanent employee status.

permissions Users of a networked system are granted a number of facilities by the SYSTEM ADMINISTRATOR when they are first registered with the system. These are known as permissions. There are a variety of permissions that can be provided, ranging from which computers in the network can be used to the files that a user is allowed to access. The system administrator is given the most comprehensive set of permissions.

persistent cookie A COOKIE which stays on a CLIENT computer after the session which established it has been completed. A typical use for a persistent cookie is to place some information on the client that a SERVER can reuse when a new session starts: for example, some personal details such as the name of the user and his or her credit card number.

personal area network A network which is used in the home to connect devices as diverse as computers, televisions, burglar alarms, and ovens.

personal assistant An AGENT that operates in a limited domain of a computing system helping an individual with some task that normally involves the processing of large amounts of interrelated data: for example, EMAIL agents which organize emails that have been sent to a particular user.

Personal Computer Memory Card International Association A successful standardization effort initiated by a number of MODEM manufacturers during the 1980s to define a standard for small interface PC CARDS. Such cards have expanded from their original use as MODEMs and embraced hardware devices such as sound cards, memory, and GLOBAL POSITIONING SYSTEM cards.

personal digital assistant A generic term describing small, hand-held computers. Originally personal digital assistants had limited functions mainly centred around personal organization such as a diary or an address book.

However, they are now very sophisticated devices which provide, amongst other facilities, access to the Internet.

personal identification number A number given to a user which enables them to access a networked facility such as a bank's ATM machine. Such numbers provide a form of AUTHENTICATION. Almost invariably abbreviated to PIN.

personalization services An Internet service which offers information or a service customized to the user. For example, there are a number of news services which provide customized news and the major search engines provide the facilities to produce personal HOME PAGES which are refreshed with CONTENT on a periodic basis.

personalized newspaper An electronic newspaper delivered to an Internet user with CONTENT that that user has expressed an interest in: for example, feature stories about a specific software technology.

personal Web site A WEB SITE produced by a single person. It could be a page which is oriented towards business and includes details such as a CV; a more personal Web site oriented to the home and which included interests, hobbies, details of the site owner's family, and links to the personal Web site of each member of that family; or it could be a page oriented towards an individual's particular interests.

personal Web site builder A program, usually driven by a WIZARD, which makes the development of a PERSONAL WEB SITE a semi-automatic process.

PFY Abbreviation for Pimply Faced Youth used in EMAILS and NEWSGROUPS.

PGML *See* PRECISION GRAPHICS MARKUP LANGUAGE.

PGP *See* PRETTY GOOD PRIVACY.

ph Abbreviation for phonebook. phs are found in many educational establishment sites containing directories of staff. Such listings are similar to those associated with FINGER and have often been the target of ADDRESS HARVESTERS in search of email addresses that can be SPAMMED.

phacker 1. Someone who gains illegal access to a phone system, usually in order to make free calls. **2**. Occasionally used to describe someone who taps phone calls. *See also* PHREAKING.

phage A program, inserted illegally into a computer network, which alters the functioning of another program. For example, a phage might infect a word processing program in such a way that whenever the word processor writes to a FILE the file is deleted.

phase of the moon A term associated with descriptions of unreliable software or hardware. For example: 'I really believe that that computer will only work during a particular phase of the moon.'

PHP A DYNAMIC PAGE technology similar to JAVA SERVER PAGES. Its main advantage over the latter is that it has an excellent set of interfaces which enable PHP programmers to use the facilities of a RELATIONAL DATABASE system.

phrase search A search using a SEARCH ENGINE which looks for documents that contain specific phrases or sentences.

phreaking The process of illegally entering the telephone system in order to make free phone calls. Occasionally this term is used to describe an intrusion into any type of network.

physical address Every device in a network is identified by a unique pattern of bits known as a physical address. On the Internet the INTERNET PROTOCOL ADDRESS needs to be converted to this address before a program can initiate a data transfer to a computer. *See also* ADDRESS RESOLUTION PROTOCOL, INTERNET DOMAIN NAME SERVICE and NAME RESOLUTION.

physical layer The layer in the OSI REFERENCE MODEL which is closest to the computers connected to a network. It carries out the process of sending data to the electrical circuits and transmission lines that make up the network.

physical medium The term given to the actual hardware—cables, satellite links, or other transmission media—over which physical communication in a network occurs. In all LAYERED ARCHITECTURES

this is the lowest layer and two computers communicating with each other and sending data have these layers as PEERS.

PIBCAK Abbreviation for Problem Is Between Chair and Keyboard used in EMAILS and NEWSGROUPS. An indication that there is a problem with the user of a computer. *See also* PEBCAK.

PICS *See* PLATFORM FOR INTERNET CONTENT SELECTION.

picture element The longer and very infrequently used version of PIXEL.

piggy back attack An attack on a computer network where the intruder monitors the activity of a user of the network. When the user issues a LOG OUT the intruder cancels it and then proceeds to masquerade as the user.

pig tail A short length of cable that is used to connect one connector type to another.

PIN *See* PERSONAL IDENTIFICATION NUMBER.

PING *See* PACKET INTERNET GROPER.

ping flooding Another name for a PING STORM.

ping o' death An attack on many operating systems in 1996 which disabled a number of computers and embarrassed a number of operating system vendors. It made many computers crash by overflowing the memory that was allocated to TCP-IP communication. The term is now used to describe any human-created event that causes a system to CRASH. *See also* PING FLOODING and PING STORM.

ping storm The disruption of a network by means of flooding it with PING messages. Recently used by Serbian nationalists to disrupt the NATO computer network. *See also* PING FLOODING.

PITA Abbreviation for Pain In The Ass used in EMAILS and NEWSGROUPS.

pixel Abbreviation for picture element. A pixel is a single point on a visual display device such as a monitor. Graphics devices display pictures which can consist of thousands of pixels arranged in rows and columns. A variety of colours are displayed using pixels. For example, in 8-bit colour mode, a colour monitor uses 8 bits for each pixel, with each integer that can be formed from 8 bits being assigned a colour; this means that 256 colours can be displayed.

pixel shim A small graphic which is usually invisible and which is used in order to force a BROWSER to format a WEB PAGE in a way that the browser was not intended to do. *See also* SINGLE-PIXEL GIF.

P JPEG Abbreviation for PROGRESSIVE JPEG.

PKI *See* PUBLIC KEY INFRASTRUCTURE.

PKZIP A popular SHAREWARE utility which compresses files prior to their being sent over a network or being archived.

plagiarism The process of reusing material found in any medium. The ease with which material can be CUT AND PASTED from the WORLD WIDE WEB has led to a major increase in plagiarism with entities such as graphics, APPLETS and animations being reused. A number of legal cases in the Western world have established the fact that media on the Web are no different from, say, printed media, and that unauthorized copying from such media is illegal. The flip side to this is that many owners of WEB SITES are usually happy for their material to be copied in exchange for, say, a mention of their Web site in the site that contains the copied material. However, the important point is that permission has to be granted.

plain old telephone system A term used to describe a telephone system unenhanced by computer-transmission-related technology such as INTEGRATED SERVICES DIGITAL NETWORK. Often abbreviated to POTS.

plain text Text which is to be encrypted before it is sent over a network. *See* ENCRYPTION. The text that is produced is known as the CIPHER TEXT.

plan file A file which contains personal information such as a user's EMAIL ADDRESS.

platform A term synonymous with OPERATING SYSTEM. However, it is occasionally used in other contexts such as when referring to Java system software as the Java platform.

platform-dependent Used to describe software that can only be used on one particular operating system such as UNIX.

Platform for Internet Content Selection A standard used to mark WEB SITES to indicate their suitability for groups such as children. It involves the developer of a Web site inserting information taken from a RATING VOCABULARY into the META-TAGS used in the HOME PAGE of the site. Software known as BLOCKING SOFTWARE examines these tags and, based on a number of preset parameters, either denies or allows access to the site by a BROWSER.

pling A term used to describe the exclamation mark character.

PLOKTA *See* PRESS LOTS OF KEYS TO ABORT.

PLONK Abbreviation for Person with Little Or No Knowledge used in CHAT ROOMS, EMAILS, and NEWSGROUPS. Used as a derogatory term, as distinct from NEWBIE.

PLS A HAKSPEK abbreviation for PLeaSe used in CHAT ROOMS, EMAILS, and NEWSGROUPS.

plug-in 1. Software that can be added to a BROWSER in order to view or execute some Web content that it is currently not able to access. For example, in the early days of the programming language JAVA, the browsers that were available were initially incapable of executing Java APPLETS. However, both Netscape and Microsoft produced plug-ins which executed applets very soon after the first release of the Java system. Plug-in software can be categorized into five areas: 3D and animation, business and utilities, presentations, audio and video, and image viewing. A typical 3D and animation plug-in enables a browser to play animations, such as those produced by Shockwave software from Macromedia. A typical business plug-in might allow the browser to access up-to-the-minute news, weather, and financial information. A typical plug-in might enable multimedia presentations

to be displayed on a browser. A typical audio/video plug-in might allow the user of a browser to listen to RealAudio broadcasts. A typical image viewer plug-in might enable a browser to display images in a new or unusual format. The process of adding a plug-in to a browser is a very simple process once the plug-in has been DOWNLOADed.
2. The term is also sometimes used in connection with non-browser software: for example, a database management information system may have a plug-in which enables it to handle object-oriented data.

PM Abbreviation for Private Message used in EMAILS and NEWSGROUPS.

pmail A jargon term for the conventional, paper-based mail service. A less abusive term than SNAIL MAIL. A contraction of paper mail.

PMFJI Abbreviation for Pardon Me For Jumping In used in CHAT ROOMS and NEWSGROUPS.

PNG *See* PORTABLE NETWORK GRAPHIC.

POAHF Abbreviation for Put On A Happy Face used in CHAT ROOMS, EMAILS, and NEWSGROUPS.

POB *See* PRISONER OF BILL.

point 1. To place a BROWSER cursor over a HYPERLINK to another WEB SITE and then clicking. This results in the document referenced in the hyperlink being displayed by the browser.
2. A unit of measurement for displayed text equal to approximately 0.35 mm (0.5 in).

Point Listing A popular WEB SITE which contains links to other Web sites chosen for their superiority of content and structure. *See also* COOL SITE OF THE DAY, BEST OF THE WEB, and HOT LIST.

point of presence A local access point to a major international or national telecommunications network.

point-to-point network A type of network, the opposite of a BROADCAST NETWORK, in which when a message is sent from one computer to another, it usually has to be sent via other computers in the network. A point-to-point network

consists of many connections between individual pairs of computers. As a general rule, large networks such as WIDE AREA NETWORKS are organized in this fashion. This type of network is sometimes called a store and forward network or a packet switched network.

Point-to-Point Protocol A PROTOCOL, like the SERIAL LINE INTERNET PROTOCOL, which governs the transmission of data over a SERIAL LINE. It supports ASYNCHRONOUS COMMUNICATION and also contains error detection facilities. It is often abbreviated to PPP.

Point-to-Point Tunneling Protocol® A PROTOCOL which enables remote users to access a LOCAL AREA NETWORK. It works by storing the protocol within messages sent via TCP-IP and enables companies to develop VIRTUAL PRIVATE NETWORKS. The protocol was developed by the Microsoft Corporation and a number of modem manufacturers. It is often abbreviated to PPTP.

point-to-point video conferencing VIDEO CONFERENCING which involves only two participants.

policy certification authority An organization which has been sanctioned to issue SECURITY CERTIFICATES to a CERTIFICATE AUTHORITY.

policy file A FILE which contains text describing the current security policies enforced in a network. Such files are usually set up by a SYSTEM ADMINISTRATOR. The file is consulted whenever a component of the system attempts to carry out an action which might compromise the current security policy. For example, a typical entry in such a file might prohibit the transfer of APPLETS into the system: a browser which was about to transfer a WEB PAGE containing an applet would consult this file before carrying out a page transfer and would be forbidden to carry out the transfer.

politeness window Many SPIDERS visit a WEB SERVER when they are cataloguing a site for a period known as the politeness window. They do this in order not to place too much additional processing load on the server.

polling 1. The process of checking a hardware device to see if some event has occurred. For example, a computer may poll a transmission line to see if any data is ready to be transferred from the line. Polling is normally carried out at regular intervals. **2**. A term used in a software context to describe the process whereby one program sends regular messages to another program in order to check whether the second program has data for it or to check on the state of the second program.

polymorphic virus A virus which changes its form each time it infects a computer. This is achieved by changing the program code of the virus although the function of the code stays the same. This makes these viruses very difficult to detect by VIRUS DETECTION SOFTWARE which looks for viruses based on pattern matching against a known structure. These viruses are also known as SELF-MUTATING VIRUSES.

POM Acronym for PHASE OF THE MOON: for example, 'My computer is behaving strangely, it must be the POM.'

Ponzi scheme An Internet scam named after the twentieth-century confidence trickster who invented it. It is based on asking investors to send money to the person running the scheme. He or she then promises to pay a very high interest rate. Interest payments are paid for a short time, usually from the funds paid by other investors. However, the interest rate paid by the perpetrators of a Ponzi scheme is so high that it collapses in debt very quickly. SPAM is the usual way of promoting such schemes.

POP *See* POST OFFICE PROTOCOL.

POP3 Version 3 of the POST OFFICE PROTOCOL (POP), a simple PROTOCOL used to transport EMAIL.

populated segment A cable in a network that has one or more NODES attached. It is also known as a TRUNK SEGMENT. *See also* LINK SEGMENT.

port A logical concept rather than a hardware concept. It represents a way of identifying a conduit through which data can flow into and out of a computer. A number of ports are known as DEDICATED PORTS and are reserved for certain services. For example, port 80 is usually the port which BROWSERS connect into in order to retrieve WEB PAGES. The combination of INTERNET PROTOCOL ADDRESS and port is known as an Internet SOCKET.

Portable Document Format A format which retains the visual integrity of a document. The format was developed by the Adobe Corporation which provides a free reader known as the Adobe Acrobat Reader. Many other document formats can be converted into the Portable Document Format and, consequently, a company using a heterogeneous collection of software for developing documents can enable their staff to read such documents easily even if they are not equipped with the software used to create them. Documents using this format can be read by BROWSERS; this enables a WEB DESIGNer to take advantage of the more flexible layout facilities than are available in the HYPERTEXT MARKUP LANGUAGE. It is often abbreviated to PDF.

Portable Network Graphic A relatively new graphic format which was developed when problems emerged with the copyright of the GRAPHICS INTERCHANGE FORMAT (GIF). It is a BITMAPPED GRAPHIC format which has been defined by the WORLD WIDE WEB CONSORTIUM. It is currently seen as a possible patent-free replacement for the currently popular GIF format. It is usually abbreviated to PNG.

port address A number which identifies a PORT. The port number forms one part of a SOCKET ADDRESS. Port numbers below 1,024 are used for services such as the FILE TRANSFER PROTOCOL; numbers above this can be used by applications. *See* DEDICATED PORT.

portal A WEB SITE which acts as a starting point for users of the WORLD WIDE WEB. Portals provide very large amounts of CONTENT and services such as FREE EMAIL, PERSONALIZATION SERVICES, and NEWS FEEDS. A typical portal is YAHOO, a SEARCH ENGINE which contains a massive amount of catalogue content and pointers to many other services. Many portals have grown out of search engines. *See also* VER-TICAL PORTAL.

positioning algorithm An ALGORITHM used to order the results of a SEARCH QUERY processed by a SEARCH ENGINE. The ideal positioning algorithm orders the results in the degree of relevance to the user. There are a number of metrics used in these algorithms, including the degree to which KEYWORDS are in proximity and PAGE POPULARITY. Most algorithms are proprietary and secret.

post To submit a contribution (a POSTING) to a NEWSGROUP.

postcardware SHAREWARE for which the developer only wants to be sent a postcard from the buyer's town or city as payment.

posting A contribution to a NEWSGROUP. For example the user of a newsgroup devoted to BROWSERS may make a posting about some of the problems that he or she has encountered with the latest version of a particular browser. Also known as an ARTICLE. Users of a newsgroup can make comments on a posting, and these are known as FOLLOW-UP postings. A posting with a series of follow-up postings are collectively known as a THREAD.

postmaster The person in an organization who is responsible for EMAIL. A postmaster can usually be contacted by sending an email to postmaster@domain name.

Post Office Protocol A very simple PROTOCOL which mediates between client computers running EMAIL software and an EMAIL SERVER. The protocol consists of a series of messages which can be sent to and received from the server. For example, the message STAT, when sent from the client, interrogates the server about the number of email messages that are waiting for the user. This protocol is very straightforward and efficient and, consequently, there are a large number of organizations currently using it. It is, however, limited: for example, it does not allow the user to transfer a subset of emails from a MAILBOX and is not suitable for users who have multiple computers to access mail.

Post, Telegraph and Telephone A term used to describe a nationalized tele-communications company which often provides a monopoly service within a country. The term is usually abbreviated to PTT.

POTS See PLAIN OLD TELEPHONE SYSTEM.

POV Abbreviation for Point Of View used in EMAILS and NEWSGROUPS.

PPP *See* POINT-TO-POINT PROTOCOL.

PPTP *See* POINT-TO-POINT TUNNELING PROTOCOL.

precision A metric used to quantify the success of a query made to a SEARCH ENGINE; it represents the ratio of the documents recalled from a SEARCH QUERY which contained the search words to the number which satisfied the query, but were not retrieved.

Precision Graphics Markup Language A two-dimensional VECTOR GRAPHICS standard developed by a consortium which included Adobe, IBM, and Sun Microsystems. Graphics using this standard can be displayed in BROWSERS. Usually abbreviated to PGML.

presentation layer The role of the presentation layer within the OSI REFERENCE MODEL is to convert data that is produced or consumed by applications residing in the application layer to a common format, so that the other layers in the model are able to understand it. For example, it converts ASCII- or EBCDIC-based data to a common format. The conversion takes place through what is known as a common network programming language. This layer also carried out the reverse process: converting the internal form of data into a form which an application such as a NEWSREADER or WEB SERVER can understand.

press lots of keys to abort To attempt to exit from a program which has crashed or stopped. By pressing a large number of keys simultaneously the user hopes to create a condition where the program will terminate. Sometimes one or more of these keys has been programmed to cause termination. Often abbreviated to PLOKTA.

Pretty Good Privacy An ENCRYPTION scheme developed by Phil Zimmerman. It is a scheme which is good enough for personal use, for example for encrypting mail messages. In its early days there was a major controversy over this scheme when the US government claimed that it was so powerful that it could be used by a hostile power. This controversy has now ended. Often abbreviated to PGP.

PRI *See* PRIMARY RATE INTERFACE.

primary backup server A SERVER which is kept in reserve and only used if another server malfunctions. For example, a commercial company will keep a second WEB SERVER in reserve to be quickly deployed when a problem occurs with the main Web server. *See also* DATA REPLICATION and MIRROR SITE.

Primary Rate Interface A high capacity version of the INTEGRATED SERVICES DIGITAL NETWORK technology.

primary server The first SERVER that is used when an attempt is made to discover the INTERNET PROTOCOL ADDRESS of a DOMAIN NAME. It is usually associated with another server—the SECONDARY SERVER—which is used if there are any problems with the primary server.

printing discussion A discussion often carried out on a NEWSGROUP which is pointless, time-consuming, and arcane.

prisoner of Bill A term of derision sometimes used by non-users of Microsoft products to describe those who do use them. The connotation is that they are locked into a Microsoft upgrade path. Often abbreviated to POB.

Privacy Enhanced Mail A standard for securing EMAIL which can employ either PUBLIC KEY ENCRYPTION or SYMMETRIC KEY ENCRYPTION. Its use is decreasing as it is being superseded by the more comprehensive SECURE MULTIMEDIA INTERNET MAIL EXTENSIONS technology.

private chat The use of a CHAT ROOM facility to carry on a private REAL TIME conversation with another user. It suffers from one problem: to carry out a private conversation with someone it is necessary to LOG-IN to a CHAT CHANNEL in order to discover whether that person is on line. Software systems known generically as INSTANT MESSAGING systems have mostly overcome this problem.

private key One of the two keys involved in PUBLIC KEY ENCRYPTION. This is the key that is used by the receiver of an encrypted message to decrypt it. The encrypted message is sent using a PUBLIC KEY.

private key encryption The ENCRYPTION of a message using a key which is only known to the sender and the recipient. This form of encryption is far and away the most popular on the Internet. It is in contrast to the use of PUBLIC KEYS which partly use a known KEY.

private packet radio The use of a private wireless network to provide wireless facilities to access a computer network.

pro In 2000 seven new DOMAIN NAMES were created. pro was one of these. It is intended for use by professionals.

profile The rules used by a FILTER to reject some content sent to a user of the Internet. For example, a filter which rejects SPAM emails might have a profile which states that certain words such as 'fortune' and 'dollars' are rejected. The collection of screening rules is also known as a SCRIPT.

Progressive JPEG A graphical format very similar to the JOINT PHOTOGRAPHIC EXPERTS GROUP format. The major difference is that pictures developed using this format can be gradually displayed in the same way as INTERLACED GIF graphics. When a progressive JPEG image is loaded, the viewer gradually sees the image emerge from a sort of graphic fog until it becomes totally clear.

Project Gutenberg A FREEWARE project which has the aim of providing free copies of classic books to users of the Internet. It is one of the longest-standing projects on the Internet and has as its goal the provision of 10,000 books by 2002. *See also* ELECTRONIC LIBRARY.

prolly A marginal shortening of the word 'probably'. It is used in CHAT ROOMS, EMAILS and NEWSGROUPS in order to save time typing.

promiscuous mode A NETWORK INTER-FACE CARD can normally only read data from packets destined for the computer in which it has been fitted. However, such cards can be placed in promiscuous mode, when they can read all the packets travelling around a network. This is a technique used by CRACKERS who wish to read unauthorized data.

prompt The action of a computer when it asks for some input. For example, before accessing a database it may ask for a password. This is usually displayed in a text field in a WINDOW. In COMMAND LANGUAGE interfaces the term usually refers to the character or set of characters displayed to indicate that some typing is required from the user.

propeller head A term synonymous with GEEK: someone who has an extremely good knowledge of computer technology. *See also* ALPHA GEEK.

proposed standard An Internet standard document originated by the INTERNET ENGINEERING TASK FORCE which originally saw life as a REQUEST FOR COMMENT. It is the first solid draft of a standard. The INTERNET SOCIETY insist that a proposed standard must remain in this state for at least six months, long enough for two sample implementations of the standard to be developed and tested in order to check it out. Once the implementations have been rigorously checked the standard becomes a DRAFT STANDARD.

proprietary protocol A PROTOCOL confined to a particular proprietary set of software or hardware. This is in contrast to Internet protocols which are completely open.

protocol A set of rules and a vocabulary that define how two computers on a network communicate with each other. In order to understand this, a good analogy can be made with the way chess players communicate, either by correspondence or over a computer network. Each move in a game of chess is defined by a notation that specifies the piece that is moved, its initial position, and its final position. This notation, together with the rules used to define what is or what is not a valid move, represents a protocol for playing chess. Protocols are used in a network in the same way. For example, a protocol known as HTTP governs the interaction between a WEB SERVER and CLIENTS which are running BROWSERS that view WEB PAGES. This protocol enables a browser to communicate with the server in order, for example, to let the server know which page the user of the browser requires. There are also a wide variety of protocols used for the provision of email services. These control functions such as the reading, sending, and deletion of emails. Protocols also use facilities provided by other protocols. For example, the FILE TRANSFER PROTOCOL, used to transfer files over a network, employs the TCP-IP protocol that is at the heart of the Internet. The use of one protocol by another has given rise to the term PROTOCOL STACK.

protocol converter A hardware device or program which converts messages expressed in one PROTOCOL to the same message expressed in another protocol.

protocol data unit Sometimes a network has to transfer the data in an INTERFACE DATA UNIT in smaller units, these are known as protocol data units. Often abbreviated to PDU.

protocol header The part of a DATAGRAM which contains information that is essential to the correct transfer of the datagram from one computer to another. For example, in TCP-IP it contains the INTERNET PROTOCOL ADDRESS of the destination computer.

protocol stack The collection of protocols in a layered network architecture, together with the hierarchic relationship between the protocols. This relationship is characterized by the fact that one protocol makes use of another; for example, in the TCP-IP model, the HYPERTEXT TRANSFER PROTOCOL makes use of the INTERNET PROTOCOL to carry out the transfer of WEB PAGES from a WEB SERVER to a BROWSER. The term is often abbreviated to STACK.

protocol suite A collection of PROTOCOLS that are associated with a particular network architecture. For example, TCP-IP is associated with a number of individual protocols which carry out functions such as network management and DOMAIN NAME lookup. It is often referred to by the term PROTOCOL STACK to stress the hierarchic relationship between protocols.

prowler A DAEMON which is periodically executed in order to carry out some maintenance task such as cleaning up the file store of a computer or collection of computers.

proximity operator An operator used in a QUERY processed by a SEARCH ENGINE. It indicates that documents which contain words physically close to each other should be retrieved. For example, the query 'Java NEAR C++' retrieves all the documents which contain the word Java and the term C++ in which the words are close together.

proxy An entity that stands in for or acts as a front end for another entity. For example, a document processing system may store copies of pages which do not contain any of the graphics found on the original pages. This might mean that such pages could be retrieved very quickly from a network, since graphics can occupy a large amount of memory. If a reader wanted to access a graphic then he or she would click a special icon on the page. The icon acts as a proxy for the pages referred to.

proxy server A server, usually a CACHING WEB SERVER, that helps to implement a FIREWALL around a CLOSED NETWORK. It is a server which is accessible by the general public and which dispenses WEB PAGES stored inside the closed network. Any request for a Web page from outside the closed network is checked by the Web server to ensure that it is a page that can be sent to an outside user. If the page is in the server's CACHE then it is sent immediately; if not, the page is retrieved from a safe Web server inside the closed network. In this way the proxy server acts as a secure front end to a vulnerable server. If a CRACKER wished to infiltrate the closed network, he or she would have to attack the proxy server first. A proxy Web server is often used in conjunction

with a FIREWALL ROUTER; this configuration is known as a SCREENED HOST FIREWALL. Proxy servers are also used to provide fast access to cached Web pages. *See* CACHING WEB SERVER. A proxy server does not have to implement a firewall; it could just be used to speed up access to Web pages.

ps A FILE EXTENSION for postscript files.

PSA or Professional Services Automation A generic term applied to software that is used to manage people in an organization, for example software which coordinates diaries.

pseudo An abbreviation of pseudonym. It is the fake identity that some users of NEWSGROUPS adopt in order to ensure that other users do not know who they are, particularly if they hold unfashionable opinions.

pseudo flaw An apparent loophole or TRAPDOOR that has been inserted into an OPERATING SYSTEM in order to trap unauthorized intruders who access a network. *See also* FLYTRAP and WEB TRAP.

psychedelicware Software that displays complicated moving graphics. Such graphics are often similar to those produced by artists associated with the hippy movement of the 1960s.

PTT *See* POST, TELEGRAPH AND TELEPHONE.

pubic directory Jargon used to refer to a collection of files associated with pornography. It is often used to refer to a WEB SITE devoted to this subject. *See also* WANKWARE. A play on the term PUBLIC DIRECTORY.

pubic key Derived from PUBLIC KEY. This is a KEY given to users of pornography sites and allows them unlimited access to the sites, usually in exchange for a payment.

public directory The area in the file store of a server that is generally accessible to users without having to go through ACCESS CONTROLS such as quoting a PASSWORD. Such directories are used for storing files that can be accessed using the FILE TRANSFER PROTOCOL.

public domain Used to describe a product which has been released for unconditional use to anyone who wishes to use or modify it.

public domain software Software which is easily accessible by users of the Internet. Usually it is SHAREWARE or FREE-WARE.

public key One of the two keys involved in PUBLIC KEY ENCRYPTION. This is the key that is made publicly available to anyone who wants to send a message. The message is decrypted using a PRIVATE KEY by the person who made the public key available.

public key encryption An alternative to SYMMETRIC KEY ENCRYPTION. It uses two keys: a PUBLIC KEY and a PRIVATE KEY. The former, as the name suggests, can be made available to parties other than the sender or receiver of a message that is undergoing ENCRYPTION. The latter is used by the receiver of the message. The receiver of a message broadcasts the public key; this is used to encrypt a message; the receiver then uses the private key to apply DECRYPTION to the message in order to convert it to its original form. The advantage of this form of transmission is that there is no need to transmit keys using a secure transmission medium. The disadvantage is that it is much slower compared to symmetric key encryption. Much communication over the Internet is two way and in practice two sets of public and private keys are employed by the sender and recipient of messages. In practice, public key encryption is not used for the bulk transmission of messages. It is used for short messages or as a medium for transmitting SECRET KEYS used in SYM-METRIC KEY ENCRYPTION. For example, the SECURE SOCKETS LAYER uses PUBLIC KEY EN-CRYPTION to send the keys involved in the SYMMETRIC KEY ENCRYPTION scheme used for sending secure data across the Internet.

public key infrastructure The set of procedures, standards, and software necessary to provide services associated with PUBLIC KEY ENCRYPTION and DIGITAL SIGNATURES. The main purpose of a public key infrastructure is to maintain and administer the KEYS and digital signatures that are registered with it.

public switched telephone network A term used to describe the network that was originally designed to carry voice transmissions and which first used analogue technology. It is sometimes abbreviated to PSTN.

publicity attack An attack on a computer system which is made in order to achieve fame rather than for criminal intent.

puff To decompress data which has been compressed using HUFFMAN CODING. *See also* INFLATE and DEFLATE.

pull advertising The process whereby customers are attracted to a WEB SITE by means of non-direct communication. An example of this is the use of BANNER ADVERTS found on SEARCH ENGINES. This is in contrast to PUSH ADVERTISING in which technologies such as EMAIL are used to spread an advertising message.

pulling glass Laying down high transmission rate, fibreoptic cable for a network.

pull technology A technology in which the user asks for some response from a computer: this is in contrast to PUSH TECH-NOLOGY, in which the computer sends data without being prompted to do so. The best example of pull technology is when a WEB PAGE is loaded into a BROWSER window only when a user requests it.

pump and dump Another name for SHARE RAMPING. It is derived from the action of fraudsters who talk up a share (pump) and then sell it at an inflated profit when its price rises as a result of the pumping (dump).

punctuation flame A FLAME which refers to a POSTING to a NEWSGROUP criticizing the poor punctuation. Usually the flame does not respond to any of the points made in the original posting.

punting A synonym for FLOODING.

purchase intermediary A third-party company that administers an ASSOCIATE PROGRAM based on a PAY-BY-PURCHASE MODEL. Typically this company provides links or custom interfaces to the affiliates of the program and carries out the accounting process involved in tracking and paying these affiliates. *See also* CLICK INTERMEDIARY.

push advertising The process of communicating advertising material to an Internet user without the user making an explicit request for the material. A good example of this form of advertising is SPAMMING.

push technology A technology whereby data is transmitted to users on an ongoing basis without them explicitly asking for it. For example, a news channel updates news information on a user's DESKTOP, continually in response to breaking news. This technology is in contrast to PULL TECHNOLOGY where the user explicitly asks for data or information.

pyramid scheme A scam in which users of the Internet are drawn into a process of recruiting other users, who in turn recruit others, and so on. Such schemes have been part of the conventional commercial world for some time: however, the Internet, with its ability to put hundreds of thousands of users in touch with each other easily, has provided a fillip to a practice that was declining in the 1990s. A typical pyramid scheme involves users recruiting other users to sell a product and keeping a commission based on their sales. The second layer of users then recruit others and keep some part of their commission. Each participant in a pyramid operation pays an initial registration fee to the initiators of the scheme. After a short time the laws of economics kick in and the schemes collapse under their own weight, with the creators of the scheme usually disappearing.

Python An extensible OBJECT-ORIENTED PROGRAMMING LANGUAGE. It is particularly suited to the rapid development required for Internet applications.

Q

QoS *See* QUALITY OF SERVICE.

quality of service The ability of a network to deliver predictable and guaranteed transmission speeds. The better the quality of service, the higher the probability that the transmission speed will reach and exceed some published figure. Often abbreviated to QoS.

quantization The process used to convert a continuous ANALOGUE SIGNAL, such as a video signal, into a fixed binary form. As an example, assume that the signal varies from 0 to 0.32 volts and that it will be stored in 32-bit words within a computer memory. The process of quantization involves converting a voltage such as 0.09 volts into binary 9 by applying a simple mathematical transformation. Quantization is the key process involved in ANALOGUE TO DIGITAL CONVERSION.

quarantine area An area on a computer where suspicious FILES which could contain VIRUSES are stored. They are placed there by ANTI-VIRUS SOFTWARE.

query A line of text used to extract data from a DATABASE. The most frequent use of queries on the Internet involves the QUERY LANGUAGES used by search engines to locate information in a site or in the WORLD WIDE WEB. Queries expressed in such languages consist of keywords separated by BOOLEAN CONNECTIVES. For example, the query 'fibre optic' AND 'computer' would find all the documents which contain the two adjacent words 'fibre' and 'optic' and the word 'computer'.

query language A language used to select data from a database satisfying various criteria. For example, such a language might be used to extract all the employees in a database who earn more than a specified salary. The two main query languages found on the Internet or in DISTRIBUTED SYSTEMS are SQL, a language used to access and retrieve data in large structured databases, and the simple query languages involving KEYWORDS and BOOLEAN CONNECTIVES used in SEARCH ENGINES.

quoted text When replying to an EMAIL it is often useful to include part or whole of the original message. The part of an email which contains this is known as quoted text. Including quoted text is often overdone and leads to POSTINGS and emails becoming bloated to the point where it is difficult to discern what the real text of the posting or email is. *See also* PASTE BOMB and INCLUDE WAR.

R

rabbit A term sometimes used for a RABBIT PROGRAM.

rabbit program A synonym for BACTERIA.

race condition What occurs when a number of programs rely on certain timing conditions. For example, a program can only execute and carry out its task when a second program has completed. If the first program tries to execute before the second program has completed then anomalous results occur. Almost invariably race conditions give rise to anomalous behaviour.

radio button A small circular WIDGET used to select options within a WEB PAGE or a WINDOW and which can exist in an on or off state. Normally radio buttons are grouped and made mutually exclusive: only one of the buttons is allowed to be on.

radio frequency interference Signals which are emitted by a piece of electrical equipment when it carries rapidly changing signals. Such signals can affect unprotected circuits and cause them to malfunction. The vast majority of industrialized nations have laws which specify the maximum amount of interference which can be emitted by an item of equipment and the maximum level of interference that an item can withstand before it malfunctions. Often abbreviated to RFI.

radio site A WEB SITE which plays radio programmes. There are a number of sites which provide links to hundreds of radio channels.

RAID *See* REDUNDANT ARRAY OF INEXPENSIVE DISKS.

Rambutan An ENCRYPTION ALGORITHM used by the British government and its agencies.

ramp up To increase: for example, 'I am trying to ramp up my enthusiasm for what John posted last week.'

ranking service A service providing advice on how to make sure that a particular WEB SITE is prominently displayed when a query is made to a SEARCH ENGINE.

rapid prototyping One of the principal software development models in software engineering and the main one used by the developers of WEB SITES. It consists of rapidly building a mock-up of a site, showing it to the customer and then progressing though a cycle of criticisms and change until the customer is satisfied. It is particularly suited to the rapid development demanded by companies which take advantage of Internet technology, as it is much faster than conventional models which require the generation of large amounts of documentation.

RARP *See* REVERSE ADDRESS RESOLUTION PROTOCOL.

RASCi One of a number of CONTENT RATING SYSTEMS.

rasterbate Jargon, used to describe the act of perfecting a RASTER GRAPHIC, usually well past the point where changes become noticeable.

raster burn The eye strain that occurs after staring at a graphics device for too long.

raster graphic A rather dated synonym for BITMAPPED GRAPHIC.

rating vocabulary A set of words used to rate a WEB SITE for content. Elements taken from a rating vocabulary are inserted into the HOME PAGE of a site in order to indicate its content and suitability for various categories of users such as children. There are a number of internationally recognized rating vocabularies in existence. They are used by BLOCKING SOFTWARE which prevents users from accessing a Web site.

rave 1. To prolong an argument in an Internet forum such as a NEWSGROUP well after others have decided that the topic discussed is dead.

2. An argument which is well beyond the realms of reason.

RC2 A BLOCK CIPHER developed by the company RSA Security.

RC4 A STREAM CIPHER developed by the company RSA Security.

RC5 A BLOCK CIPHER which has been developed by the company RSA Security.

RDF or Resource Description Framework A way of describing a web site which has been developed by the WORLD WIDE WEB CONSORTIUM. The standard for this framework defines how a Web site makes information about itself available, for example the structure of the site and copyright information which concerns the web pages stored on the site.

reach A metric used in WEB ADVERTISING. It is the number of visitors who have viewed a particular BANNER ADVERT.

reactive agent A simple AGENT which reacts to stimuli and provides a simple service to a user. Examples include an agent which informs a user when an EMAIL has arrived, an agent which informs a user when a meeting is due to start, an agent which emails a user when a WEB SITE has been updated, and an agent which informs a user when a book has arrived in a bookshop and is being dispatched. Such agents are very easy to program and are becoming very common on the Internet.

readme file A FILE which is often included in the release of a software product. It normally contains information such as the list of bugs eradicated in the release, last-minute information, and installation instructions. Such files are usually stored in a simple character format.

read-only user A derogatory term, often used by programmers, to refer to users of networks such as the Internet who only access it for the purposes of reading text, such as the text found in WEB PAGES, POSTINGS, or EMAIL messages.

RealAudio® An important STREAMING TECHNOLOGY for audio developed by a company called Progressive Networks. It enables a sound clip to be heard as it is being DOWNLOADed to a computer. Before the development of this technology a sound clip had to be fully loaded into a computer before it could be played, which led to long delays.

reality distortion field Used to indicate delusion: for example, 'If you think that Sally's suggestion about changing the browser defaults is going to make a difference, then you must be in a reality distortion field.' The term is normally atibuted to Steve Jobs, one of the founders of Macintosh computers.

Real Name® UNIFORM RESOURCE LOCATORS are notoriously difficult to remember. The Real Name system was developed in order to overcome this. It allows the user to refer to a WEB SITE by an easily remembered set of words. For example, the company Acme Widgets might have as its real name AcmeWidgets. It is in operation at the ALTA VISTA search engine in order to aid the searching process and to find Web sites by means of brand names.

real time The immediate response to events as they happen. For example, an ECOMMERCE application which takes a product order and responds with an acknowledgement or a message indicating that an item is out of stock while the user is logged on is a real-time system. A program which checks if an item is in stock and emails the user some hours later is not a real-time system.

real-time chat This is ONLINE CHAT which occurs in REAL TIME.

reboot To start up a computer, usually after some catastrophic condition has occurred or after maintenance has been carried out. Rebooting is usually carried out by a simple program which is executed when the computer is switched on. *See* BOOT.

rec This abbreviation designates those NEWSGROUPS which discuss recreational events. In 1997 the Internet Ad Hoc committee proposed a number of new names for DOMAINS and rec is one of these.

recall A metric used to quantify the success of a query: it represents the ratio of the documents recalled from a SEARCH QUERY to the number which actually matched the query.

reciprocal link A HYPERLINK placed in a WEB PAGE to a second site which also contains a hyperlink to the site in which the page is contained.

Reclaim the Networks A group of Internet users who are opposed to the WORLD WIDE WEB and any commercial uses of the Internet. *See* CYBER LUDDITE.

Recreational Software Advisory Council A group which was formed in the 1990s in order to respond to US government criticisms of the violence and excessive sex found in computer games. One of its main products was a content rating system which was adopted for the Internet by the WORLD WIDE WEB CONSORTIUM. The standard is known as RSACI.

Red, Green, And Blue These are the colours which can be combined to form another colour. The amounts of each colour in a PIXEL is known as the RGB VALUE.

redirection The process of transferring a BROWSER from one WEB PAGE to another without the user carrying out any task such as using the mouse to CLICK a HYPERLINK. Redirection can be carried out by a WEB SERVER via text included in a METATAG which is to be exited. The usual reason for redirection is that the WEB SITE being visited has moved to a new location.

redirection script A CGI SCRIPT which is executed when a BROWSER tries to download a page that has been moved from its original location in a WEB SERVER. It returns the location of the moved page back to the browser that requested it and hence the moved page is displayed.

redirection site A WEB SITE which provides facilities for developing a Web site anywhere in the world and which allows users to access the site just by typing in the DOMAIN NAME. In this way the site can be moved around and does not tie the user to a particular INTERNET SERVICE PROVIDER.

Redundant Array of Inexpensive Disks A technology used in distributed applications which is designed to allow a computer to recover its data when a crash occurs. It is based on storing a number of copies of the same data. It is often referred to as RAID. *See also* DATA REPLICATION and MIRROR SITE. The technology is based on the parallel reading and writing of data.

referer or **referrer** The address of the UNIFORM RESOURCE LOCATOR of a page which contains a HYPERLINK to the current WEB PAGE that is being browsed.

refer link An item found in an entry in a LOG FILE which refers to the URL of the page containing the link that has been browsed by a user. This data is often used by commercial companies to gauge the habits and predilections of customers.

reformatting attack An attack on a computer installation which results in one or more hard disks being reformatted, with all the files stored on those disks effectively being deleted.

regional registry A regional organization responsible for allocating DOMAIN NAMES for the Internet and INTERNET PROTOCOL ADDRESSES. An example of this is RÉSEAUX IP EUROPÉENNE NETWORK CO-ORDINATION CENTRE which is responsible for Europe, the Middle East and parts of Africa.

registrar A short term for a DOMAIN NAME REGISTRAR: an organization authorized to register DOMAIN NAMES on behalf of companies and individuals.

registration The process of informing a SEARCH ENGINE that a new WEB PAGE or WEB SITE has been created. Individual search engines have pages which can be accessed to carry out the registration process; the alternative is to carry out MULTIPLE SEARCH ENGINE SUBMISSION.

registration form A FORM found on a WEB PAGE in an ECOMMERCE site asking visitors to provide information which can be subsequently used to identify them. Such forms are also used to store basic details of a visitor, such as credit card data, which is used in transactions. Registration forms are often employed in conjunction with a mechanism which stores a COOKIE.

registry An organization responsible for allocating DOMAIN NAMES for the Internet and INTERNET PROTOCOL ADDRESSES.

rehi A word occasionally used in CHAT ROOMS meaning 'hello again'.

relational database A DATABASE in which the individual records are aggregated together into a table. Relational database technology is now the major technology for holding the type of data required in ECOMMERCE applications. For example, an online bookseller stores details of each book that it sells in a relational database, with each record representing an individual book.

relative link A HYPERLINK in a WEB PAGE that does not include the full path to the destination document referred to in the URL part of the link. The destination document is referenced with respect to the folder in which it is contained. The advantage to doing this is that relatively linked pages are much more immune to changes in the structure of a WEB SITE and require less change when, for example, a folder is moved.

relay rape The process of illegally using a MAIL SERVER to send SPAM.

relevance feedback A feature of some SEARCH ENGINES such as SEARCHKING which allows the user to communicate to the search engine that a particular document was relevant. This information is then used to search for further documents. It was originally used in the WIDE AREA INFORMATION SERVERS.

relevancy algorithm An ALGORITHM used by a SEARCH ENGINE to decide whether a particular WEB PAGE is relevant to a SEARCH QUERY that has been typed in by the user. Such algorithms are highly secret: revealing their details would mean that developers who submit their Web pages to a search algorithm would tailor their pages to be prominently displayed when a query is made.

religious war An argument, which usually takes place in a NEWSGROUP, in which the participants take violent, uncompromising positions. A typical religious war is that between the proponents of Microsoft's Windows operating system and non-Windows systems such as LINUX.

remote access Access to a network by a user who is not directly connected to the network. This form of access is usually implemented via some form of DIAL-UP ACCESS.

remote access concentrator A system usually used by an INTERNET SERVICE PROVIDER to provide REMOTE ACCESS to their SERVERS. *See also* DIAL-UP ACCESS.

remote access server A SERVER which acts as a FRONT END to a network. It provides an access point to users of the network who use DIAL-UP ACCESS and effectively acts as a very powerful switch.

remote execution service A service found on TCP-IP networks which allows users to execute programs on another computer without incurring the overheads associated with facilities such as TELNET. It is often abbreviated to REX.

Remote Method Invocation A DISTRIBUTED OBJECT technology associated with the JAVA programming language. It enables an object written in Java to communicate with another Java object on another computer. The objects that communicate must be programmed in Java; this is in contrast to CORBA, another distributed object technology, where the objects can be developed in a variety of programming languages. Remote Method Invocation technology does not use an INTERFACE DEFINITION LANGUAGE. The term is often abbreviated to RMI.

remote network monitor A device, possibly a special-purpose piece of hardware or a computer, which collects information about network traffic.

remote procedure call A technology that enables a programmer to write program code which, when executed on one computer, results in the execution of other code on another computer to which it is connected. For example, such code would enable a CLIENT to execute an application program running on a SERVER. It allows data to be sent from one computer to another to be processed and result data to be sent back.

repeater A hardware device which amplifies signals as they travel down a cable. A network usually contains a number of repeaters. Such devices enable the length of a network to be extended.

repetitive sequence suppression A COMPRESSION technique using ENTROPY CODING which relies on recognizing sequences of the same data. For example, if a file contains large amounts of white space, then each run of white space is represented by a token which indicates the number of space characters in the run.

replay attack An attack on a computer network in which an intruder intercepts a message which has been sent from one entity on a network to another: for example, a client sending a financial transaction to a server. The intruder records the transaction and then sends it on to its destination.

replicated data server A SERVER which hosts a database that is replicated on other servers. Such a server carries out a number of functions: it broadcasts changes to its data to other replicated servers, it queues up changes to its database in the order in which they are made, and it disallows any processing on the database until it is back in synchronization with the databases stored on the other replicated servers.

replication A technique used for networks which require to be working continually and where the failure of an individual computer would adversely affect the network. There are two main types of replication: DATA REPLICATION where identical data is stored on a number of SERVERS, and computer duplication where a number of computers are executed in parallel, checking each other's results; when one disagrees it is assumed to be malfunctioning and is temporarily retired.

replication manager A program which keeps a number of identical DATABASES in step. It monitors updates to each database and then rebroadcasts them to all the other replicated databases.

replication transparency A DISTRIBUTED SYSTEM often employs DATA REPLICATION to ensure a fast response from databases and to enable the system to be resilient to hardware errors. Replication transparency is the term used to describe the fact that the user should be unaware that data is replicated.

request Used in WEB ADVERTISING to describe a connection to an ECOMMERCE site which successfully retrieves the content stored at that site.

Request for Comment A document, often known as an RFC, which contains details of a proposed INTERNET STANDARD or the modification of an existing standard. Requests for Comment are produced by the INTERNET ENGINEERING TASK FORCE (IETF). An RFC represents a draft for a standard; this is discussed on the Internet and in formal meetings of the working group tasked by the IETF to develop it. Eventually the Request For Comment is transformed into a document known as an INTERNET DRAFT.

Réseaux IP Européenne Network Coordination Centre A European organization which manages the dispensing of INTERNET PROTOCOL ADDRESSES to Europe, the Middle East and parts of Africa. It is one of three organizations around the world which does this, the others being the AMERICAN REGISTRY FOR INTERNET NUMBERS and the ASIA PACIFIC NETWORK INFORMATION CENTRE.

resolver Software which enables clients to look up a DOMAIN NAME and discover the INTERNET PROTOCOL ADDRESS of a computer.

response bot A BOT which carries out a conversation with a human user of the Internet in such a way that, for a time, the user believes he or she is conversing with another person. *See also* CHATTERBOT and ELIZA EFFECT.

response time The time difference between the end of a single interaction with a computer and when the results of the interaction are returned to the screen. There are a number of factors which determine response time in a network: these include LATENCY, the loading on the network on which the computer is situated, the BANDWIDTH of connections, and the nature of the task to be carried out by the computer.

restricted file system A collection of files associated with an ACCESS CONTROL mechanism such as a PASSWORD. The mechanisms should restrict access to highly confidential files or allow public files to be changed by only a small number of users.

resubmission The process of repeatedly submitting a WEB PAGE to a SEARCH ENGINE. Sometimes there is a legitimate reason for this: a page may have drastically changed. However, it is common for unscrupulous Web developers to carry out a number of resubmissions in order to discover the RELEVANCY ALGORITHM used by the search engine.

retransmission timeout An event that occurs when data has been sent to a remote computer on a network and no ACKNOWLEDGEMENT has been received after a specific period of time. Usually when this occurs the sender of the data retransmits it.

retrocomputing The process of developing and running software that simulates programs and computers from another era. There are two reasons for retrocomputing: one serious and one less serious. The first is to extend the life of software that runs on obsolete computers; the second is as an elaborate practical joke.

retronym A word which describes an entity or idea which precedes newer versions. For example, SNAIL MAIL is a retronym for EMAIL.

retro virus A VIRUS which deletes files and works in such a way that even the BACKUP copies of files in a computer network become infected.

return from the dead A term used to describe an Internet user who has started accessing the network again after a long absence.

Reverse Address Resolution Protocol Sometimes a computer needs to know its INTERNET PROTOCOL ADDRESS:

for example, when it has been dynamically assigned this address by another computer. In order to discover this, the computer employs a PROTOCOL which forms part of TCP-IP known as the Reverse Address Resolution Protocol.

reverse auction site A WEB SITE which provides information about a product wanted by a user and how much they wish to pay; the owners of the site then try and find a supplier who will meet this price.

reverse slash A name sometimes used for the character '\'. Also known as a BACKSLASH.

REX *See* REMOTE EXECUTION SERVICE.

RFC *See* REQUEST FOR COMMENT.

RFI *See* RADIO FREQUENCY INTERFERENCE.

RGB Acronym for RED, GREEN, AND BLUE.

RGB value The value of the RED, GREEN, AND BLUE components found in a PIXEL.

Richard Petty syndrome An American term used to describe the overuse of promotional material and logos on a commercial WEB SITE. Petty was a racing driver who, like most drivers, wore overalls festooned with commercial logos. *See also* BLENDO PAGE, EYE TRASH, and ANGRY FRUIT SALAD.

rich media Used to describe any advertising medium other than text which is dynamic, such as ANIMATIONS used as a form of advertising.

ringmaster Someone who coordinates the linking of a number of WEB SITES in a WEB RING.

ring network A way of structuring a network so that the computers are connected together in a ring. The term is something of a misnomer since there is no physical transmission line connecting the computers and ending up at the first computer in the ring. The ring is found in the central hardware that is used to manage the network.

RIP *See* ROUTING INFORMATION PROTOCOL.

ripper A program that copies the contents of a compact disc and stores it on a computer. The signal is copied directly and does not have to be converted to analog form in order to traverse the computer's sound card.

RISKS forum A very popular online discussion forum which concerns itself with problems with systems. Problems of privacy and security in DISTRIBUTED SYSTEMS are one of the most frequent items posted to this forum.

Rivest Shamir Adelman Key Encryption Algorithm The major PUBLIC KEY ENCRYPTION algorithm currently used on the vast majority of networks. The algorithm is symmetric in that its PUBLIC KEY can be used for decrypting messages produced using its PRIVATE KEY and vice versa. The key for this algorithm consists of two integers. It is used in conjunction with other algorithms such as MESSAGE DIGEST 5 and SECURE HASH ALGORITHM 1 for DIGITAL SIGNATURES. It is also used to transmit keys employed in SYMMETRIC KEY ENCRYPTION prior to the keys being used.

RIW Abbreviation for Read It and Weep used in EMAILS and NEWSGROUPS.

RJ-45 The standard connectors used to connect UNSHIELDED TWISTED PAIR CABLES to devices in a network.

RMI See REMOTE METHOD INVOCATION.

RMON See REMOTE NETWORK MONITOR.

robocanceller Synonym for a CANCELBOT.

robomoderation The use of a BOT to moderate a NEWSGROUP. Such bots can only carry out very limited functions such as not allowing very lengthy POSTINGS or postings in which certain words occur.

robot A program which traverses a number of WEB PAGES following the HYPERLINKS and carrying out some process such as checking whether any Web pages have changed since the last visit. The most popular robots are SPIDERS used by SEARCH ENGINES that collect data stored in the databases used by the search engines for retrieving documents which match search criteria. The term is often abbreviated to BOT.

robots exclusion standard A standard which is used to define data stored in a text file associated with a WEB SITE. The text in the file describes the access privileges of ROBOTS visiting the page: for example, the text could forbid all access to the Web site by robots or restrict it to a small number of pages.

ROFL Abbreviation for Rolling On the Floor Laughing used in NEWSGROUPS.

ROFLUTS Abbreviation for Rolling On The Floor Unable To Speak used in CHAT ROOMS, EMAILS, and NEWSGROUPS. One of a number of abbreviations connected with rolling on the floor including ROTFL.

rogue ISP An INTERNET SERVICE PROVIDER that has been set up in order to carry out some criminal or near criminal act such as sending SPAM or garnering the credit card details of potential customers.

rollover An advanced graphical technique found on WEB PAGES. It is used when a Web designer wants a graphic to change when an event associated with a mouse occurs. A common use of rollovers is to provide a visual indication when a mouse pointer is over an area of a graphic which has a HYPERLINK associated with it. For example, the graphic might be a map with a number of cities whose names change colour when the mouse traverses the area associated with a hyperlink. Rollovers can be associated with a number of mouse events such as a mouse being clicked down, being clicked up, or being moved outside the area of the embedded link. They are created by using a simple scripting language such as JAVASCRIPT. Programming statements in the language are embedded in the HTML code of a Web page: these statements sense when a mouse event occurs and change the graphic associated with the hyperlinked area. For example, changing from a graphic which has a name displayed in one colour to a near identical graphic where the name is displayed in another colour. Rollovers can be programmed by hand but there are an increasing number of tools which automate the process and which do not require the user to know a programming language. A number of graphics programs and WYSIWYG EDITORS also incorporate this facility.

room temperature IQ A derogatory term used to describe the intellectual capabilities of a user with little intelligence. The temperature is, of course, expressed in centigrade.

root server A NAME SERVER that is used to resolve TOP-LEVEL DOMAINS in the INTERNET DOMAIN NAME SERVICE.

ROT13 A very weak ENCRYPTION scheme used in NEWSGROUPS and other similar public forums to hide material such as pornographic remarks from sensitive users. The encryption process is very simple: each letter in the alphabet is replaced by one which is thirteen letters further on from it. Any letters in the last half of the alphabet are mapped onto those in the first half.

ROTFL Abbreviation for Rolling On The Floor Laughing or Rolls On The Floor Laughing used in CHAT ROOMS, EMAILS, and NEWSGROUPS. One of a number of rolling on the floor abbreviations: for example, ROFLUTS.

ROTFLMAO Abbreviation for Rolling On the Floor Laughing My Ass Off used in CHAT ROOMS, EMAILS, and NEWSGROUPS.

round trip time A metric which measures the current loading on a computer network. It is found by timing the passage of a signal from a computer to another remote computer and back. This is usually carried out by means of a PING utility.

router A device, often a dedicated computer, used to link two networks. It takes packets of data, determines their destination, and passes them on to the network for which they are intended. A typical use for a router is in a SCREENED HOST FIREWALL.

router droppings When a ROUTER is unable to find the destination of an EMAIL message it adds a large amount of fairly cryptic information to the end of the email which enables an expert to diagnose the problem. This information is known as router droppings.

route tracing The process of discovering the path taken by data through the Internet. It is often applied to a SPAM EMAIL in order to alert the INTERNET SERVICE PROVIDER to the spammer. There are a number of software tools which help in this task.

routing When PACKETS of data are sent from one computer to another on a network, individual computers in the network have to decide the path the data should take via a number of intermediate computers. This is known as routing.

routing algorithm A set of procedures used when a computer in a STORE AND FORWARD NETWORK has to send a PACKET of data to another computer which may be the final destination or may be an intermediate computer. There are two types of algorithms: ADAPTIVE ROUTING ALGORITHMS which use traffic conditions, and NON-ADAPTIVE ROUTING ALGORITHMS where the route a packet takes is calculated in advance.

Routing Information Protocol A PROTOCOL that GATEWAYS use to exchange information about ROUTING by examining the ROUTING TABLES in each of the gateways.

routing table A table which contains details about the topology of a network. It has details of every computer in the network together with the connections between them. More sophisticated tables also contain dynamic data which describes the state of the network in terms of the amount of traffic passing though the transmission media joining each computer. A routing table is used to determine an optimal path from a source computer to a destination computer on the network. *See also* ROUTING. It is also a table associated with a FIREWALL ROUTER which contains the IP ADDRESS and PORT number of the computer sending a packet and the computer receiving a packet and specifies, based on this data, whether or not the packet is to be rejected by the router.

RPC *See* REMOTE PROCEDURE CALL.

RPG 1. Abbreviation for Role Playing Games used in CHAT ROOMS, EMAILS, and NEWSGROUPS.

2. Abbreviation for an early, primitive programming language known as Report Program Generator.

RS-232-C A standard for interfacing a computer and a MODEM which defines entities at a PHYSICAL LAYER. It was developed by a body known as the Electronic Industries Association, which is made up of electrical and electronics manufacturers. The standard is also known as CCITT V24.

RS-449 A standard for interfacing a computer and a MODEM which defines entities at a PHYSICAL LAYER. It is, in effect, three standards and is intended to be an improvement on the RS-232-C standard.

RSA *See* RIVEST SHAMIR ADELMAN KEY ENCRYPTION ALGORITHM.

RSAC *See* RECREATIONAL SOFTWARE ADVISORY COUNCIL.

RSACi A content rating standard developed by the WORLD WIDE WEB CONSORTIUM which allows parents, for example, to restrict access to particular Web sites by their children. The standard was developed from one initially devised by the RECREATIONAL SOFTWARE ADVISORY COUNCIL.

RSBE One of the first SEARCH ENGINES to be based on a BOT. It was also the first to use a ranking index to provide information about the relevance of a retrieved WEB SITE to a particular search. It is now of only historical interest.

RSN Abbreviation for Real Soon Now used in CHAT ROOMS, EMAILS and NEWSGROUPS. Usually used cynically to describe the actions of software companies who announce the immediate release of a product, only for it to be delayed by many months.

RSVP Acronym which predates the Internet. It is used in CHAT ROOMS, EMAILS and NEWSGROUPS. Its translation is Répondez S'il Vous Plait or, in English, please reply.

RTFAQ Abbreviation for Read the FAQ used in CHAT ROOMS, EMAILS, and NEWS-GROUPS. Usually used in response to someone who has asked a question that has been asked many times in the past. A polite example of one of a 'Read The' abbreviations. These include RTPR and RTM.

RTM Abbreviation for Read the Manual or Read the Message used in CHAT ROOMS, EMAILS, and NEWSGROUPS. A less polite version is RTFM (Read the Fucking Manual/ Message). One of a number of 'Read The' abbreviations. These include RTFAQ.

RTPR Abbreviation for Read The Press Release used in CHAT ROOMS, EMAILS, and NEWSGROUPS. One of a number of 'Read The' acronyms. These include RTFAQ and RTM. Usually written as a sarcastic response to a user who is baffled by the fact that a software product does not contain a function that he or she expects.

RTSC Abbreviation for Read The SOURCE CODE used in CHAT ROOMS, EMAILS, and NEWSGROUPS. One of a number of 'Read The' abbreviations. These include RTFB and RTM. It is usually written in response to a user who asks a question about a software product which cannot be resolved by looking in the manuals. The source code of a piece of software is the listing of the programming instructions used to implement the software.

RTW Abbreviation for Release To Web. Used to describe the fact that a WEB SITE which was under development is now ready to be placed on a WEB SERVER and made available for general use.

rubbage A word constructed from the words 'garbage' and 'rubbish' used in POSTINGS to NEWSGROUPS and EMAIL messages. *See also* GUBBISH.

rule A TRIGGER which, when executed, carries out a check on the data stored in a DATABASE SERVER when the data is changed. For example, a trigger may check that a valid post code or zip code has been entered in a database of addresses when a new address has been inserted into the database.

S

sacrificial computer Synonymous with SACRIFICIAL HOST.

sacrificial host 1. A SERVER which is placed outside an organization's computer network to provide a service which, if it was inside the network, would compromise network security. For example, an FTP SERVER might be used as a sacrificial host. **2**. A term used to describe a computer used by a SECURITY OFFICER or SYSTEM ADMINISTRATOR to lure an intruder, in order to provide enough time for clues about the intruder's identity to be garnered. *See also* FLYTRAP and WEB TRAP.

Safe For Kids One of a number of CONTENT RATING SYSTEMS.

safe surfing Technologies used to filter out CONTENT from WEB SITES which is unsuitable for certain categories of audience, usually children.

salami attack An attack on a computer network which involves the intruder siphoning off small amounts of money from a file and placing them in another file that he or she can access; for example, a file that holds their bank account details. A typical salami attack would add a small amount to a debit which the account holder would not check, such as a debit which represented a service charge. This small increase in debit (often a few pence or a few cents) would then be credited to the perpetrator's bank account. An unsophisticated banking system which just checked that debits and credits matched would be unable to detect this type of fraud. The name 'salami attack' comes from the fact that salami is cut into into very thin slices. It is also known as salami shaving.

salting The process of adding random digits to a PASSWORD in order to increase its size and hence make it more resistant to a DICTIONARY ATTACK.

sandbox A technique whereby a program executing on a computer in a network is isolated from the system around it so that it cannot do any damage or violate any security policy. The best example of this technique is the security technology used to execute APPLETS written in the JAVA programming language. Such programs have major restrictions placed on their execution and are only executed within a security sandbox.

SAP *See* SERVICE ACCESS POINT.

SATAN Acronym for Security Administrator Tool for Analysing Networks. A tool that SYSTEM ADMINISTRATORS can use for examining their networks to detect whether there are any security flaws. The tool has proved very controversial when it is used outside the network rather than by a SYSTEM ADMINISTRATOR and is readily available to anyone who uses the Internet. Consequently it can be, and has been, used by CRACKERS attempting to infiltrate a computer network.

Savvysearch A METASEARCH ENGINE which has consistently appeared at the top of a number of surveys of such engines. Not only can it search using conventional search engines but it can also use specialized search engines such as those which index sport WEB SITES.

scag The destruction of data on a permanent storage medium such as a hard disk.

scanned image An image that has been created using a hardware device known as a scanner. Scanned images are often used on the World Wide Web. However, they often need to be improved and retouched by a graphics program before they are published.

scanner 1. A form of VIRUS DETECTION SOFTWARE. It scans the memory of a computer looking for known code patterns associated with VIRUSES. Scanners can be executed continuously or can be scheduled to be executed at frequent intervals. **2**. A hardware device which converts hard-copy images such as magazine photographs into graphic FILES. *See* SCANNED IMAGE.

scanning attack A particular type of BRUTE FORCE ATTACK on a computer system. It involves the use of a program known as a WAR DIALLER. This generates a large number of sequences of characters that could be telephone numbers or passwords. A typical scanning attack would involve the program being set up to dial a long series of telephone numbers; any numbers giving some indication of a modem being used are stored. After a scanning session an intruder dials these numbers and attempts to break in using a variety of techniques including trying well-known passwords.

sci An abbreviation which designates those NEWSGROUPS that discuss scientific research and scientific issues.

Scooter The name of the SPIDER that is used by the ALTA VISTA search engine.

screenager A young user of the Internet. The term is usually used to describe someone who is a frequent user.

screened host firewall A FIREWALL which is implemented using a FIREWALL ROUTER and a PROXY SERVER, with the router acting as a front end to the server. The firewall router first screens off any accesses which are disallowed to a closed network, apart from WEB PAGE accesses and secure accesses to services such as EMAIL. The Web accesses are then passed to the proxy server which acts as a front end to the Web server that actually dispenses the Web pages. There are thus two layers of security that a CRACKER has to circumnavigate before accessing the Web server inside the closed network.

screening router A synonym for FIREWALL ROUTER.

script 1. A series of programming statements which can be executed usually within a WEB SERVER. The term is really synonymous with 'program' but is normally restricted to code written in INTERPRETED PROGRAMMING LANGUAGES such as PERL rather than COMPILED PROGRAMMING LANGUAGES such as JAVA.
2. The rules that are used by FILTERS to

reject content sent to a user of the Internet, such as a filter which rejects SPAM email.

scripting language A programming language used to develop SCRIPTS ranging from a full-scale programming language such as PERL, to a small, special-purpose language used to carry out a specific task such as constructing a FILTER.

script kiddie A CRACKER, usually young and technologically inexperienced, who tries to carry out some illegal act such as entering a forbidden network. Often script kiddies, because of their technological naïveté, will use knowledge about vulnerabilities discovered by others.

scroll bar A bar on the side of a BROWSER window used to display the contents of a WEB PAGE that is not currently visible in the window.

scrolling The process of moving the SCROLL BAR of a BROWSER in order to see that part of a WEB PAGE that is not currently displayed. The same process is used with other software systems such as a word processor.

scud email A public EMAIL, usually abusive, which damages the reputation of the sender more than the recipient.

scudgram A packet of data targeted at one specific computer on a network and intended to disrupt a service provided by the computer. The scudgram may be the first part of a DENIAL OF SERVICE ATTACK.

SDH *See* SYNCHRONOUS DIGITAL HIERARCHY.

SDK *See* SOFTWARE DEVELOPER'S KIT.

SDV *See* SWITCHED DIGITAL VIDEO.

sea A FILE EXTENSION for files which are condensed into an archive by the Macintosh OPERATING SYSTEM.

search bot A BOT which carries out a searching function, such as looking for reviews of a particular software product.

search directory A WEB SITE which looks just like a SEARCH ENGINE but is organized as a series of directories rather than a set of loosely coupled files. The best-known example of such a site is YAHOO where content is vetted by human editors before being entered into a directory. Many search directories are specialized and are often devoted to one subject such as kayaking, Internet crime, or a particular computer technology such as LINUX.

search engine The Internet and that part of it known as the WORLD WIDE WEB is huge and still growing (*See* INTERNET STATISTICS). This means that the user who wishes to find some item of information can be at a severe disadvantage. Search engines were developed in order to speed up searches within the Internet. The first search engine was known as ARCHIE. It was developed in 1990 to search the evolving Internet for FTP files. The next major advance was a tool known as VERONICA which searched GOPHER servers that contained text databases. This was followed by the program which bears the most resemblance to current search engines, the WORLD WIDE WANDERER, a primitive BOT which wandered around the Web tracking its growth. This program was controversial in that when it visited a WEB SITE it slowed down the performance of the network on which the site resided. This was followed by more sophisticated searchers such as the WWW WORM, JUMPSTATION and RSBE. The huge growth of the Web in the mid 1990s spawned a new generation of search engines that are active today, such as LYCOS, YAHOO, ALTA VISTA, and HOTBOT. A search engine is effectively an index to a large number of Web sites. Most of the current search engines provide a submission mechanism which allows the developer of a Web site to register that site with the search engine. After registration the engine automatically indexes the site URL by means of KEYWORDs. These keywords are then used in a KEYWORD SEARCH by users who wish to find some information. So in response to a query such as 'Christmas + Card', a search engine returns with the URL of all the sites which contain the keywords 'Christmas' and 'Card'. Search engines are not just confined to Web sites. They can search for information in a wide variety of repositories and can, for example, carry out EMAIL SEARCHes and NEWSGROUP SEARCHes. Most search en-

gines carry out automatic indexing of Web sites; although one or two rely on human indexers, YAHOO being the best known of these. Given the explosion of information on the Internet it is not surprising that search engines are able only to partially index the information that is available: most surveys put the proportion indexed on the World Wide Web at somewhere between 25 and 35 per cent of the available material. Because of this, a number of METASEARCH ENGINES have been developed. These search engines submit a search to a collection of existing search engines and collect all the responses from them. In the early days of the Internet such engines were controversial among the owners of existing search engines since they did not display the BANNER ADVERTISing that was the main source of revenue of the search engine companies. Current metasearch engines include METACRAWLER and SAVVYSEARCH. The partial indexing of the Internet has also given rise to large numbers of SPECIALIZED SEARCH ENGINES. These are search engines which have links to a collection of thematically connected databases and Web sites: for example, those containing data about William Shakespeare. The vast majority of these engines consist of a number of Web pages with links to external Web sites combined with a search program running on the SERVER on which they are stored. Search engines normally use a restricted syntax for queries consisting of keywords and BOOLEAN CONNECTIVES such as AND and OR. Most of them can accept queries expressed in natural language, although the mechanism for discovering the intent of the query is usually very primitive. There are a number of specialized natural-language search engines whose interpretation of natural-language queries is more sophisticated. Probably the best known of these is ASK JEEVES. Search engines receive a huge variety of queries. A typical snapshot of a few seconds of the queries being received by Ask Jeeves included questions on the location of a map of Worcestershire, a site holding a dictionary of cat diseases, the URL of a site to download a computer game, the location of a map of the campus of an American university, the location of a site dedicated to Marilyn Monroe, and where to seek advice on detecting heart disease. *See also* SEARCH ENGINE SUBMISSION, MULTIPLE SEARCH ENGINE SUBMISSION, METATAG, SPAMDEX, and METACONTENT.

search engine submission The process of submitting a WEB SITE to a SEARCH ENGINE so that it can be indexed and hence be retrieved by users of that search engine. The process of submission to a search engine is usually very simple: a forms-based WEB PAGE asks for details of the site, such as the UNIFORM RESOURCE LOCATOR and a ROBOT normally visits the site indexing any significant words that it finds. Some sites do not use robots but employ human indexers who visit the site using a BROWSER. For a site to have a good chance of being noticed, it is necessary to use METATAGS inside the HTML code of the site to place keywords which describe the site and to embed a short description of it. Web sites can be submitted to a number of search engines at the same time. For this *see* MULTIPLE SEARCH ENGINE SUBMISSION.

Searchking A small SEARCH ENGINE. It is unusual in that it allows its users to vote on the relevancy of the results of a query. This voting information is then used to improve its searches.

search page A WEB PAGE which contains facilities for searching the WEB SITE it is embedded in. Often search facilities are embedded in the HOME PAGE of a site but if the search process is particularly complex then a special search page is developed.

search query A query processed by a SEARCH ENGINE which returns a list of WEB PAGES that closely match the query. Such a query is expressed in a query language whose statements contain a list of KEYWORDS separated by BOOLEAN CONNECTIVES.

search space Usually used in conjunction with SEARCH ENGINES to designate the collection of data that such programs access in order to respond to a query. Sometimes, though, the term is used to describe any searchable database.

SearchUK One of the best SEARCH ENGINES targeted at British CONTENT.

SEC *See* SECURITY AND EXCHANGE COMMISSION.

secondary server A SERVER which acts as BACKUP to a PRIMARY SERVER that implements part of the INTERNET DOMAIN NAME SERVICE. *See also* ADDITIONAL SERVER.

second-generation Web site A WEB SITE which includes both text and GRAPHIC IMAGES and which makes heavy use of the HYPERTEXT MARKUP LANGUAGE facilities for TABLES in displaying the text and graphics on a WEB PAGE in a visually pleasing way. *See also* FIRST-GENERATION WEB SITE, THIRD-GENERATION WEB SITE, and FOURTH-GENERATION WEB SITE.

second-level domain The DOMAIN which lies below the TOP-LEVEL DOMAIN in the INTERNET DOMAIN NAME SERVICE. For example, in open.sys.com, sys would be the second-level domain. *See also* HIERARCHICAL NAMING.

secret key A KEY used in ENCRYPTION methods that employ SYMMETRIC KEY ENCRYPTION. The adjective 'secret' is used to describe the fact that only the sender and recipient of a message should know the key.

Secured Electronic Transaction Standard A standard for DIGITAL CERTIFICATES which provide authentication for credit card purchases over the Internet. It was developed by a number of credit card companies including Visa and Mastercard. It uses version 3 of the X509 certificate standard.

Secure Hash Algorithm 1 A MESSAGE DIGEST algorithm that has been developed by the US government. It produces a value that is 160 bits long. The INTERNET ENGINEERING TASK FORCE has selected it for its PUBLIC KEY INFRASTRUCTURE.

Secure HTTP A security PROTOCOL similar to the SECURE SOCKETS LAYER. It was developed by a company called Enterprise Integration Technology. The major difference between this protocol and the Secure Sockets Layer (SSL) protocol is that Secure HTTP is built on top of the HTTP protocol while SSL is a separate protocol.

Currently SSL is much more popular, mainly because it was the first of the two to be released.

Secure Multimedia Internet Mail Extensions A sophisticated standard for secure EMAIL which relies on a number of technologies developed by RSA Security, one of the leading Internet security companies. It uses DIGITAL CERTIFICATES and hence requires some form of CERTIFICATE AUTHORITY to make it work. It is occasionally abbreviated to S/MIME.

secure server A WEB SERVER which is protected by a number of security devices, usually via a SCREENED HOST FIREWALL.

Secure Sockets Layer The most common security PROTOCOL used on the WORLD WIDE WEB and commonly known as SSL. It was originally developed by the Netscape Corporation, but is now supported by all the major BROWSERS. It is a flexible protocol that is able to use a variety of encryption schemes ranging from those suitable for domestic use to those which can be used for the highest classified government data interchange.

Secure Telnet A version of the TELNET program which is cryptographically protected. It is used to transfer sensitive files over a network.

secure URL A UNIFORM RESOURCE LOCATOR associated with the SECURE SOCKETS LAYER. Such URLs are designated SHTTP rather than the normal HTTP and identify secure sites or Web pages.

Security and Exchange Commission A US government agency responsible for administering federal security law. Increasingly it has concerned itself with crime on the Internet. It is often abbreviated to SEC.

security certificate This is a form of digital certification which provides evidence that a particular entity on the Internet is associated with a PUBLIC KEY. The entity can be a SERVER, company, individual, or a CERTIFICATE AUTHORITY. The best-known standard for security certificates is X509.

security management A subdiscipline of NETWORK MANAGEMENT. It consists of

managing the access to a network using both software and hardware. Typical devices for this are PROXY SERVERS, PASSWORDS, and CRYPTOGRAPHY. An important part of this activity is the granting and monitoring of ACCESS RIGHTS to users.

security officer Large computer networks require so much effort in securing them that this function is often carried out by specialized members of staff known as security officers. They are responsible for a large number of tasks including ensuring the security of PASSWORD FILES, checking the state of a network for security weaknesses, and using software tools which check for intrusions. On smaller networks the functions of a security officer are usually carried out by the SYSTEM ADMINISTRATOR or NETWORK ADMINISTRATOR.

segment A section of cable found in a network which connects together devices such as GATEWAYS and computers. *See also* POPULATED SEGMENT and LINK SEGMENT.

select box A visual WIDGET which allows a user to select a number of options. Clicking on a select box displays the options in a form similar to a MENU.

selective flooding A form of routing that is based on FLOODING where a packet is sent out on all the transmission lines connected to a computer apart from the line from which it arrived. Selective flooding only uses those lines which are connected to computers that are approximately in the same direction as the recipient computer.

self-extracting archive Another name for a SELF-EXTRACTING FILE. It is usually used to describe a number of files which have been compressed and collected together.

self-extracting file This is a FILE which does not require the use of a decompression utility to be decompressed. All that is required is for it to be double clicked. A number of COMPRESSION programs allow the user the option of creating such a file. It is sometimes called a self-extracting archive.

self-mutating virus Synonym for POLY-
MORPHIC VIRUS.

self-toast To contradict oneself. *See also*
TOAST.

send storm A flood of messages from
INTERNET RELAY CHAT which comes when
a user is carrying out some other activity
such as reading EMAIL.

September that never ended Used by
veterans of NEWSGROUPS to refer to September 1993 when America Online made
access to newsgroups possible. According
to these veterans the quality of discussion
on the newsgroups markedly declined.
The term arose from the fact that prior to
this date there was a periodic decline in the
quality of newsgroup discussion around
September due to an influx of college
students starting their studies and being
provided with Internet accounts by their
universities. These students, being un-
accustomed to the conventions of newsgroups, temporarily lowered the level of
discussion until they became used to the
mores and standards of newsgroups.

serendipity search A search of the
Web, often using a SEARCH ENGINE,
which finds interesting material which
was not the object of the search.

serial equivalence Used in DISTRIBUTED
SYSTEM technology to describe the effect
that a number of parallel or nested TRANS-
ACTIONS have on the state of such a system.
When such transactions are carried out
their effect is said to be serially equivalent
if the state of the system is the same as
if they were carried out sequentially.

serialization The process whereby data
which is normally aggregated is split into
its components ready to be sent via a communication medium: for example the process of collecting together the data in an
OBJECT using a form of serialization
known as MARSHALLING.

serial line A communication line in
which BITS are transferred one at a time.

Serial Line Internet Protocol A PROTO-
COL which enables the use of TCP-IP over a
simple serial line, for example a phone
line. It is a very simple protocol which
suffers from a number of drawbacks: for

example, it does not provide for AUTHEN-
TICATION, it does not carry out any error
detection, and it is not an approved Internet standard, so that there are many incompatible versions in existence. *See also*
POINT-TO-POINT PROTOCOL

Serial Line IP An alternative name for
SERIAL LINE INTERNET PROTOCOL.

serial port A socket at the back of a computer into which connectors are plugged
that enable the computer to send data into
a SERIAL LINE.

server The combination of computer
and software in a network which carries
out a specialized service. Usually such
computers are powerful and optimized
for the particular service that they carry
out. There are a wide variety of servers
including WEB SERVERS, which receive requests from BROWSERS for WEB PAGES; FILE
SERVERS, which deliver stored files; DATA-
BASE SERVERS, which satisfy requests for
data which correspond to some QUERY;
NAME SERVERS, which map a symbolic
name into a system resource; and FTP
SERVERS which enable users to employ
FTP SOFTWARE to retrieve files. Often the
term is used to describe a collection of
software which provides a service. There
are a number of SERVER APIS available for
programming servers.

server API An API which enables applications such as ECOMMERCE programs to
interact with a WEB SERVER. Such APIs are
intended to address some of the performance problems associated with standard
CGI PROGRAMMING. Server APIs are usually
associated with a specific Web server
vendor. Two of the best known are Netscape's NSAPI and Microsoft's ISAPI.

server farm A collection of SERVERS
maintained by a central enterprise. The
enterprise rents space on the servers to
smaller organizations which are not big
enough to buy or hire their own server.
The term was initially popularized by the
Intel Corporation.

server parsed HTML A FILE which contains HYPERTEXT MARKUP LANGUAGE code
together with special-purpose instructions to the server to carry out some
task. Often this task is to replace the

non-standard instructions with further HTML code. There are a number of technologies which can be described using this term, including SERVER SIDE INCLUDES and ACTIVE SERVER PAGES.

server push Alternative term for PUSH TECHNOLOGY.

server side image map An IMAGE MAP in which the actions associated with the embedded HYPERLINKS are processed by the WEB SERVER which stores the WEB PAGE in which the image is embedded. When a user clicks on an area inside a server side image map the server is sent the coordinates of the click. It then discovers which WEB PAGE is referenced by the area in which the coordinates are contained and then sends it back to the BROWSER for viewing. Server side image maps were used extensively in the early days of the Web. They differ from CLIENT SIDE IMAGE MAPS where the browser itself carries out the processing required. The details of an image map are stored in an IMAGE MAP DEFINITION FILE on the WEB SERVER. This file is consulted to find the destination URL associated with the area of the image map that has been clicked.

server side include A point in an HTML PAGE which is left blank for a WEB SERVER to insert some data. For example, the point may represent a position in the page where the date of the last modification to the document is to be inserted. When the server finds a server side include, it inserts this information before sending the page back to the BROWSER that requested it. This is rather old technology which has been superseded by technologies such as ACTIVE SERVER PAGES and JAVA SERVER PAGES.

service access point A point in a LAYER of a LAYERED ARCHITECTURE where a network service is provided and where the layer above the layer which provides the service can access it. So, for example, if a layer offers EMAIL services, the service access point is the interface which provides software facilities to process emails. The term is sometimes abbreviated to SAP.

service primitive In a network LAYERED

ARCHITECTURE, when one LAYER requires another layer to carry out a service, the communication between the layers is carried out by service primitives. There are four categories of primitives: those that request a service, those that inform an ENTITY that an event has occurred, those that represent responses to a service request, and those that confirm that the data associated with a request has arrived. So, for example, a layer that sends an EMAIL requests that the email is sent, is informed that this has taken place, receives data about the event, and responds to the event by signalling to another layer that the event has been successful.

service provider In a LAYERED ARCHITECTURE a LAYER which provides a service such as error checking to another layer is known as a service provider. It is also a shortened version of the term INTERNET SERVICE PROVIDER.

service user In a LAYERED ARCHITECTURE a LAYER which requires some service such as error checking from another layer is known as a service user.

servlet A collection of code written in JAVA which carries out a SERVER function such as processing a FORM written using the HYPERTEXT MARKUP LANGUAGE and filled in by a user requesting some data and sending that data back to the user. Servlets, which were developed by Sun Microsystems, are the Java replacement for languages such as PERL which were used for CGI PROGRAMMING. When the APPLICATION PROGRAMMING INTERFACE for servlets was first released the only SERVER that could support them was a little-used one developed by Sun. However, many of the most popular servers, including APACHE, now support this technology either directly or via add-on software.

session hijacking An alternative name for a PIGGY BACK ATTACK.

session layer A layer within the OSI REFERENCE MODEL. It carries out the process of organizing and monitoring the transfer of data between applications such as NEWSREADERS and WEB SERVERS which reside in the APPLICATION LAYER. It also keeps track of the progress of data transfers. If an error in transmission has occurred then it is the function of this layer to inform the applications involved. This layer is also capable of synchronizing communication between two applications when, for example, transmission is temporarily interrupted.

SET *See* SECURED ELECTRONIC TRANSACTION STANDARD.

SETE Abbreviation for Smiling Ear To Ear used in CHAT ROOMS, EMAILS, and NEWSGROUPS.

SF Abbreviation for Surfer Friendly used in EMAILS and NEWSGROUPS. Usually used to describe WEB SITES which have a low incidence of graphics that slow down access to the site, or a well-structured site with the paths through it adequately signposted.

SGML Acronym for STANDARDIZED GENERAL MARKUP LANGUAGE.

SHA1 *See* SECURE HASH ALGORITHM 1.

shadow password file The UNIX operating system stores PASSWORDS in a file that has been encrypted and which every user can access. This has led to a number of intrusions based on reading this file and decrypting it. A way to get over this is to use a shadow password file which contains details about users, but to store the password file in a file which is highly secure.

shallow link A HYPERLINK which lies close to the top of a WEB SITE: that is, a link which you can reach without clicking on many higher-level links. The shallowest link is to a HOME PAGE. *See also* BANDWIDTH THEFT.

share ramping The process of influencing the share price of a company and then taking advantage of it, for example by buying shares in a company when they are at a low price and then starting a rumour that the company is being taken over. When the share price rises, the shares are sold at a profit. This is not a new scam but technologies such as NEWSGROUPS and BULLETIN BOARDS have made it much easier to spread rumours. Also known as PUMP AND DUMP. *See also* BOOK RAMPING.

shareware Software that can be DOWNLOADED at no initial cost. After a specified period, if the user of the software wishes to continue using it, then he or she buys it. There are a number of mechanisms used to enforce this. One is to release time-limited versions which stop performing after a specified period. Many shareware schemes, however, rely on trust.

sheesh A term used to describe derisive POSTINGS on NEWSGROUPS. An alternative to FURRFU.

shelfware A derogatory term for software that is purchased but, because of its inadequacies, is never used.

shell virus A VIRUS which infects a computer by wrapping itself around code which already exists, such as the OPERATING SYSTEM code which writes to a FILE. Whenever a program attempts to use the enclosed code the virus code is executed.

SHID Abbreviation for Slaps Head In Disgust used in CHAT ROOMS, EMAILS, and NEWSGROUPS.

shielded twisted pair cable Cable which contains shielding that helps minimize the effect of electrical interference. The shielding is quite bulky and can make installation difficult. The term is often abbreviated to STP.

shim A small piece of data inserted into a program or a file in order to achieve a particular effect. *See, for example,* PIXEL SHIM: a PIXEL inserted into a WEB PAGE in order to achieve a formatting effect. It has its origins in engineering, especially in the engineering of aircraft and mechanical devices.

shopping bot A BOT which helps a user shop on the Internet. A typical shopping bot might access a number of different shops for a particular product and provide information about its various prices.

shopping cart A metaphor used in ECOMMERCE sites selling products such as books or clothes. The user is able to navigate through catalog pages which describe the products on sale and can pick a product to buy, usually by clicking a button or entering some details on a FORM. This item is then added to the shopping cart. When the user wishes to complete their transactions they visit a CHECKOUT PAGE which provides information on the items sold, their price, and postage rates. ECOMMERCE SITE BUILDER software almost invariably uses the shopping cart metaphor.

shopping reassurance scheme A scheme, usually run by an independent organization, which certifies that an ecommerce company follows a code of practice, for example by not debiting a credit card until goods are sent to a customer.

shopping trolley A British term for SHOPPING CART.

shortcut An icon placed on the DESKTOP of a computer in order to enable quicker access to the FOLDER or program that the icon represents.

shortest path routing A form of ROUTING which attempts to send PACKETS of data over a network in such a way that the path taken from the sending computer to the recipient computer is minimized. The path can be measured in either physical distance or in the number of HOPS. This form of routing uses a NON-ADAPTIVE ROUTING ALGORITHM.

shorthand Acronyms and abbreviations used in EMAIL communication, CHAT ROOMS, and NEWSGROUPS. For example, IMHO means In My Humble Opinion. *See also* FASGROLIA and ABBREVIATION.

short message service A service offered by mobile phone systems. It enables the user of a mobile telephone to key in text and then send it to another phone user. Because the display of a conventional mobile phone is so small such messages are often found liberally sprinkled with ABBREVIATIONS. The term is often abbreviated to SMS. There are now a number of WEB SITES which allow users to send such messages to mobile phones.

shoulder surfing The act of looking over a user's shoulder in order to learn important information that is being typed in, such as a PASSWORD or a credit card number.

shouting The users of NEWSGROUPS or senders of EMAIL often capitalize whole words when they want to vociferously make a point. This is known as shouting.

shovelware 1. A WEB SITE which only contains material that has been cut and pasted from existing sites. **2**. Material found on a Web site which has been constructed by using existing hardcopy materials without any thought about WEB DESIGN. Such sites were prevalent during the early life of the WORLD WIDE WEB but with new design standards being set by THIRD-GENERATION WEB SITES and FOURTH-GENERATION WEB SITES their incidence is declining.

shriek The ! character. *See also* PLING.

shtml 1. Abbreviation used as a FILE EXTENSION for files which include HYPERTEXT MARKUP LANGUAGE text and which require SERVER SIDE INCLUDES. **2**. Abbreviation for SERVER PARSED HTML.

SHTTP *See* SECURE HTTP.

Sidewinder The name of the SPIDER used by the INFOSEEK SEARCH ENGINE.

sig Abbreviation for SIGNATURE FILE.

SIG Abbreviation for SPECIAL INTEREST GROUP.

sig file A commonly used abbreviation for SIGNATURE FILE.

SIG quote A pithy, relevant, or wise saying stored in a SIG FILE and appended to the end of an EMAIL message. *See also* FORTUNE COOKIE.

signal to noise ratio The ratio formed by dividing the useful data carried by a transmission line by any other signals on that line. This quantity is usually expressed in decibels.

signature file A FILE whose contents are appended to an EMAIL. It normally contains information about the sender, such as his or her name, affiliation, and phone number. Sometimes it contains a pithy saying similar to a MESSAGE OF THE DAY and known as a SIG QUOTE. Such files will occasionally contain ASCII ART. It is often abbreviated to SIG FILE.

Silicon Valley An area in California south-west of San Francisco famed for the quality and quantity of IT products.

siliwood A jargon term used to describe the MEDIA CONVERGENCE between film, television, and networking.

silly walk A series of unnecessary, time-consuming, or illogical steps to carry out some hardware- or software-related tasks: for example, 'I had to silly walk around 25 windows in order to get this software installed on my computer.' Derived from the silly walk sketch in the now defunct Monty Python television series.

silver surfer An older user of the Internet, usually someone over 50. *See also* GREY MATTER.

similarity measure A metric that is used to judge how closely the results of a query to a SEARCH ENGINE match the user's requirements.

Simple Mail Transfer Protocol An EMAIL standard. It is one of the most popular email protocols and forms the basis of a large amount of Internet mail traffic. It has been written so that mail delivered using the protocol is able to interact with a wide variety of incompatible mail servers. The main function of the Simple Mail Transfer Protocol, or SMTP as it is often known, is to specify how email messages are entered and stored on a MAIL SERVER, and how email servers collaborate to deliver a message to a recipient.

Simple Network Management Protocol A PROTOCOL used to coordinate devices such as computers, GATEWAYS, ROUTERS, and MULTIPLEXORS. It provides monitoring and controlling functions, such as detecting error conditions and uses the USER DATAGRAM PROTOCOL to carry out these functions. It is often abbreviated to SNMP.

Simple Network Paging Protocol A PROTOCOL used to deliver messages to the users of personal pagers. It is occasionally abbreviated to SNPP.

simplex communication Transmission in a network where data can only travel in one direction.

single-mode fibre Fibre optic cabling where light propagates in a straight line. In order to do this the diameter of the cable has to be of the order of a few wavelengths of light. This is in contrast to MULTIMODE FIBRE where different rays of light bounce around the cable at different angles.

single-pixel GIF A HACK sometimes carried out by WEB PAGE designers when they are unable to place some text or a graphic at a particular point using the normal facilities of the HYPERTEXT MARKUP LANGUAGE. It involves placing a small graphic in a Web page. As WYSIWYG EDITORS become more and more sophisticated there is less of a need for such workarounds.

siphoning An illegal technique used to redirect WORLD WIDE WEB traffic to another site. A popular way of doing this is to copy a number of WEB PAGES belonging to a particular organization, replace some of the HYPERLINKS with links to a different site to which visitors are to be redirected, and then submit these new pages to a SEARCH ENGINE.

SITD Abbreviation for Still In The Dark used in EMAILS and NEWSGROUPS.

site A location on the Internet which contains data or information. A location which contains WEB PAGES is known as a WEB SITE, and a site which contains files that can be accessed by the FILE TRANSFER PROTOCOL (FTP) is known as an FTP site. The data at a site can vary from files of character data to SOUND CLIPS.

site administration software A general term used to describe software that enables a WEBMASTER to make sure that a WEB SITE is running smoothly. It includes software that enables the site to be transferred to an FTP SERVER, checks HYPERLINKS for ORPHAN PAGES, checks for DEAD LINKS, to check that pages appear the same on different BROWSERS, and administers the work of a team developing a number of WEB PAGES.

site caching The process of periodically copying frequently used WEB PAGES from an external WEB SERVER to a local CACHING PROXY SERVER or FILE SERVER within an

INTRANET. This is done to speed up access to the pages by the users of the intranet and is achieved because access is usually via a fast LOCAL AREA NETWORK to the server, rather than via low-BANDWIDTH external transmission lines. The only disadvantage to this simple technique is that between downloading times the Web pages may become out of date. *See also* BROWSER CACHING and CACHING.

site manager A tool which manages a WEB SITE. It provides facilities such as viewing the site as a SITE MAP, moving WEB PAGES around the site in such a way that the HYPERLINKS in these pages are modified to reflect this, and launching an HTML EDITOR when a page is clicked in one of the displays used by the software.

site map A graphical display of the structure of a WEB SITE showing the folders and WEB PAGES contained in the site. Such a display also shows the HYPERLINKS which join pages in the site. Site maps can be stand-alone software tools or can be integrated into advanced HTML AUTHORS or HTML EDITORS.

site ranking The ordering applied by a SEARCH ENGINE to the various sites that it presents to the user who has typed in a query. The search engine uses a proprietary algorithm which promotes those sites that best match the query.

site submission The process whereby the UNIFORM RESOURCE LOCATOR and other details of a WEB SITE are communicated to a SEARCH ENGINE. Usually this process is fairly simple, as most search engines only require the URL and the EMAIL address of a contact. After submission a SPIDER or human indexer visits the site and places it in the database maintained by the search engine. *See also* MULTIPLE SEARCH ENGINE SUBMISSION.

skin A jargon term used to describe a CUSTOMIZABLE GRAPHICAL USER INTERFACE: a program which enables a user to change the look and feel of an existing user interface.

Skipjack A classified ENCRYPTION ALGORITHM developed by the NATIONAL SECURITY AGENCY and used within the CLIPPER encryption chip.

skulking Synonymous with LURKING.

slag 1. The useless material which is retrieved when trawling for information on the Web.
2. To maliciously increase the response time of a network by flooding it with data. *Also see* BITSLAG.

slash The character /. Users of the Internet see this character frequently in UNIFORM RESOURCE LOCATORS where it is used to separate the DIRECTORY names which identify where a WEB PAGE is stored on a WEB SERVER.

slashdot effect The effect that occurs when one WEB SITE is linked via a HYPERLINK from another, very popular Web site. This often overloads the server containing the first Web site so that access to it becomes very slow. The name arose from sites being overwhelmed when they were mentioned in slashdot.org, a popular NEWS SITE read by many technical staff.

Sliding Window Protocol A protocol used by the TRANSMISSION CONTROL PROTOCOL which sends data into a network. The protocol varies the number of packets that are sent out at each transmission depending on the current network conditions: if the network is heavily loaded then a small number are sent; if the network is lightly loaded then many more are sent. The collection of packets sent is known as a WINDOW. This protocol is occasionally referred to as the SLOW START PROTOCOL.

SLIP *See* SERIAL LINE INTERNET PROTOCOL.

slow infector A VIRUS similar to a FAST INFECTOR which only infects files when they are modified or created. They do this in order to trick ANTI-VIRUS SOFTWARE into identifying the modifications as legal.

slow mail A term for mail delivered by the postal service. *See also* SNAIL MAIL and DEAD TREE.

slow start protocol A synonym for the SLIDING WINDOW PROTOCOL.

small office home office Used to categorize businesses which are small to medium-sized and is usually applied to companies who have fewer than ten employees. It is often abbreviated to SOHO. *See also* SME.

small-to-medium enterprise An English counterpart to SMALL OFFICE HOME OFFICE, describing companies which have a small workforce.

smart card A credit-card-sized piece of plastic which contains a small microprocessor and a small amount of data. Smart cards are used for a number of purposes: they can be used to hold ELECTRONIC TOKENS, they can contain personal details, or they can be employed as an AUTHENTICATION medium for validating a user's identify. They often have metal contacts on their surface so that they can be connected to an electronic device capable of reading their data.

SMDS *See* SWITCHED MULTIMEGABIT DATA SERVICES.

SME *See* SMALL-TO-MEDIUM ENTERPRISE.

smiley Another name for an EMOTICON.

smiley face One of the most commonly occurring EMOTICONS. It indicates happiness and is written as :-)

SMIME *See* SECURE MULTIMEDIA INTERNET MAIL EXTENSIONS. It is sometimes written as S/MIME and sometimes as S-MIME.

SMS *See* SHORT MESSAGE SERVICE.

SMTP *See* SIMPLE MAIL TRANSFER PROTOCOL.

smurfing Attacking a computer network by instructing one or more computers in the network to BROADCAST frequent PING messages to all the other computers in the network. An example of a DENIAL OF SERVICE ATTACK. *See also* PING STORM and PING FLOODING.

SNA *See* SYSTEMS NETWORK ARCHITECTURE.

snail mail A derogatory term used to describe the conventional, paper-based mail system. *See also* SNAIL MAIL, PMAIL, and DEAD TREE.

snapshot tool A generic term for programs used by SYSTEM ADMINISTRATORS to audit a computer system for security weaknesses: for example, checking for

passwords which can be easily guessed, or checking that the file used for passwords can only be written to by the system administrator. They are also known as STATIC AUDIT TOOLS.

snarf To copy a FILE illicitly without the owner's permission.

sneaker net Jargon used to refer to the manual transfer of files via a transportable medium such as a floppy disk from one computer on a network to another. The term is derived from the footwear used by the person carrying out the transfer.

snert An invitation or overture of a sexual nature. Snerts are usually found in CHAT ROOMS and in EMAIL.

sniffer A hardware and software package which captures data being transferred over a network. There are number of sniffers which are used legally, for example in identifying CHOKE POINTS, but they can also be used for criminal acts such as capturing PASSWORDS and credit card details.

snivitz A small transitory problem with a piece of hardware or software.

SNMP *See* SIMPLE NETWORK MANAGEMENT PROTOCOL.

SNPP *See* SIMPLE NETWORK PAGING PROTOCOL.

SNR Abbreviation for Signal To Noise Ratio used in EMAILS and NEWSGROUPS.

SO 1. Abbreviation for Significant Other used in CHAT ROOMS, EMAILS, and NEWSGROUPS.
2. Abbreviation for SECURITY OFFICER.

soc An abbreviation which designates those NEWSGROUPS that discuss social research and social issues.

sociomedia Software designed for a social purpose. The best example of this is NEWSGROUP software.

socket An entry or exit point for data in a computer which is connected to a TCP-IP network. If a programmer wants to develop a program which reads data from a network, then he or she programmatically sets up a socket on the computer which is going to receive the data. This socket is then referenced in any program which carries out the data transfer. In Java a socket is created by specifying the PORT number through which data transfer is to occur. A socket is a logical concept not a hardware concept.

socket address The unique address which identifies a SOCKET on a computer. It is made up by combining the INTERNET PROTOCOL ADDRESS and a PORT ADDRESS, where the port address designates the port that is to receive or transmit data.

sock puppet A pseudonym adopted by someone who has made a POSTING to a NEWSGROUP and then follows it up with a supportive posting using the pseudonym. The process is carried out in order to give the impression that the poster's opinions are supported by others. *See also* BOOK RAMPING.

soft boot A BOOT which only starts up part of a computer's system.

software copyright Until the late 1990s the only way of obtaining legal protection for software was by copyright. This was easy as no formal procedures were required since the copyright existed as soon as the software was created. However, copyright is a weak safeguard compared with a patent where ownership can be proved relatively easily and it is possible to sue without having to prove that copying has taken place. Unfortunately, getting a patent for software was a very difficult process. However, the late 1990s saw a liberalization of American practice and a number of computer programs and business processes have won patents.

software developer's kit A generic term used to describe any collection of software released by the developer of a software product in order to provide other developers with programming facilities that enable them to modify the functions of the product. It is also used to describe a collection of software, associated with a particular programming language, which is used to develop programs: for example, software which compiles SOURCE CODE into MACHINE CODE, execution software, and testing software.

software patent Until relatively recently this was a contradiction in terms. Until the late 1990s it proved very difficult to gain a patent for software in either the US or the European courts. This state of affairs has been much criticized, as a patent is easy to enforce in law since it is officially registered and no proof of copying is necessary. However, in the late 1990s, US law was liberalized and a number of landmark cases allowed the patenting of software and business processes. *See also* SOFTWARE COPYRIGHT.

software piracy The process of copying commercial software and making it available to the general user community, either at a small fee or free. This has always been a problem in computing, but it was previously confined to companies. However, the rise of the Internet in the 1990s and the ease with which an FTP SERVER can be deployed has meant that there has been an increase in this activity. There are a number of motives for it including commercial gain, the pleasure gained from CRACKING the security technology associated with a software product, and the idealistic view that all software should be free. *See* WAREZ, WAREZ DOODZ, and FREE SOFTWARE FOUNDATION.

SOHF Abbreviation for Sense Of Humour Failure used in EMAILS and NEWSGROUPS. Usually applied to a user who takes everything that is written in a newsgroup seriously.

SOHO *See* SMALL OFFICE HOME OFFICE.

soliton A special type of pulsing that is used with light signals in a fibre optic transmission line in order to reduce DISPERSION.

solution A word appended onto a computer term as a marketing ploy. It implies that a product can solve certain commercial problems: for example, 'ECOMMERCE solution'.

SOMY Abbreviation for Sick Of Me Yet used in EMAILS and NEWSGROUPS.

SONET *See* SYNCHRONOUS OPTICAL NETWORK.

sorcerer's apprentice mode When a bug in a PROTOCOL causes a message to be reproduced a number of times. Each of these messages then encounters the bug again and further messages are generated. The large numbers of messages can shut down a whole system. The term is derived from a traditional story, retold by Goethe and put to music by Paul Dukas. Walt Disney popularized the story by animating it in *Fantasia* where a young Mickey Mouse (the sorcerer's apprentice) creates a large number of animated buckets and brushes which cause a huge flood.

SorG Abbreviation for Straight or Gay? used in CHAT ROOMS.

SOT Abbreviation for Short Of Time used in CHAT ROOMS.

SOTMG Abbreviation for Short Of Time Must Go used in CHAT ROOMS.

sound card A hardware card which is found in a computer which provides sound facilities.

sound clip A FILE stored using an audio format associated with a WEB PAGE. When some action occurs, such as the page being first displayed or when a BUTTON is clicked, the clip plays on the loudspeakers of the computer hosting the browser. Sound clips can occupy a large amount of memory and hence should be used with caution as they slow the DOWNLOAD time of a page.

sound player A PLUG-IN which enables a BROWSER to play sounds which have been DOWNLOADed as part of a WEB PAGE. *See also* SOUND CLIP and MP3.

source code The text developed by a computer programmer. The source code is converted into MACHINE CODE by a COMPILER.

source encoding A generic term used to describe compression methods that take advantage of some characteristic of the data to be compressed which is related to the application. For example, video files consist of data which represent each frame of the video, with each frame differing only slightly from the previous one. Because of this, such files can be stored as an initial frame followed by data which describes the difference between each individual frame.

source route Data which describes the route an EMAIL message should take when being sent to its destination. The route is determined at the point where it is sent rather than at the various computers it meets as it traverses the Internet. This form of addressing is now rarely seen.

spacehog A synonym for bloatware.

spam 1. Commercial EMAIL which is unsolicited. The derivation of the term is a little misty: popular opinion says it came from a sketch in the Monty Python television show in which a large number of Vikings demanded spam at a snack bar and ended up repeatedly chanting the words 'spam, spam, spam'. Most spam is commercial in nature, offering services such as pornography, PYRAMID SCHEMES, lists of 'useful' information such as addresses of cheap auctions, and free software. Spam is often part of some criminal enterprise such as a PONZI SCHEME. Users of the Internet who send spam usually obtain the EMAIL ADDRESSES from list vendors who gather them from a number of sources. These sources include WEB PAGES where a user has placed an email address, user directories maintained by an INTERNET SERVICE PROVIDER, POSTINGS to NEWSGROUPS, and information generated by participation in CHAT ROOMS. Spam list vendors construct these lists using special software known as ADDRESS HARVESTERS; these are a type of BOT which scour the Internet looking for email addresses. Spam is increasingly becoming a problem, but there are a number of ways an Internet user can minimize the amount of spam they receive. First, have two email addresses, one which is not circulated widely or made publicly known and one which is used to post to newsgroups and which is never read. Any messages sent to the latter are deleted by the Internet service provider responsible for your mail after a period of time. The second solution is not to put your email address in public places such as Web pages and the members' directories maintained by Internet service providers. The third solution is to use an ANONYMOUS REMAILER SERVICE when posting to a newsgroup. The fourth solution is to use ANTI-SPAM SOFTWARE which prevents most spam reaching your email reader.

2. The term used to describe an attack on a computer in which the BUFFERS used by the OPERATING SYSTEM have been caused to overflow.

spam attractor An alternative name for a SPAM MAGNET.

spamblock Users of the Internet who send SPAM often obtain the EMAIL ADDRESSES they use from companies who use special-purpose tools known as ADDRESS HARVESTERS. These tools can examine the POSTINGS in NEWSGROUPS and WEB PAGES for email addresses. A spamblock is a way of defeating these tools: it consists of writing the text of the address in such a way that someone who genuinely wants to send an email is able to do so, yet it is written in such a way that a harvester is unable to detect the text. An example of this is 'd.c.ince is my name and email me at now.ac.uk.'

spamdex Another name for INDEX SPAMMING.

spamdexing The process of adding extraneous material to a WEB PAGE in order to have it ranked more highly by SEARCH ENGINES. Also known as SPOOFING and KEYWORD STUFFING.

spamhaus A jargon term used to describe a company which sells lists of EMAIL ADDRESSES to SPAMMERS. These addresses are usually obtained by the use of mechanized tools known as ADDRESS HARVESTERS.

spam magnet A service offered to individuals who are about to divulge their email address to a WEB SITE, perhaps via a GUEST BOOK. The company that offers a spam magnet service provides a special email address to be used when interacting with the suspected Web site. After some time it is possible to access the Web site of the company that provided the spam magnet to see whether it has attracted any SPAM. Sometimes this service is called a SPAM ATTRACTOR service.

spamming The process of sending large amounts of unsolicited EMAIL to a group of users, usually for some commercial purpose. *See* SPAM.

spamvertise The process of advertising a product or service using SPAM.

special interest group A group of users who use EMAIL to exchange views and information on a particular topic, often of a technical nature such as a particular OPERATING SYSTEM.

specialized search engine A SEARCH ENGINE associated with a particular topic such as Shakespearean studies. It functions very much like a conventional search engine, but it only searches a small area of the Internet: connected with the topic it deals with.

spelling flame A FLAME which refers to a POSTING to a NEWSGROUP and which criticizes the poor spelling in the posting. Usually the flame does not respond to any of the points made in the original posting.

spew To produce a large amount of irrelevant text in POSTINGS to a NEWSGROUP or in a CHAT ROOM.

SPH *See* SERVER PARSED HTML.

spider A program which wanders around the Internet looking for new resources such as recently released WEB SITES. These programs, also known as BOTS or wanderers, are used by SEARCH ENGINES although a number of user-driven spiders can be found on SHARE WARE sites. When a developer registers a site with a search engine the engine often sends a spider to the site to index it and produce data which is stored in the search engine's database.

splash page A WEB PAGE that is displayed for a few seconds followed by the display of the HOME PAGE. Such pages are viewed with approbation by many users and abomination by others.

splash screen A graphic which is initially shown when a program such as a word processor is started. Such a screen contains fancy graphics, the name of the company that developed the software, and version information. The screen usually disappears after a few seconds; this is in contrast to the screens associated with NAGWARE.

spod A derogatory term for a user of a MULTIUSER DUNGEON system who has no social skills at all.

spoiler A POSTING which contains details of the plot of a book or film or provides the answer to a puzzle. Spoilers, as their name suggests, spoil the enjoyment of contributors to newsgroups and are discouraged. If it is necessary to send a spoiler there are a number of conventions that should be adopted, such as placing the word 'spoiler' in the header of a posting. *See also* SPOILER SPACE.

spoiler space Space in a POSTING to a NEWSGROUP or EMAIL which precedes part of the text of a SPOILER. Such text usually gives away the plot of a film or book and is preceded by some textual warning that this is about to happen. Spoiler space is inserted so that when the user is reading the email or posting he or she does not inadvertently see the spoiling text.

spoofer A program which is used to gain unauthorized access to a site on a network. The program usually does this by pretending to be an authorized user or by taking over an authorized user's online session with a computer. *See also* SPOOFING.

Spoofing 1. Assuming the identity of an existing user in order to discover information associated with that user or information that the user is allowed to access: a technique used by CRACKERS. When the spoofing involves an INTERNET PROTOCOL ADDRESS the process is known as IP SPOOFING.
2. A technique that reduces the transmission traffic through networks by having hardware such as BRIDGES and ROUTERS carry out some of the functions of a computer on the network.
3. A synonym for SPAMDEXING.

sprawl site A huge, badly organized WEB SITE which is difficult to navigate. Often the site has started off being very well organized but has degenerated as new material has been added.

SQL *See* STRUCTURED QUERY LANGUAGE.

SQL server A DATABASE SERVER which responds to queries sent to it in the query language known as SQL. The server decodes the query, discovers what data is required, extracts it from the databases that it holds, and sends it back to the client that issued the query.

squammer Someone who buys a domain name in anticipation of it being useful to companies in the future. When this happens it is usually sold at an inflated price.

squirt the bird American jargon term for the process of sending data to a satellite.

SSL *See* SECURE SOCKETS LAYER.

SSMA Abbreviation for Some Such Meaningless Acronym used in EMAILS and NEWSGROUPS.

SSP Abbreviation for STORAGE SERVICE PROVIDER.

stack 1. A short version of the term PROTOCOL STACK.
2. A term used by computer scientists for a data structure in which the last item added to the structure is the first to be removed.

stack attack A form of DENIAL OF SERVICE ATTACK. The stack of a computer is an area of memory where a running program keeps the data necessary for its correct functioning. A stack attack involves embedding a program in a WEB PAGE which consumes huge amounts of stack memory. Eventually such a program terminates with some error message, but before this happens the BROWSER viewing the page that contains the program becomes unusable.

staircase A word synonymous with JAGGIES.

stalker site A WEB SITE devoted to one person, usually someone in the entertainment industry. Such a site is normally constructed by an obsessive fan.

stand-alone Adjective used to describe a computer that is not connected to a network.

Standard for Robot Exclusion A number of the early BOTS and SPIDERS used by SEARCH ENGINES caused problems when they visited WEB SITES, for example, they would reduce the access time of other users. This standard specifies a number of measures which attempt to alleviate these problems.

Standardized General Markup Language A markup language, known as SGML, developed for the design of languages for the formatting, storage, and access of large corpora of documents. It is a very large and complex language, and the standard reference work on it runs to 662 pages of text. It has been a very successful technology in that it has been extensively adopted by large organizations which generate voluminous quantities of documentation, such as IBM and the US Department of Defense. It is included in this work since it is the parent of the HYPERTEXT MARKUP LANGUAGE.

star network A network centred on a hardware device called a CONCENTRATOR. Each computer in the network is connected to the concentrator which has the function of routing packets of data from one device on the network to another. It acts very much like an airline hub.

start page The WEB PAGE that appears when a BROWSER is first executed. The default start page is normally the HOME PAGE of the browser developer's WEB SITE.

start-up file A FILE held on a computer which is processed and executed when the computer is first started up. Often the file contains instructions which set up the computer for use. This file is often targeted by VIRUSES.

stateful protocol A PROTOCOL which is able to remember and store details of the interactions which it governs. A good example of such a protocol is the FILE TRANSFER PROTOCOL which, for example, remembers the identity of the client that is using it to DOWNLOAD files. Stateful protocols differ from STATELESS PROTOCOLS such as the HYPERTEXT TRANSFER PROTOCOL used for transferring WEB PAGES to BROWSERS.

stateful server A SERVER which keeps data about previous requests for a service which can then be used for subsequent requests. The best example of such a server is an FTP SERVER. *See also* STATELESS SERVER.

stateless protocol A PROTOCOL which is incapable of remembering the results and data associated with the interactions it governs. Probably the best-known state-less protocol is the HYPERTEXT TRANSFER PROTOCOL used for transferring WEB PAGES from a WEB SERVER to a BROWSER. This protocol cannot remember the result of a previous instruction to transfer a page. There are a number of devices which have been used to overcome this problem: for example, in the case of HTTP, one solution is to embed a COOKIE on a client machine which holds data to keep track of the interactions.

stateless server A server which stores no data from one request to another. In effect, after a service request has been completed, it discards the data associated with the request. This simplifies the design of such servers. However, it severely limits the type of services which can be provided. The best example of a stateless server is a WEB SERVER. The stateless nature of such servers has meant that considerable effort has been expanded on server side technologies such as SERVLETS and client side software developed from COOKIE technology to overcome the inherent limitations of the HYPERTEXT TRANSFER PROTOCOL. A server which does keep state information between requests is known as a STATEFUL SERVER.

static audit tool Another name for a SNAPSHOT TOOL.

static IP This refers to the fact that when you log on to the Internet your INTERNET PROTOCOL ADDRESS always remains the same rather than being assigned dynamically.

static page A WEB PAGE which does not change during the process of being retrieved and sent to a BROWSER. This is in contrast to DYNAMIC PAGES which are altered before being sent: for example, by including dynamic data from a database.

static routing This is when ROUTING in a network is carried out without any reference to traffic conditions. When a ROUTER uses static routing to discover which computer to send a PACKET to, it consults a table of data which defines which route to take.

statistical attack An attack on a database to which users are allowed limited access: for example, access in order to calculate information such as averages. A statistical attack uses this information to discover data that is secret. For example, a database containing employee details may be used by others to calculate the average salary of employees based on particular criteria. If a user discovered a criterion which only holds for one employee, and uses this information to find the average salary of all employees having that criterion, then the employee's salary could be easily discovered.

statistical encoding A COMPRESSION technique using ENTROPY CODING which recognizes statistical patterns in the data to be compressed and takes advantage of these patterns to carry out the compression. For example, the data may contain the character 'e' a large number of times. A technique which uses this knowledge might represent this character using a small number of BITS.

status bar A small area at the bottom of a BROWSER window which contains textual messages. Typical messages inform the user that a WEB SERVER has been found and the progress of the DOWNLOAD of the current WEB PAGE.

stealth script A CGI SCRIPT used to redirect a visitor to another WEB PAGE depending on who the visitor is. For example, stealth scripts are used to implement AGENT NAME DELIVERY where a SEARCH ENGINE is directed to a special page which contains material that makes sure that the engine ranks the page highly.

stealth virus A type of virus which attempts to nullify or confuse any attempt to detect it. It does this by infecting the code of the computer that could be used by VIRUS DETECTION SOFTWARE so that this code does not spot the presence of the virus. For example, a number of stealth viruses infect the code used for reading the contents of FILES so that they ignore the presence of a virus in a file.

steganography The process of sending a secret message by embedding it within some text or graphics. For example, many graphic image formats have spare bits which can be used to place the text of a secret message.

Stel *See* SECURE TELNET.

stemmer A computer program which determines the stem of a word. For example it is able to determine the stem 'cat' from the word 'cats'. Such programs are employed in SEARCH ENGINES to construct efficient queries of the databases maintained by the search engines.

stemming The returning of documents which contain words that are prefixed by a search term provided by the user of a SEARCH ENGINE. For example, a search engine which uses stemming responds to a query containing the keyword 'run' with all words starting with 'run', such as 'running' and 'runner'.

sticky content 1. CONTENT in a WEB SITE which is organized so well and is so interesting to read that users who access the site stay there for a considerable time.
2. The content of those sites which only contain links to pages which form part of the site.

stock bot A BOT which carries out tasks associated with online share trading, such as monitoring share prices and notifying the user when unusual behaviour in a share or group of shares is detected.

stone age Used to describe the period starting with the invention of the first computer (1949) up to the mid-1950s.

stop word A word used in a SEARCH QUERY that is ignored by a SEARCH ENGINE because it is so common, such as the word 'the'.

storage service provider A company that offers secure storage facilities for FILES owned by other customer companies. The more sophisticated companies will have systems which will automatically access customer files and store them; less sophisticated companies will require their customers to DOWNLOAD their files. Often abbreviated to SSP.

store 1. In 1997 the Internet Ad Hoc committee proposed a number of new names for DOMAINS. store is one of these. It represents vendors or merchants.
2. To write data to a permanent medium such as a CD ROM.

store and forward network A primitive network wholly implemented via the telephone network. During the day each computer in the network stores data and messages meant for the other computers. At night the computers connect up and send the data and messages to each other. FIDONET is an example of such a network.

stored procedure A collection of program statements which are stored on a DATABASE SERVER. They can be executed programmatically by a client. They were originally developed by a company called Sybase in order to speed up access to databases held on networks. The mechanisms they use are similar to those used in REMOTE PROCEDURE CALL.

storyboarding A process used in the development of a WEB SITE which involves the designer and colleagues simulating a particular set of visits to the site in order to gain ideas about how the site should be structured. The term is derived from one used in the movie industry.

stream cipher An ALGORITHM used in symmetric key encryption which transforms data one character at a time. One of the best known stream cipher algorithms is the RC4 algorithm developed by the US government. *See also* BLOCK CIPHER.

streaming audio A technology that allows the user of a BROWSER to listen to a sound clip in real time as it is being downloaded to the browser.

streaming technology Technology that transfers media to a BROWSER and plays them in real time, not after the whole file has been received by the browser. *See* STREAMING AUDIO and STREAMING VIDEO.

streaming video A technology that allows the user of a BROWSER to view a video clip in real time as it is being DOWNLOADed to the browser.

string A sequence of characters usually enclosed within single or double quotation marks.

strong encryption An ENCRYPTION ALGORITHM which cannot be broken within a time frame that would enable the breaker to take advantage of the information that has been encrypted.

Structured Query Language A QUERY LANGUAGE used to extract data from a database. It is usually referred to as SQL. It is often embedded within another language such as JAVA. The vast majority of databases held in distributed systems now accept SQL queries. *See also* SQL SERVER.

stub network A network which only passes data to and from the computers connected to it. Even if such a network is connected to other networks it does not pass any data to or from these.

STW Abbreviation for Search The Web used in EMAILS and NEWSGROUPS.

style guide A set of guidelines for a WEB SITE which defines a standard look and feel for WEB PAGES. The contents of a style guide are usually implemented using TEMPLATES.

style sheet A document which defines the structure and look of another document. For example, a word processor might contain a style sheet which specifies the format of a standard business letter. Each time a business letter is required, the style sheet is applied to the text to turn it into the format defined by the style sheet. HTML version 4 supports a style sheet via the CASCADING STYLE SHEETS facility. A style sheet which is used to generate WEB PAGES is often referred to as a TEMPLATE.

subject drift This is what happens in a NEWSGROUP when the contributors to a THREAD drift away from the main topic.

subject tree A hierarchic way of organizing the subjects covered by WEB SITES. A number of SEARCH ENGINES provide facilities whereby such trees can be traversed in order to home in on a particular subject. The most well known search engine that does this is YAHOO.

submission address The EMAIL address used to send a message to users who have subscribed to a MAILING LIST.

subnet A short and frequently used version of SUBNETWORK.

subnet address The INTERNET PROTOCOL ADDRESS partly consists of data which identifies a SUBNETWORK. This data is known as the subnet address.

subnet mask The set of BITS used to determine the SUBNET to which a packet of data is to be sent.

subnetwork A smaller network which is connected to the Internet. Typically these networks would be LOCAL AREA NETWORKS maintained by a commercial, educational, or governmental organization.

subroutine A section of code which executed from another section of code. Once the subroutine has been executed, control is returned to the code that executed it.

subscribe To notify a MAILING LIST SERVER of a wish to receive EMAILS associated with the mailing list. It is also used to describe the process of adding a particular NEWSGROUP to the list of groups that you frequently access.

substitution cipher A form of ENCRYPTION which substitutes symbols in a PLAIN TEXT with other symbols. Such ciphers are usually very easy to crack. *See* ROT13.

sucking mud Used to describe a SERVER that has crashed or is behaving in an anomalous way. It is derived from oil field jargon when a pump is shut down and it starts pumping mud rather than crude oil.

suck site A WEB SITE which is dedicated to complaints about a specific company or product. It gets its name by the fact that the word 'suck' often appears in the UNIFORM RESOURCE LOCATOR of the site.

super searcher Another name for a CYBRARIAN.

super source quench A PACKET of data which effectively disconnects a computer from the Internet by telling the computer to send data to itself.

Superstitial® An emerging advertising technology used on the WORLD WIDE WEB. Superstitial adverts are highly interactive non-banner adverts which minimize the DOWNLOAD problems associated with normal BANNER ADVERTS, they are usually displayed when a user takes a break from surfing.

superzapping Virtually every network has a member of staff known as a SYSTEM ADMINISTRATOR who has the highest level of privileges in the system. For example, he or she is allowed to read, delete, and create files in any part of the system. Superzapping is the name given to the process whereby an unauthorized intruder manages to gain these privileges and use them in a criminal way by, for example, stealing the PASSWORDS of the network users. The term is derived from the Superzap program, a utility program developed by IBM which allowed MAINFRAME COMPUTER administrators to override normal security measures in order to react to some emergency such as a failed device.

supply chain A chain of links between supplier and consumers in a BUSINESS TO BUSINESS system. For example, a two link system exists when a company supplies subcomponents to another company which assembles them into components and then supplies them to a third company which assembles the components into a product. Supply chains are major consumers of resources and the advent of DISTRIBUTED SYSTEMS which link businesses together has made a major impact in terms of financial savings.

support site A WEB SITE which is used by an enterprise to support their customers. Normally such sites are maintained by companies who sell IT products such as software and hardware peripherals. Typically a support site contains press releases, FREQUENTLY ASKED QUESTIONS, DOWNLOADS of new versions of software, and EMAIL LINKS which enable the visitor to contact support staff.

surf To access a number of WEB PAGES using a BROWSER.

SWAG An American abbreviation for Scientific Wild Ass Guess used in EMAILS and NEWSGROUPS.

swap image An image which appears when some mouse event occurs that is associated with an existing image displayed in a BROWSER window. For example, a swap image might be displayed when a mouse travels over the existing image or when the mouse is clicked within the image. In this case the swap image might replace the whole of the existing image or only a part of it. Swap images are used in the development of ROLLOVERS.

swap space An area of memory used to hold data which is currently not required by a program. This area is usually found on a slow storage medium such as a hard disk. When the data is required it is copied into the memory used by the program.

swap space attack A DENIAL OF SERVICE ATTACK which is based on overwhelming an area of memory known as a SWAP SPACE. A browser usually has a relatively small amount of main memory available for the storage of data. When this memory is exhausted and more data is created then the old data is copied out to a slow memory device, usually some form of backing storage. When the old data is required again it is brought back in, with existing data being copied out. This type of attack creates large amounts of data and results in a massive traffic between the browser and the slow memory device, with the browser being disabled to the point where it becomes unusable. A swap space attack also impacts on other programs running on the computer executing the browser that has been attacked. *See also* STACK ATTACK.

SWDYT Abbreviation for So What Do You Think? used in CHAT ROOMS, EMAILS, and NEWSGROUPS.

switched connection A connection to a computer network that is established only when the user of a program requires it. The best example of such a connection is the one made when a user employs a telephone line to dial in to the Internet.

Switched Digital Video A technology that is used to carry video signals over fibre optic cables.

Switched Multimegabit Data Services A transmission technology which operates at speeds comparable to T3 CARRIER speeds, by splitting packets into fixed CELLS. It was regarded as a stop gap solution until better technologies came along and is now drastically declining in use.

SWL Acronym used in EMAILS and NEWSGROUPS. Its translation is Screaming With Laughter.

symmetric key encryption A form of ENCRYPTION where the same KEY is used to encrypt and decrypt the text that is to be sent. This means that the sender and the receiver must have exchanged this key some time before the message has been sent and that this transfer must occur over a secure channel. The key used for symmetric key encryption is often known as a SECRET KEY. The algorithms used for encryption with this type of scheme can be either BLOCK CIPHER algorithms or STREAM CIPHER algorithms. The former encrypt a block of data at a time, while the latter encrypt data on a character-by-character basis. Symmetric key encryption algorithms are usually much more efficient than their main competitor, the algorithms used in PUBLIC KEY ENCRYPTION. The most popular algorithms and technologies associated with symmetric key encryption in current use include the DIGITAL SIGNATURE STANDARD, RSA, and the DIFFIE HELLMAN KEY AGREEMENT. *See also* DATA ENCRYPTION STANDARD, RC2, RC4, RC5, and INTERNATIONAL DATA ENCRYPTION ALGORITHM.

SYN flooding A form of DENIAL OF SERVICE ATTACK which attempts to set up a large number of random connections to a computer on a network which is running the INTERNET PROTOCOL. Each connection requires the computer to devote resources to the connection, but after a time resources become so scarce that the performance of the computer that is being connected degrades and it denies any legitimate requests from real users. There were a small number of famous SYN flooding attacks in the 1990s, but TCP-IP software has now been amended to make them much more difficult to carry out.

synchronous communication The transmission of data where each character of data is sent at a time determined by the timing of previous characters. This is in contrast to ASYNCHRONOUS COMMUNICATION.

synchronous computer-mediated conferencing A form of computer conferencing where the participants have to come together at one time. A good example of this type of conferencing is INTERNET RELAY CHAT, where interactions are very much like those that occur during face-to-face conversations. This is in contrast to ASYNCHRONOUS COMPUTER-MEDI-ATED CONFERENCING where participants do not need to come together and where messages can be sent and read at will.

synchronous data transfer The transfer of data between two devices on a network where they both carry out a predetermined set of interactions based on a clock. The sending of collections of data by a computer, where every collection is sent periodically and where the ACKNOWLEDGEMENT from the destination computer has to be received by a certain time, is an example of this form of data transfer.

Synchronous Digital Hierarchy An optical fibre transmission standard that was developed by the CONSULTATIVE COM-MITTEE FOR INTERNATIONAL TELEPHONE AND TELEGRAPH that was similar to the SYNCHRONOUS OPTICAL NETWORK technology. It was the loser in the competition for optical standards with SONET. It is often abbreviated to SDH.

Synchronous Optical Network An optical fibre communications technology used to transfer network data. The developers of this technology had four aims: to enable a number of carriers to work together, to connect incompatible systems, to enable the MULTIPLEXING of many digital signals, and to make system maintenance easy. Often abbreviated to SONET.

syndicated content CONTENT which has been developed for sale to WEB SITES, for example, a page which contains IT industry comment from a well-respected expert. It is the electronic equivalent of syndicated material found in printed publications such as newspapers.

synonym ring A collection of words which are related to another word used in a search, usually with the search being carried out using a SEARCH ENGINE. A synonym ring is used to broaden the search.

SYS 1. Abbreviation for See You Soon used in CHAT ROOMS, EMAILS, and NEWS-GROUPS.
2. Occasionally used as an abbreviation for SYSTEM OPERATOR.

sysop Abbreviation for SYSTEM OPERATOR.

system administrator Someone who administers a small network, often one which contains a large central computer and many DUMB TERMINALS. Many of the functions of the system administrator are similar to those of a NETWORK ADMINIS-TRATOR, but since the network being administered is small, specific functions such as performance monitoring and altering the configuration of a network are carried out less frequently, with tasks such as updating software and registering new users predominating.

system log A FILE which contains information about the accesses that the users of a DISTRIBUTED SYSTEM make to its resources. Such a log can be configured to contain a huge amount of information about every access to every resource, or it can be configured to contain limited but highly revealing information such as the time pattern of log-ins made by certain users. Security tools can examine such logs and discover abnormal behaviour, such as a user logging in at unusual times of the day, suggesting that an intruder is masquerading as a regular user. *See also* LOG FILE and WEB LOG FILE.

system operator The MODERATOR of an INTERNET RELAY CHAT room. It is often abbreviated to op or sysop.

Systems Network Architecture A proprietary seven-layer protocol developed for IBM mainframe systems, now defunct. It is regarded by historians of the Internet as one of the major influences on the OSI REFERENCE MODEL.

T1 carrier A form of telephone line transmission which employs 24 channels of voice data. It can be used for digital data: however, in this case, only 23 channels are used, the remaining channel being used for synchronization.

T2 carrier A form of transmission which is implemented by MULTIPLEXING four streams of data from T1 CARRIERS. This enables the speed of transmission to be increased by just under a factor of four.

T3 carrier A form of transmission which is implemented by MULTIPLEXING seven streams of data from T2 CARRIERS. This enables the speed of transmission to be increased by just under a factor of seven.

T4 carrier A form of transmission which is implemented by MULTIPLEXING six streams of data from T3 CARRIERS. This enables the speed of transmission to be increased by just under a factor of six.

tab delimited file A FILE in which the individual items in the file are separated by tab characters. *See also* COMMA DELIMITED FILE.

table A facility in HTML which allows a user to develop conventional tables such as statistical tables using the <TABLE> TAG. For example, it allows the developer to specify the number of rows and columns, the width of rows and columns, and the background colours to the table. The main use of the TABLE facility, however, is for the placement of graphics and text. Early versions of HTML did not provide enough facilities to enable graphic designers to carry out the precise placement of graphics and text, so they had to use tables. Although tables were not originally intended for this, they had just enough power to provide a facility which came close to that found in conventional desktop publishing software, albeit at the cost of some arcane HACKS and SHIMS. Increasingly WYSIWYG EDITORS are providing more precise layout facilities using

modern features of HTML such as LAYERS, so the use of tables as a layout device is expected to decline greatly.

tag Some text placed in a file described by a markup language which either informs some formatting software to carry out a display or conveys some structural information. In the two most important MARKUP LANGUAGES used on the Internet, HYPERTEXT MARKUP LANGUAGE and the EXTENSIBLE MARKUP LANGUAGE, tags are introduced by the < character and terminated by the > character, as in the HTML tag <P> which instructs a BROWSER to display the line break at the end of a paragraph. In HTML, tags are used for display, while in the Extensible Markup Language they are used to indicate structure.

Tagged Image File Format An image format which is often used to transfer graphics from one computer to another. It is often abbreviated to TIFF.

tail circuit *See* TAIL LINE.

tailgating The process of listening in to an interactive session on a network, cancelling the LOG OUT issued by the user and continuing the session masquerading as the user. It is also known as a PIGGY BACK ATTACK. It is usually carried out for criminal reasons.

tail line A communication line which connects two MODEMS. Also known as a tail circuit.

talk A system which combines many of the features of a MULTIUSER DIMENSION and INTERNET RELAY CHAT. It effectively acts as a real-time CHAT ROOM. Sometimes a talk system is referred to as a LIVE NEWSGROUP or as a virtual community. It also designates those NEWSGROUPS that discuss controversial social issues.

talk bomb A malicious computer program illegally introduced into a network which floods users' screens with random characters.

tampering The unauthorized changing of data on a computer system, such as changing the value of an account balance. It is also known as DATA DIDDLING.

TANSTAAFL Abbreviation for There Ain't No Such Thing As A Free Lunch used in EMAILS and NEWSGROUPS.

tar A FILE EXTENSION for files which are condensed into an archive by the UNIX operating system.

tar pit A trap set for SPAMMERs. To set this trap it is necessary to develop a WEB PAGE which contains a large number of EMAIL ADDRESSES. Such a page attracts the attention of a spammer's ADDRESS HARVESTER. Hidden within the page are some addresses which are associated with a MAIL SERVER with an inordinately slow response time, usually numbered in days. When the spammer attempts to send an EMAIL to the server nothing happens and the spammer's mail program HANGS. *See also* WEB TRAP, FLYTRAP, and SPAM MAGNET.

Tbase10 ETHERNET wiring which uses twisted pair copper. It is also known as TENBASE10 wiring.

Tbase2 Thin wire ETHERNET cabling that uses cheap coaxial cable. It is also called THIN ETHERNET, TENBASE2, or THINNET.

Tbase5 This was the first cabling used in ETHERNETS. It had a large physical diameter and computers were connected into it via connections known as VAMPIRE TAPS which necessitated a pin being forced into the cable. It is also known as THICK ETHERNET, THICKNET, or TENBASE5.

TCOY Abbreviation used in CHAT ROOMS, EMAILS, and NEWSGROUPS. Its translation is Take Care of Yourself. It is usually used to finish a communication.

TCP *See* TRANSMISSION CONTROL PROTOCOL.

TCP-IP The set of protocols which enable communication over the Internet. The impression given by this name is that there are only two protocols involved: the TRANSMISSION CONTROL PROTOCOL (TCP) and the INTERNET PROTOCOL (IP). There are in fact many more, including the UN-RELIABLE DATAGRAM PROTOCOL and the INTERNET CONTROL MESSAGE PROTOCOL. Sometimes written as TCP/IP.

TCSEC *See* TRUSTED COMPUTER SECURITY EVALUATION CRITERIA.

teamware Another name for GROUPWARE.

techie Someone who has either hardware or software skills. *See also* GEEK, ALPHA GEEK, and ANORAK.

technical attack An attack on a computer network which is carried out by avoiding the hardware and software protection mechanisms of a computer system rather than by taking advantage of system users, for instance by stealing a password from a diary.

technobabble Speech or written text which is heavily larded with ABBREVIATIONS and technical words to the point where it becomes barely understandable. *See also* WEBLISH.

technocentrism An over-identification with computer technology at the expense of human relationships.

technology butler A member of staff of a hotel, usually a large expensive hotel, who has the job of helping guests with their communication, software, and hardware problems.

Technology Without an Interesting Name A de facto standard for scanner software and hardware. Sometimes abbreviated to TWAIN.

technophile A supporter and evangelist of technology, usually computer technology.

teergrube Another name for a TAR PIT.

telecommuting An alternative term for TELEWORKING.

teleconference A meeting using network technology such as CU SEEME.

telecottage A room or a building, usually in a remote community, which contains computers and communications equipment. Telecottages are used by members of that community for work or for pleasure.

telecottaging A term sometimes used for TELEWORKING or TELECOMMUTING with the implication that the worker is based in an rural environment.

telemedicine A term which covers a number of applications of network technology in medicine, ranging from sites which provide medical advice to users who type a query into a FORM embedded in a WEB PAGE, to the use of video technology over ultrafast networks to enable remote diagnosis.

telepresence A term for technologies which enable the user of a networked computer to be part of the network as if they are located within the physical area of the network. This involves everything from conferencing to the use of video links.

teleworking The process of using a network, usually the Internet, for working at a distance from the usual place of employment. Staff who carry out teleworking use facilities such as EMAIL, the WORLD WIDE WEB, and NEWSGROUPS to keep in touch with other workers.

Telnet An acronym for TELecommunications NETwork program. It was a program originally developed to allow users to log-in to other computers on a network. The interface to Telnet is very simple: all it usually consists of is a window which allows sequences of characters including an account name and a password to be typed in, in order to gain access to a remote computer. Virtually all the versions of Telnet allow the user to specify the remote computer, either in DOTTED QUAD NOTATION or via a symbolic name, and the port through which they want to be connected. Telnet relies on a DEDICATED PORT (port 23) to function. As well as using special-purpose Telnet software it is also possible to use Telnet HYPERLINKS embedded in WEB PAGES.

Telnet link A HYPERLINK embedded in a WEB PAGE which, when clicked by a mouse, initiates a TELNET session that enables a user to transfer files to the computer which is acting as the Web client. Displaying Telnet sessions on BROWSER windows has been problematic for browser developers: as a consequence many sites do not support this type of link.

TEMPEST Used to describe the capture of sensitive data that can be extracted from the EMANATIONS emitted by visual display equipment. Usually this is carried out for illegal purposes such as discovering details of bank accounts.

template A skeletal WEB PAGE which contains entities such as a NAVIGATION BAR which are to appear in every page found at a WEB SITE. New pages are then created from this Web page. Many modern HTML EDITORS have facilities for defining templates and reusing them time and time again.

Tenbase10 An alternative name for TBASE10 wiring.

Tenbase2 Another name for TBASE2 wiring.

Tenbase5 An alternative name for TBASE5 wiring.

ten-finger interface Sometimes there are very good reasons why two networks cannot be connected, such as those associated with security. One way of transferring data from one network to another is for the data from the first network to be displayed on a screen which is then read by a human operator who types it into the second network. This is known as a ten-finger interface. *See also* SNEAKER NET.

TEOTWAWKI Abbreviation for The End Of The World As We Know It used in CHAT ROOMS, EMAILS, and NEWSGROUPS.

term broadening The process of replacing a word used in a SEARCH QUERY by more abstract words in order to broaden the search space examined by a SEARCH ENGINE.

term narrowing The process of replacing a broad, descriptive word in a SEARCH QUERY by one which is more specific. This enables the user of a SEARCH ENGINE to home in on a particular set of results.

terminal A device consisting of a keyboard and a monitor that allows the user to contact and send data and messages to another computer on a network. A rather dated term which is rapidly going out of use.

terminal emulation The process of using a computer to pretend to or to emulate a TERMINAL, often a DUMB TERMINAL. This is usually achieved using emulation software.

terminal server A SERVER which provides access to a TCP-IP network for DUMB TERMINALS. Such a server usually uses some subset of the TCP-IP protocol to enable the terminal to log-in to the network and to access it.

terminator A hardware device which is placed at the end of a transmission line in a network. Its function is to absorb signals so that they do not bounce back into the network and cause errors.

text anchor A section of text in an HTML document which, when clicked by the user of a BROWSER, displays the WEB PAGE referred to by the URL associated with the anchor. Text anchors can appear by themselves on a Web page or can be embedded in normal text. *See also* GRAPHIC ANCHOR, and IMAGE MAP.

text area A term sometimes used for a TEXT BOX. It often refers to a text box which has space for more than one row of text.

text box A rectangular area found in a WINDOW or a WEB PAGE into which text can be typed, for example when communicating a PASSWORD.

text file A FILE which contains only printable characters. For example it contains none of the control or interpretation characters used by a word processor.

text GIF A GIF graphic which contains only text with no other graphic embellishments. It is used when a Web designer is confident that the font employed for the text is not be found on the BROWSER which accesses the WEB PAGE where the graphic is found. Such GIF graphics are used for normal typographical purposes such as for headings and subheadings which, if the font is popular, is normally expressed in the HYPERTEXT MARKUP LANGUAGE.

text messaging A technology which enables mobile telephone users to send text messages to each other. Such messages are cheaper than normal phone calls. Because of the restricted nature of the phone's screen, users often have to resort to the use of ABBREVIATIONS in order to communicate. One popular name for this form of technology is SHORT MESSAGE SERVICE.

text-to-speech Usually employed as an adjective to describe technology that is used to convert text stored in files into simulated speech. This technology is often used by call centres when, for example, variable text such as a date is to be spoken.

TFH Abbreviation for Thread From Hell used in CHAT ROOMS, EMAILS, and NEWSGROUPS. This refers to a THREAD on a discussion group which rambles on even though most participants of the group are totally disinterested in it.

TFTP *See* TRIVIAL FILE TRANSFER PROTOCOL.

The Cyberskills Association A group of companies and education providers which was set up with pump priming money by the British government to promote awareness of the importance of Internet skills.

The Great Renaming In 1987 a number of NEWSGROUP administrators decided to reorganize the relatively small number of newsgroups that were then in existence; in particular they decided on the HIERARCHICAL NAMING convention that is currently used. This was known as the Great Renaming.

thesaurus A FILE which contains list of words. Each word in the list is associated with a number of other words semantically similar to it. A thesaurus is normally used by SEARCH ENGINES and word processors.

thick client A CLIENT which contains a lot of program code, with the client carrying out a large number of its functions rather than the SERVER which it connects to. Thick clients have the disadvantage of having to be frequently updated, a complicated task if there are a large number of them spread around a network.

thick ethernet An alternative term for TBASE5 wiring.

thicknet A term occasionally used to describe thick COAXIAL CABLE.

thin client A CLIENT which contains a small amount of code compared to the quantity of code found on the SERVER which provides the service to the client. Thin clients are associated with FAT SERVERS. They have the advantage of not needing to be updated very frequently; this is in contrast to THICK CLIENTS.

thin ethernet Another name for TBASE2 wiring.

thinnet A slang term for TBASE2 wiring.

thin server The SERVER side of a CLIENT SERVER COMPUTING application where the bulk of the code resides on the client. A FILE SERVER is a good example of a thin server.

third-generation Web site A WEB SITE which includes both text, GRAPHIC IMAGES, ANIMATIONS, and EXECUTABLE CONTENT such as APPLETS. Such Web sites started appearing in the mid-1990s. See also FIRST-GENERATION WEB SITE, SECOND-GENERATION WEB SITE, and FOURTH-GENERATION WEB SITE.

third-level domain The domain which lies below the SECOND-LEVEL DOMAIN in the INTERNET DOMAIN NAME SERVICE. For example in the domain open.sys.deep.com, sys would be the third-level domain. See also HIERARCHICAL NAMING.

third-party processor A company which carries out normal credit card tasks such as authorization and account debiting for an organization—usually a bank or finance house—that issues credit cards.

thread A series of POSTINGS to a NEWSGROUP which all refer to one topic. The term is also used in software development to refer to a segment of code which can be executed in parallel with other segments.

three-dimensional graphics Graphics which are displayed in three dimensions. There has been a paucity of graphics which display pictures in three dimension on the Internet. This has been because of the amount of BANDWIDTH that such graphics occupy, resulting in slow DOWNLOAD times. However, the late 1990s saw a resurgence in this technology due to an increase in bandwidth and also due to a rise in the number of technologies which take cognizance of problems with downloading, such as STREAMING TECHNOLOGY. See also VIRTUAL REALITY MODELLING LANGUAGE.

three-tier model A model of CLIENT SERVER COMPUTING where much of the functionality of a system resides in a software layer which is interposed between the software found on the CLIENT (the first layer) and the software found on the SERVER (the second layer). An example of this type of model is a database application which responds to queries entered by staff who use client computers. The middle tier would be sent different messages by the client depending on the functionality required. It would then decode these messages and ask software which resided on the server to satisfy the request. The data that satisfied the request would then be sent back through this layer to the clients. Because much of the functionality of the application lies in the middle tier, changes to the system can be achieved quickly and efficiently. For example, a change to the database software on the server only requires small changes to the software in the middle tier that communicated the clients' intentions. Systems built using the three-tier model are more robust and extensible than those built using a TWO-TIER MODEL.

throughput The amount of data that can be transferred through a network within a certain time period. See also BANDWIDTH.

throwaway account An ACCOUNT which is acquired from an INTERNET SERVICE PROVIDER for the sole purpose of sending SPAM. Such accounts are temporary: they are used for a number of spams and then either the ISP shuts them down or the perpetrator of the spam moves to another throwaway account.

throwaway email address An EMAIL address which is used to receive unwanted emails. One way to minimize the amount of SPAM received is to use such an address when POSTING to a NEWSGROUP. Spammers who use ADDRESS HARVESTERS would pick up this address and then direct spam mail to it. If email directed to this address is never read, then, theoretically, there is no problem with spam. After a time any emails to this address are deleted by the INTERNET SERVICE PROVIDER which normally uses programs to release file space from user accounts with unread mail that has been in existence for some time. With the increase in the number of providers supplying multiple email addresses this has become a feasible way of handling unwanted email.

thumb The slider on a SCROLL BAR used to browse through the contents of a window. It is used in a BROWSER to read the text of a WEB PAGE.

thumbnail image A small graphic embedded in a WEB PAGE. Normally the thumbnail contains a HYPERLINK to a much larger version of the graphic. Thumbnails are used to expedite the fast loading of a WEB PAGE since a small image occupies very much less memory than a large one. If a user wants to see the large image, all he or she needs do is click the thumbnail. Those users who are not interested in the image are not bothered by a long download time when the page containing the thumbnail is transferred to the browser across a network.

Thunderbolt A highly secure ENCRYPTION ALGORITHM used by the British government.

TIA Abbreviation for Thanks In Advance used in EMAILS and NEWSGROUPS.

TIAIL Abbreviation for Think I Am In Love used in CHAT ROOMS, EMAILS, and NEWSGROUPS.

TIC Abbreviation for Tongue In Cheek used in CHAT ROOMS, EMAILS, and NEWSGROUPS.

tick box A WIDGET which allows a user to select whether a particular option or mode is to be switched on or off. A tick box is shaped like a box and displays a tick when the option is on. Usually tick boxes are used in conjunction with a number of other tick boxes.

tickler email An EMAIL which is sent out in order to check a connection to an email user or to a MAILING LIST. It usually contains a request for a brief reply.

Tier 1 ISP An INTERNET SERVICE PROVIDER with a direct connection to the Internet. *See also* TIER N ISP.

tiered service A commercial service offered by an ECOMMERCE organization on the WORLD WIDE WEB which has a number of levels of charging. For example, a company running a WEB SITE that offers stock price information may offer end-of-day prices free, hourly prices for a small fee, and continually updated prices for a much larger fee.

tier n ISP An INTERNET SERVICE PROVIDER with a connection to a tier n-1 service provider. For example, a tier 2 ISP has a connection to a TIER 1 ISP.

TIFF *See* TAGGED IMAGE FILE FORMAT.

tiger team A team of HACKERS who are hired to explore the weaknesses of a network by a company.

tilde The $\sim$ character.

TILII Abbreviation for Tell It Like It Is used in CHAT ROOMS, EMAILS and NEWSGROUPS.

time bomb A program illegally inserted into a computer which, at a specified time, carries out some destructive act such as deleting important files. Reputedly these programs are often planted by disgruntled employees who have left the company whose computer they have infected with the time bomb.

time server A SERVER used to coordinate the local clocks on the servers connected to a network.

time stamp Time data attached to a message or TRANSACTION in a DISTRIBUTED SYSTEM which provides information about when they were created. Time stamps are occasionally referred to by the jargon term NONCE.

time stamping certificate A DIGITAL CERTIFICATE which provides validation that a certain event occurred at or after a specific time. There are a number of uses for this technology including the process of establishing copyright.

time to live The time period that a DATA-GRAM can remain on a TCP-IP network before it is destroyed.

timing attack An attack on a system which is based on the attacker timing how long the ENCRYPTION and DECRYPTION process takes.

TLA A self-referential abbreviation for Three Letter Acronym used in EMAILS and NEWSGROUPS.

TLS *See* TRANSPORT LAYER SECURITY.

TMI Abbreviation for Too Much Information used in CHAT ROOMS, EMAILS, and NEWSGROUPS.

TMTOWTDI Abbreviation for There's More Than One Way To Do It used in CHAT ROOMS, EMAILS, and NEWSGROUPS. Invented by Larry Wall, the author of the PERL programming language.

TNT Abbreviation for To the Next Time used in EMAILS and NEWSGROUPS, normally for finishing a message or POSTING.

TNX Abbreviation for Thanks used in CHAT ROOMS, EMAILS, and NEWSGROUPS.

toast Used either as a verb or a noun in connection with the CRASH of a computer in a network, for example, 'The satellite computer is toast' or 'I have toasted the satellite computer.' Similar in use to the word FRIED.

toasternet Jargon used to describe a low-cost network used by a small community.

token A form of DIGITAL CASH generated by an enterprise, usually a bank, which is used as payment for a product bought over the Internet. The token is validated by the issuer applying a digital stamp. When the customer who holds the tokens wishes to make a payment for a product he or she sends the serial number of the tokens that are used. These are sent to the issuer by the merchant, who is then credited with a sum equal to the token amounts, and the tokens are withdrawn from circulation. Any attempt to respend them fails. Tokens and token payment schemes are still in their infancy and are currently experimental.

token card A small hardware device which often resembles a pocket calculator or credit card and which generates ONE-TIME PASSWORDS.

token ring A PROTOCOL developed by IBM for LOCAL AREA NETWORKS that is based on the passing of packets known as tokens around a network.

toll connecting trunk The name given to a transmission line which joins an END OFFICE to a TOLL OFFICE.

toll office A major exchange in a telephone system which is connected to a number of END OFFICE exchanges.

Tomcat This is a prototype WEB SERVER which forms part of the APACHE project. It is an implementation designed for testing SERVLETS and JAVA SERVER PAGES.

toolbar A collection of icons displayed horizontally on a WINDOW. Each icon corresponds to one FUNCTION of the software which can be exercised by the user: for example, the toolbar on a BROWSER contains an icon which enables the user to stop the transfer of a WEB PAGE.

Toolkit Without an Interesting Name An alternative name for TECHNOLOGY WITHOUT AN INTERESTING NAME.

TOPCA Abbreviation for Till Our Paths Cross Again used in EMAILS and NEWSGROUPS. It is usually used to terminate a message.

Topclick A small SEARCH ENGINE which prides itself on respecting the privacy of its users. For example, it does not issue information about its visitors and does not store COOKIES.

topic drift This occurs in a NEWSGROUP when a POSTING in a THREAD drifts away from the original point of the discussion. A MODERATOR may attempt to bring back the thread or even KILL it.

top-level domain The domain which lies at the top of a HIERARCHICAL NAMING scheme. For example, in the INTERNET DOMAIN NAME SERVICE there are a number of top-level domains such as COM, EDU, GOV, and NET.

topology The layout of a computer network in terms of the number and type of connections made between the computers and the types of computer used.

tortoise site A WEB SITE which contains pages that have such a large amount of processor-intensive technology embedded in them that it takes a long time to DOWN-LOAD pages from the site into a BROWSER. Such technology includes VIDEO CLIPS and ANIMATIONS. *See also* ANGRY FRUIT SALAD and DANCING BALONEY.

tossing out The ejection of someone from an ISP for violating CHAT ROOM rules or some other violation of the ISP's conditions of service.

tourist The user of a NETWORK such as an EXTRANET or INTRANET who is a guest and who has not been allocated an account.

tourist information Information produced by a program which is not directly useful, but provides some information about the functioning of the program. The blue bar which is shown at the bottom of a BROWSER as it DOWNLOADS a WEB PAGE, giving an indication of how far the download has proceeded, is an example of tourist information.

TOY Abbreviation for Thinking Of You used in CHAT ROOMS, EMAILS, and NEWS-GROUPS.

TP *See* TRANSACTION PROCESSING.

TP monitor A common name for a TRANSACTION PROCESSING MONITOR.

TPA *See* TRADING PARTNER AGREEMENT.

TPTB Abbreviation for The Powers That Be used in CHAT ROOMS, EMAILS, and NEWS-GROUPS.

tracker A program which tracks events on the Internet and informs users if something they are interested in has happened. For example DEJANEWS has a tracker which notifies a user when nominated topics are mentioned in a POSTING to a NEWSGROUP.

trading partner A company involved in sending or receiving data which is defined by an ELECTRONIC DATA INTERCHANGE standard.

trading partner agreement An agreement between two companies who wish to do business together: for example, to jointly develop and market some product. If the companies need to exchange some data over a network then they enter into a trading partner agreement. This describes what data will be passed between the companies and the format of this data. Companies have found producing such an agreement a slow process—certainly too slow for the current commercial climate where speed is of the essence in bringing products to market. Because of this, a number of EDI standards have been proposed. Almost certainly the most advanced of these is OPEN EDI.

traffic The data flowing through a network, including EMAILS, pages transferred from a WEB SERVER to a BROWSER, or large FILES being dispensed by FILE SERVERS. It can also include data which is used by the network in order to carry out its function: for example, MESSAGES sent between servers holding replicated databases which keep the databases in step.

traffic control The process of modifying the parameters or TOPOLOGY of a network in order to adjust the traffic flow. This can be a fairly frequent process if the network is a large one. The major aim of traffic control is to avoid CHOKE POINTS.

traffic logging system A system comprising hardware and software which writes data about the traffic in a network to a log file. Such data can then be used by a NETWORK ADMINISTRATOR to carry out the process of TRAFFIC CONTROL.

transaction An action which is associated with a database. That action might be the execution of a QUERY, such as finding those customers in a banking database who have an overdraft, or it may be an update in which the database changes, such as a transaction which updates a manufacturing database when some new components have been delivered. A transaction which is associated with a series of databases on a number of servers is known as a DISTRIBUTED TRANSACTION. Making sure that a transaction which consists of a number of smaller transactions is carried out correctly is a complex process which is carried out by software known as TRANSACTION PROCESSING MONITORS.

transactional certificate A DIGITAL CERTIFICATE which demonstrates that a certain incident has occurred. For example, such a certificate might be associated with the transmission of an EMAIL in order to authenticate the fact that the sender of the email was who he or she claimed to be.

transactional commerce Applications which integrate real-time interactivity with information held in an ECOMMERCE organization's database. An example of this type of application occurs in the delivery industry, where a customer can track a parcel via a WEB PAGE in real time by consulting the dispatch database of the company carrying out the deliveries.

transactional email An email which allows the recipient to buy goods without visiting a website. The body of the email will usually contain items for sale and include facilities for selecting an item to buy and submitting an order. Proponents of this form of e-commerce claim that it is much more successful than commercial Web sites.

transaction processing The process of executing a TRANSACTION so that it leaves a DISTRIBUTED SYSTEM in the proper state. For example, a transaction often consists of a number of other transactions and the software that carries out transaction processing should ensure that no transaction interferes with another transaction to leave the system in an erroneous state. *See also* TRANSACTION PROCESSING MONITOR and ACID.

transaction processing monitor A program which administers TRANSACTIONS that affect a number of databases. Typical functions that a transaction monitor carries out include sending transactions to servers to execute them, balancing the load across a number of servers, and enforcing the ACID properties of transactions. They are frequently referred to as TP monitors.

transaction server A SERVER that contains a database. The CLIENT that communicates with the server executes a program on the server which then initiates statements written in the STRUC-TURED QUERY LANGUAGE that return with the data requested by the client.

transfer interrupted A message that is sometimes displayed when the DOWNLOAD of a WEB PAGE into a BROWSER is interrupted, usually because of a system error or because the user has manually stopped the download.

transform encoding A SOURCE ENCODING technique used to achieve COMPRESSION of data. It uses a mathematical function to characterize the data, the function being stored in a much smaller memory than the data. Transform encoding is often used to compress images.

transit network A network which passes traffic to and from other networks as well as carrying messages and data for the computers that are connected to it.

Transmission Control Protocol A major protocol within TCP-IP. It carries out the process of assembling data from applications that run on the Internet, collecting up this data into packets and ensuring that they are transferred safely to their destination. It works in conjunction with the INTERNET PROTOCOL (IP).

transmission line A WIDE AREA NETWORK consists of switching elements, which direct the flow of PACKETS in the network, and transmission lines. These transmission lines can be implemented in a wide variety of media ranging from wireless transmission bands to phone lines. They are also known as CIRCUITS, CHANNELS, or TRUNKS.

transmission rate A little-used term to describe the rate at which data flows through a network.

transparency The property that makes the user of a network unaware of the fact that they are interacting with a network. The truly transparent system gives the impression to the user that they are interacting with a single computer. An example of transparency occurs when a system consists of data which is replicated over a number of SERVERS. When a user interacts with this data, he or she should be unaware of which file they are using and which server is servicing their requests.

transparent GIF A GIF graphic which has one colour designated as a transparent colour. When a BROWSER displays the graphic the colour becomes the same as the browser background and hence provides a transparent effect. Transparency was one of the major features introduced in the GIF89A standard.

transport layer A layer in the OSI REFERENCE MODEL and the TCP-IP architecture. It carries out the process of establishing, prioritizing, maintaining, and terminating the communication between two computers on a network. It also has the function of checking that data sent from one computer to another has correctly reached its destination.

Transport Layer Security An effort by the INTERNET ENGINEERING TASK FORCE to standardize the SECURE SOCKETS LAYER (SSL). The documents so far released by the IETF on this standard indicate that it will be very similar to SSL and backward compatible with it.

transposition cipher A form of ENCRYPTION which involves the scrambling of symbols in a PLAIN TEXT. When this process is applied twice it is known as a DOUBLE TRANSPOSITION CIPHER.

trapdoor A device placed in an ENCRYPTION scheme that allows someone to read easily any messages that have been encrypted. There has, for example, been a suspicion in the computing community that there is a trapdoor within the DATA ENCRYPTION STANDARD developed by the US government which allows agencies of the government to read messages.

tree network A network TOPOLOGY which contains features of a BUS NETWORK and a STAR NETWORK. It consists of groups of devices connected to a CONCENTRATOR with each group attached to a bus.

treeware Anything made from paper including books, manuals, and letters. *See also* SNAIL MAIL *and* PMAIL.

trellis coding A technique used in MODEMS in order to reduce the number of errors in transmission.

trep A short version of entrepreneur. *See also* ENTREPRENERD.

trigger An action taken by a DATABASE SERVER when data stored in the SERVER is changed. For example, when a new customer is entered into a bank database, a trigger is activated which sends information about the customer and the client which carried out the process of creating the customer, to an AUDIT FILE. A trigger which carries out data validation, for example checking that a user has typed in a correct account number for a banking application, is known as a RULE.

Triple DES An ENCRYPTION scheme which involves applying the DES algorithm to a text three times.

tripwire software Software which monitors system activities and informs a SYSTEM ADMINISTRATOR whenever an unusual event happens, for example a user trying to LOG-IN a number of times and failing. Such software can be easily modified to cater for different events and their different frequencies.

Trivial File Transfer Protocol A protocol which is used to transfer files over the Internet. It is one of the simplest and fastest protocols for this, although it has severe limitations. The main one is that since it is based on the USER DATAGRAM PROTOCOL there is no error checking: if an error occurs during a transfer, then the transfer normally fails completely. The main use for this protocol is for loading an operating system onto a computer in a network which does not already have an operating system installed and hence cannot make use of the powerful FTP protocol. *See* FILE TRANSFER PROTOCOL *and* DOWNLOAD. Often abbreviated to TFTP.

Trojan horse A VIRUS which infects a computer by masquerading as a normal system entity. For example, a virus which infects a computer by purporting to be a text file containing a Christmas card attached to an EMAIL is an example of a Trojan horse.

troll A member of a NEWSGROUP who makes deliberately provocative comments in order to provoke a FLAME WAR. The term derives from mainstream 'trolling', a style of fishing in which one trails bait through a likely spot hoping for a bite.

trunk An alternative name for a TRANS-MISSION LINE.

trunk segment Another name for a POPULATED SEGMENT.

Trusted Computer Security Evaluation Criteria A document published by the US Department of Defense which contains criteria used for evaluating the degree of security in a networked system. It characterizes security from D (the minimum) to A1 (very secure). Most OPERATING SYSTEMS and NETWORK OPERATING SYSTEMS are classified at the C2 level. It is also known as the Orange Book and is often abbreviated to TCSEC.

trusted third party An organization which interposes itself between two other entities who might themselves be individuals, companies, or other organizations. The two entities trust the third party to carry out some process which is in the best interests of all of them. For example, there are a number of trusted third parties who hold goods that are submitted for auction, check that they meet the description given by the goods' vendor, and only release the goods to the buyer and the funds to the vendor when the buyer has paid. Another example of this type of service is a KEY ESCROW service.

TTFN Abbreviation for Ta Ta For Now used in CHAT ROOMS, EMAILS, and NEWSGROUPS. It is usually used to sign off a message or POSTING.

TTL *See* TIME TO LIVE.

TTP *See* TRUSTED THIRD PARTY.

TTT Abbreviation for To The Top or Thought That Too used in CHAT ROOMS, EMAILS, and NEWSGROUPS.

TTYL Abbreviation for Talk To You Later used in CHAT ROOMS. It is usually used to sign off.

tunnelling The process of sending data expressed in one PROTOCOL but embedding the data within another protocol. One use of tunnelling is to send transmissions expressed in one protocol over the Internet embedded in the INTERNET PROTOCOL.

tunnelling router A ROUTER which allows two similar networks which are of the same type—for example they may be ETHERNETS—to communicate via a third different network. In order to do this they embed the message in a PACKET which is directed by the tunnelling router to its destination via the third network. The tunnelling router must hence have the capability of understanding the two PROTOCOLS: the protocol for the networks which are the sender and the destination and the protocol for the intermediary network.

turning blue Used to describe someone who has become a permanent employee of the Microsoft Corporation, named after the blue badge such employees wear. *See* BLUE BADGE.

TWAIN *See* TECHNOLOGY WITHOUT AN INTERESTING NAME or TOOLKIT WITHOUT AN INTERESTING NAME.

tweening A computer-supported ANIMATION technique where the computer fills in intermediate frames in an animation given a start frame and a finish frame. For example, if the start frame shows a person standing at a certain point and the end frame shows them in the air, the computer would then fill in (or tween) the frames which show the person jumping. *See also* MORPHING.

twiddle A jargon term for the TILDE character ~.

twink Slang for a user with limited intellectual capabilities.

twisted pair cabling Cabling that contains two wires twisted together and is surrounded by an insulating material. The wires are twisted together in order to reduce electrical interference. Such wires can achieve speeds of several Mbits/s over a small number of kilometres. There are two sorts of twisted cable: UNSHIELDED TWISTED PAIR CABLE and SHIELDED TWISTED PAIR CABLE.

two-phase commit protocol A PROTOCOL used when a DISTRIBUTED TRANSACTION contains a number of operations which require a number of SERVERS to operate in conjunction with each other. The transaction ensures that if all the servers involved in the transaction are able to carry out their part then the transaction is carried out; if one or more servers are unable to carry out their part, then the transaction is aborted.

two-tier model A model of CLIENT SERVER COMPUTING where the logic for an application is either found in the graphical user interface of the CLIENT or in a database found on the server. This architecture is being gradually superseded by the THREE-TIER MODEL which is more robust and more extensible.

TX Abbreviation for Thanks used in CHAT ROOMS, EMAILS, and NEWSGROUPS.

typo domain A DOMAIN which has almost the same name as another more famous domain, but which contains typographic differences, such as micros0ft.com. Domains such as these are used to attract customers who might have visited the better-known domain.

typo pirate A user who registers a TYPO DOMAIN.

TYVM Abbreviation for Thank You Very Much used in CHAT ROOMS, EMAILS, and NEWSGROUPS.

ubiquitous computing Used to describe a future where computers are so numerous they affect every action we take. This includes computers that are part of our clothing and which monitor our vital functions, computers which control traffic, computers which are integrated with television sets, and computers that control our homes.

UDP *See* UNRELIABLE DATAGRAM PROTOCOL.

unconfirmed service A service which is provided by a LAYER in a LAYERED ARCHITECTURE such as the INTERNET LAYERED ARCHITECTURE where some confirmatory response from an entity is not required. For example, disconnecting a computer in a network is an unconfirmed service.

under mouse arrest Describes a customer of an ISP who has been suspended for violating the rules of the ISP: for example, for carrying out SPAMMING or exhibiting objectionable behaviour in a CHAT ROOM.

Undernet An INTERNET RELAY CHAT network which seceded from the IRC network.

undocumented feature A FUNCTION of a computer program which is not described in any of its documentation. There are a number of reasons why programs have undocumented features, ranging from incompetence in developing user documentation, to the fact that the feature has not been adequately tested by the developer, who feels that it should not currently be used by customers.

unicast address One of the main groups of addresses used in the IPV6 PROTOCOL.

Unicode A standard for a set of characters which is intended to support written texts expressed in a large number of languages from Europe, America, Asia, India, and the Pacific Rim. Version 2 of the standard contains 38,885 different characters.

uniform resource citation A set of pairs of data which describe an object embedded in a WEB SITE. They describe properties such as the author of the site and the copyright status of the site.

uniform resource locator More commonly referred to as a URL. An address used by Web BROWSERS in order to locate a resource on the Web. An anchor in a WEB PAGE specifies the URL a browser will transfer to when the link associated with the URL is clicked. There are three parts to a URL: the protocol designator that specifies which protocol is to be used, the location of the WEB SERVER on which a resource is held, and a path name to that resource through the file system of the server. So, for example, the UNIFORM RESOURCE LOCATOR address http://www. op.ac.uk/SWeb/M874 refers to the protocol HTTP that is used for transferring Web pages; the server location is designated by the name of the Web server (www) and the DOMAIN where it can be found (op. ac.uk); and the final part designates the path to the file M874, the HOME PAGE file, which is in the directory SWeb. This is the normal format of a URL, sometimes extra information is added associated with queries that might be processed by programs which interact with the COMMON GATEWAY INTERFACE. The URL might also differ in that another PROTOCOL might be specified: for example, ftp would replace http if the link was to an FTP SERVER rather than to another Web page.

uninstall To remove a program from a computer so that it cannot be executed again. It is also used in a non-technical sense when it means to be sacked, as in 'I was uninstalled from my company yesterday.'

unique visitor A term used in WEB ADVERTISING to describe a visitor to a WEB SITE who can be identified by information provided by them, usually via a REGISTRATION FORM.

universal messaging service A service which provides the user with a single phone number to which FAXes and voice messages can be sent. The service then converts them into EMAILS and sends them to the user.

UNIX One of the earliest and longest-lasting OPERATING SYSTEMS. It has an entry in this dictionary for two reasons. The first is historical: most of the protocols that are used on the Internet, including the TRANSMISSION CONTROL PROTOCOL and the INTERNET PROTOCOL, were initially developed for UNIX since its program code was readily available and because it is an easy operating system to modify. The second reason is that one of its derivatives, BSD UNIX, has become one of the two most common Internet programming platforms. *See also* LINUX.

unmarshalling This is the opposite of MARSHALLING: it is the process whereby data which has been sent over a network is reconstituted into its original form. For example, if an object produced by an OBJECT-ORIENTED PROGRAMMING LANGUAGE has been marshalled into a form suitable for transmission to another computer, it is unmarshalled and returned to its original form by software on the computer to which it is sent.

unmoderated newsgroup A NEWS-GROUP to which POSTINGS are sent without any filtering being applied to check, for example, that the posting is relevant to the subject of the newsgroup. *See also* MODERATED NEWSGROUP.

UnPC Abbreviation for UnPolitically Correct used in CHAT ROOMS, EMAILS, and NEWSGROUPS.

Unreliable Datagram Protocol A term sometimes used for the USER DATA PROTOCOL.

unshielded twisted pair cable The cable that is used to connect devices in a LOCAL AREA NETWORK. It is often referred to as UTP and it consists of four pairs of cables which are twisted with a different number of pairs per inch in order to minimize interference. A major disadvantage of this type of cable is that it may react to radio or electrical interference. A version

of this cabling known as SHIELDED TWISTED PAIR CABLE has been developed to overcome the problems with electrical interference.

unzip The process of decompressing a file which has been compressed using ZIP technology.

update bot A BOT that notifies a user when a specific event has occurred which is associated with a change in a stored data. For example, a bot which notifies a user when a new book on a particular subject is published would be placed in this category, as would a bot which informs a user when a WEB SITE is updated.

upgrade fever The irresistible urge to upgrade to more powerful hardware or more function-laden software even when there is no logical reason for such a decision.

upload The process of copying a FILE from a CLIENT to a SERVER; it is the opposite of DOWNLOAD. For example, when you transfer a WEB SITE which has been prepared on a CLIENT to the WEB SERVER that is to host the site, this is called uploading the site to the Web server.

URC *See* UNIFORM RESOURCE CITATION.

URL *See* UNIFORM RESOURCE LOCATOR.

URL redirection The process whereby a visitor to a WEB PAGE is redirected to another page—often after a short delay. The main reason for URL redirection occurring is because the address of the WEB SITE being accessed has changed. The process of redirection can be carried out by the WEB SERVER or by text placed in a METATAG in the old HOME PAGE of the Web site.

usage software Software that discovers details of the use that is made of a WEB SITE. Such software provides data such as the most frequently visited page in a site, the way visitors move through a Web site, and where visitors come from. This information is primarily used for marketing purposes, although it can also be used to optimize a Web site for performance. *See also* WEB LOG FILE.

Usenet The collective term given to the NEWSGROUPS which are accessible via the Internet. There are now over 35,000 of these groups. They are organized using HIERARCHICAL NAMING, with a root name designating the nature of the discussions that occurs in such a group. For example, the newsgroups starting with the name comp are all devoted to computing topics. Users access Usenet newsgroups using NEWSREADERS and contribute POSTINGS (also known as ARTICLES). Some newsgroups are MODERATED NEWSGROUPS while others are UNMODERATED NEWS-GROUPS. A set of postings on a particular topic is known as a THREAD. In the early days of the Internet there were a number of predictions which stated that there would be no more than ten postings to Usenet newsgroups per day. This has now been greatly exceeded.

Usenet death penalty A sanction against computers and users who send SPAM to Usenet NEWSGROUPS. It effectively bars them from sending anything to a newsgroup.

User Datagram Protocol A term that is usually employed for the USER DATA PROTOCOL.

User Data Protocol An Internet PROTO-COL used for transporting data across a TCP-IP network. Its main advantage is speed. However, it suffers from the fact that it does not provide any facilities for reliability checking. This means that if data is sent using this protocol there is no guarantee that it will arrive correctly, or in the order in which it is sent out. Some applications do use the protocol, but they normally have error checking programmed into them or transport data for which it is unimportant if a small amount is lost, such as voice data. A notable Internet application which uses this protocol is the DOMAIN NAME SERVICE.

user group A collection of users who are allowed collective access to a set of resources in a DISTRIBUTED SYSTEM. For example, the members of the accounting department of a company may be given permission to read files which contain the financial data that they all require in order to carry out their job.

user identifier A unique set of characters given to the user of a computer system or network which uniquely identifies the user. Also called a USER NAME.

user name A unique set of characters given to the user of a computer system or network which uniquely identifies the user. Also called a user identifier.

UTC *See* COORDINATED UNIVERSAL TIME.

UTP *See* UNSHIELDED TWISTED PAIR CABLE.

UUCP A freely available tool for transferring files and sending mail on the UNIX operating system.

UUDECODE A method for converting an ASCII file to a BINARY FILE. *See also* UUEN-CODE.

UUENCODE A tool for converting BINARY FILES to ASCII format. One use for the tool is for posting FILES to NEWSGROUPS.

V2V Abbreviation for Voice to Voice used in CHAT ROOMS, EMAILS, and NEWSGROUPS. It is usually used to invite another user to either meet or phone the sender.

vaccine An anti-virus program which checks that programs on a computer have not been modified by a VIRUS.

validating XML parser A program which checks the source of a document expressed in the EXTENSIBLE MARKUP LANGUAGE against its DOCUMENT TYPE DEFINITION (DTD). It checks, for example, that the source syntactically matches the description given in the DTD and provides facilities for program code to be executed when various TAGS are encountered. This is in contrast to NON-VALIDATING XML PARSERS which carry out a rudimentary validation.

value-added network A network which is formed when two or more enterprises want to communicate with each other in order to add value to a service or a product. It normally involves connecting two or more CLOSED NETWORKS together with Internet technology. An example of a value-added network would be one which connected a manufacturer with the suppliers of components used in the products made by the manufacturer. The term is often used to denote the fact that the networks are connected across a publicly accessible network such as the Internet, although it has been used for VALUE-ADDED PRIVATE NETWORKS.

value-added private network This is a VALUE-ADDED NETWORK which is not connected using a publicly accessible network such as the Internet.

vampire tap A connection that was made to a TBASE5 cable. It involved a pin being forced into the cable in order for it to contact the central conductor.

VAN *See* VALUE-ADDED NETWORK.

vandalware Software which has been developed for malicious intent: for example, VIRUS software. Also known as MALWARE.

vanilla An adjective used to describe the basic version of a piece of software or hardware with no sophisticated FUNCTIONS or features.

vanity domain A DOMAIN which has the same name as its owner, such as George-Williams@George.co.uk.

Vannevar A completely inaccurate technological prediction or concept. Named after the distinguished American researcher Vannevar Bush who predicted that computers would need to be the size of the Empire State Building in order to cope with the heat dissipation demands of their vacuum tubes. To be fair to Bush, he was very accurate with other technologies. For example, he predicted the use of HYPERMEDIA and an interpretation of some of his works would ascribe to him a prediction of the WORLD WIDE WEB.

vapourware A product, usually software, which has been announced but has not yet been released to customers.

VBScript A subset of the programming language Visual Basic, a language developed by Microsoft. The main use of VBScript is for BROWSER programming where it is a competitor to JAVASCRIPT. It is used to add intelligence to Web pages or to enhance the pages in some way, for example by providing ANIMATION facilities. VBScript, along with Javascript, tends to be the language chosen when programming simple browser enhancements.

VCalendar A standard for a data interchange format which allows applications concerned with calendar and task functions to swap data. For example, it would allow one meeting scheduler and diary system to interchange data with a different system developed by another vendor.

VCard A standard for the interchange of data normally found on business cards, such as the holder's name, address, and telephone number. *See also* VCALENDAR.

vector graphic A graphic which is stored as a series of mathematical instructions which are then used to draw the picture. Drawing a vector graphic is more complicated than drawing a BITMAPPED GRAPHIC. However, vector graphics have one big advantage over bitmapped graphics: they can be scaled without any loss of resolution. Vector graphic formats are not directly supported on BROWSERS as opposed to GIF and JPEG graphics which are both bitmapped; however, they are supported indirectly via PLUG-INS.

vector image Another name for a VECTOR GRAPHIC.

Veronica An early SEARCH ENGINE developed at the University of Nevada. Its main use was to search for documents on the embryonic Internet. It is now of only historical significance.

version control The administration and maintenance of a number of files used in a system as it is being developed or as it evolves. Version control is not restricted to the Internet: it has been one of the central disciplines of software project management since the 1960s. Normally version control has been confined to the maintenance of information on software, but the advent of large WEB SITES has meant that many of the disciplines associated with version control are being applied to WEB PAGES. There are a number of programs which carry out version control of HTML files: they are either stand-alone software or are integrated into an HTML EDITOR or HTML AUTHOR. A typical tool maintains information including the version number of the page, which designer is currently working on the page, the changes that are currently being applied, and the date when the page is due for completion.

version rollback attack An attack on a computer system which uses an insecure feature of an old version of a PROTOCOL. This occurs because new versions of protocols will often contain many of the features and software of an old version.

vertical application A software system developed for a specific set of customers, such as a practice management system for doctors.

vertical portal A PORTAL which has more focused content than a normal portal. For example, a portal which concentrated on travel information and holiday bookings would be described as a vertical portal.

verti port A commonly used contraction of VERTICAL PORTAL.

vesting The ownership of maturing stock options in a company. As the time to maturity gets closer staff who are vested often start to mentally disengage themselves from their work.

video clip A series of images which are animated by a program. A WEB SITE sometimes contains video clips which are animated by means of a PLUG-IN. Video clips should be used with discretion, as they can occupy a large amount of space and hence slow down the loading of the WEB PAGE in which they are embedded. STREAMING TECHNOLOGY aims to minimize this problem.

video conferencing The process of conducting a conference between two or more participants over a network in such a way that the faces and upper bodies of the participants are visible. POINT-TO-POINT VIDEO CONFERENCING involves just two participants, while MULTIPOINT VIDEO CONFERENCING involves three or more. The most popular technology for video conferencing is currently CU SEEME.

video on demand The use of a network to provide individual users with the ability to view, stop, and rewind a video using a device connected to the network, where the video is stored and dispensed from a central location. This ideal can only be reached if each viewer has a separate copy of the video. This places major storage, transmission rate, and software demands upon a network.

video plug-in A PLUG-IN used to enable BROWSERS to display VIDEO CLIPS.

video streaming The animation of a VIDEO CLIP as it is being sent to a BROWSER in REAL TIME. This improves the LOAD TIME of the WEB PAGE over that experienced with older video technologies where the whole of the video clip had to be transferred to the browser before it could be played.

viewer An application which displays text or graphics that has been produced using an internal format such as the GRAPHICS INTERCHANGE FORMAT or the PORTABLE DOCUMENT FORMAT. These are HELPER APPLICATIONS or PLUG-INS which often work in conjunction with a BROWSER.

viral marketing Used to describe the word-of-mouth marketing of a product or service using the Internet. A good example of this approach was the marketing of the *HotMail* free email service. Subscribers to this service could only send emails with advertising messages extolling the virtues of *HotMail* at the bottom of the email text.

virtual Adjective used to describe an experience or entity which is a simulation of something real: for example, VIRTUAL COMMUNITY and VIRTUAL CORPORATION. As the entries in this dictionary testify, it is a fairly commonly used adjective.

virtual bank A bank which has no physical branches but carries out business over the Internet and via automatic teller machines.

virtual community A group of network users who are linked by some specific area of interest such as GENEALOGY. A variety of technologies are used to link members of such communities together including EMAILS, BULLETIN BOARDS, MAILING LISTS, and NEWSGROUPS. They are also known as an ONLINE COMMUNITY.

virtual corporation A company which is formed from one or more companies, often to carry out a specific business project such as the development of a new plane. Virtual corporations formed from physically distant companies have been made possible by much of the technology associated with the Internet, WORLD WIDE WEB, and DISTRIBUTED SYSTEMS. Indeed it would be impossible to create anything but the most trivial virtual corporation without such technology.

virtual dial-up A form of access to the Internet which supports the use of PROTOCOLS other than TCP-IP.

virtual museum A WEB SITE run by a conventional museum which displays its works graphically.

Virtual PIN An unusual method of carrying out financial transactions over the Internet. It was devised by the company Virtual Holdings. A customer is given a virtual PIN which identifies them. The buying cycle for purchasing is as follows: the purchaser sends an order to a vendor together with his or her virtual PIN; the vendor transmits this PIN to an authorization company; the authorization company then contacts the customer asking if the vendor's charge is known to the customer; if the customer replies with the word YES then the transaction is allowed but if the reply is FRAUD then the transaction is illegal. This form of security relies on the huge difficulty in intercepting a number of different but related email messages.

virtual private line A service offered by a telephone company which offers many of the facilities of a DEDICATED LINE and which seems to the user to be a dedicated connection. However, the connection switches traffic over a number of telephone circuits. Such a connection is offered at a lower cost than a true dedicated connection.

virtual private network A network made up of two or more CLOSED NETWORKS linked together within an OPEN NETWORK such as the Internet. Such networks are used when an enterprise wants to substitute expensive leased phone lines that are used to connect networks which are physically separate for Internet connections. The links that are established between two closed networks employ

AUTHENTICATION technologies and EN-CRYPTION to ensure security, with the SECURE SOCKETS LAYER being a popular choice.

virtual reality The combination of animation, sound, and graphics which simulate some physical location such as a supermarket or the inside of a passenger plane. A typical use for this technology would be for an online supermarket where the customer walks around the shelves of the supermarket by clicking a mouse. *See* VIRTUAL REALITY MODELLING LANGUAGE.

Virtual Reality Modelling Language A programming language, often referred to as VRML, used to define three-dimensional VIRTUAL WORLDS which can be viewed using a conventional BROWSER or a VRML BROWSER. VRML is the three-dimensional equivalent of languages such as the HYPERTEXT MARKUP LANGUAGE and the STANDARDIZED GENERAL MARKUP LANGUAGE which deal with two dimensions. A typical application for VRML would be in providing the virtual environment of a supermarket which a shopper can wander around by using a mouse to choose the direction they want to travel. VRML worlds can be viewed in a conventional browser using a VRML PLUG-IN. Although programs can be developed in the language using a simple text editor, most users of VRML employ a VRML AUTHOR.

virtual reality theme park A collection of VIRTUAL REALITY programs found in the same place, for example as links in a WEB PAGE.

virtual safe deposit box An online service that offers secure electronic storage of documents or programs.

virtual server An account on a host server which is usually linked to the DOMAIN NAME associated with the server. The domain of any WEB SITE hosted by the server is preceded by the domain name of the company owning the real server. This is a cheap alternative to running your own WEB SERVER although response times to clients running BROWSERS are slower.

virtual store front Used in ECOMMERCE circles to describe WEB PAGES which present products for sale. Often a HOME PAGE acts as a virtual store front.

virtual world A product of VIRTUAL REALITY technology such as the VIRTUAL REALITY MODELLING LANGUAGE.

virus A computer program which enters a computer, usually via a network connection, and carries out a malicious act. This can range from the less serious, such as displaying a SPLASH SCREEN with an obscene message, to the potentially disastrous, such as deleting all the files on the computer's hard drive. A virus which enters a computer masquerading as something else such as an EMAIL from a friend or a useful program is known as a TROJAN HORSE. There are a number of categories of virus, including ADD-ON VIRUS, SHELL VIRUS, and INTRUSIVE VIRUS. Since 1996 the number of reported viruses found on the Internet has tripled.

virus detection software Programs which detect the intrusion of VIRUSES into a computer system. This type of software can be categorized into two types: software that is continually executed while a computer is running and software which is periodically executed to check for the presence of viruses. There are four main virus detection programs: ACTIVITY MONITORS, APPLICATION MONITORS, SCANNERS, and INTEGRITY CHECKERS.

virus signature Data written to an infected computer by a VIRUS which has infected it. Many viruses try and infect a computer time and time again and the virus signature is used by a virus to determine whether there is any need for re-infection.

visit The act of accessing a WEB SITE using a BROWSER. This access might involve the reading of a number of WEB PAGES. Sometimes it is used synonymously with HIT. Information about visits is useful to a company carrying out ECOMMERCE since, combined with other data such as the number of electronic orders made from the site, it provides information about marketing effectiveness.

Visual J++ The name of the version of JAVA which has been developed by Microsoft. It has been the subject of much controversy as Sun Microsystems, the original developer of the language, has claimed that it is a non-standard implementation which is designed to wreck the major design idea behind Java—that of portability over a number of OPERATING SYSTEMS.

visual tag A TAG in a MARKUP LANGUAGE which is used to format text. For example the <H1> tag in the HYPERTEXT MARKUP LANGUAGE displays its text in a large font. This type of tag differs from those tags such as METATAGS which just provide auxiliary information.

VJ++ *See* VISUAL J++.

voice grade line A technical term for a telephone line.

voice jail system A VOICE MAIL SYSTEM that is so badly designed and has so many sublevels that the user either gets lost or gives up.

voice mail system A computer-controlled system for the reception of phone calls. It takes the person who has phoned through a series of questions until the service that is required is located. A voice mail system either senses keys being pressed on the caller's telephone or recognizes simple words such as 'yes'.

voice over IP A technical term for INTERNET TELEPHONY. Often abbreviated to VOIP.

voice recognition The process of recognizing the individual words which are spoken into a microphone. This technology made great strides in the 1990s and is incorporated into technologies such as VOICE MAIL SYSTEMS and UNIVERSAL MESSAGING SERVICES.

VOIP *See* VOICE OVER IP.

vortal An abbreviation for a VERTICAL PORTAL.

VPL *See* VIRTUAL PRIVATE LINE.

VPN *See* VIRTUAL PRIVATE NETWORK.

VRML *See* VIRTUAL REALITY MODELLING LANGUAGE.

VRML author A program used to create three-dimensional worlds using the VIRTUAL REALITY MODELLING LANGUAGE VRML.

VRML browser A special-purpose BROWSER which has been optimized so that it can view efficiently three-dimensional VIRTUAL WORLDS created using the VIRTUAL REALITY MODELLING LANGUAGE VRML.

VRML plug-in A PLUG-IN which enables a BROWSER to display the three-dimensional worlds developed using the VIRTUAL REALITY MODELLING LANGUAGE VRML.

VRWeb A BROWSER which can be used to examine three-dimensional worlds created by the VIRTUAL REALITY MODELLING LANGUAGE.

VSP or Vertical Service Provider A systems developer that produces applications for one specific area of the economy, for example banking.

VXML or Voice Extensible Markup Language A language defined by IBM, Lucent Technologies and Motorola which allows a user to interact with the Internet, primarily the Web, using voice commands.

vulture capitalist A derogatory term for a venture capitalist who takes advantage of the inventor of a particular technology or product.

W3 A frequently used abbreviation for the WORLD WIDE WEB.

W3C *See* WORLD WIDE WEB CONSORTIUM.

WAG Abbreviation for Wild Ass Guess used in CHAT ROOMS, EMAILS, and NEWS-GROUPS.

WAIS *See* WIDE AREA INFORMATION SERVERS.

wallet A technology used within a BROWSER when transactions are carried out over the Internet using a credit card. When a customer uses a credit card for a purchase he or she uses a PIN. This is passed from the merchant's computer system to the credit card company's computer, which decodes the PIN, retrieves the credit card holder's account, and then either authorizes or rejects the transaction. If it is authorized the merchant's account with the credit card company is increased by the amount of the transaction minus a transaction charge. An alternative wallet technology involves the ENCRYPTION of the credit card number and the use of a DIGITAL SIGNATURE. The use of wallet technology is more secure than conventional means of processing, in that it prevents the merchant's staff knowing the credit card number and using it for unauthorized transactions.

wallpaper The pattern shown on computer screens on which WINDOWS and other visual objects are placed.

WAMBAM *See* WEB APPLICATION MEETS BRICKS AND MORTAR.

WAN *See* WIDE AREA NETWORK.

WAN2 A HAKSPEK abbreviation for Want to used in CHAT ROOMS, EMAILS, and NEWS-GROUPS.

wanderer Another name for a SPIDER.

wankware Jargon for pornographic material found on the Internet. It usually refers to pictures and animations. *See also* PUBIC DIRECTORY.

WAP *See* WIRELESS APPLICATION PROTOCOL.

war dialler A program capable of producing long lists of numbers or other characters. They are used to generate entities such as telephone numbers or PASSWORDS for an intruder who wishes to enter a computer network illegally. *See also* SCANNING ATTACK.

war dialling Another name for a SCANNING ATTACK.

warez The collection of illegal files often found in a DEPOSITORY DIRECTORY. A typical warez file will contain pirated software.

warez doodz A group of Internet users who routinely crack the security protection of commercial software and post illegal copies on WAREZ sites. Such software has been modified so that anyone can use it without, for example, quoting a security PASSWORD or key.

warez kiddies A term of abuse for WAREZ DOODZ.

warlording The process of removing a SIG FILE from a user. There are a number of reasons why a SYSTEM ADMINISTRATOR might carry this out: two common reasons are that the file is too big or it contains obscene or racially offensive material. The term is derived from the nickname of the user who was reputedly the first to have his file removed.

warm boot The process of BOOTING a computer while its circuits and devices are warm. This normally occurs when the computer CRASHES during operation.

wavelength The distance between successive maxima or minima of an electromagnetic wave.

Wavelet A graphics COMPRESSION technology which holds out high promise for the future. It is still in the development labs but some early software, including

PLUG-INS for popular BROWSERS, have been developed.

WB Abbreviation for Welcome Back used in CHAT ROOMS, EMAILS, and NEWSGROUPS.

WBMP *See* WIRELESS BIT MAP.

WBS Abbreviation for Write Back Soon used in CHAT ROOMS, EMAILS, and NEWSGROUPS.

WCA Abbreviation for Who Cares Anyway used in CHAT ROOMS, EMAILS, and NEWSGROUPS.

WDALYIC Abbreviation for Who Died And Left You In Charge? used in CHAT ROOMS, EMAILS, and NEWSGROUPS.

WDYS Abbreviation for What Did You Say? used in CHAT ROOMS, EMAILS, and NEWSGROUPS.

WE Abbreviation for WhatEver used in CHAT ROOMS, EMAILS, and NEWSGROUPS.

weak encryption An ENCRYPTION ALGORITHM which can be broken within a time frame that would enable the breaker to take advantage of the information that has been encrypted.

wearable computing The integration of computers with clothing or other wearable artefacts such as sunglasses. The proponents of wearable computing claim that the PC has not fulfilled its usability promise and that the only solution is to more fully integrate the human user and the computer. This is still a research area within MOBILE COMPUTING.

weasel A naive or inexperienced user of the Internet.

weasel text A message found on a WEB SITE which explains why some facility of the site has been deleted.

Web A term that is often used when referring to the WORLD WIDE WEB.

web In 1997 the Internet Ad Hoc committee proposed a number of new names for DOMAINS. web is one of these and it represents Web services.

Web accelerator A utility which speeds up access to the WORLD WIDE WEB. It does this by trying to guess which WEB PAGES will be loaded while a user is browsing a page which contains links to these pages.

Web advertising The process of advertising a product or service on the WORLD WIDE WEB. This is normally carried out by means of BANNER ADVERTS which are DOWNLOADed from an ADVERT SERVER.

Web application meets bricks and mortar The development of WEB SITES by traditional companies such as Blackwell's Bookshops and Lands' End.

Web-based newsgroup service A service which provides an alternative to using a NEWSREADER. A Web-based newsgroup service accesses stored archives of NEWSGROUP postings on the Web. There are two advantages to using a Web-based service: first, POSTINGS can be accessed on any computer that has a browser; and, second, such services often contain massive archives which stretch well into the past, while many NEWSGROUP SERVERS delete postings after a few weeks or even a few days. The major disadvantage is that access using a browser is slower than that experienced by the user of a newsreader who connects to a newsgroup server. The most famous example of this type of service is DEJANEWS.

Web broker A financial broker who sells stocks and shares via the WORLD WIDE WEB.

WebbelGanger Someone or something that appears during a Web search using a SEARCH ENGINE, but is not what you are searching for.

Web brownout The decline in speed of Web access that occurs as more and more users employ the technology and more and more sites include material such as video clips which take a long time to DOWNLOAD.

Web cache A temporary store of WEB PAGES that a browser has examined. By keeping these pages in a file the browser enables the user to revisit a page without having to retransfer the page across the Internet. This speeds up the access to these pages.

Web cam Short for Web camera. A small, relatively cheap camera which broadcasts moving pictures on a WEB PAGE. For example, such a camera might broadcast scenes of traffic passing over a bridge, wild animals, or even everyday life in one room of a house. WEB SITES which feature Web cam pictures are often called Web cam sites.

Webcasting The use of the WORLD WIDE WEB for BROADCASTING material regularly to subscribers.

Webcrawler An early SEARCH ENGINE. It is of historical significance because it was one of the first engines to use a BOT to carry out its indexing and because it enabled users to access the full text of a WEB PAGE: previous search engines had just stored the first hundred words of a page.

Web design The process of developing a series of WEB PAGES which satisfy a number of different criteria. The first is that the pages should look good, they should be uncluttered, they declare their intent, and the material on the pages can be read easily. The second criterion is that the user of the pages is able to navigate effortlessly between pages and knows where they are in the WEB SITE which contains the pages at all times. The third criterion is that the pages should DOWN-LOAD quickly. Reconciling these three criteria requires design skills of the highest order.

WebDAV This is a standard for collaborative authoring on the Web which has been developed by the INTERNET ENGINEERING TASK FORCE. It specifies the sort of facilities needed on the Web for Collaborative working. A typical use for tools based on the standard would be to develop joint business plans when two or more companies collaborate on some joint venture.

Web designer Someone who has overall responsibility for the organization and presentational features of a WEB SITE. Web designers must have a large number of skills. They should be good visual designers, have a knowledge of the technical aspects of WEB PAGE construction, be experts in the information aspects of visual presentation, and be able to relate easily to customers.

Web developer Someone who carries out the technical tasks necessary to construct a WEB SITE, such as writing the HYPERTEXT MARKUP LANGUAGE code and programming APPLETS. A Web developer often works in tandem with a WEB DE-SIGNER. Sometimes the role of Web developer is combined with that of Web designer.

Web email The use of the WORLD WIDE WEB to send EMAIL messages. The big advantage of this form of email access is that it can be used anywhere: a user who normally sends mail from a computer at their business can employ it when physically located away from that computer. *See* WEB EMAIL GATEWAY.

Web email gateway A WEB SITE or WEB PAGE which allows users to send conventional EMAIL. Such gateways do not have the detailed and extensive functions of an EMAIL PROGRAM and it is very difficult to integrate them with a conventional email program. For example, mail that has been sent using a Web gateway has to be physically copied into the sent folder associated with the program.

Web end A WEB SITE which is a dead end in that it contains useless links or no links at all. A typical Web end is one which has been developed by a student as an exercise. *See also* CUL DE SITE.

Webertising A jargon term for WEB AD-VERTISING.

Web farm A WEB SITE which mainly contains HYPERLINKS to other sites. Often these sites are devoted to specialized topics and are a first stop for anyone wishing to learn about the topic. They are useful resources but they lack the power of a GURU SITE.

Web font Currently when a designer produces a WEB PAGE he or she specifies the fonts that are required for the page using the facilities of HTML. When the page is displayed, the BROWSER looks at the fonts that are currently installed in the client computer. If the right ones are installed, they are used: if not they are substituted by fonts which are closest to the ones used. This FONT SUBSTITUTION can mean that the design balance of the page can be spoiled. Because of this, Web designers resort to a number of strategies. The two most common are keeping to fonts which will almost invariably be implemented, such as Times Roman, and using TEXT GIFS. In order to overcome the problems of font substitution the WORLD WIDE WEB CONSORTIUM is developing a standard whereby fonts can be embedded into a Web page using CASCADING STYLE SHEETS. Such fonts are known either as EMBEDDED FONTS or DYNAMIC FONTS. The former term is used by the Microsoft Corporation while the latter is used by the Netscape Corporation.

Web graffiti The modification to a WEB PAGE which has been the subject of unauthorized alteration. There are a number of motives for this electronic version of daubing walls and buildings with paint. It is carried out by a variety of users including hackers who enjoy the challenge of CRACKING a secure site, disgruntled ex-employees of the company whose site has been altered, and members of protest groups. A recent software utility Third Voice has, controversially, provided a means of carrying out this process with ease. It consists of a tool which can be used to deface a Web page and a PLUG-IN for a browser. Any browser which uses this plug-in sees the additions made to the site by the users of the tool.

Web guru A WEB DEVELOPER or WEB DESIGNER in a company who is responsible for the company WEB SITE. The term is also used to describe someone who has a very high level of expertise in Web technology.

Webhead A frequent contributor to the WORLD WIDE WEB.

Web hippy Someone who espouses the views of the hippy movement of the 1960s with special reference to the WORLD WIDE WEB. For example, a Web hippy stresses freedom of expression and ready access to all information on the Web.

Webify A verb used for the process of placing an existing document on the WORLD WIDE WEB.

Webisodics Online soap operas which are published on a WEB SITE in short fragments.

Web kiosk A kiosk which can be used by members of the public for accessing the WORLD WIDE WEB, usually for a charge.

Weblish 1. The combination of acronyms, abbreviations and HAKSPEK terms used to communicate via EMAIL. It has arisen because of a need to communicate quickly and distinguished by a lack of punctuation and poor spelling.
2. To publish on the WORLD WIDE WEB.

Weblog A WEB SITE which is a cross between a BULLETIN BOARD and an ONLINE COMMUNITY. Users of a Weblog post details of interesting WEB PAGES and exchange views on the topic covered by the Weblog.

Web log file A FILE which contains important information about the accesses to WEB PAGES made by users. For example, every time a BROWSER requests a page, an entry is automatically made in this file by a WEB SERVER, containing information such as the time at which the access was made, the address of the computer on which the browser was running, and the transfer time of the page. Such information is exceptionally useful. For example, a WEBMASTER is able to use it to judge whether certain pages should be kept in a fast storage medium in order to optimize them. A company is able to use the information to judge which pages are popular and which pages are hardly visited. They can then adjust marketing tactics and the structure of their WEB SITE. Web log files are also increasingly being used to monitor employees' use of the Web: for example, to detect those who visit computer game sites during office hours. The development of software tools for analysing log files has become a major business, and such tools are often referred to as WEB LOGGING TOOLS. There are a number of formats which define the contents of Web log files: what data is in the file and the order it appears. The most common is the COMMON LOGFILE FORMAT which was defined by the NATIONAL CENTER FOR SUPERCOMPUTING APPLICATIONS. Microsoft have also defined a similar format known as the IIS STANDARD LOG FILE FORMAT which is associated with their IIS server. The WORLD WIDE WEB CONSORTIUM have also defined a format which is particularly suited to analysis, and this is known as the EXTENDED LOGFILE FORMAT. There is also an experimental format known as the EXTENSIBLE LOG FORMAT based on XML. The aim of the developers of this format is to standardize log file formats over every Web server.

Web logging tool A tool which accesses a WEB LOG FILE and produces summary reports based on the contents of the file. Typical reports include the number of HITS that a WEB PAGE receives, a list of popular pages in ascending or descending order and a breakdown in terms of DOMAINS of the users who have visited the site. The more sophisticated tools offer a variety of formats for these reports ranging from those written in HTML to those which can be read and displayed by a word processor or spreadsheet program. Advanced tools also allow users to customize the reports that are produced. The development of these tools is a burgeoning Internet industry. At one time their users were mainly WEBMASTERS interested in obtaining information which enabled them to optimize their WEB SITE, but the user base has now shifted to marketing staff who are interested in the way customers access pages on ELECTRONIC COMMERCE sites.

Webmail A jargon term for WEB EMAIL.

Webmaster The name given to a member of staff who is responsible for a WEB SITE. The duties of a Webmaster can be quite diverse. In a large organization they are responsible for the maintenance of the files used on WEB PAGES and usually carry out programming of CGI SCRIPTS. In smaller organizations they may be called on to carry out WEB DESIGN and construct Web pages using HTML and even develop the content of Web pages. Occasionally known as a Webmeister.

Web mining The use of a BOT to carry out some information gathering on the Web. A typical Web mining application is that of a company marketing a particular product scanning a number of WEB SITES in order to discover references to that product in order to effectively market it.

Webmistress A female WEBMASTER.

Webmonkey An unskilled, often incompetent WEB DESIGNER. *See also* BOBO THE WEBMONKEY.

Web navigation The process of moving from one WEB PAGE to another on the same WEB SITE or another Web site using HYPERLINKS. *See also* CLICKSTREAM and NAVIGATION BAR.

Webonomics The economics of making money and creating wealth using the Internet, in particular the WORLD WIDE WEB.

Web page The collection of text, graphics, sound, and video that corresponds to a single window of scrollable material displayed by a browser. A WEB SITE contains a number of Web pages, each of which is written in the HYPERTEXT MARKUP LANGUAGE; one of these pages is designated the HOME PAGE for the site.

Web police A US voluntary organization that processes reports on possible Internet irregularities, investigates them, and, if they prove to be criminal, notifies some criminal agency.

Web ring A collection of WEB SITES with a common theme which are linked together using HYPERLINKS. The person responsible for coordinating these sites is sometimes called a RINGMASTER. *See also* LINK SWAPPING.

Web rot The process whereby a poorly maintained WEB SITE degrades, in that it increasingly contains links to pages which do not exist. ALSO SEE COBWEB SITE and ORPHAN PAGE.

Web Search A METASEARCH ENGINE to which listings can be submitted directly. It has a very flexible way of displaying results which can be customized.

Web server A program which responds to requests to fetch WEB PAGES expressed in the HYPERTEXT TRANSFER PROTOCOL. It effectively acts as a FILE SERVER for files containing Web pages. There are a large number of different Web servers on the market, but the vast majority are only used by a small percentage of organizations, with servers such as APACHE dominating. A Web server maintains a cache containing a series of pages held in fast access memory that can be sent to a CLIENT running a BROWSER very quickly, without the delay encountered in reading the pages from a FILE medium. A Web server also writes entries to a WEB LOG FILE which holds data about the requests made for Web pages. There are a number of ways of programming a Web server, and one of the most popular involves the use of the COMMON GATEWAY INTERFACE which is an interface to the server's software. Another programming technology that can be used is SERVLETS: snippets of JAVA code which can be loaded into a Web server.

Web server performance metric The performance of a WEB SERVER can be judged by a number of key metrics. The first is the number of connections a server can handle efficiently per minute or per hour. The second is the throughput: the number of bytes of data transferred to browsers over a period of time. The third is the average ROUND TRIP TIME, which stretches from the time a request is made to a Web server to the time the final byte of the request has been sent to the client that made the request.

Web server tuning The process carried out by a WEBMASTER to optimize the performance of a WEB SERVER. This involves decisions such as choosing a CACHING POLICY, deciding on the location of WEB PAGES within the server, and selecting the number of HTTP DAEMONS to create.

Web site This is the term used for a set of linked themed pages which are stored on a WEB SERVER. Such a server can host one Web site or, in the case of an INTERNET SERVICE PROVIDER, can host a large number of sites. Access to a Web site is usually via a HOME PAGE.

Web site promotion The process whereby a WEB SITE advertises itself to attract visitors. There are a number of ways of doing this. The first is to register with a number of SEARCH ENGINES, which can be done via SEARCH ENGINE SUBMISSION sites or MULTIPLE SEARCH ENGINE SUBMISSION sites. Another way is to submit the site to BEST OF THE WEB or COOL SITE

OF THE DAY sites. A third way is to announce a site in one of a number of specialized NEWSGROUPS known as ANNOUNCEMENT NEWSGROUPS set up to announce commercial ventures. A fourth way is to contact the owners of other similar sites in order to see whether they will carry out LINK SWAPPING with you or make your Web site part of a WEB RING. A fifth way is to notify paper-based periodicals that cover the area which your Web site is concerned with: newspapers and magazines often have a short Web site listing section.

Websmith Another name for a WEB DESIGNER.

Webstone benchmark A set of laboratory tests which evaluate the performance of a WEB SERVER. There are a number of Webstone benchmarks in existence, all providing a heterogeneous mix of Web server requests, ranging from those which are simple and require very little data to be returned by the server, to those which require large amounts of data. Such tests are normally used to carry out comparisons between Web servers. The name is a pun on the Whetstone tests used to compare the performance of computer systems.

Web trap A WEB SITE or a series of Web sites used to trap intruders who attempt to infiltrate a network. Such intruders are lured into the Web trap where their interaction with the WEB PAGES in the trap might betray their identity. For example, they may inadvertently provide a PASSWORD. This is also known as a MIRROR WORLD.

Web TV The use of a television set to access the WORLD WIDE WEB. All that is required is a television, a communication line, and a Web TV terminal. This is the first attempt to overcome consumer resistance to using the World Wide Web arising from the fear of using a computer.

Web wrap agreement The licensing agreement that a user enters into before downloading software from the Internet.

Web year The period during which the economic growth of companies that use the WORLD WIDE WEB increases compared with conventional companies. A number of commentators have posited that a Web year is approximately one seventh of a calendar year.

Webzine A magazine which can be found on the WORLD WIDE WEB.

wedging Introducing WORMS into a network. It is also occasionally known as FLOODING.

WEG Abbreviation for Wicked Evil Grin used in CHAT ROOMS, EMAILS, and NEWS-GROUPS.

welcome page A term for both a HOME PAGE and a SPLASH PAGE.

well-known port A synonym for DEDI-CATED PORT.

we mail An EMAIL ADDRESS owned by two people which can be used to send mail to each of them.

WfM *See* WIRED FOR MANAGEMENT.

whack a mole 1. To close INTERSTITIAL ADVERT windows that appear on WEB SITES which offer some ECOMMERCE facility. Such windows often generate new windows, with the user clicking them very quickly in order to keep a clear screen: a process similar to that involved in the computer game Whack a Mole which involves continuously hitting the heads of moles which appear above ground level.
2. To continually shut down THROWAWAY ACCOUNTS that are used by SPAMMERS, the implication here being that as soon as one is closed down another appears.

whacker A HACKER who enjoys delving into the details of a piece of software and pushing it to its limits.

what you get is what you never thought you had A jibe against WYSIWYG systems which show the contents of a screen in a different way from the paper version.

what you see is all you get A derogatory term used by hard-core HACKERS to describe WYSIWYG software which they are unable to modify for specific purposes not catered for in the original software. The term was originally coined by Brian

Kernighan of Bell Labs to indicate that WYSIWYG systems might throw away information in a document that could be useful in other contexts.

whispers Private conversations that start up in a CHAT ROOM.

white board A shared area on a computer screen which can be accessed by clients who can send messages or draw graphics. A concept that is sometimes found in TEAMWARE.

white board attack An attack on a computer network which relies on data that can be physically discovered rather than electronically discovered: for example, the use of a PASSWORD written on a white board in an office. *See also* DRAWER ATTACK.

white hat A HACKER who has been hired to prevent illegal acts such as entering a forbidden network. *See also* BLACK HAT.

white page service A service associated with PEOPLE FINDING. There are a diverse number of white page services dealing with finding addresses, phone numbers, and EMAIL addresses.

Whois Whois is an Internet utility which enables a user to find out information about an INTERNET SERVICE PROVIDER, DOMAIN NAMES, and addresses. Web interfaces to this utility are very simple: all they usually consist of is a text box into which is typed the name about which information is required. The utility can be used by CRACKERS to infiltrate a system and so it is usually disabled.

WIBNI Abbreviation for Wouldn't It Be Nice If used in CHAT ROOMS, EMAILS, and NEWSGROUPS.

Wide Area Information Servers An early SEARCH ENGINE which used KEYWORD-based searches to look for documents on the Internet. It has now been superseded by more modern search engines such as ALTA VISTA.

wide area network A network, often known as a WAN, that spans a large area such as a country or a continent. Such networks are normally organized as POINT-TO-POINT NETWORKS. The Internet is the largest wide area network in existence.

wideband A medium-speed transmission medium.

wide distribution When an EMAIL has been sent to a very large number of people, for example every employee in a company, it is said to have a wide distribution.

widget A visual object such as a BUTTON that appears in WEB PAGES or in the interfaces to other programs.

wildcard A character used in a SEARCH QUERY that can stand for a variety of STRINGS. The asterisk character is often used as a wild card so, for example, a search for Dav* would retrieve words such as Dave, David, Davina, and Davies.

Window 1. A collection of PACKETS of data that is to be transmitted into a network. *See* SLIDING WINDOW PROTOCOL.
2. A frame displayed on a computer monitor which contains visual entities such as BUTTONS.

window attack A form of DENIAL OF SERVICE ATTACK which relies on the fact that administering visible widgets such as WINDOWS and BUTTONS on a screen consumes a large amount of resources. A typical example of a window attack might involve the creation of a large number of windows displayed on a screen. The amount of resources required to manage such a large number of windows can easily render a computer inoperable.

Windows Metafiles A graphics format developed by the Microsoft Corporation which attempts to combine the advantages of both BITMAPPED GRAPHICS and VECTOR GRAPHICS. The format is usually used for CLIP ART which needs to be resized.

winkey The name given to the EMOTICON ;-)

WinSock A SOCKET associated with one of the Windows operating systems marketed by Microsoft. It is a Windows implementation of the Berkeley sockets API.

wired A term which was once used to describe someone who was under the influence of drugs; it is now used to describe someone who is proficient in Internet technologies and alive to the possibilities they offer.

Wired One of the first and most influential magazines to draw attention to the Internet and its power. In its early days the Internet featured very heavily although there has been a slight disengagement from this topic in the last few years. Wired was also one of the first companies to use adverts on a WEB SITE.

Wired For Management An open standard for systems which allow administrators to automate the management of CLIENT computers using a network. Using this technology clients, even MOBILE CLIENTS, can be configured and updated from a central location.

wirehead 1. A hardware expert, particularly one who has expertise in communications hardware.
2. An expert in LOCAL AREA NETWORK technology.

Wireless Application Protocol A mobile PROTOCOL which allows the user of a mobile phone to browse WEB PAGES written in the MARKUP LANGUAGE known as WML. This is the first tentative step towards transferring the cable-based Web to a wireless network. It is often abbreviated to WAP.

Wireless Bit Map A graphic format intended for mobile computing devices such as PERSONAL DIGITAL ASSISTANTS.

Wireless Markup Language A cutdown version of the HYPERTEXT MARKUP LANGUAGE. It is used for developing WEB PAGES which can be accessed using a mobile phone and is compatible with the WIRELESS APPLICATION PROTOCOL.

wireless network LOCAL AREA NETWORKS usually use cabling for connecting devices. However, there is another alternative: wireless or infrared transmission. Each device on a network which uses this form of communication is connected to its own transmitter and receiver and communicates using the same protocols that are used in cable access. Such networks are employed when users move around a building or where the building might be unsuitable for cable transmission, such as an old building with strict regulations about what modifications can be made to its fabric. Such wireless networks are expensive, have poor security, and are easily affected by electrical interference. As well as these local area uses for wireless technology there are a number of technologies that allow the mobile user to connect into networks, including CIRCUIT SWITCHED CELLULAR, CELLULAR DIGITAL PACKET DATA, and PRIVATE PACKET RADIO.

wiretap To read the traffic which flows along a transmission medium. This is normally carried out by a physically invasive means such as by cutting a cable and routing it through a small portable computer. Also used as an alternative to VAMPIRE TAP.

wizard 1. A type of program which gradually takes a user through a complicated task. Wizards are normally associated with tasks such as installing software, creating a database, or constructing a complicated structure such as a table in a word processor.
2. Occasionally used for a technical expert as an alternative to terms such as GEEK and ALPHA GEEK.

WMF *See* WINDOWS METAFILES.

WML *See* WIRELESS MARKUP LANGUAGE.

wok on the wall A small microwave antenna.

word of mouse The spread of information via the Internet. For example, a previously little-known film may become a hit because of word of mouse.

word spamming The process of repeating certain words time and time again in a WEB PAGE in order to ensure that the page is high on the list of retrieved UNIFORM RESOURCE LOCATORS produced by a SEARCH ENGINE. This is a practice frowned upon by the developers of search engines who delete any reference to pages which have been word spammed. *See also* SPAMDEX.

work factor The amount of work required to break a scheme that uses CRYPTOGRAPHY.

workflow The process whereby items of work move from one person to another in an organization. Communication technology and TEAMWARE have brought about large efficiencies in this area.

workgroup computing The use of software to facilitate team working.

workstation A very powerful computer which, while being of the size of a PC, exceeds it in terms of processor power and storage capacity.

world wide wait A derogatory term for the WORLD WIDE WEB used by those who suffer from low-speed connections.

World Wide Wanderer One of the first BOTS used on the WORLD WIDE WEB. It was originally developed to track the Web's growth and was designed by Mathew Gray. At first it counted only WEB SERVERS, but was quickly redesigned to capture URLS. Its database of HYPERLINKS was called the Wandex and was the first Web database. The Wanderer created a furore because early versions caused network degradation. Its appearance coincided with the first arguments about whether such bots were a good thing for the Internet. It has now passed into history.

World Wide Web The collection of WEB SITES which are stored on the WEB SERVERS contained in the Internet. It is known as the Web because each site will usually contains HYPERLINKS to other sites, thus mimicking the structure of a spider's web. The technologies used in the World Wide Web were first developed locally by the English computer scientist Tim Berners-Lee at the CONSEIL EUROPÉEN POUR LA RECHERCHE NUCLÉAIRE (CERN) for an internal documentation project. Gradually the main ideas of this project percolated outwards to other research organizations and universities, prompted by the success of technologies such as the WIDE AREA INFORMATION SERVERS facility and GOPHER. The main fillip to the growth of the Web took place when the BROWSER known as MOSAIC was developed at the NATIONAL CENTER FOR SUPERCOMPUTING APPLICATIONS. The technology accelerated in the 1990s with more commercial browsers being developed and with the further development of the language used to develop WEB PAGES: the HYPERTEXT MARKUP LANGUAGE, commonly known as HTML. The 1990s saw an explosion in the use of the World Wide Web by commercial companies and a new booming area of the economy known as ECOMMERCE appeared. The 1990s also saw a huge increase in technological developments: more and more powerful WEB SERVERS, the appearance of PLUG-INS which increased the ability of WEB DESIGNERS to present content, the rise of the JAVA programming language which enabled EXECUTABLE CONTENT known as APPLETS to be incorporated into Web pages; the development of technologies such as the SECURE SOCKETS LAYER which provide facilities for the transfer of sensitive data across the World Wide Web; the development and improvement of a wide variety of SEARCH ENGINES; the integration of Web sites with other media including telephony; and the release of HTML AUTHORS which enabled individuals with little knowledge of Web technology to produce sophisticated Web pages.

World Wide Web Consortium A collection of hardware companies, software companies, content providers, corporations, government organizations, and educational institutions which specify standards for Web technologies such as HTML, XML, and CASCADING STYLE SHEETS. It was set up in 1994 and was based at the Massachusetts Institute of Technology's Computer Science Lab. It is now also hosted by two other institutions: Keio University in Japan and the French National Institute for Research in Computer Science. It is the initiator and repository of Web technology standards and reference software such as the AMAYA experimental BROWSER and the JIGSAW experimental SERVER. It issues standards, sample code, and reference implementations which are freely available at regular intervals. The standards that have been developed have to go through a formal process of being working drafts, proposed recommendations and finally recommendations. The W3C, as it is often known, is independent of software and hardware vendors and is funded by membership fees, research funds, and external contracts.

World Wide Web Worm One of the first indexing programs. It was developed in 1994 by Oliver McBryan and was used to catalogue CONTENT on the WORLD WIDE WEB. Many of the original ideas behind this program have survived in more modern WORMS currently found on the Internet. It is sometimes confused with the INTERNET WORM, a virus which was unleashed into the Internet in the 1980s.

worm 1. A computer program that propagates itself from one computer to another on a network. The most famous of these was the INTERNET WORM.
2. A program which accesses the Internet, usually the WORLD WIDE WEB, catalogues the WEB SITES that it visits and constructs databases used by a SEARCH ENGINE.

wormhole A point in the Internet where traffic originating from a PACKET RADIO network enters. For example, email sent across a packet radio network needs to enter a wormhole before it can be sent to an Internet user.

worst of the web A generic term used to refer to WEB SITES which are devoted to detecting and showing poor Web content and design. These sites are your best starting point for seeing how not to develop a Web site. They document sites which contain distracting content, poor design, uninteresting content, execrable taste, and random structure.

wrapper software Software which is used to surround elderly software so that it can be employed in a modern system. For example, there are a huge number of database systems in existence which contain data such as stock levels, purchase orders, and delivery notes. If an ECOMMERCE developer wanted to interface a Web-based system with such software then wrapper software would be used to enclose the elderly software. The wrapper software is able to communicate with the software used for the ecommerce application and the database at the same time.

wry face One of the most commonly occurring EMOTICONS. It is written as :-/

WTG Abbreviation for Way To Go used in CHAT ROOMS, EMAILS, and NEWSGROUPS.

WWW Worm *See* WORLD WIDE WEB WORM.

WYGIWYNTYH Abbreviation for WHAT YOU GET IS WHAT YOU NEVER THOUGHT YOU HAD.

WYRN Acronym used in CHAT ROOMS. Its translation is What's Your Real Name.

WYS Abbreviation for Whatever You Say used in CHAT ROOMS, EMAILS, and NEWS-GROUPS.

WYSIAYG *See* WHAT YOU SEE IS ALL YOU GET.

WYSIWYG Acronym for What You See Is What You Get. Usually used to describe editing software where the visual appearance of the object being edited is shown directly in the window of the editor to which changes are applied. *See* WYSIWYG EDITOR.

WYSIWYG author A synonym for WYSIWYG EDITOR.

WYSIWYG editor An editor which produces Web pages. It is different from an HTML EDITOR in that it displays how a page will look in the window that is used for editing. WYSIWYG editors have now become very sophisticated and use textual layers for the layout of material on a page. The most sophisticated editors also offer a plethora of other facilities including the checking of HYPERLINKS, the semi-automatic insertion of ROLLOVERS, site transfer using facilities normally found in FTP SOFT-WARE, automated TABLE development, automated FRAME development, the development of IMAGE MAPS, the use of HTML TEMPLATES, and the construction of animations.

WYT Abbreviation for Whatever You Think used in CHAT ROOMS, EMAILS, and NEWSGROUPS.

X400 A standard for EMAIL developed by the International Standards Organization. The development of this standard was a long process and it was released just as the Internet was exploding in size and well after a number of TCP-IP-based MAIL PROGRAMS had been released. The consequence is that the number of X400 users is very much smaller than users of protocols such as SMTP, and is confined to governmental users. X400 is associated with a sister standard, X500, which specifies DIRECTORY SERVICES. It is expected that this standard will be obsolete by 2005.

X500 A standard for DIRECTORY SERVICES which is a sister to the X400 standard for EMAIL. The standard was developed by the International Standards Organization and is regarded as being influential in the development of DIRECTORY ACCESS PROTOCOLS including the LIGHTWEIGHT DIRECTORY ACCESS PROTOCOL. The aim of the X500 standard is to enable organizations to make available a large amount of data about their network, the people that use it, and the resources on the network. *See also* LIGHTWEIGHT DIRECTORY ACCESS PROTOCOL.

X500 server A SERVER which administers an X500 directory service. Such a server waits for requests for information from remote clients. If it can satisfy a query—for example, the details of a member of staff in the organization that runs the server—it does so. If not, it either invokes other servers which are under its control or redirects the client making the request to another X500 server.

X509 This is the most popular standard for SECURITY CERTIFICATES. It contains information such as the PUBLIC KEY associated with some Internet entity, its name, and a unique registration number.

XBRL Abbreviation for EXTENSIBLE BUSINESS REPORTING LANGUAGE.

X consumer Someone who views adult material on WEB SITES.

XFDL *See* EXTENSIBLE FORMS DESCRIPTION LANGUAGE.

XHTML *See* EXTENSIBLE HYPERTEXT MARKUP LANGUAGE.

XLF *See* EXTENSIBLE LOG FORMAT.

XML *See* EXTENSIBLE MARKUP LANGUAGE.

XML Schema A proposed replacement for DOCUMENT TYPE DEFINITIONS used to define documents written in the EXTENSIBLE MARKUP LANGUAGE. It is a much richer language which allows the developer facilities to define more sophisticated documents than is currently possible.

Xmodem A PROTOCOL for transferring files using DIAL-UP ACCESS.

XSL *See* EXTENSIBLE STYLE LANGUAGE.

XSLT *See* EXTENSIBLE STYLE LANGUAGE TRANSFORMATION.

YA Abbreviation for Yet Another used in CHAT ROOMS, EMAILS, and NEWSGROUPS.

YABA Abbreviation for Yet Another Bloody Acronym used in CHAT ROOMS, EMAILS, and NEWSGROUPS.

YAFIYGI Abbreviation for You Asked For It You Got It used in CHAT ROOMS, EMAILS, and NEWSGROUPS.

Yahoo One of the most popular SEARCH ENGINES on the WORLD WIDE WEB. It is unusual in that it uses human indexers to categorize and catalogue a site rather than a SPIDER. There is a junior version known as YAHOOLIGANS. It is very difficult for a site to get listed in Yahoo. Once listed, however, the TRAFFIC to your site increases greatly.

Yahooligans Part of the SEARCH ENGINE known as YAHOO that is dedicated to children. It provides CONTENT that parents can be sure is safe.

YBS Abbreviation for You'll Be Sorry used in CHAT ROOMS, EMAILS, and NEWSGROUPS.

YDKM Abbreviation for You Don't Know Me used in CHAT ROOMS, EMAILS, and NEWSGROUPS.

Yellow Book A computing industry standard which defines the format of CD ROMs. It extends the Red Book standard used for audio CDs.

yellow page service 1. A service provided by a WEB SITE which is analogous to the yellow pages found in a telephone directory.
2. The name given to a service which allowed users to log-in to multiple computers without having separate accounts and passwords. It was originally used in conjunction with REMOTE PROCEDURE CALL services and renamed as NETWORK INFORMATION SERVICE.

YGMTPO Abbreviation for You Greatly Misunderstand The Purpose Of used in CHAT ROOMS, EMAILS, and NEWSGROUPS.

YHBT Abbreviation for You Have Been TROLLed used in NEWSGROUPS.

YMMV Abbreviation for Your Mileage May Vary used in CHAT ROOMS, EMAILS, and NEWSGROUPS.

yoyo mode When a computer in a network alternates rapidly between being available for use and GOING DOWN.

YOYOW Abbreviation for You Own Your Own Words used in CHAT ROOMS, EMAILS, and NEWSGROUPS.

YSYD Abbreviation for Yes Sure You Do used in CHAT ROOMS, EMAILS, and NEWSGROUPS.

YTTT Abbreviation for You Telling The Truth? used in CHAT ROOMS, EMAILS, and NEWSGROUPS.

YWIA Abbreviation for You're Welcome In Advance used in CHAT ROOMS, EMAILS, and NEWSGROUPS.

Z

Zemma's law Zemma's law concerns POSTINGS to newsgroups. It is 'that there is nothing you can say (in a newsgroup) that won't offend somebody.'

Zen mail This is EMAIL which arrives with no message attached to it. Usually this occurs because of a user error or a system error.

zine A shortened form of EZINE or WEB-ZINE.

zip The process of compressing a FILE using LEMPEL ZIV WELSH CODING. The term is derived from the name of an early commercial product that did this. The term is often used when the method employed for COMPRESSION is not in fact based on Lempel Ziv Welsh Coding.

zip file A FILE that has been compressed using LEMPEL ZIV WELSH CODING.

zip software A generic term that is used to describe software that compresses files using LEMPEL ZIV WELSH CODING.

zipperhead A user with a closed mind.

zone The area of the Internet administered by a particular NAME SERVER which forms part of the INTERNET DOMAIN NAME SERVICE. Details of the zone are stored in a FILE known as the ZONE FILE.

zone file A FILE containing details of the ZONE administered by a NAME SERVER which takes part in the INTERNET DOMAIN NAME SERVICE.

zone of service The geographical area for which a network provides a service. The zone of service of the Internet is the whole world.

zoom To home in on and display a section of a graphic or document at a larger magnification than the original.

Z order The order in which layers are placed in a graphic or a WEB PAGE. For example, the CASCADING STYLE SHEETS facility allows blocks of text to be placed one on top of another. The order in which they are placed is known as the Z order. The term comes from the fact that the *x* and *y* coordinate systems describe horizontal and vertical ordering in a graphic, while the *z* coordinate system defines ordering in a direction ninety degrees to both these.

APPENDIX 1 Country Codes

AD	Andorra	BS	Bahamas
AE	United Arab Emirates	BT	Bhutan
AF	Afghanistan	BV	Bouvet Island
AG	Antigua and Barbuda	BW	Botswana
AI	Anguilla	BY	Belarus
AL	Albania	BZ	Belize
AM	Armenia	CA	Canada
AN	Netherlands Antilles	CC	Cocos (Keeling) Islands
AO	Angola	CF	Central African Republic
AQ	Antarctica	CG	Congo
AR	Argentina	CH	Switzerland
AS	American Samoa	CI	Côte d'Ivoire (Ivory Coast)
AT	Austria	CK	Cook Islands
AU	Australia	CL	Chile
AW	Aruba	CM	Cameroon
AZ	Azerbaijan	CN	China
BA	Bosnia and Herzegovina	CO	Colombia
BB	Barbados	CR	Costa Rica
BD	Bangladesh	CS	Czechoslovakia (former)
BE	Belgium	CU	Cuba
BF	Burkina Faso	CV	Cape Verde
BG	Bulgaria	CX	Christmas Island
BH	Bahrain	CY	Cyprus
BI	Burundi	CZ	Czech Republic
BJ	Benin	DE	Germany
BM	Bermuda	DJ	Djibouti
BN	Brunei Darussalam	DK	Denmark
BO	Bolivia	DM	Dominica
BR	Brazil	DO	Dominican Republic

DZ	Algeria	GW	Guinea-Bissau
EC	Ecuador	GY	Guyana
EE	Estonia	HK	Hong Kong
EG	Egypt	HM	Heard and McDonald Islands
EH	Western Sahara	HN	Honduras
ER	Eritrea	HR	Croatia (Hrvatska)
ES	Spain	HT	Haiti
ET	Ethiopia	HU	Hungary
FI	Finland	ID	Indonesia
FJ	Fiji	IE	Ireland
FK	Falkland Islands (Malvinas)	IL	Israel
FM	Micronesia	IN	India
FO	Faroe Islands	IO	British Indian Ocean Territory
FR	France	IQ	Iraq
FX	France, Metropolitan	IR	Iran
GA	Gabon	IS	Iceland
GB	Great Britain (UK)	IT	Italy
GD	Grenada	JM	Jamaica
GE	Georgia	JO	Jordan
GF	French Guiana	JP	Japan
GH	Ghana	KE	Kenya
GI	Gibraltar	KG	Kyrgyzstan
GL	Greenland	KH	Cambodia
GM	Gambia	KI	Kiribati
GN	Guinea	KM	Comoros
GP	Guadeloupe	KN	Saint Kitts and Nevis
GQ	Equatorial Guinea	KP	Korea (North)
GR	Greece	KR	Korea (South)
GS	South Georgia and South Sandwich Islands	KW	Kuwait
		KY	Cayman Islands
GT	Guatemala	KZ	Kazakhstan
GU	Guam	LA	Laos

LB	Lebanon	NC	New Caledonia
LC	Saint Lucia	NE	Niger
LI	Liechtenstein	NF	Norfolk Island
LK	Sri Lanka	NG	Nigeria
LR	Liberia	NI	Nicaragua
LS	Lesotho	NL	Netherlands
LT	Lithuania	NO	Norway
LU	Luxembourg	NP	Nepal
LV	Latvia	NR	Nauru
LY	Libya	NT	Neutral Zone
MA	Morocco	NU	Niue
MC	Monaco	NZ	New Zealand (Aotearoa)
MD	Moldova	OM	Oman
MG	Madagascar	PA	Panama
MH	Marshall Islands	PE	Peru
MK	Macedonia	PF	French Polynesia
ML	Mali	PG	Papua New Guinea
MM	Myanmar	PH	Philippines
MN	Mongolia	PK	Pakistan
MO	Macau	PL	Poland
MP	Northern Mariana Islands	PM	St Pierre and Miquelon
MQ	Martinique	PN	Pitcairn
MR	Mauritania	PR	Puerto Rico
MS	Montserrat	PT	Portugal
MT	Malta	PW	Palau
MU	Mauritius	PY	Paraguay
MV	Maldives	QA	Qatar
MW	Malawi	RE	Reunion
MX	Mexico	RO	Romania
MY	Malaysia	RU	Russian Federation
MZ	Mozambique	RW	Rwanda
NA	Namibia	SA	Saudi Arabia

SB	Solomon Islands	TP	East Timor
SC	Seychelles	TR	Turkey
SD	Sudan	TT	Trinidad and Tobago
SE	Sweden	TV	Tuvalu
SG	Singapore	TW	Taiwan
SH	St Helena	TZ	Tanzania
SI	Slovenia	UA	Ukraine
SJ	Svalbard and Jan Mayen Islands	UG	Uganda
SK	Slovak Republic	UK	United Kingdom
SL	Sierra Leone	UM	US Minor Outlying Islands
SM	San Marino	UY	Uruguay
SN	Senegal	UZ	Uzbekistan
SO	Somalia	US	United States
SR	Surinam	VA	Vatican City State (Holy See)
ST	Sao Tome and Principe	VC	Saint Vincent and the Grenadines
SU	USSR (former)	VE	Venezuela
SV	El Salvador	VG	Virgin Islands (British)
SY	Syria	VI	Virgin Islands (US)
SZ	Swaziland	VN	Viet Nam
TC	Turks and Caicos Islands	VU	Vanuatu
TD	Chad	WF	Wallis and Futuna Islands
TF	French Southern Territories	WS	Samoa
TG	Togo	YE	Yemen
TH	Thailand	YT	Mayotte
TJ	Tajikistan	YU	Yugoslavia
TK	Tokelau	ZA	South Africa
TM	Turkmenistan	ZM	Zambia
TN	Tunisia	ZR	Zaire
TO	Tonga	ZW	Zimbabwe

APPENDIX 2 Popular Emoticons

:-)	Happiness
:-(	Sad
:,-(	Sad and crying
;-)	I've just made a sarcastic statement
>:->	Used for flirting
:*)	I'm drunk
:-D	I'm laughing
:-I	I'm apathetic
:-0	I'm surprised
:-/	I'm annoyed

APPENDIX 3 Popular Chat Room, Email, and Newsgroup Abbreviations

AFAIC	As far As I'm Concerned
AFAIK	As Far As I Know
AFK	Away From Keyboard
AKA	Also Known As
ASAP	As Soon As Possible
BAK	Back At Keyboard
BBL	Be Back Later
BFN	Bye For Now
BOHICA	Bend Over, Here It Comes Again!
BRB	Be Right Back
BTW	By The Way
CU	See You
CUL8R	See You Later
EFLA	Extended Four Letter Acronym!
FAQ	Frequently Asked Question
FC	Fingers Crossed
FCFS	First Come First Served
FUCT	Failed Under Continuous Testing
FWIW	For What It's Worth
FYI	For Your Information
GMTA	Great Minds Think Alike
GTRM	Going To Read Mail
GR&D	Grinning, Running, and Ducking
HSIK	How Should I Know
HTH	Happy To Help or Hope This Helps
IAE	In Any Event
IIRC	If I Recall Correctly
ILF	I'll Look Forward
IMCO	In My Considered Opinion
IMHO	In My Humble Opinion
IMNSHO	In My Not So Humble Opinion
IMO	In My Opinion
INAL	I'm Not A Lawyer
IOW	In Other Words
IRL	In Real Life
IYKWIM	If You Know What I mean
JFYI	Just For Your Information
L8R	Later
LMAO	Laughing My Ass Off
LOEL	Laughing Out Extremely Loud
LOL	Laughing Out Loud
ML	Mailing List
NBD	No Big Deal
NIFOC	Nude In Front Of Computer
NIFOK	Naked In Front of the Keyboard
NOYB	None Of Your Business
NRN	No Reply Necessary
OIC	Oh, I See!
OOH	Out Of Hand
OTOH	On The Other Hand
PITA	Pain In The Ass
PMFJI	Pardon Me For Jumping In
PMJI	Pardon My Jumping In
POV	Point Of View
PTB	Powers That Be
ROFL	Rolling On Floor Laughing
ROTF	Rolling On The Floor
ROTFL	Rolling On the Floor Laughing
RSN	Real Soon Now
RTM	Read The Manual or Read the Message
SEP	Someone Else's Problem
SITD	Still In The Dark
SOL	Smiling Out Loud
TANJ	There Ain't No Justice
TANSTAAFL	There Ain't No Such Thing As A Free Lunch
TBH	To Be Honest
TIA	Thanks In Advance
TIC	Tongue In Cheek
TLA	Three-Letter Acronyms
TLTBT	Too Ludicrous To Be True
TPTB	The Powers That Be
TTFN	Ta Ta For Now
TTYL	Talk To You Later
WIC	Where I'm Concerned
WRT	With respect to
WTH	What The Heck or What the Hell
WYSIWYG	What You See Is What You Get
YMMV	Your Mileage May Vary

Oxford Paperback Reference

A Dictionary of Chemistry

Over 4,200 entries covering all aspects of chemistry, including physical chemistry and biochemistry.

'It should be in every classroom and library ... the reader is drawn inevitably from one entry to the next merely to satisfy curiosity.'

School Science Review

A Dictionary of Physics

Ranging from crystal defects to the solar system, 3,500 clear and concise entries cover all commonly encountered terms and concepts of physics.

A Dictionary of Biology

The perfect guide for those studying biology – with over 4,700 entries on key terms from biology, biochemistry, medicine, and palaeontology.

'lives up to its expectations; the entries are concise, but explanatory'

Biologist

'ideally suited to students of biology, at either secondary or university level, or as a general reference source for anyone with an interest in the life sciences'

Journal of Anatomy

Oxford Paperback Reference

A Dictionary of Psychology
Andrew M. Colman

Over 10,500 authoritative entries make up the most wide-ranging dictionary of psychology available.

'impressive ... certainly to be recommended'
Times Higher Educational Supplement

'Comprehensive, sound, readable, and up-to-date, this is probably the best single-volume dictionary of its kind.'
Library Journal

A Dictionary of Economics
John Black

Fully up-to-date and jargon-free coverage of economics. Over 2,500 terms on all aspects of economic theory and practice.

A Dictionary of Law

An ideal source of legal terminology for systems based on English law. Over 4,000 clear and concise entries.

'The entries are clearly drafted and succinctly written ... Precision for the professional is combined with a layman's enlightenment.'
Times Literary Supplement

More Social Science titles from OUP

The Globalization of World Politics
John Baylis and Steve Smith

The essential introduction for all students of international relations.

'The best introduction to the subject by far. A classic of its kind.'
Dr David Baker, University of Warwick

Macroeconomics
A European Text
Michael Burda and Charles Wyplosz

'Burda and Wyplosz's best-selling text stands out for the breadth of its coverage, the clarity of its exposition, and the topicality of its examples. Students seeking a comprehensive guide to modern macroeconomics need look no further.'
Charles Bean, Chief Economist, Bank of England

Economics
Richard Lipsey and Alec Chrystal

The classic introduction to economics, revised every few years to include the latest topical issues and examples.

VISIT THE COMPANION WEB SITES FOR THESE CLASSIC TEXTBOOKS AT:

www.oup.com/uk/booksites